A Handbook of
Psychological
Assessment
in Business

A HANDBOOK OF
PSYCHOLOGICAL ASSESSMENT IN BUSINESS

Edited by
CURTISS P. HANSEN and
KELLEY A. CONRAD

HF
5549
H2975
1991

QUORUM BOOKS
New York • Westport, Connecticut • London

Library of Congress Cataloging-in-Publication Data

A Handbook of psychological assessment in business / edited by Curtiss
P. Hansen and Kelley A. Conrad.
    p. cm.
  Includes bibliographical references and index.
  ISBN 0–89930–565–2 (alk. paper)
  1. Personnel management—Psychological aspects. 2. Psychology,
Industrial. 3. Prediction of occupational success.
4. Psychological tests. I. Hansen, Curtiss P. II. Conrad,
Kelley A.
HF5549.H2975   1991
658.3'001'9—dc20   91–6822

British Library Cataloguing in Publication Data is available.

Library of Congress Catalog Card Number: 91–6822
ISBN: 0–89930–565–2

First published in 1991

Quorum Books, One Madison Avenue, New York, NY 10010
An imprint of Greenwood Publishing Group, Inc.

Printed in the United States of America

The paper used in this book complies with the
Permanent Paper Standard issued by the National
Information Standards Organization (Z39.48–1984).

10 9 8 7 6 5 4 3 2 1

Contents

Part Five: Users of Psychological Assessments

Part Six: The Future of Psychological Assessment

Exhibits

Preface

Psychological assessment is a term that conjures different images for different people. For some people, it evokes a clinical setting and, perhaps, the psychiatrist's infamous couch. For others, it simply refers to the process of trying to understand another person in a systematic manner. What might be perplexing for both types of people is the linking of psychological assessment with the world of business. What could the assessment of a person from a psychological perspective possibly have to do with the transactions of business?

Although business is certainly concerned with making money, it is not an abstract entity or force. Business is people doing things for specific purposes. It is people interacting to achieve goals, and it is people solving problems to improve situations. In a more familiar vein, it is an employee providing service to a customer, and a boss giving instructions to a subordinate. In all cases, business is about people.

To improve a business, therefore, a manager would be wise to focus on improving the people within the business. Better employees will have better relationships, be better problem-solvers, provide better customer service, and be better leaders. There are two ways to go about obtaining better employees. One way is to train and develop employees once they are on the job. However, this tactic is usually a hit-or-miss proposition, with more misses than hits. It is very difficult to change an adult's behavior patterns, be it planning, time management, organization, sensitivity to others, negotiating methods, or a host of other training seminar topics.

The best approach to obtaining top employees is the second way, which is to determine and select the kind of employee the business needs while the employee is still an applicant. To quote an old adage, "You can't make a silk purse out of a sow's ear." Unfortunately, many managers do not have the time or expertise to probe beyond the resume glitter and preformulated interview responses from multiple candidates. Hiring decisions are often made with a fair amount of uncertainty.

Managers often feel that they must restrict the job requirements to concrete and technical ones such as "five years of management experience," or "knowledge of the East Coast fastener market." While these considerations are certainly important, they are not enough to ensure that you have hired the best person for the job. What is more important in determining whether or not the candidate will be a success is the degree to which that candidate fits the profile of personal characteristics required for success in that position. This profile must be carefully defined and will include personal traits often thought of as psychological qualities. Employees do not usually fail on the job because of concrete or technical mistakes. Rather, a person is more likely to get fired because someone in a position of influence thinks the employee is a "jerk," or lacks one of a number of vital personal qualities (e.g., "he has no guts"; "she's not a likeable person"; "he's a pompous windbag"; "he doesn't know how to put his best foot forward").

It should be obvious now where psychological assessment fits into the picture. Personal characteristics become more critical for success the higher one rises in an organization. Managers, executives, and even human resources professionals are not equipped to assess these often subtle personality-related traits. To do an accurate and thorough job of candidate or employee assessment, the services of a psychologist who specializes in business psychological assessment are needed. Unlike other psychologists in clinical settings, the business psychologist does not perform psychotherapy or mental health evaluations, but is there to assess people in terms of future job performance and company fit.

This book is an introduction to psychological assessment in business. It is written for managers in all functional areas, but particularly for human resources executives. It is a reference book for all companies currently using or contemplating use of psychological assessments. It is also written to managers unfamiliar with the method, who might be experiencing difficulty selecting successful employees.

Our intent in this book is not to teach you how to do a psychological assessment, but how to more effectively utilize the services of a psychologist consultant. It is a useful handbook for a company that is considering hiring an in-house psychologist to provide promotion evaluations and developmental assessment. Likewise, a manager who is contemplating using the services of an outside psychologist consultant will find this book to be a welcome road map. For the company whose top managers are reluctant to use a business psychologist due to a vague sense that the services do not seem businesslike, or that the employees will feel threatened, the material presented here should provide a clear direction and certainty that the psychologist's work will add value to the company and its employees.

The book is organized into six parts. The first part explains what psychological assessment is, the process for using the technique, the context in which it is used, the history of psychological assessment in business, and the research conducted to date on the method. The second part presents an in-depth look at the components of a psychological assessment, and concludes with an analysis of the results of a typical psychological assessment, expressed in a written report.

The third part of the book consists of 12 chapters illustrating the multitude of psychological assessment applications in business. These include its use with first-level supervisors, middle managers, top executives, sales professionals, technical personnel, and advertising and marketing professionals. In addition, this section explores how psychological assessments can be useful in career and personal development, in international business settings, and when used to assess the characteristics of an entire group of managers.

Part four presents brief profiles of three of the oldest psychological consulting firms in the United States. The directors of these firms describe their histories and approach to using psychological assessments when consulting with business. Part five presents the other side of the coin. Here, the human resources directors of four companies that are long-time users of psychological assessments describe their experiences in using the method. Finally, the sixth part discusses the legal considerations in using psychological assessments in business decisions, as well as how psychological assessment will be useful in the business environment of the future.

Most of the chapter authors for parts one, two, three, and six are psychologists with many years of business consulting experience, specifically in the area of psychological assessment. Authors were chosen to write chapters about topics of which they are particularly knowledgeable. This book presents a number of different viewpoints on the subject of psychological assessment. While the basic structure of the method is similar from psychologist to psychologist, different consulting firms and psychologists use various types of interviews, tests, and feedback procedures to achieve the same goals. This contrast in styles is illustrated by the highly structured approach of HRStrategies, Inc. (John Arnold, Chapter 7) compared to the seemingly unstructured approach of RHR International (Chapter 9). Yet, both arrive at useful information about an employee's or job candidate's strengths and weaknesses in terms of a particular job placement.

_____ **Part One**

*Introduction to
Psychological Assessment*

What Is Psychological Assessment?

Curtiss P. Hansen

A BUSINESS SCENARIO: THE TERMINATION DECISION

Three vice-presidents of the Frugal Fastener Corporation have met to discuss the performance and future of Tom Fielding, assistant vice-president and director of West Coast marketing. The three managers are Phyllis Clay, controller; George Townsend, national sales manager; and Fred Anderson, director of marketing. They are reviewing Tom Fielding, who was hired almost one year ago after a lengthy search. Tom reports to Fred Anderson.

Fred: I wanted to meet with both of you today before I talk with Tom Fielding later this week. As you are aware, I have been less than happy with Tom and his work since we hired him. However, I want to get your perspectives on Tom just in case I'm missing something or am making too much out of the differences in our personalities. Both of you have worked closely with Tom over the past six months—what do you think?

George: I'm in your corner on this one, Fred. Tom has been a thorn in my side since day one. Well, maybe not from day one, but at least in the last six months. All it took was time for our "real world" expectations to wear down that MBA polish. I've been in sales for more years than I care to think about and I know that you can't learn the ropes of sales and marketing from a book!

Phyllis: But George, you were the one who felt most strongly that we should hire him a year ago!

George: Yeah, well, I guess that's true, but . . . he put on a good show then. He fooled me. He had so many good ideas and seemed to have the capability to put them into action. But it never happened. He would sell us on a new program and then get lost in the details. Meanwhile, I'd get my troops geared up for the new campaign but with no marketing support to back them up. And Bill [the president] wonders why my numbers look so bad!

Fred: As I recall, we all felt very favorable about Tom initially. It seems that we overestimated his ability to navigate in a large company. He did a good job of developing a plan and selling it to us in presentations. However, he seems to expect everything to simply fall into place after he gets agreement on a concept. When he runs into any opposition, he backs off and gets angry in his office. Then, rather than addressing the concerns of others, he simply gets more documentation to support his position.

Phyllis: From my perspective, his strength is in his attention to the smaller details, such as in documenting everything he does. He's the one manager around here that I don't have to be constantly chasing down to get information. His reports are always on time and done accurately.

George: That's because the rest of us are too busy trying to make money for the company to worry about some nit-picky report!

Fred: I think that gets at part of the problem with Tom. Another problem area that is becoming critical is his inability to manage his staff. In the last three months, I've had half of his people marching into my office complaining about the way he is running the West Coast marketing operation.

George: Or not running it, to be more correct. His idea of delegation is to announce a general plan at a meeting, and then expect everyone to know what he wants them to do and by when.

Fred: I've talked with him at length on several occasions already. On some things he promises to make changes, but on most issues he argues with me, and tries to blame the problems on other people.

George: Tell him that a manager's job at Frugal Fastener is to solve problems, not refer them to someone else. I get so sick of hearing him tell me that "it's not my job." This is not a huge company—sometimes we all have to sweep up the mess on the floor. Fielding's a prima donna who we don't need around here.

Phyllis: Let's not be hasty, George. We have a lot invested in Tom that would go to waste if we were to release him. Maybe we need to think in terms of how we can develop his weaker areas.

Fred: Tom has definite rough edges, but they're not unlike those I've seen in other new MBAs. The main problem is that he brought a big corporation mentality with him. He just doesn't fit into our smaller, less specialized culture. We wanted a marketing generalist with a down-to-earth, team approach. Instead we got a specialist who is an independent producer with no interest in people management.

George: Then why did we hire him in the first place if he was so obviously wrong for the job? What are we, a bunch of dummies?

Phyllis: We hired him because we were impressed with his ideas. Unfortunately, because we needed new ideas, we didn't weigh the pros and cons of these other issues at the time.

Fred: Well, it seems that we are all in agreement that Tom is not doing the job that needs to be done. The question now is, what do we do about him? If I understand both of you, George would probably volunteer to help Tom clear out his desk and then escort him to the exit. Phyllis sees potential in Tom and would vote to work on developing him into the type of manager we want. Is this correct?

George: Well, I don't know that I would have put it quite that way, but yes, I vote that we fire him.

Phyllis: I would like to discuss the possibility of further development—you know, give him the benefit of the doubt.

Fred: I understand your point, Phyllis. To let Tom go means that we have lost a great deal of time and money. . . .

George: And to not let him go means that we will continue to lose time and money. We're launching a new product next month with no marketing.

Fred: That's clearly understood, George, and I do agree with you. It would be nice if we could develop Tom so that we could benefit from his good ideas, but that's not possible. We obviously do not have a training and development staff, and we do not have the time to spend on intensive one-on-one developmental supervision. Besides, there's no way that Tom would respond favorably to such an arrangement. My guess is that he is as unhappy with us as we are with him. My decision is that we make a clean break. I will tell him on Wednesday.

George: And let's hope that we don't have to go through all this again with the next person.

EPILOGUE

Regarding George's closing remark, maybe they will or maybe they won't have to go through their year-long misadventure with a Tom Fielding again. They certainly have learned a lot from this experience. They now have a greater understanding about why Tom failed at Frugal Fastener Corporation. However, will that be enough to prevent them from focusing on one or two salient characteristics of a marketing director candidate while ignoring other aspects that may prove critical later? Maybe. They can certainly hope that this will not be the case.

Then again, perhaps there is a better way they can go about selecting their next director. This book is about a better way. It is called psychological assessment.

DEFINITION OF PSYCHOLOGICAL ASSESSMENT

Broadly speaking, psychological assessment is the measurement and description of a person's personality, behavior, and intellectual characteristics by a person with psychological training. The psychological assessment as a technique was developed and originally performed primarily in clinical and counseling settings. In these contexts, the goal of the assessor (usually a clinical psychologist, psychiatrist, or social worker) is to evaluate the individual's characteristics in relation to a desired outcome such as success in therapy or adjustment in daily living.

Assessments have since been found to be valuable in the business world. In a business context, psychological assessment is generally conducted by a psychologist for the purpose of evaluating an individual in terms of specific criteria. The criteria differ from those in the mental health situation by being work-related. For example, a psychologist might do an assessment on each of several candidates for an open managerial position. The psychologist would evaluate each candidate in terms of the personality and behavioral characteristics deemed important for success in this particular managerial position.

In addition to this use of psychological assessment as a selection tool, it is often used for developmental purposes. A current employee might go through the assessment as a way to identify developmental weaknesses that need to be addressed before being considered for a future promotion.

It is also important to take into consideration the *process* in which the assessment is embedded. The psychological assessment is not a stand-alone product to be purchased from a vendor. It must be integrated into the organization's culture and requires active management. To fully understand the value of psychological assessment in business settings, it is critical that this overall process is discussed and understood throughout the organization. The remainder of this chapter presents each component of the overall psychological assessment process, as well as how the assessment fits into a company's operational and strategic plans.

It should be noted, though, that the description in this chapter is of a generic psychological assessment process. As the reader will discover when the following chapters are explored, there are many variations on this theme. Although there are differences, most providers of psychological assessment services structure their work in a way that is quite similar to the structure described in this chapter.

GETTING TO KNOW THE COMPANY

One of the major purposes of conducting a psychological assessment in a business setting is to assess the fit of an individual to a particular job and to the overall company culture. To do this, the psychologist must accomplish two things. First, the psychologist needs to thoroughly understand the knowledge, skills, abilities (KSAs) and other characteristics required for successful performance on the job. This information is obtained from job descriptions, job analysis documents, and discussions with the hiring manager and job incumbents. For many positions such as those in the technical, sales, and first-level supervisory areas, this information might be sufficient for the psychologist to conduct a good psychological assessment.

Second, beyond the details of the basic job requirements, the psychologist must understand the context of the work to be done, and the nature of all interrelated positions. At the middle and upper management levels, for example, a position is often defined to some extent by the incumbent. Therefore, to understand these positions, the psychologist must understand the individuals who currently hold the positions.

Most psychological assessments are done at the middle and upper management levels. Because this group of executives creates and defines a company's culture, a psychologist will understand the dynamics of the company by getting to know this group.

For many psychologists who conduct assessments in business, the first step in working with a new company is to have each key manager go through a psychological assessment. While this assessment might vary in its degree of formality and exhaustiveness, it is essential that the psychologist get a good reading on the company as a whole, and on each executive's strengths, limitations, personality and management style, aspirations, interpersonal skills, and so forth. This information is important for the psychologist to have for all possible applications of the psychological assessment, whether it be external selection, career counseling, professional development, or internal promotion.

DEFINING THE COMPANY'S NEEDS

The next stage in the relationship between the psychologist consultant and the client company is characterized by the definition of needs and the setting of specific goals. This process often occurs during the course of a psychologist's initial assessment interviews with the company's key personnel. Needs will vary from company to company. While an organization's initial goal may be stated as, "Tell us which candidate will make the best manager," the psychologist will need to do further probing to flesh out this bare-bones objective.

What does "best manager" mean? It could mean "the person who is most like our current management staff." Or it might refer to someone with new ideas and a different style of management than is currently in place. Does it mean, "Find someone with long-term potential who can run the company in ten years"? Or is a turnaround specialist the real hope? These are questions that must be addressed before the psychologist can assess the candidates in a way that is meaningful for the company.

Sometimes the organization's needs are not clearly understood or articulated by management. It is not unusual for a consulting psychologist to be called in for what appears to be a routine selection assessment, only to find a dysfunctional management team. In such cases, the psychologist may wisely propose that each senior manager work with the psychologist in a series of developmental sessions before the new executive is chosen. This work might result in several team building sessions to address interpersonal issues that surfaced during the individual assessment work.

In a similar context, the assessment services of a psychologist might be requested in order to "fix" a manager who is floundering. While the assessment reveals the manager's strengths and limitations, it also frequently discloses that the manager is not failing in isolation. That is, the manager's performance efforts are entwined with the behaviors and attitudes of other managers, most notably those of the superior. To thoroughly address the manager's difficulties, the psychologist must also make the superior aware of his or her contribution to the subordinate's problems. This situation is delicate because the superior might be the person who called in the psychologist to fix the problem with the employee. It takes an exceptionally well-balanced executive to hear of his or her own culpability and deal with it in a positive manner.

Management's expectations regarding what a psychologist can do for the company are sometimes unrealistic. Many managers treat consulting psychologists as if they are magicians or mind readers. These managers expect the psychologist to perform incredible feats when it relates to the assessment of people and prediction of future performance. Unfortunately, such managers can become quite disillusioned when they discover that the psychologist is sometimes off-base on a judgment.

Worse still is the executive who treats everything the psychologist says as absolute truth, regardless of the person's own experience in the matter. To illustrate this point, I was once consulting with the president of a medium-size company on a "team assessment" of the vice-presidents reporting to the president. I had completed psychological assessments on all vice-presidents, and had dictated brief reports on each person. Because I was in a hurry, my usually efficient secretary mixed up some of the pages in two of the reports. As my review session with the president began, I noted that he referred to me as "doctor" a dozen times in five minutes, emphasizing my title to match the level of expertise he was expecting. During my review of the finance vice-president's assessment (whose report was correctly assembled), the president agreed enthusiastically with all my observations and conclusions about the man.

We then moved on to the manufacturing vice-president, whose report had in it pages from the marketing vice-president's report. As I presented my conclusions about the vice-president of manufacturing using the written report as a discussion outline, the president continued to be in agreement with my observations, and even volunteered several behavioral examples to support my conclusions. When I detected the error midway through our discussion of this vice-president, it was the president who was most embarrassed (even though I was quite red-faced!). The president had known the manufacturing executive as a friend and colleague for twenty years, yet did not recognize when the statements being reviewed were totally inappropriate.

The point for managers to understand is that a psychologist who consults to business is a professional trained in the art of assessing people in business settings. Experience in doing this work makes the psychologist probably better equipped than any other person to provide objective assessments of job candidates and key employees for targeted business purposes. However, like any professional with expertise in a given field, a business psychologist can make errors of judgment. A manager needs to view the results from a psychological assessment as information to be discussed and evaluated in light of what the company knows about the individual.

On the other hand, some executives are suspicious of psychologists because of the media's often negative portrayal of the profession. Obviously, neither extreme helps the psychologist do the job for the company. The most useful attitude for a manager to have in using the services of a business psychologist is to be open-minded and objective. A rational approach to identifying needs and setting goals works much better than mysticism or cynicism.

THE PERSONAL INTERVIEW

The one-on-one personal interview of the job candidate or employee is the cornerstone of the psychological assessment. While interview length, style, content and method will vary from psychologist to psychologist, all practitioners of psychological assessment use the interview as their primary tool in reaching conclusions about the individual being assessed. Chapter 4 looks at the interview in depth; this section presents an overview of the types of interviews commonly found in assessment situations.

The one-on-one interview can last between one hour and four hours. Most psychologists' interviews would fall in the one-and-a-half hours to two hours range. This amount of time is considerably longer than for the typical employment interview as conducted by a company's human resources representative or by the hiring manager. These latter interviews may range from ten minutes to an hour. Typically, when a psychologist is not involved, the candidate is interviewed briefly by a number of managers and human resources employees. These interviews are often not well-planned or coordinated; consequently the candidate may be asked the same basic questions by each interviewer.

Most managers are not trained to do effective interviews. They often feel "out of their element" in an interview situation. While human resources professionals usually have some training in basic interviewing skills, they rarely have the time to do a thorough interview assessment of each candidate for every job opening. In addition, there invariably will be internal political pressures that affect the objectivity of their conclusions. It is very difficult for even the most competent human resources interviewer to contradict the opinion or wishes of a higher ranking company executive regarding the potential of a given candidate. One value of an external psychologist consultant or a high-ranking internal psychologist is the greater capacity of that person to be objective when evaluating candidates.

The Structure of the Interview

Interviews vary as to how structured or unstructured they are. Both sides of the structure continuum have their assets and drawbacks, and there are psychologist interviewers who represent every point along this continuum. Early in the history of psychological assessment, psychologists tended to conduct unstructured and loose interviews. They would basically sit down with a candidate and chat about anything. In this style of interview, the content is relatively inconsequential. What is important are more intangible aspects such as the following:

How well does the person communicate?

Does the person take charge or wait to be asked a question?

Is the person polite and accommodating, or expressive and self-involved?

Is the person uncomfortable without a clear agenda in the interview?

Is the person nervous or confident?

Does the person have a sense of humor?

Does the person seem to like interacting with another person?

Does the person "play politics" in the interview, or "throw caution to the wind"?

Is the person likeable? Will others get along with the person?

Can the person "hold his own" when challenged?

The above list contains only a few of the questions and concerns running through the mind of the psychologist conducting an unstructured interview. Any topic is fair game, provided that it yields information about the candidate that is relevant to some aspect of the job. This type of interview has the advantage of extreme flexibility; the interviewer can go in whatever direction seems fruitful at the moment. The unstructured interview casts the psychologist as an artist.

Unfortunately, an interview of this type can be an unsettling experience for the candidate who sees no relationship between the questions and the job. In addition, highly unstructured interviews are difficult if not impossible to defend when legally challenged (see Chapter 26).

At the other end of the continuum is the structured interview. By structure, it is meant that the questions asked are determined before the interview begins.

Job-related topics are identified and questions relevant to these topics are formulated. All candidates are asked the same set of questions. The role of the interviewer is to ask these questions and record the responses. This approach to interviewing casts the interviewer as a technician.

A structured interview has the advantage of being easy to administer and amenable to legal defense if challenged in court. It also enables a company to have different interviewers interviewing different candidates for the same job, while allowing the interviewers to clearly compare all candidates for that job against the same criteria.

The main disadvantage of a structured interview is that it is essentially the same as handing candidates a list of the interview questions and having them write down the answers. There really is no need to have an interviewer because the unique dynamics of the interview have been removed. The interviewer is not allowed to assess less tangible (but equally job-related) candidate characteristics as communication quality, interpersonal style, and self-confidence. The assessment of these traits is generally considered too subjective and, thus, unreliable by proponents of the structured interview approach.

Very few practitioners of psychological assessment conduct rigidly structured interviews. Although the ideal interview style is probably somewhere in the middle of the unstructured–structured continuum, many psychologists I know conduct interviews that are more unstructured than structured.

Topics Generally Covered in the Psychological Assessment Interview

This section reviews many of the subject areas often discussed in the psychological assessment interview. The list is not exhaustive, but is designed to give the reader a feel for what transpires in a business psychologist's interview of a candidate or employee. It should be kept in mind that the ethical psychologist will only ask questions regarding issues that are in some manner related to the knowledge, skills, abilities, and other personal characteristics required for success in the position. While it may not be immediately apparent to the interviewee or casual observer how a given area of inquiry relates to the job, the psychologist should be able to provide an understandable rationale for the questions asked.

Education. In inquiring about a candidate's educational background, several issues will be applicable to most jobs. How relevant are the candidate's educational experiences to the needs of the job? What does the candidate's description of his or her study methods and habits indicate for performance on the job? How consistent was the person's educational progress? Was there a clear goal in mind that was pursued until achieved? How purposeful was the curriculum? Were "easy" courses taken to raise the individual's grade point average? Was education viewed as a positive learning experience or as a necessary evil to achieve a desired end? Who or what motivated the candidate to go into the chosen major study area? Did the person work while attending college, and who financed the education? Why were certain extracurricular activities chosen?

Unfortunately, many inexperienced interviewers tend to ask questions such as, "What was your grade point average in college?" Or, "What courses have you taken?" These questions are a waste of time because the answers can be obtained elsewhere. A better line of questioning would allow the psychologist to come to a conclusion about the following issues.

Work Experience. This is the most important area of inquiry. However, as in the previous section, a simple recounting of companies, positions, and dates can be obtained from a resume. Asking "whys" and "hows" about these things is likely to be more fruitful. The psychologist will generally be concerned about addressing the following issues.

Are the candidate's past work experiences relevant to the position in question? Is the progression of jobs sensible? Is the person operating from an overall career game plan? What are the reasons for leaving the current or last job? What does the candidate say about past employers, bosses and co-workers? What does the individual get from a job—power, pleasure, money, variety? Is there any evidence of achievements on past jobs? What aspects of the work does the person feel best about? Does the candidate have a history of showing initiative in work activities?

Interpersonal Orientation. How comfortable is the candidate in dealing with people? Is the candidate a loner or a team player by nature? Is the individual a leader or follower? What are the person's strengths and limitations in working with people? Questions about a variety of topics will reveal the answers to these questions.

Family History. Many business psychologists spend a great deal of time inquiring into this area. Questions about the person's family background can be quite revealing about the candidate's character and likely future course of behavior. For example, it is unlikely that a bricklayer's child will have had the necessary developmental experiences while growing up to become an advertising executive. This actuarial observation is not to denigrate bricklayers, but only to acknowledge the basic psychological fact that people do not change substantially once the foundation is poured in childhood and adolescence.

However, as revealing as this area can be, it is difficult to ask questions about a candidate's family and upbringing and still stay within the legal parameters. Several issues that are desirable to address are as follows. Was there an appropriate role model for the candidate when growing up? Was there stability in the family of origin? In the candidate's current family?

Personal Assessment and Goals. This area is also of critical importance to assess accurately. Unfortunately, it is an area that is not accessible to direct questioning. For example, in a job selection situation, if you ask candidates if they are confident, you will invariably receive an affirmative response. Important personal characteristics such as self-confidence must be assessed indirectly and by inference. This is one area where the psychologist's experience and expertise in human behavior becomes a major factor in accurately assessing the candidate. Some issues that the psychologist will need to resolve during the interview are as follows.

How is the candidate's self-assessment similar to and different from the psychologist's perceptions of the person during the course of the interview? Are the candidate's personal traits similar to those required for success on the job? Does the individual have a "fatal flaw" (i.e., shyness in a sales candidate)? Does the person believe that success is more a matter of good fortune and "being in the right place," rather than hard work and personal commitment? Does the candidate have a history of setting realistic, but difficult goals? Does the individual's conduct during the interview suggest self-acceptance and maturity? Does the candidate seem able to learn from mistakes rather than be overwhelmed by them?

Activities and Interests. A discussion about the candidate's special hobbies and avocations can be enlightening. Often, a casual question about a person's favorite sporting activity can cause a candidate to relax and put away the formal interview persona for a moment. It is then that the psychologist can get clues regarding the following issues.

Is the person a spectator or a "doer" in life? Are the candidate's interests stable and congruent with other aspects of his or her life, or do they change from month-to-month, according to the current fashion? Does the individual have one main non-work interest or several? Do the person's interests involve other people or are they solitary activities? Do favorite interests often take precedence over work and family responsibilities?

Interest in the Position. Why is the person applying for the position? Or, if the individual is a current employee, why is the employee in that job? Do the reasons offered make sense in light of the other information gained from the candidate during the interview? Is the job part of an overall game plan, or is it just a means to get more money?

PSYCHOLOGICAL TESTING

The majority of consulting business psychologists use psychological tests when conducting a psychological assessment. Chapter 5 describes the use of psychological tests in detail. This section briefly presents some reasons why tests are employed, and the types of tests that are commonly used. Broadly speaking, a psychological test is an exercise that reveals some of the individual's personal characteristics. Psychologists give psychological tests when assessing people in business settings for several reasons. One, it is a quick and economical way to gather much information about a person. Two, it is another source of information about the individual that is quite distinct from the interview, reference letters, and school transcripts. Three, some tests provide measures of job-related abilities. Four, some tests are hard to "fake well" because the purposes of the test are unknown to the test-taker.

Psychologists vary as to the number of tests given to a candidate and the weight placed on the tests' results for the final evaluation. Some psychologists only use tests for confirmation of the impressions and conclusions gained during the interview. Other psychologists give an extensive battery of tests and look for consistency among the results of the various tests in order to arrive at final conclusions about the person. Ideally, the information gained through testing should be carefully weighed with all other sources of information. The quality of the information should dictate how much weight to place on it. Also, for each area of assessment, congruence among as many measures as possible should be sought before reaching a conclusion.

Types of Psychological Tests

Almost every type of psychological test created has been used at one time or another in business settings. Often the familiarity of the psychologist with a particular test determines its usage rather than the requirements of the job. This practice is clearly not in accordance with current legal and professional guidelines. Because the practice continues, a manager using a psychologist to do assessments should ask how the tests used are job-related.

The majority of psychological tests were created for clinical usage and purposes. Some of these tests have been successfully used and validated in business settings. However, many tests are grossly inappropriate for use in the screening of job applicants for all but high-risk occupations (e.g., nuclear power plant operator, air traffic controller). For example, the Minnesota Multiphasic Personality Inventory (MMPI), a well-known test that many psychologists are trained to use, is designed to assess an individual's degree of psychopathological maladjustment. Many of the questions on the MMPI are offensive and invasive to someone applying for a business job. The MMPI is not a valid predictor of general job performance, nor of specific job requirements for all but a few high-risk jobs. Yet it continues to be used regularly by many psychologists working in business.

In recent years, there have been many new psychological tests developed that are specifically designed for use in business settings. These tests often use business-related language and assess characteristics commonly required of employees in a variety of positions. A top-notch business psychologist will be aware of these newer instruments and will have incorporated those tests most applicable to the psychological assessment process.

Personality Tests. A personality test is a useful adjunct to the information and impressions garnered in the interview. It can provide an in-depth overview of the person as a whole. However, of all the different types of tests, personality tests are most likely to be viewed as lacking in job-relatedness by the candidate.

Two kinds of personality tests are used by psychologists. These are typically called objective and projective tests. An objective personality test is a paper-and-pencil inventory of questions or items that the test-taker answers, rates, or endorses. Examples of these tests are the MMPI, 16 Personality Factor, Myers-

Briggs, and California Personality Inventory. Responses to objective personality tests are grouped into multiple scales representing a variety of personality characteristics. The tests are useful in business assessments to the extent that the personality scales are related to the requirements of the job.

A projective personality test can come under a variety of guises. Some require paper-and-pencil (projective drawings, incomplete sentences), while others require the person to view an ambiguous stimulus and "project" onto it what it seems to look like (Rorschach Ink Blot, Thematic Apperception Test). The use of projective tests in personnel selection is a controversial issue. These tests are not well-accepted by business people because the test-taker has no idea what is being assessed and has no control over how a response may be interpreted. Although once widely used by psychologists in industry, very few business psychologists now use projective tests in selection work.

Cognitive Ability Tests. Cognitive ability tests are widely used by most psychologists who do psychological assessments in business. These problem-solving tests provide an estimate of intellectual strengths and limitations, and have been found to be powerful predictors of job performance for a wide variety of positions. A well-known cognitive ability test is the Wonderlic Personnel Test. The Wonderlic and similar tests are not "IQ" tests, nor are they achievement tests. They are brief measures of a person's ability to work his or her way through a variety of problems in a limited amount of time. The problems typically deal with arithmetic, logic, spatial reasoning, basic algebra, word definitions, and verbal analogies.

Some cognitive ability tests measure specific abilities such as reading comprehension, vocabulary, math proficiency, or mechanical reasoning. These tests can be combined into batteries that will assess the specific requirements of a particular job. Full IQ tests such as the Wechsler Adult Intelligence Scale-Revised are usually given only in full-day assessments.

Job Sample Tests. A job sample test directly measures a person's performance in doing an important part of the job in question. An example would be a typing test given to applicants for a clerical position. Job sample tests are not often used in psychological assessments because the higher level positions for which psychological assessment is most often used are not amenable to discrete job samples. On occasion, though, a psychologist might have an assessee complete an "in-basket" test. This would usually occur in the context of a day-long assessment. The in-basket is a type of job sample test in that it directly assesses a constellation of job behaviors common to all managerial jobs.

Interest Inventories. Interest inventories are designed to identify occupational interests and directions. They have not been found to be of much use in psychological assessments for selection purposes, and are not usually given as part of a test battery. However, a test such as the Strong-Campbell Interest Inventory or the Kuder Interest Inventory can be of great value when conducting an assessment for developmental or career counseling purposes.

ORAL FEEDBACK TO THE REQUESTING MANAGER

The psychologist has now completed the following components of the psychological assessment process: the top management team and its philosophy have become known; the company's needs and expectations have been defined; and the candidate or employee has been interviewed and given a battery of psychological tests. Now it is time for the psychologist to step back, think about the information gathered, and develop conclusions about the individual.

When this has been accomplished, the psychologist will then contact the manager who requested the psychological assessment. The contact might be by phone or in person. The purpose of the contact is to orally brief the manager on the results of the psychological assessment. This briefing generally centers around the most pressing concern of the manager regarding the assessed individual. However, it might also include a brief overview of the assessee's personality, intelligence, and potential within the company.

If the person was seen in the context of a selection decision, the conversation might be quickly oriented toward a "yes-or-no" determination, with succinct descriptive reasons later given in support of the opinion. On the other hand, if the assessee is an employee who was seen for developmental purposes, the conversation between psychologist and requesting manager might be less targeted and more descriptive of broad strengths and limitations.

It is during the oral feedback session that the manager is likely to get the most honest and valid impressions from the psychologist. This is true for several reasons. First, the psychologist will usually be speaking at a time that is fairly close to the time of the interview. In fact, the oral briefing may be immediately after the candidate interview. This situation contrasts to the recollection and reliance on notes that must be done later when the psychologist finds time to sit down and write a formal report on the individual.

Second, the psychologist is more likely to give an uncensored accounting of his true impressions and judgments when the information is given orally. Access to and interpretation of a written report cannot be controlled by the psychologist once it is given to the client company. Most business psychologists word their written psychological assessment reports carefully so as to avoid misinterpretations and undue concerns should the assessee or other employees see the report. For this reason, the written report is most often a "softer" version of the oral feedback briefing.

In general, the oral feedback should be succinct in presenting the highlights of the assessment. The experienced business psychologist does not use psychological jargon, but speaks in everyday language. The effective psychologist will allow time for the manager to digest the conclusions presented, and to formulate questions. The psychologist knows that a deeper understanding about the company's needs and expectations can be gained from the requesting manager's impromptu questions during the feedback phase. These evolving issues can then be addressed in the subsequent written report or in a future one-to-one discussion.

The content of the oral feedback will contain a listing of the assessee's strengths and weaknesses relevant to the requirements of the job (if it is a selection assessment), or to the current job and potential future positions (if it is a developmental assessment). If there are several candidates for one position, the merits and drawbacks of each candidate relative to the others in meeting the job requirements may be discussed.

THE WRITTEN PSYCHOLOGICAL ASSESSMENT REPORT

Once the oral feedback to the requesting manager is completed, the psychologist will usually write a report detailing impressions and conclusions about the assessee. This report will be more elaborate and formal than the oral feedback. It will contain a number of sections, each discussing a particular dimension of the individual. While there are many variations in the style and content of psychological assessment reports depending on the psychologist or consulting firm, almost all reports have in common the following areas.

An overall description of the individual's intellectual functioning is usually presented. This might be followed by an analysis of the assessee's personality. Most reports have a section discussing how the individual gets along with other people. If the position is managerial in nature, the report might contain a section analyzing the person's capacity for effective leadership. Often, an overall conclusion or summary is included. Many psychologists include a point-by-point list of developmental strengths and weaknesses in their reports. An in-depth discussion of the psychological assessment report with illustrative examples is presented in Chapter 6.

FEEDBACK TO THE ASSESSEE

When a psychologist conducts a psychological assessment with an employee of a requesting company, it is common practice to do a follow-up feedback session with that employee. If the assessment was done as part of a promotion process and the employee was given the promotion, the psychologist should spend a good amount of time reviewing all aspects of the assessment results. The purpose of this feedback meeting is to provide the promoted employee with as much personal and job-relevant insight as possible. Generally, employees in this position are quite open to receiving both positive and negative feedback.

Many business psychologists prefer to have the new manager present at the feedback session. The employee may be given a copy of the assessment report to read as the psychologist goes through the report point-by-point. The value of having the new manager present is that the feedback session can become a developmental and performance planning meeting. If consensus is reached on most of the major points coming out of the assessment, then the employee and manager will be focusing on the same current needs and future objectives.

Chapters 16 and 17 discuss in greater detail the application of the psychological assessment in developmental contexts.

A different situation exists when the psychologist meets with a candidate who was rejected for a position. While feedback is also important in this situation, the former candidate is less likely to be open about his or her faults. The psychologist should try to present the reasons why the individual was not selected for the position (as far as the psychological assessment had a bearing on the decision) in a manner that is constructive and future-oriented. If the rejected candidate is not a current employee of the requesting company, then most psychologists provide no feedback unless the former candidate returns to the company requesting this information.

THE CONTEXTS AND USES OF PSYCHOLOGICAL ASSESSMENT

As indicated in this chapter, the primary use of psychological assessment in business is in the context of selecting an employee for a particular position. Undoubtedly, the majority of psychological assessments are done for this purpose. However, there are several other important uses of the method. This chapter has also briefly discussed the use of psychological assessment as a tool to help develop an employee. In this context, the psychologist attempts to identify developmental weaknesses that are or will hinder the employee from reaching full potential. The discussion of this information is designed to impart a greater self-understanding to the assessee so that the employee can more quickly change self-defeating behaviors and improve upon existing skills.

A third use of psychological assessment is related to the above. In a career counseling context, the psychological assessment can be used to help determine whether a technical professional would be suited for a move into management. This use is of obvious benefit to a company because it can help eliminate costly placement errors.

Another application of psychological assessment is in the diagnosis and re-mediation of performance problems. For example, an executive with a talented but erratic subordinate could choose to have the individual evaluated by a business psychologist rather than resorting to termination. Working with the psychologist through the assessment process, the executive and subordinate could begin managing the problem areas.

Finally, psychological assessment is a tool that can be used by a top executive who is new to a company and wants to get a quick "read" on the managers reporting to him or her. In this context, the assessment is termed a management audit. The process generally requires all members of the top management team to go through psychological assessments. The goal is to not only develop profiles of each individual manager, but to capture the management culture of the company with its collective strengths and weaknesses. The management audit is the topic of Chapter 18.

CONCLUSION: REVISITING THE FRUGAL FASTENER COMPANY

Returning to the vignette that opened this chapter, what advice could we now give to Fred Anderson, director of marketing and the boss of the failing Tom Fielding? In the best of all situations, it would have been ideal if Fred had contacted a business psychologist before he hired Tom. The psychologist would have worked with Fred and the other key managers to develop a clear understanding of their expectations for successful performance from the person to be hired. The psychologist would have applied expertise as an evaluator of business personnel in an in-depth assessment of each candidate for the West Coast marketing director position. By going through this process before Tom was selected, Frugal Fastener could have avoided its great loss of time, money, and opportunities.

Even after Tom was hired, though, the assessment services of a psychologist could have been helpful in ameliorating the problem situation. An assessment conducted soon after the problematic behaviors became noticeable would have clarified the exact nature and extent of the performance incongruities. In addition, the evaluation may well have revealed aspects of George's, Phyllis's and Fred's behaviors that contributed to Tom's demise at Frugal Fastener. Managers rarely fail in isolation. The psychologist might have recommended that a management audit be conducted after carefully interviewing Tom and comparing the situation from both Tom's perspective and the view provided initially by Tom's boss, Fred Anderson. A management audit could have led to a series of problem identification meetings and, eventually, to several solid team-building sessions.

Psychological assessment is a powerful tool for the selection and development of key personnel, as well as for the identification of human resource-related organizational problems. It is a process that has been used by hundreds of companies for many years. The following chapters in this book take a detailed look at the psychological assessment, and describe its many applications in the business world. Most of the chapters were written by experienced business psychologists who are experts in the field of psychological assessment. Some of the chapters were written by executives in companies that use psychological assessments.

2

The History of Psychological Assessment in Business

Curtiss P. Hansen

INTRODUCTION

The use of psychological assessments in business settings extends back to the late 1930s. While isolated examples of psychologists or psychiatrists assessing employees can be found before this time, the few industrial psychologists of that era focused on group-level issues rather than assessments of individual employees or candidates. It was not until around World War II that psychological assessment as a business in itself came into being.

Prior to World War II, almost all psychologists taught and conducted research in colleges and universities. A handful of psychologists were consulting to business during the late 1930s. During World War II, many psychologists were hired full time by the military. A primary function of these psychologists was to assess the "fitness" of military personnel for specific duties and positions. The tools used in these assessments were primarily paper-and-pencil tests, supplemented by a face-to-face discussion of the results.

When the war ended, many of these psychologists left the military. Most returned to academia, although some decided that the business world could benefit from the skills they had developed in the military. Some of these psychologists took positions with large companies, while others joined together and christened some of the first psychological consulting firms working primarily with business. These firms drew some academic psychologists into their ranks. A few professors simply began consulting to business as a side activity once the ball started rolling.

The specialty area backgrounds of these first business psychologists were predominantly clinical. That is, they were trained to diagnose, treat, and conduct research in mental illness. Many of these psychologists took the tools of their clinical trade into the business world, only to discover that their methods did not fit very well. For example, the MMPI, a clinical test designed to detect various types of emotional disorder, was widely used in business. Similar instruments and interview approaches were used during these early years.

Eventually, psychologists who consulted to companies learned the language of business and the characteristics of business people. Many of the post–World War II business executives had been military officers during the war. Some of these men had worked with psychologists and were familiar with their assessment abilities. These and other managers gradually began to view the assessment and advisement functions of the business psychologist as aids in recognizing and remediating the managers' personal and professional areas of ineffectiveness. Thus, those psychologists with a military background or some experience actually working in a business setting fared the best. During the late 1940s and early 1950s, the field of industrial psychology began to gel, and psychological approaches to numerous business problems were codified.

The psychological assessments done in the late 1940s and the 1950s were generally of two types. One was similar to the "fitness for duty" reports common in the military. These assessments were often conducted by company psychologists on applicants for industrial jobs. The assessments generally consisted of a brief clinical interview followed (or preceded) by a battery of paper-and-pencil tests. Many psychologists would also administer projective tests such as the Rorschach Ink Blot or Worthington Incomplete Sentences.

The second type of psychological assessment conducted during the early years was an "executive appraisal." It is this type that is most similar to the modern psychological assessment, described in Chapter 1. These assessments were almost always conducted with the incumbents of top executive jobs in small to large companies, or with candidates for such positions. There was a greater focus on family history, childhood experiences, and early relationships with one's mother and father than there is currently. The spirit of the time for many psychologists was captured by Sigmund Freud's psychoanalytic approach to understanding people. Even business psychology was not immune to its influence. In addition, the business climate favored the "organization man," so conformity and loyalty were desirable traits sought in the assessment.

Executive appraisals were almost always conducted by outside psychologists. They were the bricks and mortar that built the psychological consulting firms of that time. One of the first and the most successful of these firms was, and is Rohrer, Hibler & Replogle (RH&R). RH&R began in the 1930s when Perry Rohrer, Francis Hibler, and Fred Replogle left their employer, a management engineering firm, to found their own firm in Chicago. As discussed in Chapter 19, RH&R (now known as RHR International) quickly grew from one office to several in the Midwest. Gradually, the firm expanded nationwide and, more recently, worldwide.

Many of the early RH&R psychologists left the company to start their own firms once they became proficient in the tools of the trade. For example, in 1952,

Edward Glaser left the Los Angeles office of RH&R to found Edward Glaser & Associates. Glaser's firm quickly expanded and continues to function today. Bill Humber and Paul Mundie also left RH&R in the early 1950s to found Humber, Mundie & McClary in Milwaukee, Wisconsin. Their firm soon expanded to three offices and is today one of the most respected business consulting firms in the Midwest. William, Lynde & Williams, headquartered in Boston, is another firm whose principals were once employed by Rohrer, Hibler & Replogle.

Some of the psychologists in academia organized university-affiliated institutes that provided, among other services, psychological assessments to business and government clients. An example of this arrangement was the Psychological Research Services Institute at Case Western Reserve University. In addition to providing assessments, this institute conducted research on the dynamics and effectiveness of psychological assessment.

During the 1960s, 1970s, and 1980s, psychological consultants to business proliferated. Although many of these consultants specialize in areas other than psychological assessment (stress management, for example), there are dozens of small firms providing assessment services to business. In addition, many of the large accounting and financial management consulting firms such as Arthur Anderson and Ernst & Young have added psychologists to their staffs and are offering psychological assessment services.

Some of these providers are good, some are bad. Because there is no official credentialing process for entry and practice in this field, anyone can adopt the name "psychological business consultant," or other official sounding title. It is illegal in most states, however, to use the title psychologist or consulting psychologist without having a license. To avoid getting stung by an unqualified practitioner, many executives seek word-of-mouth referrals from their counterparts in other businesses when considering hiring a consultant for evaluation purposes. The good consultants are confident enough in their assessment abilities to provide a trial assessment of the executive who is considering using the services. For most business people, this process is a true test of the method's potential value to the company.

AN INTERVIEW WITH THREE SENIOR PSYCHOLOGISTS

This section is an interview with three senior practitioners of psychological assessment who had a hand in the development of the method in the 1940s. These psychologists, now in their 70s, are W. J. Humber, Edward Glaser, and Richard Porter. In this discussion, the three men talk about psychological assessment, the role of a business psychologist, the qualities of a good manager, and a historical perspective on the field of psychological consultation to management and organizations. A brief description of each man's career precedes the interview.

W. J. Humber, Ph.D.

Dr. Humber earned a Ph.D. in Social Psychology from the University of Minnesota in 1941. He completed a one-year internship at Kalamazoo State Hospital in Michigan in 1942 and joined the psychology department at Lawrence University soon after. With co-author Richard Dewey, Humber published a widely used social psychology textbook, *The Development of Human Behavior*, in 1951. After 12 printings, the book was revised in 1966. He has also published a number of articles in professional and trade journals.

Dr. Humber joined the Chicago psychological consulting firm of Rohrer, Hibler & Replogle in 1945. After mastering the trade of psychological assessment, he left RH&R in 1952 with Paul Mundie, and they joined John McClary to found Humber, Mundie & McClary (HM&M) in Milwaukee. HM&M was modeled after RH&R, and provided similar services to management.

Dr. Humber holds an ABPP Diplomate in Clinical Psychology, and is a Fellow of the American Psychological Association. He was a founder and first president of the Wisconsin Psychological Association. Although he is 78 years old now, he continues to work full time conducting assessments and consulting to senior management.

Edward Glaser, Ph.D.

Dr. Glaser earned his Ph.D. in Social-Clinical Psychology from Columbia University in 1940. After graduation, he worked for the U.S. Public Health Service on an experimental project at the Federal Reformatory in Ohio. For two years, he worked on a program to rehabilitate psychopaths incarcerated in the prison. Glaser was a line officer during World War II from 1942 through early 1946. During his military service, he used his psychological training in various assignments. After his naval service, he resumed his psychology career by joining RH&R in Los Angeles in 1946. Following a disagreement with RH&R management over assessment procedures, he left the firm in 1955 to found Edward Glaser & Associates. He has published numerous articles on the psychological assessment method in professional journals. Dr. Glaser is now semi-retired but works personally with selected clients. He is also chairman of the board for the Human Interaction Research Institute.

J. Richard Porter, Ph.D.

Dr. Porter earned a Ph.D. in Psychology from the University of Pittsburgh in 1951. His first professional assignment was as head of the Mobile Trainee Acceptance Center in 1943. This project was sponsored by the War Manpower Commission and the U.S. Office of Education. Its purpose was to determine if psychological tests could be useful in placing people in war-related jobs. Later that year, he was called into military service, and spent the next three years as a naval officer.

When the war ended, Dr. Porter completed his doctorate, then returned to his previous position in Pittsburgh. The trainee acceptance project, however, was no longer government funded, but was now funded by various private foundations and grants from businesses. Its mission now was to develop better selection methods for nonmilitary organizations. Gradually, the "project" grew to become a consulting firm with multiple contracts, employing many psychologists. This firm, Psychological Service of Pittsburgh (recently changed to PSP Human Resource Development), employed Frederick Herzberg as its research director. While at PSP Herzberg developed the two-factor theory of motivation. Porter spent his entire career with PSP as the firm's overall director. He is now retired.

The Interview

Dr. Hansen: What was the field of psychological consultation to management like when you began your careers?

Dr. Porter: In those early years, there were few guidelines. Two of my colleagues founded similar firms in Cleveland and Philadelphia. The three of us met from time to time to discuss problems and procedures.

Dr. Humber: I was one of the first psychologists hired at RH&R. I had a lot of respect for those fellows, but they were very, very new at this themselves. They had a definite structure set up, even in the beginning. There were many activities that we had to pass on because they didn't fit into the philosophy of the firm, even though they may have been useful to the client.

Dr. Glaser: It was different at RH&R than at other firms that employed psychologists. Their philosophy was to start at the top of the company, to get to know the culture-shapers.

Dr. Humber: Yes, you had to evaluate the CEO before you did anything else. The younger psychologists have gotten away from this policy, which is probably not a good thing. It lessens your impact in a company. However, it is harder today to deal directly with the top in large companies. One reason for this is the greater role and influence of the human resource department. Back then, there was no such thing. Companies had an employment office and that was it.

Dr. Hansen: How were psychologists used by management when you started out?

Dr. Porter: As a non-RH&R trained psychologist, my perspective is a bit different. Management used our (PSP) psychologists primarily to select clerical, technical, and trades people. There was a heavy reliance on psychological test data. Gradually, the field changed. Although tests were still used in the selection of trade level employees, the psychologist consultant began to set up procedures and trained technicians in the company to do the testing and interpreting of results under the direction of the psychologist. Our psychologists then turned to the assessment of managerial level people, and became involved in executive and managerial counseling. More emphasis was placed on the problems of the organization—how it functions and how it can be changed. Gradually, the role of the psychologist changed from that of tester to problem solver, with expertise in a variety of areas.

Dr. Glaser: RH&R, and later my own firm, was always focused on the top management level. Our primary concern was helping management identify and solve immediate problems, and to help them better appreciate their long-term needs. Beginning with the assessment process, we could watch how managers operated, gauge their impact on others, make suggestions, and try to give them some insight into their selves. We tried to be helpful in developing their careers as executives.

Dr. Humber: Originally, there was more romance in the business. The entrepreneurs of those days were intrigued with the contributions psychologists had made in the war effort and felt there could be considerable transfer of those skills to business. There was a good feeling of mutual adventure and high expectations for change and progress in human relationships within the industrial world.

Dr. Hansen: How were psychological tests used in the business sector when you began your careers?

Dr. Glaser: RH&R used very few psychological tests. The assessment was based more on the clinical interpretation of the interview. A timed problem-solving test of 36 problems was used. They also used a brief, homegrown personality inventory.

Dr. Humber: To not use tests was really bucking the trend back then. Everything that psychologists did was in the area of measurement. In the schools you were taught that everything that exists can be measured. That was the theme song. Although Perry Rohrer didn't call it a clinical approach, he was interested in getting to know the individual. His idea was to look at the person and not at test results. In fact, he hardly ever used a test. Tests were strictly a support. Emphasis was on the personal history and how to predict a man's future from looking at his past.

Dr. Porter: Because one of PSP's main goals was to find better uses of psychological tests in the selection and placement of employees, we were quite involved in this area. Tests have changed greatly over the past 45 years. Better measures have been developed and the way they are used has changed. Back in 1943, there were very few tests available that could be used with a nonpsychiatric population. Among cognitive ability measures, there was the ACE for high-level managers, the Otis for middle-level personnel, and the Beta (a nonverbal test) for people with limited reading skills. The personality measures available were the Bell Adjustment Inventory and the Bernreuter Personality Test. Gradually, multiple factor tests began appearing, such as the Guilford–Zimmerman Temperament Survey.

Dr. Hansen: What is your definition of a psychological assessment?

Dr. Glaser: It is an attempt to understand and assess an individual with reference to five behavioral areas of interest to the company. These are: intellectual characteristics, emotional makeup, skill in interpersonal relations, insight into self and others, and ability to organize and direct. The focus is on assessing those things that bear upon executive development.

Dr. Porter: The psychological assessment provides the individual being assessed an opportunity to describe his interests, values, abilities, personality, and motivation so that job assignments can be made that will maximize his strengths, and allow him to advance to the highest level that he is capable of attaining. The psychological assessment in the business setting is geared to job placement and advancement. It is normally conducted with people who are, or have been, successfully employed. The question to answer is whether the individual will be successful in the job situation for which he is being considered. What is his potential, where can he make the greatest contribution, and what will it take to keep him happy?

Dr. Humber: Before you can define what it is, you have to know the purpose of the assessment. In most industrial situations, it is to obtain enough clinical, projective, and psychometric information to be able to make a prediction of a candidate's behavior in a particular business culture. If the assessment is completed for the individual's own use, then it is for the purpose of providing the person the opportunity to gain insights into himself, his interests, and what will have the most impact on his life satisfaction.

Dr. Hansen: How does a psychological assessment in a business setting differ from an assessment in a clinical setting?

Dr. Humber: The main difference is that in the industrial setting the candidate is advised, or should be advised, that the assessment is being done for the purpose of predicting his behavior and contributions in a particular industrial or organizational culture. Whereas in a clinical setting, the assessment is done in terms of the person's present life circumstances, examining the assets and liabilities the person brings to his opportunities in life.

Dr. Porter: In a clinical setting, the emphasis may be more on adjustment problems, and tests of that nature may be given to diagnose the problem and determine a course of therapy.

Dr. Glaser: Also, a psychological assessment is usually shorter in business. A long assessment would be about five hours for a top executive, though most are much shorter.

Dr. Hansen: How is the psychological assessment useful to management?

Dr. Glaser: It can help identify people with a better chance of doing the type of job that the company wants done. Pick out people who want to stay with the company.

Dr. Porter: The psychological assessment is useful to management in that it provides a picture of how the individual sees himself, what his values and motivations are, which environment he is most likely to be successful in, and where his strengths lie.

Dr. Hansen: How do you know that your conclusions are accurate and valid?

Dr. Porter: The validity of assessments on a group of applicants for the same position is straightforward. Performance on the job is the criterion—it may be a rating of overall performance, rate of advancement, turnover, or whatever management views as most important to the company. The specific predictions for this group of employees is then statistically related to the criterion, which will show the level of the assessment's validity. The process is less clear in executive assessments, though. Because there may be only one person in the job, a statistical validation is not possible. However, if the executives recommended tend not to work out, management will not be happy with the assessment results, and the psychologist will be less likely to do business with that company in the future. The psychologists who are accurate stay in business.

Dr. Glaser: I agree with Dr. Porter's comments. It is important to follow up with companies so that performance data is obtained on the people who were assessed and then hired. For those employees who did not work out satisfactorily, the psychologist should review the report in light of actual job performance, and look for what may have been missed or interpreted incorrectly. Learn and grow.

Dr. Humber: Validity in statistical terms is a moving target. My own satisfactions and comfort derive from those client relationships that are long-lasting, mutually productive, and satisfying to both the candidate and employer. Validity and reliability of the assessment are closely related to the psychologist's knowledge of the real expectations of the corporation's executives as opposed to their simply stated objectives. Assessments made without such a knowledgeable relationship of the culture and expectations of the hiring institution are probably substantially less valid than those made under the most favorable circumstances. The validity of the assessment is related not only to the skill of the psychologist, but also to the character and quality of the culture in which the candidate will work. A good professional psychologist will enhance the validity of his recommendations by following up on the candidate's employment. This discussion points out the need for the company and the psychologist to develop a continuing and hopefully long relationship. The psychologist should support the candidate in achieving satisfaction and productivity in the new job. If the culture needs change or improvement to motivate the candidate, the psychologist will attend to these modifications. Thus, the complete psychologist will do more than make a recommendation. He or she will work with the candidate and the company to maximize the candidate's effectiveness in the new job. I realize this view of assessment validity is quite different from the statistical approach discussed by Dr. Porter. However, I feel that this view is essential to ensure that our method remains valid and useful.

Dr. Hansen: Some companies feel that their own top managers can do a better job than an outside psychologist in assessing candidates for top management positions. How do you respond to this?

Dr. Glaser: Managers are not qualified to dig into a person's values and background. However, the psychologist's assessment should be used in combination with the manager's impressions. Most companies will screen out the less desirable applicants and only send the final candidates to the psychologist. The manager's evaluations should be used, though they are not likely to be as comprehensive as the psychologist's.

Dr. Humber: I agree. Undoubtedly, there are some managers who do a first-rate job of selecting and developing their own personnel. Probably most managers believe that since they are successful in managing money they are equally competent in making assessments of individuals. In reality, a psychologist has some advantages, including, of course, training in applying psychological procedures to assessment situations in organizations. For one thing, the psychologist is a guest in the company he is serving. His home is elsewhere and he is not totally dependent on the organization he serves. He can function with greater objectivity because he is less emotionally involved. In short, he sees assessments in a larger perspective and without personal involvement.

Dr. Porter: There is no question that top managers can provide useful, even critical judgments in the assessment of candidates for top management. This is particularly so if the candidate has worked for the company for many years, perhaps even worked for the manager doing the assessment. But this is not enough. How many times have highly productive people been promoted, only to fail in the new assignment? Most sophisticated managers want to know more about how a candidate will do in the new position, especially if it is in a different environment. This is not a question of whether the manager can make a better assessment than the outside psychologist, but rather that the best assessment will be the result of both methods used in conjunction. I would recommend that the manager and psychologist review each other's data and come to a joint recommendation.

Dr. Hansen: What makes a good manager?

Dr. Humber: Well, that depends on the situation. Some people will be a good manager in one place but will fail in a different environment. I saw a man the other day who presented himself well, was bright and eager to do something big with his ideas. However, the company that sent him over is looking for managers who are efficient and obedient, people they can control easily. So for this company, he is not a good manager, but for a different company he could one day be their president.

Dr. Porter: It is difficult to generalize across all managers and all situations, but there are some commonalities among good managers. Their verbal skills tend to be average or above, and they are good at logical reasoning. They have better than average "people" skills. They get satisfaction working through and directing others, rather than just what they can do themselves. They react to frustration and pressure rationally, rather than emotionally.

Dr. Hansen: What have you found in your assessments of managers to be the "make or break" attributes that determine the future of a young manager?

Dr. Porter: The ability to get along with people is the key for young managers. Anybody can get along with people who are easy to get along with. That's no measure of the person's skill in this area. How does he get along with people who are difficult to deal with? That is the key.

Dr. Glaser: The critical factor is whether he has skill in inviting his people to participate in contributing to decisions and solutions. Does he often ask his people, "What can we do here?" or "What ideas and suggestions do you have for dealing with this?" Another important quality is being able to look at the broad picture and see what really bears upon the matter.

Dr. Humber: Hard work is not enough. Those who move ahead in management positions are the people who do more than others, who go out of their way in terms of extending themselves positively with imagination and leadership. The people who get ahead and become valuable to the company are the ones who know how to listen, who understand what the boss needs or wants conspicuously or subtly, and who contribute toward meeting those needs.

Dr. Hansen: How do most managers view psychologists?

Dr. Glaser: The company invited you (the psychologist) in and is paying your bills, so this indicates that they see you as valuable. This perception of value can be quickly destroyed if you make too many recommendation errors or violate the manager's confidence.

Dr. Porter: Managers who work with psychologists probably view them differently from those who do not have such a relationship. Also, it depends on the type of work the psychologist does for the company. Some may be seen as testers and number crunchers, while others are viewed as counselors and problem solvers. Some are viewed as experts only in dealing with individuals, while others are seen as experts with groups or organization-wide problems.

Dr. Humber: In a really productive relationship, the top executive usually develops a certain amount of psychological "transference" to the psychologist, and views him not only as a professional support, but also as a trusted friend. This may become a very private relationship that enables the executive to function with the psychologist in an open and relaxed manner. The psychologist's observations and feedback in this type of relationship allows the executive to sharpen his wits and check the validity of his thinking. However, there may also be productive relationships with managers where things are strictly objective and technical. In these instances, the psychologist is strictly a consulting aide.

3

Psychological Assessment: A Research Literature Review

Curtiss P. Hansen

RESEARCH STUDIES ON PSYCHOLOGICAL ASSESSMENT IN BUSINESS

This chapter reviews the research that has been conducted over the years on the psychological assessment method of selecting employees. Although hundreds of companies have used assessments as part of their selection programs for managers and other employees, rarely do managers ask to see hard research data on the method. Instead, the executives in charge of authorizing a psychological assessment selection program for their companies tend to rely on their "gut feeling," the accuracy of their own personal assessments, or the recommendations from top managers at other companies. Psychologists, particularly those who do not conduct psychological assessments or who advocate a different selection technique, tend to be more scrutinizing and critical of the method from a research perspective. A research summary is provided in this chapter so that managers can supplement their intuition with knowledge of the relevant "hard" studies on psychological assessment.

Research Questions

Is the method valid? Do employees selected or promoted using psychological assessment information as a key input fare better than those chosen without such data to aid in making the decision? Surprisingly, there is very little research on this subject. This state of affairs is even more incredible considering the current and past popularity of the practice when compared to the thousands of studies conducted in the field of industrial-organizational psychology on topics of limited relevance to "real world" human resource management and organizational functioning.

Although there are many reasons why psychologists do not conduct and publish research on the validity of assessments in business, one reason is simply that it is difficult to do good research in this area. A good study would answer the following questions: Do the conclusions regarding those aspects of the candidate that were assessed accurately predict the company's evaluation of these attributes a year or more later? Did the psychologist's overall conclusion about the individual accurately predict the company's overall conclusion about the employee a year or more later? Finally, which assessment tools were most important in determining the psychologist's conclusions, and which tools were most strongly related to the company's appraisal of the employee at a later date?

To research these questions would require a year or more to do the study. One would need to investigate the assessment as a whole, as well as all the components of the assessment process. The task is made even more difficult because of the small number of assessees hired by a company in a given time period. The researcher must either collect data for several years from one company, or try to combine the assessments done in several companies.

In an academic environment where university-based research psychologists are evaluated by the number of research publications they produce each year, it is unlikely that this large and time-consuming undertaking would be completed. It is more expedient and personally beneficial for an assistant professor to research small facets of the overall psychological assessment process. Further hindering the university-based researcher is the policy of most companies and consulting firms not to release assessment-related data to those outside their organizations. Not only is this information considered confidential, it is also viewed as proprietary to the purchaser of the services. These are other reasons why there are no recent large-scale studies of the psychological assessment method's validity.

There are many studies that evaluate the validity of particular tests or interview formats in the prediction of job performance. However, over the past 40 years, only a handful of studies have dealt with the questions listed above. All but one generated results supportive of the psychological assessment as a predictor of future job performance. The most recently published research report on the topic concluded: "In general, results show positive relationships between ratings based on assessment reports and supervisory ratings" (Ryan and Sackett 1987, 460). The following sections briefly review the studies upon which this conclusion is based.

Handyside and Duncan, 1954

J. Handyside and D.C. Duncan (1954) published one of the first empirical investigations into the validity of using multiple assessment techniques to arrive at a hire/no hire decision. The subjects in this study were first-level supervisors. Four years after the group was hired, performance ratings were obtained on each supervisor. Most of the individual sources of selection information were related to job performance. However, the ability to predict performance was most powerful when the psychological tests, two lengthy interviews (with separate interviewers), panel review, and letters of recommendation were combined.

Hilton, Bolin, Parker, Taylor and Walker, 1955

The Hilton et al. research (1955) was the first major study to evaluate the accuracy of psychological assessment. The specific purposes of the study were to validate the psychologists' predictions of overall job performance, and to assess the accuracy of their predictions of specific performance dimensions. The subjects were 100 employees from 18 companies. A variety of jobs were represented, including salesmen, engineers, and accountants. About a third of the sample were managers.

The psychologists used several tests, including the Allport-Vernon-Lindzey Study of Values, Strong Vocational Interest Blank, Guilford–Zimmerman Temperament Survey, and a general cognitive ability test. Based on the personal interview and test results, the psychologists rated each employee on five scales: sociability, organizational ability, drive, overall performance, and potential for advancement. After a period of six months to two years, each employee's supervisor rated the employee on the same five scales.

This study indicated that the psychologists were accurate in their ability to predict the supervisors' ratings of employee performance. Hilton et al. concluded: "Compared with most validity findings, these results are promising and indicate that the technique [psychological assessment] has practical value" (Hilton et al. 1955, 293).

Trankel, 1959

A. Trankel (1959) studied the validity of airline pilot assessments. He concluded that combining interview information and impressions with psychological test data resulted in stronger prediction of performance than when using tests or the interview alone.

The Standard Oil Study, 1961

This study was an attempt to demonstrate the validity of psychological assessment in the prediction of mid- to upper-level managers' job performance (Laurent 1968). The research took place at Standard Oil of New Jersey and involved 443 experienced managers from different areas of the company. In 1955, the managers went through psychological assessments that included personality and cognitive ability tests, a management situations test, background survey, personal history record, and an in-depth personal interview. Four to six years later, performance data was collected on the managers. The data included ratings of managerial effectiveness by each manager's superior, position level increases, and salary progress. In addition, an overall success factor was created from the above three sources of performance outcome data.

The results of this study provided strong support for the psychological assessment method. The best combination of the predictor variables from the psychological assessment clearly differentiated the most successful from the least successful managers. For example, 42 of the 44 managers with the best assessment profiles were in the group with the highest level of rated job success.

The Case Western Reserve Studies, 1962

During the 1950s, Psychological Research Services of Case Western Reserve University provided psychological assessments to business. In 1962, several psychologists published a series of reports summarizing research on the accuracy of assessments in predicting a number of job-related personal characteristics. As described in Campbell (1962), Campbell, Otis, Liske, and Prien (1962), Huse (1962), and Otis, Campbell, and Prien (1962), the procedure required two interviewers and a separate tester/interpreter. These three psychologists rated each candidate in separate reports. A fourth psychologist then integrated the three reports into a final report.

Each candidate was rated by the psychologists on the job-relevant dimensions of supervisory ability, planning, drive and effort, persuasiveness, sociability, ability to handle complexity, originality, and overall effectiveness. A minimum of six months after the assessment, the supervisors of these employees also completed ratings on the same set of dimensions. The components of the psychological assessment were the personal interview plus a variety of paper-and-pencil personality tests, projective personality tests, interest inventories, and several cognitive ability tests (see chapters 1 and 5 for discussions of these tests).

The result of these studies was that the psychologist's original ratings of the candidates were similar to those the supervisors completed six months or more later. One area of disagreement was on the drive and effort (motivation) dimension. Otherwise, the prediction of each dimension and that of overall performance was fairly accurate.

Specific conclusions from the studies are as follows. "It appears, then, that the psychologist is to some degree able to identify or interpret the psychological requirements of unique positions, to integrate and compare this material with what is known about the psychological characteristics of the individual, and to come up with an effective prediction" (Otis, Campbell, and Prien 1962, 442). Also, "Maximum effectiveness in prediction of future job performance as represented by supervisor ratings is obtained through the use of an interview combined with the clinical interpretation of psychometric test scores" (Campbell, Otis, Liske, and Prien 1962, 72–73).

Finally, "At this point it seems reasonable to say that psychologists are able to predict the job performance of an individual in terms of interpersonal relations, intellectual functioning, and the motivation or job effort the individual brings to the job" (Otis, Campbell, and Prien 1962, 444).

Albrecht, Glaser, and Marks, 1964

This study described one company's selection assessment program for new sales managers. An assessment battery consisting of an extensive two-hour interview, personality tests, and cognitive ability tests was used. Using the results of the interview and tests, the psychologists rated and ranked the managers in terms of four performance dimensions: forecasting and budgeting, sales performance, interpersonal relations, and overall effectiveness. Using these dimensions, performance ratings were completed on each sales manager by an immediate (district) manager. Rankings were done by the regional managers and the sales managers' peers.

The results of this study were somewhat mixed. The psychologists were generally in agreement with the regional managers and the peers in their rankings of the sales managers' performance on the four dimensions. However, the psychologists' ratings of the sales managers accurately predicted only two of the four areas rated by the immediate managers. The correctly predicted dimensions were sales performance and interpersonal relations. Albrecht, Glaser, and Marks concluded that "the use of multiple assessment (psychological assessment) procedures did result in generally valid predictions" (1964, 359).

Korman Literature Review, 1968

In 1968, Abraham Korman reviewed the research literature on all predictors of managerial performance. In a section summarizing the research on psychological assessment (which he terms "judgmental prediction"), he concluded: "Judgmental prediction can do as well as actuarial (statistical) prediction in some instances and perhaps better" (Korman 1968, 312).

DeNelsky and McKee, 1969

This research is one of the few descriptions of a government agency's selection program. G. Y. DeNelsky and M. G. McKee (1969) studied the predictive value of the psychological assessment in selecting 32 CIA overseas agents. The assessment consisted of psychological tests and an interview. The psychologist rated each candidate on specific job-related personal characteristics. Performance appraisals were completed by superiors on all agents 12 to 57 months after the original assessments were done. The superiors rated each agent on the same set of personal characteristics used by the psychologists.

The ratings from the psychological assessments were strongly related to the subsequent performance appraisal ratings (validity coefficient of .32). Interestingly, the psychologists were able to predict the agents' weaknesses better than their strengths. In the prediction of weaknesses, 76 percent of the predictions were judged to be accurate, while 55 percent of the strength predictions were deemed to be valid.

In summing up this research, the authors stated: "It is reasonable to conclude that psychologists can predict competence and specific performance and personality characteristics of employees using psychological assessments. . . . This study does provide reassurance that the assessment process can result in meaningful predictions of job behavior" (DeNelsky and McKee 1969, 443–44).

Miner, 1970

Not all the research on psychological assessment has been supportive. John Miner (1970) conducted a series of studies on the method and failed to find evidence of validity. The five studies described below contain the results of psychological assessments completed on business consultant candidates for a large consulting firm. The assessments were performed by four to six psychological consulting firms.

Study One. Ten psychologists from six firms assessed a group of business consultant candidates during the 1960s. From this group, 80 consultants were hired. About one-fourth were hired against the psychologists' recommendations. The consultants' progress was tracked throughout their tenure with the company, which ranged from one month to nine years. After all the consultants from this group had left the company for one reason or other, the follow-up study was completed.

The psychologists' original "hire" or "no hire" recommendations were statistically compared to three types of performance criteria: length of tenure, increase in compensation each year, and the value of the consultant's work as rated by the immediate manager. The results failed to show a consistent relationship between the recommendations and the performance criteria. The consultants with "hire" recommendations were just as likely to do poorly as the "no hire" consultants were to do well.

Study Two. This study was a replication of the first study, except that only 53 consultants were involved. The results were similar to those obtained in the original research.

Study Three. The third study reported by Miner looked at the validity of psychological assessments on incumbent business consultants. A total of 73 consultants were assessed by 14 psychologists from five firms. The measure of success to which the psychologists' evaluations were compared was each consultant's increase in salary from year to year. However, as in the previous studies, this measure of job success was not accurately predicted by the bottom-line conclusions drawn from the psychological assessments.

Study Four. In this study, current employees were also assessed, although by different psychologists and with several additional performance indicators in the analyses. The criteria that were correlated with the psychologists' overall evaluations of each of the 34 consultants were increase in salary from year to year, ratings of overall performance by several managers, ratings of potential for advancement by several managers, and professional grade-level increases over time.

Once again, the results gave no support for the psychological assessments. In fact, there was an inverse relationship between the psychologists' recommendations and the grade-level change indicator. In other words, the lower the psychologist's evaluation of the consultant, the more likely the consultant was to have made substantial professional advancement, compared to the others in the group.

Study Five. The fifth study differed from the previous ones in that it focused on a comparison of the psychologists' recommendations. It was discovered that some psychologists tend to consistently give either favorable or unfavorable recommendations.

The author concludes that "these results provide absolutely no evidence for the predictive validity of psychological evaluations as they are currently conducted in the business world" (Miner 1970, 402). This is a sweeping statement that might be tempered by considering the following facts and possibilities.

First, all of these studies used business consultants as subjects. Given that many other researchers have obtained positive results with psychological assessments of managers, it might be that there is something peculiar to the consulting profession that makes it difficult to predict future performance. Also, it is not clear if the psychologists had experience in the assessment of consultants. It is possible that their concept of a successful consultant was actually that of a successful manager.

Second, the use of multiple psychologists from many different firms goes counter to the typical practice procedures outlined in Chapter 1. The relationship between a psychologist and the client company is necessarily an exclusive and intimate one. Simply knowing the job description for the consultant's position is not enough to let a psychologist accurately predict a candidate's future performance. The psychologist must become acquainted with the heart and soul of the organization before the candidate's personal characteristics will begin to make sense. In the research described by Miner (1970), it is extremely unlikely that this relationship developed, given the great number of psychologists involved in the studies. Thus, the psychologists' predictions were likely to have been superficial.

Third, other studies have found that some psychologists tend to be either mostly favorable or mostly negative in their assessments of candidates. However, this fact is generally not an issue for most companies that use only one psychologist because managers will perceive the degrees of favorableness in the psychologist's reports over time. What is obscured in the fifth study is the likelihood that all psychologists grouped in the "favorable" category actually described a range of favorableness in their reports. As a company continues to work with psychologists such as these, the managers will come to interpret the different degrees of favorableness as indicating a continuum from very good to mediocre. The same is true for psychologists who tend to focus on the negative in their reports. Because Miner's research had so many psychologists involved, the consulting firm's management was probably unable to perceive this phenomenon.

Personal Decisions, Inc., 1970s and 1980s

Study One. Robert Silzer (1986) reported two studies conducted by Personnel Decisions, Inc. during the 1970s and 1980s. The first of these, The Indicators of Management Success Study, involved 1,749 managers representing all levels and functions of management. The California Personality Inventory (CPI) and several cognitive ability tests were administered as possible "indicators." Psychologists used the test information as the basis of their ratings of each manager's motivation, judgment/problem-solving ability, administrative ability, communication skills, interpersonal skill, leadership ability, and degree of personal adjustment.

A large number of the psychologists' ratings and the test scores predicted management success. Among the areas rated by the psychologists, leadership ability was the most powerful indicator of success, followed by motivation. Only judgment/problem-solving ability failed to predict success. Ten CPI scales predicted management success. A manager scoring high on these scales would be a dominant person who likes to be in control of situations. The manager is interested in management and in directing the activities of others. However, the manager is also an outgoing individual with good social skills. More than a manager, this person is a leader. The manager thinks highly of his or her abilities and place in the world, and has a strong sense of personal security. The manager is able to tolerate ambiguity while working toward solutions to problems. The manager who scores high on the CPI scales enjoys challenges and needs to achieve goals, whether alone or with people.

Study Two. The Assessment Research Study was a follow-up on 208 managers from two companies who went through psychological assessments. Job performance ratings from each manager's superior were obtained eight to ten years after the psychological assessments. The superiors rated the managers on administrative and intellectual performance, work motivation, emotional and behavioral maturity, and general effectiveness.

A variety of psychological tests were used in the original psychological assessments, including the CPI, Strong-Campbell Interest Inventory (SCII), Sentence Completion, Wesman, EAS 1, 5, 6, and 7, and the Differential Aptitude Test. Based on the test results, a personal interview, and job sample exercises, the psychologists rated each manager on 38 personal characteristic dimensions. These dimensions were grouped under six headings: cognitive and skill dimensions; organizing and planning dimensions; work orientation dimensions; interpersonal dimensions; energizing and orienting dimensions; and personal adjustment dimensions.

Many of the dimensions strongly predicted the job performance ratings. Administrative performance was highly related to intellectual curiosity, organization, and the need to accomplish goals independently. Interpersonal effectiveness was best predicted by oral communication, the desire to lead, and flexibility of behavior. Ratings on the intellectual performance criterion were highly related to organization, overall intelligence, and planning.

The superiors' appraisals of the managers' work-oriented motivation correlated highly with the psychologists' assessment of need for achievement, energy, and competitive aggression. The emotional and behavioral maturity dimension was most related to the original rating of energy, practical judgment (decision quality), and organization. Finally, general management effectiveness was strongly predicted by the desire to lead, competitive aggression, and need for achievement.

The psychologists' assessment ratings were also correlated with managerial tenure (number of years with the company). Organizational commitment was the strongest predictor, while the desire to advance and long-range goal orientation were negatively related to tenure (i.e., managers who do not want promotions and who do not set long-range goals tend to stay the longest with these companies).

The dimension from the psychological assessment that was most closely related to salary increases over the years was independence, which was the strongest predictor. Organization commitment and need for security were negatively correlated with salary increases. In other words, the ''company man'' tends not to get the largest salary increases.

CHARACTERISTICS OF CURRENT PSYCHOLOGICAL ASSESSMENT PRACTICE

This section presents the results of a recent survey of 163 doctoral level, industrial-organizational psychologists regarding their practice of psychological assessment in business. The survey was conducted in late 1986 and the results were published in 1987 by Ann Marie Ryan and Paul Sackett (Ryan & Sackett 1987). The survey was conducted because of the paucity of information available about the psychological assessment and its dimensions in actual practice. The chapters comprising this book are not taught in any graduate psychology training program in the United States of which the author is aware. Psychologists who use psychological assessment are trained by the consulting firms using the method.

The Ryan and Sackett survey discovered that most psychological assessments are conducted in manufacturing industries, with banking/finance, retail, and service businesses also well-represented. Fifty-six percent of psychologists who conduct psychological assessments have their practices in cities of one million or more residents. Most assessees are white (89%) and male (76%). As discussed in Chapter 27, the latter situation will gradually change as the demographic makeup of middle and top management changes during the coming years.

Levels in the Organization and Assessments

More assessments are done at the middle-management level (34%) than at other levels within an organization. Top management assessments accounted for another 25 percent of those completed. Forty-two percent of the psychologists reported conducting assessments at the middle-management level, while 25 percent said they assessed top-level managers. Another 10 percent did assessments of sales candidates.

Reasons for Conducting Psychological Assessments

Psychological assessments are conducted for a variety of reasons, according to the psychologists who mailed back their surveys. These purposes, and the percentage of psychologists who offer assessments for that purpose, are as follows:

- Final candidate selection (83%)
- Promotion determination (76%)
- Employee development (67%)
- Career counseling (66%)
- Succession planning (47%)
- Initial applicant screening (42%)
- Outplacement counseling (30%)

Most typically, psychological assessments for final hiring selection decisions are in greatest demand. The psychologists reported that 53 percent of their assessments were of this type. A distant second were psychological assessments for promotion decisions, at 20 percent of all assessments.

Length and Prices of Psychological Assessments

The typical psychological assessment is four to eight hours long. The second most common assessment length is two to four hours. The 1986 price of a psychological assessment was in the $300 to $600 range, with an average price of $500 and a median price of $420. Price was determined by the extensiveness of the assessment and the type of feedback required, the type of assessment (i.e., selection or promotion), and the level and type of job for which the individual was being assessed. The 1991 price of an assessment is probably about $100 more than shown in the 1986 figures.

Psychological assessments conducted higher up the management hierarchy are progressively more expensive (from $352 to $723). In addition, psychological assessments for promotion and succession planning at all levels were costly ($705), while sales and nonmanagement assessments were least expensive ($342 and $265, respectively). Finally, 56 percent of the psychologists believed their prices to be about average for the local market.

Use of Tests and Interviews in Psychological Assessments

Ryan and Sackett (1987) discovered that 78 percent of the surveyed psychologists used cognitive ability tests as part of their assessments. These 127 psychologists used 61 different ability tests. The most popular test was the Watson-Glaser Critical Thinking Appraisal (38%), with the Wesman Personnel Classification Test (19%), Employee Aptitude Series (19%), and Wechsler Adult Intelligence Scale-Revised (18%) being frequent choices. Fourteen percent of the psychologists used a proprietary cognitive ability test designed by their firms.

Paper-and-pencil personality inventories were used by 78 percent of the respondents. Of this group, the 16 Personality Factor Test and Guilford–Zimmerman Temperament Survey were most popular (33% each). Other frequently used personality tests were the California Personality Inventory (28%), MMPI (20%), Myers-Briggs Type Indicator (19%), and the Edwards Personal Preference Profile (18%). Nine percent used a proprietary personality test designed by their firms.

Only 34 percent of the psychologists used projective personality tests. These 55 psychologists used 25 different projective tests. However, a sentence completion test of some type was used by the majority of psychologists who used projective tests (77%), with the Thematic Apperception Test (TAT) and Rorschach Ink Blot Test used next most often (43% and 25%, respectively).

It was more common for the psychologists to compare a candidate's test scores to a "local" normative group than to a nationwide normative sample. The local norms could be based on the test scores from all employees in a large company, or could consist of a defined group's scores, such as those of sales managers. Many of the psychologists use a combination of local and national norms when interpreting test results.

The decision of which test to use in a given situation was based upon research results for most of the survey respondents. The research could be either published in professional journals or proprietary to the consulting firm or client company. Very few psychologists endorsed a trial-and-error approach to test selection.

Finally, simulation exercises of the type usually used in assessment centers were endorsed by 38% of the psychologists. Of these, the most frequently used was some type of in-basket exercise (60%). Also used were role-plays (21%), writing exercises (14%), and business cases (12%).

Regarding the use of the personal interview, 73 percent of the psychologists reported using a semi-structured interview. Fifteen percent stated that they used a structured interview, while 11 percent endorsed the unstructured approach. The typical interview was reported to last one-and-a-half hours.

Dimensions/Categories Used in Psychological Assessments

The candidate performance dimensions assessed by the most psychologists were interpersonal skills, judgment and analytical skills, organization and planning, intelligence, supervisory skills, emotional maturity, leadership, energy, and drive. A total of 70 separate dimensions were tallied from the psychologists' lists. Each dimension was assessed by at least one psychologist. The dimensions that were judged to be most critical in predicting future overall effectiveness were work history, verbal ability, motivation, and intelligence.

Information about the Company and Position

How do psychologists get needed information about the company? Almost all respondents obtained information by interviewing employees (82%) and by informally talking with managers (81%). To get information about the position in question, most psychologists review written job descriptions (81%) or talk about the job with the supervisor (75%) or with the original company contact (81%).

What kinds of information do psychologists want to have in order to be most effective as a consultant to the company? Most of the psychologists in the survey listed the following: key position job descriptions, understanding of the company culture, performance expectations, current top executives' management style, an overview of the company's lines of business, and the purpose of the psychological assessments from the company's viewpoint. Concerning the job itself, the psychologists wanted to know the tasks, duties, knowledge, skills, and abilities required to succeed in the job; a job description; the supervisor's expectation and performance standards; the personality of the position's supervisor; and how and why past incumbents failed or succeeded in the job.

Miscellaneous Issues

When asked why a client stopped using the psychologist's services, only 16 percent of the psychologists reported client loss resulting from selection errors. Forty-five percent said that the cost of the assessment had eliminated some clients, while 61 percent stated that some clients simply stopped using psychological assessments in their businesses. Finally, 39 percent of the psychologists lost clients to other psychologists. (Psychologists were allowed to give more than one reason for loss of clients.)

Most of the psychologists felt that their psychological assessment practices conformed to the *Uniform Guidelines on Employee Selection Procedures* (1978) and the *Standards for Education and Psychological Testing* (1985). Only 6 percent of the psychologists reported ever having been sued by an assessee.

When asked what skills are required to do effective psychological assessments, the psychologists most often listed interviewing skills, listening skills, test interpretation skills, judgment, knowledge of jobs, job analysis skills, and clinical insight.

CONCLUSION

This chapter presented two areas pertaining to psychological assessments: a review of the research conducted on psychological assessment to date and a look at the characteristics of current assessment practice. After reading Part One, the manager who was previously unaware of psychological assessment and its place in business should now have a clear understanding of the method and its potential. Psychological assessment is not a fad that has suddenly come into favor. The method has been in existence for almost 50 years. It will continue to be used in the future because it meets the practical business need of understanding the work-related capacities and potential of employees and job candidates.

REFERENCES

Albrecht, P. A., Glaser, E. M., & Marks, J. (1964). Validation of a multiple-assessment procedure for managerial personnel. *Journal of Applied Psychology* 48:351–60.

American Educational Research Association, American Psychological Association, and The National Council on Measurement in Education (1985). *Standards for Education and Psychological Testing.* Washington, D.C.

Campbell, J. T. (1962). Assessment of higher-level personnel: I. Background and scope of research. *Personnel Psychology* 15:57–62.

Campbell, J. T., Otis, J. L., Liske, R. E., & Prien, E. P. (1962). Assessment of higher-level personnel: II. Validity of overall assessment process. *Personnel Psychology* 15: 63–74.

DeNelsky, G. Y., & McKee, M. G. (1969). Prediction of job performance from assessment reports: Use of a modified Q-sort technique to expand predictor and criterion variance. *Journal of Applied Psychology* 53:439–45.

Handyside, J., & Duncan, D. C. (1954). Four years later: A follow-up of an experiment in selecting supervisors. *Occupational Psychology* 28:9–23.

Hilton, A. C., Bolin, S. F., Parker, J. W., Jr., Taylor, E. K., & Walker, W. B. (1955). The validity of personnel assessments by professional psychologists. *Journal of Applied Psychology* 39:287–93.

Huse, E. F. (1962). Assessment of higher-level personnel: IV. The validity of assessment techniques based on systematically varied information. *Personnel Psychology* 15: 195–205.

Korman, A. K. (1968). The prediction of managerial performance: A review. *Personnel Psychology* 21:295–322.

Laurent, H. (1968). Research on the identification of management potential. In *Predicting Managerial Success,* edited by H. Laurent, H. D. Kolb, V. J. Bentz, & D. W. Bray. Ann Arbor, Mich.: Foundation for Research on Human Behavior, 1–34.

Miner, J. B. (1970). Psychological evaluations as predictors of consulting success. *Personnel Psychology* 23:393–405.

Otis, J. L., Campbell, J. T., & Prien, E. P. (1962). Assessments of higher-level personnel: VII. The nature of assessments. *Personnel Psychology* 15:441–46.

Ryan, A. M., & Sackett, P. R. (1987). A survey of individual assessment practices by I/O psychologists. *Personnel Psychology* 40:455–88.

Silzer, R. F. (April 1986). Predictions or Prophecies: By data or by divinity? Presented at first annual conference of the Society for Industrial and Organizational Psychology, Chicago.

Trankel, A. (1959). The psychologist as an instrument of prediction. *Journal of Applied Psychology* 43:170–75.

Uniform guidelines on employee selection procedures (August 25, 1978). *Federal Register* 43 (166), 38290–309.

_____ **Part Two**

*Components of a
Psychological Assessment*

4

The Assessment Interview

Richard E. Miller

INTRODUCTION

The assessment interview is the most widely used assessment tool for selection and promotion. The popularity of the interview makes sense. Few individuals would make a major investment—such as purchasing a home or a car—without seeing the product first. Similarly, companies want to see the candidate before making a decision to hire or to promote that person; it would be careless to do otherwise.

In addition, practically everyone can hold a conversation. The interview makes use of an ability that everyone has; no special training or techniques are seemingly required to conduct one. Nothing could be further from the truth, however, because an interview is a conversation with a purpose.

The apparent simplicity of the interview has been one of the greatest obstacles to progress in the area of employee selection. Good interviewing is a very complex task. In several minutes or several hours, the interviewer tries to obtain an accurate understanding of a lifetime of many years, of thousands of experiences producing attitudes, motives, skills, and behaviors—often unknown to the candidate—and modified at different times and in various places. Because it is so complex, the interview can be poorly done.

The purpose of this chapter is not to provide a "how to" manual for interviewers. Rather, the intent is to review some of the salient aspects of the assessment interview so that the reader can gain a better understanding of the process as a whole and evaluate his or her role as an interviewer.

THE STAKES ARE HIGH

A study conducted in 1988 by the American Management Association revealed that the median cost per hire of an exempt employee was $5,856. One of our client companies, for example, estimated that it cost $65,000 to select a certain manager. The overall amount included interviewing and selection expenses, travel, lodging, meals, and recruitment costs.

Selection costs are controlled, to a certain extent, by the selection ratio; that is, the number of candidates assessed compared with the number hired or promoted. To illustrate this point, suppose that a company has two openings for a particular job and assesses ten candidates. To determine the selection costs for each person hired, take the *total* cost of assessing all ten candidates and divide this sum by two.

If an interview produces a candidate who is hired, and that individual later turns out to be a substandard performer, the decision will cost the company a great deal in terms of inefficiency, lower than expected productivity, and poor morale. These costs can be calculated (Flamholtz 1985) and can be many times the cost of hiring the employee. Added to these are the costs of the training or break-in period when the employee is more a consumer than producer of the company's resources. If the employee must be terminated because of poor performance, add the costs of separation and outplacement.

While few companies calculate the cost of assessment errors, the point is that such errors do have a tremendous financial impact. One company hired a high-level manager who demonstrated poor judgment and was not able to perform as expected. Relocating the manager to a different work site with more limited responsibilities did not alleviate the problem. The company estimated that this mistake cost the organization one million dollars.

This example highlights the importance of doing everything possible to insure that interviews are of the highest caliber. Companies that rely on the assessment interview alone for making selection or promotion decisions rather than using an array of assessment tools are not availing themselves of all the information they could obtain and are consequently increasing the risk of erroneous decisions.

THREE FUNCTIONS OF THE INTERVIEW

During the interview, the interviewer must gain information. Because this is obvious, some interviewers believe that they have completed their responsibilities when they have obtained answers to their questions. Interviewer training often focuses upon this aspect of the interview. But there is more to be done.

The interviewer must also give information to the candidate. Usually, this information is about the job, the department and the company, possibly together with ancillary information about benefits, housing, and the community. In large companies, some of the topics may be handled by specialists.

It is best for the interviewer to first get and then give information. If this sequence is maintained, the candidate will not have the opportunity to devise a presentation on the basis of advance information. Thus, one possible source of distortion in the interview will have been reduced or eliminated.

The interviewer naturally wants to fill the job opening, but during the "giving information" phase, the job or the company should not be oversold. If anything, care should be taken to tactfully point out any limitations or concerns that might be appropriate. If the candidate joins the company only to discover that things are not as rosy as depicted by the interviewer, disappointment will follow. The company—or at least the interviewer—will face a credibility problem.

The third task of the interviewer is to generate and maintain good will. Here is an opportunity to produce positive public relations. Candidates who think they have been treated fairly and courteously by the interviewer will spread the word; those who feel they have not been treated well will tell others about their experiences. During the interview, the interviewer represents the company. To the extent that the candidate thinks the interviewer has behaved in a professional, businesslike manner and has demonstrated sincere interest in and respect for the candidate, the candidate will have a positive impression of the company.

TYPES OF INTERVIEWS

In this section, we will look at five approaches to the interview. The first three focus on content; the last two revolve around structure.

The Stress Interview

In the stress interview, one or more interviewers intentionally place the applicant under a great deal of stress. This is accomplished by:

1. Asking questions so rapidly that the applicant does not have sufficient time to compose answers;
2. Challenging what the applicant says;
3. Attempting to discredit what the applicant says;
4. Asking questions intended to cause the applicant to falter (e.g.,"If you were a garden, what would you want planted?").

Strengths. This technique can indicate how well individuals respond to social stresses. It might reveal positive attributes such as poise and a quick wit, as well as unearth negative qualities such as defensiveness, hostility, and poor reasoning.

Weaknesses. In a literal sense, the only thing that is learned from this procedure is how well the applicant responds to social stresses in an interview. The implication that the interviewer will gain a picture of how well the applicant responds to stresses in general is tenuous; people can respond differently to different types of stress.

Worse, the stress interview puts the interviewer and the prospective employer in a poor light, because few applicants will appreciate being handled roughly in the interview. Even when apologies and explanations (with smiles) are offered later, irreparable damage may have been done. The applicant will still wonder why the employer has to resort to such extraordinary tactics in order to obtain information.

The Historical Interview

The content of this type of interview focuses on the accomplishments and experience of the applicant. Questions address what, when, and where the person did certain things. Questions about the extent and type of education the applicant has had are examples of the search for historical information. A properly conducted historical interview should provide an account of what the person did from the beginning of high school to the present.

Strengths. The information obtained in the historical interview can determine whether the candidate has the appropriate education and experience for the job.

Weaknesses. If the historical format is strictly adhered to, there will be no questions regarding the applicant's feelings and attitudes or lines of inquiry designed to assess the applicant's abilities, such as leadership or judgment. For this reason, interviews often contain a behavioral component.

The Behavioral Interview

In this type of interview, inquiry is directed toward those significant behaviors that the applicant demonstrated when dealing with problems, goals, equipment, people, and tasks. Questions begin with "what" or "why" in order to invite elaboration from the applicant.

A variation of the behavioral interview is the situational interview in which one or more interviewers ask the applicant how he or she would respond to some hypothetical situation that has relevant job content. This tactic may be used to assess the applicant's knowledge of technical procedures or manner of dealing with people. The hypothetical situation is prepared well in advance of the interview and is used with all applicants for the job.

Strengths. This type of interview provides an opportunity to assess the applicant's feelings and attitudes about people in authority, co-workers, different types of work situations, and company policies. The behavioral line of inquiry can tap the applicant's abilities such as leadership, decision-making, and judgment.

Weaknesses. The behavioral interview includes questions that are designed to assess aspects of the individual that often cannot be directly observed in the limited time span of the interview. The interviewer must make inferences about personal qualities not seen or measured. This process requires a high level of skill and practice and is subject to error.

The Unstructured Interview

In the unstructured interview, the interviewer starts with a very broad question such as "Tell me about yourself," and the applicant is left to proceed in whatever manner seems best. Minimal guidance is provided to the applicant, who does practically all of the talking. People who are spontaneous and verbally adept will be comfortable and effective in this setting because they can talk about whatever they wish.

Strengths. This procedure provides some opportunity to observe how well applicants can organize their thoughts, express themselves, anticipate the interests of the interviewer, and speak persuasively.

Weaknesses. Applicants who need structure or who are not adroit with words will be at a disadvantage in this type of interview. They may seem less competent than would be the case if other types of interview were used.

The unstructured interview also is inefficient. The applicant may speak for several hours, but only a small fraction of the output may be of use to the interviewer. The disparity between the number of words spoken and the amount of information gained is the fault of the interviewer, not the applicant.

The Structured Interview

In its purest form, the structured interview requires the interviewer to ask prepared questions and to record the answers provided. No deviations from the questions are permitted.

Strengths. The advantage of the structured interview is that preparation for the interview is mandatory, because questions must be written. The use of prepared questions allows the interviewer to gain an understanding over time of what the usual responses are; when the applicant gives an atypical answer, the experienced interviewer will know to look elsewhere in the interview record to determine whether the atypical responses form a pattern.

Weaknesses. This type of interview permits little variation from the standard questions and does not allow the interviewer to take advantage of those instances when the applicant says something that begs for elaboration or more extemporaneous questions.

This obstacle may be overcome if the interviewer is permitted to ask for elaborations of the applicant's responses when it seems appropriate. The interviewer must ask the specified questions but is free to ask other questions and follow those paths that appear most fruitful.

The Ideal Interview

The following is an ideal interview from the author's point of view.

The content of the interview unfolds in a chronological manner, starting with the applicant's early experience and education. Then it moves on to the applicant's work history—including military experience, if any—starting with the earliest job and moving forward to the present. The reasons for any gaps in the educational background or employment history should be understood by the interviewer. The interview includes a discussion of the applicant's hobbies and recreational interests.

The interviewer uses a structured format but has the freedom to seek elaboration of the applicant's responses. The interviewer takes notes of significant information during the interview but does not write any evaluative remarks or conclusions until the applicant has left. The interviewer talks about 20–25 percent of the time when gaining information but maintains control over the direction of the interview. He or she feels free to challenge the applicant's responses but does so in a tactful manner.

The interviewer does not express critical or judgmental thoughts about the applicant's remarks, and does not form a final opinion about the applicant early in the interview. The ideal interview is not limited by the clock. It continues until the interviewer believes the amount and kind of information necessary to make a hiring or promotional decision has been obtained.

PREPARING FOR THE INTERVIEW

Imagine the following situation. A person has decided to go grouse hunting but has no idea what a grouse looks like. Accordingly, our hunter shoots everything that flies in the hope that a grouse might be among the group of birds killed. At the end of the day, the hunter still does not know what a grouse looks like, so he cannot conclude that he has attained his objective. The method of hunting he used was not efficient, and he cannot determine if it was effective.

Interviewers, who are hunters of a kind, can fall into the same trap. They can ask for a great deal of information from the applicant in the hope that some of this information will be the right kind. However, once the interview is over, they are unable to properly judge the value of the information they have obtained.

In my interviewer workshops, I am often asked how to evaluate the information obtained in an interview. The answer is to know what you are hunting for before you take to the field. What is done before the interview is crucial to the success of the interview and the analysis of the information obtained. The following steps should be taken prior to the interview.

Step One: Define the Job

Begin with a job analysis. According to the *Uniform Guidelines on Employee Selection Procedures*, a *job description* is "a general statement of job duties and responsibilities" and a *job analysis* is "a detailed statement of work behaviors and other information relevant to the job" (1978, 38307). While the two documents can be combined into a single unit, the importance of a job analysis is that it should produce an indication of the knowledge, skills, abilities, and traits necessary to perform a given job.

A job analysis begins by breaking a given job down into functions, which are then subdivided into tasks. A "task" is a discrete unit of work with a definite beginning and a definite end. For example, one task of an insurance sales representative might be to "make telephone calls to prospective clients." Sidney Gael (1983) suggests that tasks should be evaluated with regard to their (1) frequency, (2) level of difficulty, and (3) importance for job success.

There are a number of ways of collecting this information. Ernest McCormick (1983) lists the following:

1. Direct observation
2. Individual interviews with job incumbents
3. Group interviews with several job incumbents
4. Technical conferences with experienced people
5. Questionnaires, either structured or open-ended
6. Diaries or logs kept by employees for this purpose
7. Records of employee behaviors that characterize very good or very poor job performance (critical incidents)
8. Equipment design information
9. Available records

Step Two: Decide What Traits Are Needed for the Job

The tasks involved in a job are reviewed to determine what knowledge, skills, and abilities are required to perform these tasks. Abilities need to be further refined by determining what traits are components of the abilities. What does the "ability to sell effectively in a competitive market" require? Persistence? Persuasiveness? Energy? Assertiveness? All of these?

A list of some possible job-related traits is provided in Exhibit 4–1. When the job analysis is completed, it is preferable to have no more than six to eight traits that are considered key predictors of successful job performance. Adding more traits is misleading. As additional traits are added to the list, it becomes likely that they will not be conceptually or statistically independent of the other traits. A list of twelve traits will provide a false sense of accuracy and refinement. There will probably be a few traits that encompass the other traits. To repeat: keep the list of predictors basic.

Consider the job of applications development engineer. A job analysis revealed that the following predictors were very important for job success:

1. Effective listening
2. Willingness to follow through

Exhibit 4–1
Possible Applicant Traits

Leadership	**Organizational Sensitivity**
Initiative	Stress tolerance
Independence	Team player
Cooperation	Wears well
Flexibility	Assertiveness
Persuasiveness	Resilience
Energy	Decisiveness
Persistence	Goal oriented
Objectivity	Social confidence
Planfulness	Sensitivity to others

3. Logical thinking

4. Ability to work with a high degree of independence

5. Ability to function without short-term results

6. Sales persuasiveness

Step Three: Formulate Appropriate Interview Questions

Once the list of performance predictors is set, the next step is to formulate questions that tap the qualities sought. The formulation of questions and areas to probe in the interview will take time. The payoff is that the interviewer will have a better idea of what to look for in the interview and, just as important, will be in a position to evaluate the interview information later on.

The hunter now knows the quarry. Adequate preparation is the single most important contributor to the successful interview.

ASSESSING TRAITS IMPORTANT FOR SUCCESSFUL JOB PERFORMANCE

There are a number of traits that frequently are considered essential for successful performance in business. Some of these are listed below, along with interview assessment methods for each.

Decision-Making

Definition: Making decisions that reflect logical and objective conclusions based upon a review of available information and alternative courses of action.
Interview: Find out if the applicant shows good judgment regarding:

1. The selection of colleges and major programs
2. The selection of jobs and employers
3. The reasons for changing jobs
4. The solution of job-related problems

Oral Communication

Definition: Ability to express, completely and concisely, ideas and concepts when dealing with individuals or groups.
Interview: Check the following:

1. Experience speaking before groups in business or the community
2. Completion of courses in public speaking or presentation skills
3. Organization, clarity, and pronunciation of the applicant's ideas
4. Gestures, facial expressions, posture and eye contact

Initiative

Definition: Taking action without external prompting, self-starting, energetic in pursuit of objectives.
Interview: Look for clues in these topics:

1. Preference for close supervision versus independent action
2. Willingness to put long hours into job
3. Rapid speech and action in the interview
4. Prior experience with the initiation of projects or departments

Leadership

Definition: Use of interpersonal skills to guide or influence others toward specific objectives or desired outcomes.
Interview: Look for:

1. Nonpaid leadership positions in professional or community groups, church committees, and service clubs

2. Leadership positions in school and college

3. Persuasive manner in the interview

4. Willingness to defend opinions in the interview

Teamwork

Definition: Willingness to ask for and give information to others in order to achieve common objectives.

Interview: Determine whether the applicant:

1. Shows an openness and willingness to share information in the interview

2. Has been an active member of volunteer organizations

3. Describes the preferred work environment as one involving teamwork

4. Has been in job assignments that involved work of the project or task-force type

VALIDATION AND THE INTERVIEW PROCESS

The concept of validity is a complex one. Basically, validity addresses what a procedure measures and how well it does so. Investigations of the validity of the employment interview can be traced as far back as the second decade of this century. An old but classic journal article by E. C. Mayfield (1964) provides an excellent review of some of the earlier work.

The bulk of research suggests that the employment interview does not have strong validity. Richard Reilly and Georgia Chao (1984) found the average validity coefficient from 12 reported studies to be .19.

More recent research (Schmitt and Robertson 1990) suggests that the validity of the interview might be higher than previously indicated. However, the statistical procedure that produces these higher validities is one called "meta-analysis," which combines the data from different studies. While meta-analysis is not new, it has not been reported very much in the literature until recently. It has its supporters and detractors, and time will be the judge of whether this approach to data analysis will receive the widespread acceptance accorded more conventional statistical procedures.

The issue of validity did not become of widespread concern to the general business community until the passage of the Civil Rights Act of 1964 and the issuance of the *Uniform Guidelines on Employee Selection Procedures* in 1978. The guidelines state that a selection procedure must be justified on the grounds of "business necessity" if it has adverse impact on so-called protected groups. Business necessity normally must be established by the demonstration of validity. Note that evidence of validity is required only if the procedure has adverse impact on the hiring rates for protected groups.

The guidelines largely address the use of standardized employment tests, particularly those of the skill and aptitude type. However, the guidelines define "selection procedures" to "include the full range of assessment techniques . . . and physical, educational, and work experience requirements through informal or casual interviews and unscored application forms" (p. 38308). It is clear, then, that the employment interview does not escape the validation requirement.

There are two types of validity that are particularly suited to the interview. "Content validity" is established if it can be shown that the areas explored in the interview represent the content or activities of the job under discussion. "Predictive validity" has been demonstrated when there is evidence that the interview procedures predict future job performance.

The predictive validity of an interview could be determined in the following manner. Begin by quantifying some of your interview information. In terms of potential for the job, rate the candidate to be much more than acceptable, more than acceptable, acceptable, or unacceptable. In a sense, you have just created a four-point rating scale. Notice that you probably would not hire someone you judged to be unacceptable, so you essentially end up with a three-point rating scale for the validation study. If you use multiple interviewers for each candidate, obtain the average rating for the group of interviewers.

After time passes and your company has hired 30 to 50 people for the same job, obtain job performance ratings on a three-point scale for each employee: above average, average, below average. By using appropriate statistical tests (such as correlation coefficients or tests for differences between means), you can now determine whether there is a predictable relationship between interviewer ratings and ratings of job performance. If you have conducted a job analysis and can rate the applicant on critical job predictors, you can use the same procedure to determine whether each of these predictors is valid.

The above exposition is not intended to provide a complete treatise on how to validate the interview but rather to provide some understanding of what is involved in validation. It may be preferable to have a consulting agency conduct the validation study if you do not feel prepared to do this yourself.

Validation studies might generate problematic results. They might indicate that the interview procedures or predictor variables used by a company are not valid predictors of job performance, or that certain interviewers are much stronger in their predictive accuracy than others.

COMMON INTERVIEWER ERRORS

Whether we like it or not, the success of the interview depends upon the interviewer, not the applicant. Many interviewer errors arise from a failure to recognize and anticipate the dynamics that can occur during and after the interview. Here, then, are ten common traps of interviewers.

The Verbose Candidate

The very confident and talkative candidate can take control of the interview. When asked a question, these individuals provide long, sometimes rambling, responses that provide little in the way of content. This style results in a long interview that does not provide much useful information. With this type of candidate, the interviewer must interrupt and refocus the candidate on the question that was asked.

There are also candidates who have large and flexible vocabularies and are able to present information quite well. Be careful: strong verbal skills may hide a weakness in mathematics, judgment, or some other intellectual ability.

The "Quiet" Candidate

The individual who does not have well-developed expressive skills might appear, erroneously, to be intellectually weak. The quiet candidate offers few spontaneous comments, gives short answers to questions, and generally seems ill-at-ease in conversations. Yet this person might have favorable potential for the job, adept at quantitative or mechanical problems, while still being poor at communicating those assets. By reviewing what the applicant has done and how he or she has handled challenges in prior jobs, interviewers can determine whether the nonexpressive candidate's behavior reflects modest ability, lack of self-confidence, anxiety, or poor communication skills.

A Focus on Technical Qualifications

The interview presents an excellent opportunity to discuss and review the candidate's resume with regard to education and experience. While the appropriate education and experience are necessary for job success, they might not be sufficient. Attention must also be given to the candidate's motivation, tolerance for pressure, teamwork, leadership, organization, conceptual ability and other factors (revealed by a job analysis) that lead to the effective delivery of technical skills.

Even success in prior jobs is no guarantee that the candidate is the right person for the job under consideration. Other companies have different styles, requirements, and standards. Managers seem to be particularly prone to the error of emphasizing technical skills without giving consideration to the other factors that are important for successful performance.

Stereotypy

Stereotypy exists when some aspect of the applicant elicits a conclusion from the interviewer based upon the interviewer's personal beliefs about that particular aspect. These beliefs can have either positive or negative connotations. Discrimination and bigotry rest upon stereotypes. Stereotypy can be far more subtle, even unconscious.

To make matters worse, stereotypy usually contains some small grain of truth, which helps sustain the overgeneralization involved. If one believes that people with red hair are temperamental, one can surely find some red-haired person with a hot temper. To counteract stereotypy, the interviewer should ponder whether that reasoning would be acceptable to the attorney for the plaintiff in a court of law.

The Halo Effect

The halo effect occurs when one phase of the interview, either positive or negative, influences the interviewer's judgment with regard to subsequent phases of the interview. The result is that the interviewer is no longer making independent judgments about each job dimension. Halo effect can be reduced by the use of rating scales to assess each job dimension. Scales with three to five points are preferred. The job dimensions should have brief definitions in order to provide standards for interviewer judgments. The rating scales can be enhanced by having guidelines that indicate the amount and type of evidence required to select each point on the scale.

Suppose one job dimension you want to assess is "analysis." First, define this dimension in one or two sentences. Next, decide upon a three-point rating scale such as unacceptable, acceptable, more than acceptable. Then indicate what kind or amount of evidence you would need to rate the applicant "more than acceptable" on this dimension. Do the same for "acceptable" and "unacceptable."

Contrast Effect

Imagine the following scenario. An interviewer has four candidates for one job opening. The first three candidates have not been impressive. After interviewing the fourth candidate, the interviewer decides that (behold!) this person is an acceptable candidate. In this situation, the contrast effect may have been at work.

The contrast effect thus occurs when one or more candidates seem "good" by comparison with other candidates who are "not good." To combat the contrast effect, managers should compare every candidate against standards established by the job analysis; those who pass this acid test can then be compared with each other.

Self-Fulfilling Prophesies

Poor interviewers make their decisions about the candidate early in the interview—sometimes in the first five minutes. The remainder of the interview then becomes a search for information that supports the interviewer's conclusion, while minimizing or dismissing information that contradicts the interviewer's preconception. This type of error can be reduced by having the applicant evaluated by more than one interviewer. The interviewers then meet to compare notes and provide evidence for their conclusions from the interviews.

Overgeneralization

The interview provides a sample of the applicant's behavior and, from this standpoint, can provide useful information. However, one should be wary regarding the representativeness of this behavior sample. If an interviewer spends two hours interviewing a 40-year-old candidate, the obtained sample represents 57 ten-millionths of the candidate's lifetime of behavior to that point.

It is unwise, then, to overgeneralize from the limited behavior sample obtained from the interview. The neatly-dressed applicant might be slovenly in other respects. The nervous candidate might be a chronically nervous person, nervous only when dealing with people, or perhaps uncomfortable in interviews. Which is the correct interpretation? The answer will come only from an analysis of all other information obtained from the candidate during the interview. No one observation or bit of information can stand by itself.

Reliance on Clever Questions

Interviewing seminars and professional trade journals sometimes present lists of questions that promise to reveal all truths in the interview. These questions can vary from the thought-provoking to the bizarre.

There is nothing inherently wrong with using such questions. The fault is in the expectation that the questions will do the job of the interviewer. This expectation arises when there is a preoccupation with technique rather than objectives. As we have stated repeatedly, preparation—stemming from a job analysis—is the key to effective interviewing and supersedes technique or clever questions.

Telling the Candidate What You Want to Hear

At some point during the interview process, it often is appropriate to talk to the applicant about the job and the company. After all, the applicant has to have sufficient information to make a decision whether to accept a job offer, if one is extended.

If most of this information is provided to the candidate before or at the beginning of the interview, the astute candidate will use this information to modify comments and behavior in an attempt to meet the interviewer's expectations. If, for example, the candidate has been informed that the job requires a high degree of planning and organization, then the candidate will suggest that he or she achieves success partly through organization. The appropriate strategy is to ask your questions first, then discuss the job and the company thereafter.

INTERVIEWING: A MESSAGE FOR MANAGERS

As we suggested at the beginning of this chapter, the employment interview is a challenging and complex process. Effective interviewers are made, not born.

The ideal background for the interviewer would consist of courses in personality psychology, organizational behavior, and personnel psychology, plus a supervised practicum in interviewing. Most interviewers probably cannot claim this experience. A more practical expectation is that the interviewer will have attended a seminar on interviewing, preferably one that allowed role playing and critical observation. But this alone is not enough.

Many managers face a peculiar problem with regard to interviewing. Even though they might have taken a course or seminar on interviewing, they do not conduct enough employment interviews to develop and refine their interviewing skills. Being instructed on how to play tennis is one thing; you must play the sport frequently in order to maintain and refine the necessary skills. But many managers conduct fewer employment interviews than necessary to maintain a sharp edge. Given this circumstance, there are two things the manager can do to maintain and improve interviewing skills.

First, the manager can have a colleague sit in on the interview as an observer. This process can be repeated with different fellow employees during different interviews. The purpose of the colleague's presence is to provide the manager with candid feedback on how the interview was conducted, particularly with regard to areas of possible improvement. As a side benefit, perhaps the observer will learn something beneficial from observing the interviewer. In a similar vein, group interviews should be followed by an analysis of how the interview was conducted and what each of the individual interviewers did that was effective or ineffective.

Second, the manager can recognize and remember that there are other situations in the manager's job that require the same kinds of skills necessary for effective interviewing. Whenever the manager counsels an employee, conducts a performance appraisal, functions as a mentor, or deals with the problems of employees, there is the opportunity to use some of the skills required of the interviewer. These include advance planning, correctly formulating and selecting questions, listening, and maintaining positive and open information flow. If managers approach these situations with the same kind of preparation and skills required by the employment interview, they will continue to hone their skills, be more effective in these situations, and be better managers.

REFERENCES

Equal Employment Opportunity Commission, Civil Service Commission, Department of Labor, & Department of Justice (1978). Uniform guidelines on employee selection procedures. *Federal Register* 43: 38290–315.

Flamholtz, E. G. (1985). *Human resource accounting*, 2d ed. San Francisco: Jossey-Bass.

Gael, S. (1983). *Job analysis: A guide to assessing work activities*. San Francisco: Jossey-Bass.

Mayfield, E. C. (1964). The selection interview: A reevaluation of published research. *Personnel Psychology* 17: 293–323.

McCormick, E. J. (1983). Job and task analysis. In *Handbook of industrial and organizational psychology*, ed. by M. D. Dunnette. New York: Wiley, 651–96.

Reilly, R. R., & Chao, G. T. (1984). Alternative employee selection theories. In *Readings in professional assessment*. Washington, D.C.: International Personnel Association, 255–308.

Schmitt, N., & Robertson, I. (1990). Personnel selection. In *Annual review of psychology*, ed. by M. R. Rosenzweig and L. W. Porter, vol. 44. Palo Alto: Annual Reviews, 289–319.

5

Psychological Testing

Stephen L. Guinn

Managers admit that employee selection is one of their most difficult and yet most important business decisions. Interviews, even when handled well, provide only a small capsule of information about an applicant's potential. Obtaining a true picture of a candidate's strengths and weaknesses becomes even more difficult because of the extensive training job seekers have had in interviewing skills by outplacement and job search firms. The situation is further aggravated by the refusal of companies to provide meaningful references for fear of litigation. The cost of hiring good employees is high; the cost of making hiring mistakes is even higher.

Effective employee selection is crucial in today's flattened organizations because there is little capacity to cover an employee who is not contributing. In addition, the increased diversity of the work force creates more opportunity for bias to affect selection decisions. Add to this the increasingly sophisticated workplace equipment that requires specialized abilities. The result is that employee selection requires a scientifically sophisticated approach to meet complex demands.

Psychological testing has had a resurgence as a selection method in response to these changes because it is a more reliable and accurate method of selecting employees than any other. The financial benefits are considerable if hiring mistakes are minimized.

Reducing turnover, with the resulting recruiting and training expense savings, more than pays for the addition of testing to a selection program. The real payoff, however, comes with the stronger intellectual skills and job-relevant personality traits of employees. Exhibits 5–1 and 5–2 compare the test performance of man-

Exhibit 5–1
Comparison of Abilities of Management Candidates Tested vs. Not Tested Before Being Hired

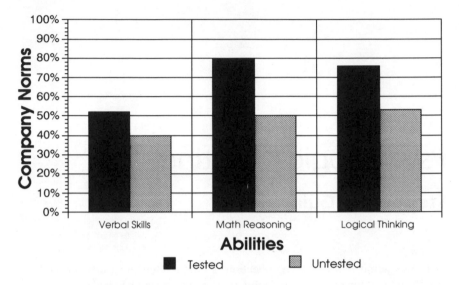

Exhibit 5–2
Comparison of Personality Characteristics of Management Candidates Tested vs. Not Tested Before Being Hired

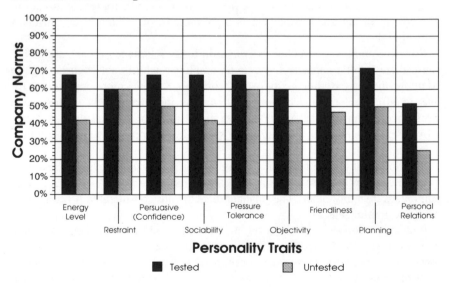

agement candidates at a *Fortune* 500 company who were psychologically tested prior to being hired versus those who were not. Those managers who were tested are clearly stronger in both their intellectual skills and key personality behaviors such as energy level, persuasiveness, planning, and personal relations. In today's business environment, a managerial work force with stronger skills and personal attributes can give the employer a competitive edge.

The higher quality of new hires also leads to productivity increases that can be calculated in dollars. In one study that shows this bottom-line contribution (Mkandawire 1975), sales representatives who were assessed and ranked through testing contributed 48 percent more in net sales revenue a year than those who were not. The subjects in the study were 40 field industrial sales representatives hired by the company during the previous year. They had been recruited very selectively and hired only after extensive interviews, then put through an intensive training program and assigned to various district offices. The purpose of the study was to determine if psychological testing, which had not been used in the selection process, could predict the success of the candidates. Each candidate was given a battery of psychological tests, and the psychological profile for each sales representative was compared with the net sales revenue attributable to that person. Thus, it was possible to compare both the effectiveness of the selection process then being used as well as the potential benefit of the addition of psychological testing. The analysis showed that, for each representative added to the sales force, there was an average increase in net sales revenue of $887,575 (actual dollars have been adjusted to 1990 values) a year, showing that the selection system, training program, and day-to-day management of the sales representatives were successful. However, the analyses also showed that if the company had also used psychological testing in hiring, the dollar contribution per salesperson would have been $1,315,114, or $427,539 more than the actual average. It should be noted that the criterion was net sales revenue, not actual profits, and the study should be repeated with a larger group to verify the findings. Nevertheless, the results do suggest that psychological testing used in conjunction with standard selection procedures makes financial sense.

Such potential rewards have led many companies, such as AT&T and Sears, to use psychological testing continually over many years. For these companies, testing has been integrated into their employee selection, career development, and succession planning programs with outstanding results. Others have shied away from psychological testing because of a lack of understanding, fear of litigation, or bad experiences with poorly run programs. Psychological testing is complex, and there are legal concerns common to all selection systems. The purpose of this chapter is to provide an understanding of how psychological testing can contribute to better human resource decision-making as well as to discuss the issues that businesses should be aware of in using tests effectively.

A BRIEF HISTORY OF PSYCHOLOGICAL TESTING

Psychological testing for job placement made its initial impact in classifying large numbers of military recruits in World War I. Paper-and-pencil tests were developed to measure the intellectual ability of soldiers for the most appropriate job placement. After the war, the use of psychological testing in business grew rapidly. In 1921, the Psychological Corporation was founded by James Cattell, a famous psychologist noted for test development. Psychological Corporation continues today as a major test publisher. During the early years of testing, Walter Bingham of the Carnegie Institute of Technology in Pittsburgh developed the Bureau of Salesmanship Research, supported by businesses interested in using psychological testing techniques. The bureau concentrated on employee selection and career development of clerical, sales, and executive personnel. The bureau was eventually disbanded, but its efforts are an example of the early application of psychological testing to the needs of business.

Psychological testing received another boost during World War II when psychologists developed a new test for the U.S. Army, the Army General Classification Test. New recruits were assigned to positions based on their ability to learn the duties required of particular military jobs that were assessed with this test. Psychologists also developed tests for the selection of aircraft pilots and soldiers in military intelligence units. Throughout the war and later, there was a great increase in the use of psychological testing in civilian life. Prior to the war in 1939, only 15 percent of businesses used psychological testing; after the war nearly three-quarters of businesses used psychological testing to some extent.

The use of psychological testing continued to grow unabated until the passage of the Civil Rights Act of 1964. As part of this act, the Equal Employment Opportunity Commission was created to investigate claims of discrimination in employment. Psychological testing came under excruciatingly intense review that required psychologists and businesses to prove, in court, that employment tests did not discriminate against protected groups. Because there was considerable legal disagreement regarding the proper use of psychological testing, the standards were often changed from court decision to court decision. As a result of this uncertainty, the use of testing declined during the 1970s. In 1978, the federal government finally developed a set of employment selection standards known as the *Uniform Guidelines on Employee Selection Procedures*.

With the publication of these guidelines, businesses and psychologists had an established set of standards for using psychological tests in employee selection. In essence, the guidelines require that psychological tests be constructed according to professional standards; that is, they must be reliable, valid measures of the skills and attributes necessary for success on the job, or they must be accurate predictors of training or job success. Another requirement is that tests not eliminate protected group members at a higher ratio than majority group members. This latter requirement is often waived if there is a systematic relationship between failure on the test and failure on the job.

While there have been refinements and exceptions by various court decisions, the guidelines have been accepted by the government, businesses, and psychologists as acceptable standards for a defensible employee selection program. As a result, there has been a rebound in the use of psychological tests for

Exhibit 5–3
Placement of Mathematical Reasoning Score as a Function of Norms Used

High School Grad	Some College	College Graduate	Graduate Training
92%	80%	65%	50%

identifying those workers who will be successful on the job. However, the employer must establish the job relevance of psychological tests; that is, show that the test measures behavior that is job-related and predictive of success on the job. While testing has many advocates in business, it frequently generates controversy among the general public, who are often less well-informed about the merits of testing.

HOW TESTS ARE USED IN BUSINESS

The most frequent uses of psychological testing in business are for employee selection and promotion. For employee selection, psychological testing can be used at all levels, from the hourly worker to the corporate executive. The tests used for each group vary according to the job requirements; each group is compared with appropriate norms or comparison groups.

Norms are determined by a reference group of similar individuals who have taken the same test. Comparison groups are called norm groups. These large groups establish the range of performance on a given test. Typically, norm groups are composed of people having similar characteristics, such as age, education, sex, or job classification. Norms become a standard against which appropriate comparisons of test scores can be made. For example, if someone scores 50 on a mathematics test, the score itself tells little about that person's ability. The score becomes meaningful only when it is compared with scores of similar individuals who have taken the test. If the average score of college graduates holding a particular job is 75, the individual with a score of 50 might not be competitive in that position. On the other hand, if the average score had been 35, a score of 50 would be extremely competitive.

Appropriate comparison groups are extremely important in the use of norms. It is not fair to compare a high school graduate's score on a mathematics test with that of a college graduate for a position requiring a high school education. However, if the high school graduate is expected to perform the same job as a college graduate, and the position requires higher mathematics for successful performance, then the comparison is fair. Exhibit 5–3 illustrates what happens to the interpretation of the same score on a mathematical reasoning test when it is compared with different norm groups based on education.

Exhibit 5–4
Score That Must Be Attained for the 50th Percentile Ranking

	Mathematical Reasoning	Verbal Skills	Logical Thinking	Percentile
Steel Company	17	34	80	50%
Bank	16	45	83	50%

THE IMPORTANCE OF APPROPRIATE NORMS

Exhibit 5–3 shows how any score on a test of mathematical reasoning can vary in its interpretation depending on the norms used. In this example, a score of 17 is compared for different educational groups. An individual who attains a score of 17 would place in very different percentiles, depending on the group with which the person is compared.

When tests are used regularly by a company, or for a specific classification, norms can be established for that company or for that job. Exhibit 5–4 shows, for instance, that the average management score for a steel company on a measure of verbal skills is 34. That score is quite competitive within the steel company, but when it is compared with the average verbal skills test score of 45 for a bank, it is not competitive and would be below the average of managers who work at that bank. Company norms for a steel company and a large bank show the relative standards for managers of their respective companies on measures of intellectual ability. For each company, the midpoint, or the 50th percentile ranking, requires a considerably different score on a test of verbal skills.

The test manuals that come with most published tests will list sets of norms that can be used to make comparisons among test-takers. Company and specific job norms, however, are much more accurate and, consequently, more useful. Job relevance of test scores is of critical importance for both their utility and for meeting legal requirements. Norms, however relevant, do not take the place of a proper validation study that shows a direct link between test scores and success or failure on a particular job.

An example of how the validation process works occurred with the start-up of a Pennsylvania manufacturing business. The company planned to hire a large number of new workers and wanted these workers to meet performance standards of an existing facility. The first task was to perform an analysis of the job so that tests selected would measure job-relevant characteristics.

The job involved complex machine operation. To establish the relevance of the tests of successful job performance, 75 experienced workers at the existing plant were given tests of mechanical comprehension, spatial relations, and numerical skills to measure intellectual abilities. They were also given tests of vocational interests and personality characteristics. Performance criteria were then obtained by having direct supervisors rate each worker by placing the employee into one of three performance categories (average, below average, or above average), based on the worker's performance level. Statistical analyses were performed to determine the relationship between the scores on the tests and performance levels.

The analyses showed that scores on the intellectual abilities tests could distinguish among performance levels of the workers. There were several scales on both the interest and personality tests that could also distinguish between better and worse machine operators. Cutoff scores were established for each test, based on the scores of experienced workers who were average or above average in performance.

As a result of this validation research, these tests are now being used for the hiring of new workers in a pre-selection testing program. The applicant's test performance is integrated into a carefully planned selection process that includes skilled interviewing techniques and reference checks. Hiring decisions, as a result, have been remarkably dependable. Indeed, only 1 of 87 employees hired was terminated for poor performance during the first six-month training and probationary period.

Psychological assessments are also used at the middle and upper levels of management to select candidates and ascertain potential for promotion. With the latter, the results are often incorporated into career development and succession planning.

Assessment at the executive level often differs from other assessments because the number of individuals hired for a position is insufficient for a validation study. In addition, objective performance criteria are typically more difficult to ascertain, because the job duties of an executive are broader in scope and evaluations are more subjective. As a result, assessments at the executive level are more individualized and cover broader strategic issues, such as leadership and management styles, political and personal relations skills, and how the individual will fit with the organization's competitive strategies.

Psychological testing at this level requires experience and understanding, not only of testing itself, but also of business issues and strategies. It is helpful when the psychologist has an in-depth knowledge of the company and the executives with whom the candidate will be working. The information is integrated with the tests results and helps target the interpretations to the company's behavioral expectations for the position.

The testing will typically assess intellectual abilities, sources of job satisfaction, and job-related personality traits. Personality traits might include management style, energy level, persuasive skills, independence, decision-making ability, grace under pressure, delegation skills, planning ability, and personal relations and political skills. Because of the complexity of executive assessment, it is more time-consuming and expensive than other assessments, and it requires extensive interviewing as well. The psychologist must be attentive to all the information available, including biographical data such as educational back-ground, work history, and previous project assignments. In many cases the norm group used as a comparison base for executive candidates will be other managers at similar levels within the company who were tested previously. Finally, the psychologist must integrate all the available information with the tests results in the final report. The information obtained through the psychological assessment is typically presented in a written descriptive report and an oral discussion with the hiring executive.

Considering the size of the investment made when an executive is hired and the expense of recruitment, many companies believe the expense of psychological assessment is worthwhile. Mistakes in hiring at the executive level are costly in out-of-pocket expense (cost of hiring is generally three times the executive's salary) as well as in lost business opportunities.

Psychological testing of top-level executives also provides valuable data about how these people compare with managers of business who are college graduates. Exhibit 5–5 shows that the verbal skills for top managers are good to outstanding. Decision-making at the executive level typically requires dealing with broad issues that require exceptionally high verbal and logical reasoning skills. Man-agers, with few exceptions, also have fair to outstanding mathematical reasoning ability. The majority also score high in logical reasoning ability, although the percentage of executives scoring above average is not as large as in the verbal or mathematical areas. Top managers have stronger intellectual skills and key personality characteristics. Testing enables a company to identify key individuals for advancement in the organization and to assure the best are hired from the outside.

Top executives share the positive personality characteristics of all successful business managers: high energy, persuasiveness, organization skills, grace under pressure, and the ability to work with others. There are some exceptions, how-ever. Top executives tend to be more dynamic, energetic, assertive, and confident than successful business managers in general. They also tend to be outgoing and have the ability to develop the loyalty of the subordinates. Other factors, of course, determine who makes it to the top levels in business, but there is definitely a similarity in the personality traits of top executives, as reported in studies conducted by PSP Human Resource Development (Sullivan 1983; Guinn 1987), Sears (Guyton 1969), AT&T (Bray 1964), and others.

The studies show, and the experiences of many companies verify, that psy-chological testing can be a valuable tool for identifying management talent early in the careers of potential managers. Psychological testing can not only identify potential for higher level management; it can also help to identify, objectively, an individual's strengths and weaknesses, which can be used for career devel-opment planning.

Psychological testing is effective for establishing pre-employment testing pro-grams for all types of positions, including supervisors, sales representatives, and management trainees. While different tests are used to fit the level of difficulty

Exhibit 5-5
Skills and Characteristics of 50 Top Level Executives Who Manage Medium to Large Companies

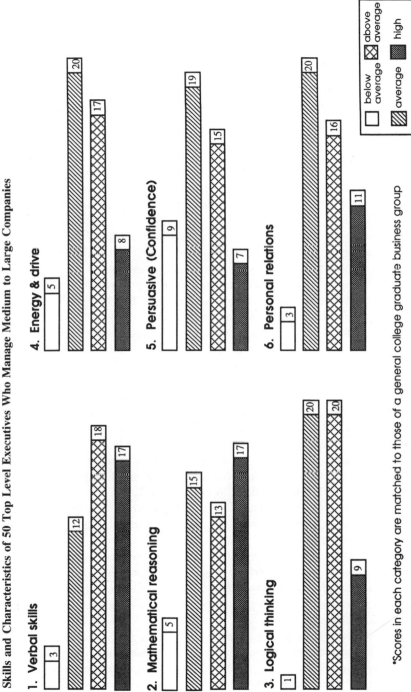

1. Verbal skills

2. Mathematical reasoning

3. Logical thinking

4. Energy & drive

5. Persuasive (Confidence)

6. Personal relations

□ below average
⊠ above average
▨ average
■ high

*Scores in each category are matched to those of a general college graduate business group and unique requirements of each position, the process and the results are equally effective.

PROFESSIONAL STANDARDS FOR PSYCHOLOGICAL TESTS

Most of the psychological tests used in business and industry are standardized tests developed by professional psychologists and testing agencies, using procedures developed and researched over many years. Psychological tests are more than mere listings of items thought up by someone because the items seemed to be relevant to the task at hand. A professional psychological test is a rigorous and sophisticated measuring device that has been developed through patient, thorough, and careful scientific research. All professional psychological tests meet certain standards that have been established by the American Psychological Association and published in the *Standards for Educational and Psychological Testing* (1985).

The use of employment testing is regulated by and must adhere to federal guidelines that are spelled out in the *Uniform Guidelines on Employee Selection Procedures* (1978). The professional use of psychological tests should also conform to *Principles for the Validation and Use of Personnel Selection Procedures* (1987) established by Division 14 of the American Psychological Association, Society for Industrial-Organizational Psychology.

These standards require that the tests meet high levels of reliability and validity. Reliability refers to the consistency of a test. Do its individual items measure the same thing, and will its scores be stable over a period of time if it is readministered? The reliability of a test is defined by how closely test scores will be identical when the test is retaken at different times. This is expressed as the degree of correlation between the first and second testing, and is expected to be .80 or higher out of a possible 1.00. The greater the number, the higher the similarity, and the greater the evidence of test reliability. Although individual's test scores should remain stable over a period of time, it is recommended that individuals be retested after three years, or sooner if they undergo training or engage in developmental efforts to improve skills.

It is important to know whether a test being used actually measures what it is purported to measure or predicts what it is expected to predict. Psychologists employ rational and criterion validity studies to make these determinations. Rational validity is used to determine if the test content actually measures what it is supposed to measure and focuses on the content of the test; it will be discussed in detail later in this section. Criterion-related validity shows to what degree a systematic relationship exists between a predictor (test) and a criterion (job performance).

There are two methods of establishing criterion validity: through a predictive validity study or through a concurrent validity study. In a predictive validity study, tests are given to new employees before or soon after they have been hired. Performance data is gathered after they have been on the job long enough to have their performance evaluated. Test scores and performance data are then correlated to determine if the tests can predict employee performance levels. While this approach is considered ideal, there are obstacles to its use. A company must be hiring sufficient numbers of employees (50 or more) in a short period of time to have a likelihood of achieving statistical significance. In addition, there is a time delay before research can be completed so that the tests can be used in hiring new workers.

The approach that is more often used in business to establish the criterion-related validity of a test for a job is a concurrent validity study. In this procedure, the test is given to experienced employees rather than to applicants or new employees. The test scores of these experienced employees are then correlated with measures of their job performance. In both the predictive and the concurrent approaches, the better workers' scores become the basis for future selection. Cutoff scores are established so that new employees will resemble the stronger performers in terms of test scores and, consequently, predicted job performance.

Whether concurrent or predictive validation research is conducted, a pool of 50 or more employees doing the same job is desirable so that statistical correlations can be made. It is possible to obtain practically useful results with a smaller number of employees, in the vicinity of 25, although the results may not be statistically significant.

There are criterion validation strategies that can be used for numbers smaller than 25 that combine small numbers of employees from similar job classifications in different locations to obtain a higher overall sample for statistical analysis. In addition, it is possible to take established research data on similar jobs where testing has been used and generalize these validation results to the position for which the tests are to be used.

Another alternative when there are small numbers of employees in a single job is rational validity, which does not use statistical correlation coefficients but, instead, focuses on the internal characteristics of the test itself. Two approaches are used for establishing rational validity: content and construct validity. Content validity is concerned with the items on the test and whether the items are representative of the sample of behavior being assessed. For example, a test of mechanical comprehension would measure mechanical concepts used on the job. Usually, content validity will not be established statistically. Instead, it will be determined by experts who analyze the requirements for the job and the behavior being measured and compare those with the items on the test. Construct validity determines what psychological characteristics are being measured. For example, if a test purportedly measures mechanical aptitude, there should be a high correlation with similar tests that measure mechanical aptitude, and frequently a low correlation with tests for different aptitudes, such as verbal or mathematical skills.

In most cases, the *Uniform Guidelines on Employee Selection Procedures* recommends that specific criterion validation studies be conducted for the jobs for which the tests will be used. The guidelines require criterion-related validation procedures; that is, the correlation of test scores with actual job performance whenever it is feasible. When it is not feasible because there are not sufficient numbers of employees in a given job classification to establish criterion-related validity, it is permissible to validate testing procedures through a rational validation approach.

In order to determine the accuracy of predictions from psychological tests, it is important to give considerable thought to the criteria that will be used to distinguish the performance of employees. Most often, performance criteria ratings are taken *not* from previous performance appraisals, but, instead, they are asked directly of supervisors, using objective measures, such as sales dollars or production quotas, when possible. When objective measures are not available, separate overall ratings might be asked of supervisors who are knowledgeable of the employees' performances.

The three most important requirements for performance data are that they be truly representative of what is expected or demanded for success on the job; that they be quantifiable, if possible; and that they be stable over a period of time. Obtaining accurate performance criteria is the most difficult part of completing successful validation studies because the criteria have significant influence on establishing both the validity and the usefulness of a test to predict an applicant's potential for successful job performance.

It is often naively assumed that testing should involve only the most superior workers so that the scores of the "best" current workers will become the basis for selecting future workers. The rationale for this approach is that the characteristics of the top workers should be the standard with which job applicants will be compared. While this is one of the desired outcomes, it is important that the research assess workers with both good and poor skills to ensure that the tests used are capable of discriminating various levels of job performance.

There will always be a margin of error in any selection system, including one using psychological tests. There will be some people hired who will not work out as predicted; there will also be some people who were predicted to be unsuccessful who would have succeeded if they had been hired. These "false positives" and "false negatives," as they are called, respectively, occur in all selection systems. However, they happen more frequently in selection programs that do not test. It is possible to set very high cutoff scores to reduce the number of false positives. The problem with this approach is that it limits the number of applicants who pass, thus screening out applicants who could be solid, competent performers. Remember that average workers are typically quite capable. Unless there is a very large applicant pool, it might not be possible for a company to hire only the top or above-average performers.

The predictive and concurrent validity procedures described are not always possible when a testing program is used for a new position or where there is a small number of workers (fewer than 25). In these situations, it might be necessary to use rational validation procedures, where one looks at the content and behavior dimensions of the job and selects available tests that measure that content and that behavior. Psychologists will also look at similar jobs in similar industries where tests have been previously validated. Using previous research for a basis of validation is known as validity generalization and might require a job analysis to verify job similarity. Working with a consulting firm that has experience with different companies in a particular industry allows this procedure to be used, because the consultant is able to draw upon previous studies for selecting appropriate tests that have already proven their predictive validity. Obviously, this saves both time and money.

Employers bear the responsibility for demonstrating the validity of all tests used for employee selection. The payoff for a company using tests, however, comes from increased employee job proficiency, fewer inaccurate personnel decisions, more effective placement of workers, and less disruption from turnover—outcomes that have a direct impact on bottom-line profitability.

SELECTING PSYCHOLOGICAL TESTS FOR USE IN BUSINESS

The determination of a candidate's suitability for a certain job has three dimensions. First, does the candidate have the *ability* to do the job; that is, does the person have the necessary experience or skills to learn the job and handle its demands? Second, is the candidate *willing* to do the job; that is, does the person possess the motivation, drive, and personal qualities necessary to achieve the results expected? Third, will the candidate *persist* in the job, that is, will the person's interests coincide with the primary job duties and lead to high job satisfaction?

To help employers secure information about candidates in these three areas and predict their potential for success, psychologists have developed specific objective tests to measure intellectual abilities, motivational/personal characteristics, and job interests.

Intellectual (Cognitive) Ability Testing

Intellectual or cognitive abilities are assessed by tests of general intelligence and tests of specific aptitudes and skills. Tests of general intelligence can be given either individually or in a group. The Wechsler Adult Intelligence Scale-Revised is the most well-known and most often used of the individually administered intelligence tests and is given mostly in educational and clinical settings. Tests that can be given either individually or to groups include the Wonderlic Personnel Test, the Slosson Intelligence Test, and the Otis Test of Mental Ability. These tests measure "general intelligence," or general cognitive ability, and are good predictors of job performance. As broad screening tools, these tests have proven very useful, particularly for jobs that require extensive training and a broad array of skills. While general intelligence tests are often used in business, many industrial psychologists prefer to use tests of specific abilities or aptitudes that can better target specific job skills. There are numerous specific ability or aptitude tests available, and the individual job requirements dictate which are selected. For example, a commonly used test for clerical accuracy is the Minnesota Clerical Test. It consists of two parts, number comparison and name comparison, and measures speed and accuracy of clerical perception.

Other examples of specific ability tests include the Computer Programmer Aptitude Battery; the Bennett Mechanical Comprehension Test; the Guilford–Zimmerman Verbal and the Guilford–Zimmerman Mathematical Tests; the Minnesota Form Board, which measures spatial relations; the PTI Numbers, which measures general shop arithmetic; the Watson–Glaser Critical Thinking Test, which measures logical thinking ability; the Differential Aptitude Test; the Short Employment Test, which measures verbal and math skills; and the Hand-Tool Dexterity Test. The General Aptitude Test Battery, used by the U.S. Employment Service, measures nine vocational aptitudes, such as general learning ability, numerical and spatial ability, and manual dexterity.

This brief listing of the more popular intellectual ability tests illustrates the variety of tests available. Selecting the most appropriate test requires a professional understanding of both the tests and the job, as well as the purpose for which the tests will be used.

Existing research suggests that specific ability tests are among the best predictors of successful performance. Intellectual tests, however, describe only part of a person and do not tell whether the person has the personal qualities for the job or will find the work satisfying.

Personality Testing

Personality tests are administered either individually or in groups. These tests are classified as either "projective" or "objective," depending on their format. Individually administered tests are typically projective; that is, the person being tested is presented with ambiguous stimuli, such as ink blots or photographs, and then asked to describe what he or she sees in the inkblots or to tell stories about the photographs. The responses are coded and incorporated into a scoring system for final interpretation. The most popular projective tests are the Rorschach Ink Blot Test and the Thematic Apperception Test (TAT). The scores from these tests, however, are typically very unstable over time and are best confined to clinical settings, rather than being used in a business environment.

The vast majority of tests given in business are objective self-report questionnaires. These tests require true or false responses to descriptive statements such as "You would go out of your way to put a new person at ease." Unlike intellectual ability tests, personality surveys do not have right and wrong answers. Instead, they describe the individual's personal characteristics such as social confidence, ability to work with others, energy level, interpersonal skills, independence, and the ability to handle criticism and stress.

There are many paper-and-pencil personality tests available. The more common include the California Personality Inventory, the Edwards Personal Preference Schedule, the Guilford–Zimmerman Temperament Survey, the Gordon Personal Profile Inventory, the Myers-Briggs Type Indicator, the Sixteen Personality Factor Questionnaire, and the Minnesota Multiphasic Personality Inventory. This last, usually referred to as the MMPI, is used most often in screening for emotional stability.

Personality inventories have proven very effective for predicting job success. In research at AT&T and Sears, correlations in the .40 to .60 range have been found in longitudinal studies covering 20 years.

The use of personality tests can be controversial, however, and the tests are perceived by some as an invasion of privacy. This issue is seldom raised by those who have taken the personality tests and received feedback on the results, with the possible exception of the MMPI. Indeed, what often goes unmentioned in emotional arguments about testing is that interviewers draw conclusions about candidates' personality characteristics in a much less systematic and objective manner and with far less accuracy than psychological tests do. Personality tests, along with tests of specific intellectual aptitudes, can be powerful tools for predicting job success.

Interest Testing

Interest or vocational tests identify job activities that people prefer. These tests have been shown to be useful for predicting long-term job satisfaction in a given occupation or position. Commonly used interest inventories include the Self-Directed Search, the Strong-Campbell Interest Inventory, the Kuder Occupational Interest Survey, the Allport Scale of Values, and the Career Assessment Inventory. All of these interest tests can be administered either individually or to groups, and many are computer-scored by the test publishers.

Both interest inventories and personality tests have one major drawback: faking responses. While most individuals give honest responses, some people will select answers based on what they expect is required of the job. As a result, interest inventories and personality tests work best when they are used in combination with cognitive or aptitude tests to determine if there is both an ability and interest in the job activity. Many of the personality tests have scales that measure faking or attempts to look good that can be used to assess the degree of untrue responses. Psychologists also try to confirm personality test scores with behavior observed during the interview.

Tests of intellectual abilities, personality characteristics, and vocational interests, when used together in a test battery, can be extremely accurate predictors of job success. They yield information to help assess whether the candidate can do the job, whether he or she will persist and be satisfied with the job, and whether the candidate has the characteristics necessary to meet the demands of the job. Combined with good interviewing and reference checks, psychological testing will greatly enhance an employee selection system.

Honesty and Integrity Testing

Honesty testing is a recent method of screening new hires for potential on-the-job theft. With the prohibition of polygraph testing in pre-employment screening, the interest in honesty testing has increased. Honesty tests often ask people about their attitudes regarding dishonest activities. There is, of course, a paradox in asking dishonest people to be honest about their dishonesty. The Reid Report and the Stanton Survey are the most commonly used honesty tests. Unfortunately, there has not been a sufficient number of independent validation studies carried out to give most of these tests the same endorsement that we can give to tests of intellectual abilities, personality characteristics, and interests.

Integrity tests are similar to personality tests in that their goal is to predict satisfactory job behavior rather than dishonesty. Research to date suggests that honesty and integrity tests are valid only when their cutoff scores are set very high. An undesirable effect of high cutoff scores is that they screen out large numbers of honest employees. Most professionals agree that more research at this stage is necessary. To be most effective, the research should be carried out by people other than the test publishers, in order to be certain about the accuracy and usefulness of honesty or integrity tests.

ESTABLISHING A TESTING PROGRAM

Ready-made tests can be purchased from a publishing house or a psychologist; new tests can be created to measure unique job requirements. Experienced industrial-organizational psychologists know which tests are appropriate for a given job, after an analysis of the job has been done. If an "off the shelf" test is not available, then a new test must be developed.

Anyone, however, can research appropriate tests through the *Mental Measurements Yearbook*, which is updated every four or five years. This book includes critical reviews of over 1,000 tests, along with determinations of reliability, validity, and the appropriate uses for each test. Test publishers provide manuals with information on reliability and validity, as well as test results from normative groups (comparison groups to whom the test has previously been given). *Tests in Print* lists tests by categories such as aptitude, interests, and personality. Names and addresses of publishers are provided by both books.

Although some have chosen to develop their own tests for specific jobs, this is a difficult and expensive venture into which not many companies enter. Tests have most often been developed and used in the civil service, for specialized knowledge jobs, and in apprenticeship programs where companies need specific tests that measure the ability to complete a training program successfully.

Creating a test is more complex than just putting together a number of items. Once a pool of items that reflect the knowledge, behavior, and information to be measured has been developed, each item must be analyzed to see how well it discriminates between high and low performers on the tests. The level of difficulty of individual items must also be determined, and research must be completed to determine the test's reliability and validity. Development of a new test requires professional skills and training and should not be undertaken haphazardly.

Testing must be administered by properly trained personnel. Test administration, which may seem like a simple and straightforward procedure, requires great attention to detail. Improperly administered tests are useless. Standardization of the testing process is necessary to maintain the reliability of testing. Test interpretation also requires professional knowledge that is usually not available in-house unless the test administrator has been professionally trained or is administering a testing program established by psychologists.

One example of poor test administration innocently occurred at a large utility company that used an otherwise valid test. The company repeatedly gave the test to the same candidates until they passed. Such a process violates the standardization of testing, particularly when the test is given frequently enough that those taking it have the opportunity to become so familiar with the tests that they eventually guess the correct answers. This testing program was rendered useless by improper administration.

Test administrators must also be attuned to the legal and scientific issues involved in a testing program. Tests must be used only for job-related purposes and not as a means of providing general information for non-job-related purposes. The interpretation of personality inventories requires a trained psychologist with a master's degree, at minimum.

Confidentiality is a prerequisite of any testing program. Test results should be kept with confidential employee records, and the only people who should have access to them are those who need to know, usually the hiring manager and key human resource professionals.

Psychological tests can be powerful predictors of job success and useful tools for employee selection or career development. However, if they are not handled correctly, they become useless to the employer or, worse, harmful to the test-takers. A shoddy testing program is worse than no testing program. Many unscrupulous or naive vendors create and sell short tests of dubious quality, but with incredible claims for enhancing a company's work force. Psychological test users must be critical and informed consumers. There are few shortcuts to a successful employee selection program, whether or not psychological tests are used.

WHEN TESTS SHOULD NOT BE USED

Testing is not always the best approach to personnel decisions. Tests should not be used, for instance, to terminate employees. Termination decisions should always be based on the employee's job performance. If an employer requests testing to get additional ammunition for the employee's dismissal, the decision to terminate that employee has already been made. Psychological assessment in this case is inappropriate and will add little worthwhile information. However, if an employee has been told of his or her imminent dismissal, testing may be useful during the separation as part of outplacement or career counseling. If, on the other hand, the employer is committed to keeping the employee with the company or on the job, psychological testing can help to determine, objectively, developmental training needs to improve the employee's performance.

Testing is also inadvisable when the tests involved are developed in-house and do not meet professional standards. The tests may appear to be job-related with appropriate content but still not meet the rigorous reliability and validity previously described. If normative comparisons have not been developed or reliability and validity determined, and if cutoff scores have been established arbitrarily, using the tests is very risky. The practice may not only be inaccurate and misleading, but also indefensible if challenged in court.

HOW TO SELECT A PROFESSIONAL TESTING FIRM

Since psychological testing is a complex enterprise fraught with problems for the nonprofessional, the use of tests should be limited to trained people with a professional background in testing. While some companies have a Ph.D.-level psychologist on staff to direct their testing programs, the employment of a full-time psychologist does not make economic sense for most companies, who find it more cost-effective to use professional consulting firms.

There are additional advantages in using an outside consulting firm. The firm may have broad experience working with many different companies, which can bring expanded perspective to addressing a client's needs. Psychological consulting firms have the expertise to select appropriate tests and provide the know-how to establish a testing program that will adhere to professional and legal guidelines. Confidentiality and test security will also be assured if an outside firm is used.

Potential clients should check the qualifications of a consulting firm carefully. A wise consumer will look for organizations with well-qualified, licensed professionals, typically at the Ph.D. level. Experience working with industries and job functions similar to those to be tested is highly desirable. Armed with the information contained in this chapter, you should be able to ask the right questions. Expect the firm to be knowledgeable regarding norms, reliability, and validity. The organizations represented in this book are quality firms that have been in business for many years and have licensed, seasoned professionals on their staffs.

With the assistance of experienced professionals, psychological testing can be integrated into a company's business strategy to improve bottom-line profitability through the hiring of a more capable work force and identification of existing talent for key positions. Recruitment, interviews, promotions, and career development are all impacted positively to give a company a competitive edge in the effective use of their human resources.

REFERENCES

Anastasi, A. (1982). *Psychological testing*, 5th ed. New York: Macmillan.

Arvey, R. D. & Campion, J. E. (1982). The employment interview: A summary and review of recent research. *Personnel Psychology* 35: 281–322.

Bray, D. W. (1964). The management progress study. *American Psychologist* 19: 419–29.

Conoley, J. C., & Kramer, J. J., eds. (1989). *The tenth mental measurements yearbook*. Lincoln, Neb.: Burros Institute of Mental Measurements.

Dunnette, M. D., ed. (1983). *Handbook of industrial and organizational psychology*. New York: Wiley.

Guinn, S. L. (July 1987). High potential bank managers: Can they be identified? *Banks in Insurance Report*, 11–13.

Guyton, T. (1969). The identification of executive potential. *Personnel Journal* 48: 866–72.

Mitchel, J. V., Jr., ed. (1983). *Tests in print*, vol. 3. Lincoln, Neb.: Burros Institute of Mental Measurements.

Mkandawire, D. S. J. (1975). Application of a decision theory model to evaluate selection tests. Ph.D. Dissertation. University of Pittsburgh.

Muchinsky, P. M. (1983). *Psychology applied to work*. Homewood, Ill.: Dorsey Press.

Principles for the validation and use of personnel selection procedures (1987), 2d ed. Berkeley: Division of Industrial-Organizational Psychology, American Psychological Association.

Standards for educational and psychological testing (1985). Washington, D. C.: American Psychological Association.

Sullivan, W. P. (1983). Have you got what it takes to get to the top? *Management Review* 72, no. 4: 8–11.

U. S. Equal Employment Opportunity Commission, Civil Service Commission, Department of Labor, & Department of Justice. (1978). Uniform guidelines on employee selection procedures. *Federal Register* 43: 38289–315.

Wigdon, A. K., & Garner, W. R., eds. (1982). *Ability testing: Uses, consequences and controversies*. Washington, D.C.: National Academy Press.

6

The Psychological Assessment Report

Curtiss P. Hansen

The most visible part of the psychological assessment process is the written report. This report is a summary of findings from the psychologist's interview and the candidate's testing. Almost all psychologists who conduct psychological assessments will produce some sort of written documentation. The length and content of a psychological assessment report will vary from firm to firm and even from psychologist to psychologist within a given firm. However, all assessment reports have several aspects in common. These include descriptions of intellectual style and ability, personality characteristics, interpersonal style, work motivation, and career direction. In addition, most reports contain a section discussing how the candidate matches up to the general and unique requirements of the position, and conclude with an overall evaluation of organization-job-person fit.

DIFFERENCES AND SIMILARITIES AMONG FIRMS

Many firms providing psychological assessment services to business pattern their written reports after the model established by Rohrer, Hibler & Replogle (RHR) in the 1940s. This is the model described in the introduction. Differences among firms are mostly those of style rather than substance.

For example, Firm A uses the following sections in its psychological assessment reports:

1. Intellectual Functioning
2. Emotional Control and Stability

3. Motivation, Drive, and Ambition

4. Interpersonal Style and Competence

5. Insight into Human Behavior

6. Leadership Style and Work Habits

7. Recommendations, Conclusions, and Prognosis

Firm B, on the other hand, uses:

1. Intellectual Characteristics

2. Emotional Makeup

3. Skill in Interpersonal Relations

4. Insight into Self and Others

5. Ability to Organize and Direct

6. Summary and Prognosis

Firm C uses a slightly different set of categories in their psychological assessment reports:

1. Intellectual Capabilities

2. Impact and Communication Skills

3. Emotional Organization

4. Human Relations Skill

5. Managerial and Administrative Style

6. Career Orientation

7. Summary

Firm D does not use category titles at all, but simply numbers each section consecutively. Finally, in reports on current employees, Firm E lists "bulleted" points under the headings "What We Know," "Looking Ahead," and "Development Recommendations." The latter firm is unique in that it clearly highlights the information that is not known about the person, but that may have a critical bearing on other conclusions.

SECTIONS OF THE PSYCHOLOGICAL ASSESSMENT REPORT

To give the reader a better understanding of the content found in the written psychological assessment report, a detailed analysis of each section is given. In addition, excerpts from actual reports are provided as illustrations.

Intellectual Capabilities

This category describes the individual's intellectual resources and how they are used. The person's actual scores from aptitude or problem-solving tests are rarely reported, although the level of performance is described. This is done for several reasons. For example, technical training is usually required to accurately interpret the scores. Also, scores from tests portray only one aspect of a person's intellectual functioning, although they are often looked upon as the totality of cognitive ability by the uninitiated.

Many individuals who score exceedingly well on mental ability tests are better suited for technical jobs without substantial management responsibilities. The "math whiz," for example, might not have the breadth of knowledge and experience or the decisive temperament necessary for success in many managerial positions. Conversely, there are highly successful managers in many organizations who perform in the average range on standardized ability tests.

The following are aspects of intellectual capability frequently commented on in psychological assessment reports.

Native Intelligence. Refers to an individual's innate or "raw" intelligence. The measured level of native intelligence is often compared and contrasted to the person's actual cognitive-related accomplishments, such as college grades. A high achiever with modest native intelligence might have more drive and ambition than a person with high intelligence who has accomplished little in life.

Intellectual Effectiveness. Refers to the type of problem-solving activity in which the individual is most likely to be comfortable and successful. Typical problem-solving situations are: administrative versus technical, abstract versus practical, structured versus unstructured, and general versus technical.

Quality of Thinking. Refers to the depth and relevance of thinking. Superficial thinking characterized by tangential or stereotyped solutions to problems lies at one end of the continuum. Penetrating, organized, and reflective thought falls at the other end of the spectrum.

Creativity. Refers to innovativeness in thinking, rather than artistic ability. It is the ability to think about things in fresh new ways, avoiding stereotyped and limited perspectives.

The following excerpt is an example of the intellectual capabilities section from a psychological assessment report.

Mr. X's overall intellectual abilities are superior when compared to managers and other professionals. He has excellent quantitative, verbal, and abstract reasoning abilities. He combines a strong analytical mind with good intuitive insight when solving problems. He has the ability to think creatively. He processes information very quickly and appears to arrive at conclusions effortlessly. He knows that he is smarter than most of the people with whom he deals, and he might cultivate an image of the intellectual tour de force. One relative weakness in his approach to problem solving is his tendency to make quick and final decisions after a first acquaintance with a problem area. While his intellectual powers will carry him to a correct conclusion most of the time, he will occasionally miss a detail and arrive at an incorrect conclusion. He is not a cautious person who feels a need to double-check his work. At times, he must consciously discipline himself to slow down and review his work. Overall, though, he is a very bright, insightful, and innovatively thinking person.

Personal Impact and Communication Skills

This section discusses how individuals present themselves in face-to-face meetings. The psychologist views a person's behavior during the interview as being representative of behavior at other times when the person is trying to create a good impression while under moderate stress. Assessing a candidate's personal impact is the most subjective area of the psychological assessment process. The psychologist must be careful to not let personal biases enter into the assessment, instead, interpreting the behaviors as would others in the company or community.

The personal impact portion of this section often includes descriptions of the individual's self-confidence in new situations, tolerance of ambiguity, handling of stress, "personableness," energy level, sense of humor, and overall interpersonal comfort. The communication skills discussion focuses primarily on the candidate's oral communication ability as evidenced in the interview. Occasionally, a description of written communication skill will be included in this section if a writing sample was obtained during the assessment.

The oral communication skills portion includes the description of the ability to present ideas clearly and convincingly, the appropriateness of language and concepts for the audience, conciseness of expression, effectiveness in speaking on a nonrehearsed topic, and overall comfort in talking. Does the candidate stay on one topic or jump around from subject to subject? Is the individual blunt or tactful in the portrayal of employers, co-workers, and friends? Is the person in tune with the interviewer, knowing when to clarify a technical concept or check for understanding?

Another important component of the oral communication portion is to evaluate listening skill. In assessing this area, the psychologist will note the quality of the candidate's understanding of the psychologist's comments. Does the person devote full attention when the psychologist speaks at length? Or does the person interrupt or seem impatient for the interviewer to finish? Does the candidate later need to have some material repeated?

The following excerpts are examples of the personal impact sections from actual psychological assessment reports.

In a first meeting, Mr. Y is consistently nervous and ill-at-ease. Although he tries to be friendly, cooperative, and agreeable, he does not appear to have the confidence that would allow him to establish rapport quickly with another person. He basically takes a passive and nonassertive stance throughout a lengthy meeting. He does not take charge of the interview, nor does he try to sell himself even when the interviewer urges him to do so. He comes across as serious and earnest, though unable to relax.

Mr. Z projects the image of a professional salesman. He is relaxed, open, and highly personable. He is a likable person who is easy to talk with because he has a sense of humor, and is extraverted and spontaneous. He adapts himself well to the personality of the other person. He is serious when they are serious, and casual when they are casual. He is naturally an expressive, gregarious person with a flair for the dramatic. He is sometimes given to exaggeration when describing things. He has excellent social skills and can be highly poised and sophisticated when the situation calls for it. While his interactions are seemingly effortless, he is actually very much in control of himself and the situation. He is a take-charge type of person with a high level of confidence and energy. However, he does not come across as aggressive or self-centered. He sells himself quite well.

An example of the oral communication section of a report is as follows:

Ms. X's oral communication skills are below average when compared to top-level managers. Although she is very verbal and expressive, she tends to treat a discussion as if it were a monologue. She often speaks in a barrage of words without giving much thought to what she is saying and how it is coming across to the other person. She becomes quite emotional about many issues. Her communication becomes disorganized in proportion to the degree of her emotional excitement. At such times, she has difficulty taking the other person's perspective and will leave out important details or change topics so quickly that it becomes impossible to follow her train of thought. Her listening skills could be improved greatly. In her urgency to say what is on her mind, she will often cut off the other person in mid-sentence. At times she will assume that she knows what the other person has to say after he has said only a few words. Sometimes her assumption is correct, but sometimes it is incorrect. At other times, she will simply ignore what the other person said or will echo a few words and change the topic to what she wants to talk about. These communication problems appear to be partly a function of nervousness and the emotion-arousing subject matter. However, they also appear to be largely attributable to her high need for dominance and control when with other people.

Emotional Organization

This section uses information about the individual from the interview and psychological testing to describe personality and emotional functioning. Only personal characteristics that have relevance for current or future job performance are included in the report. Some of the dimensions commonly described include the candidate's stability and predictability, level of adjustment to life, capacity to be open to criticism, optimism, self-esteem, confidence, assertiveness, independence, and boredom threshold.

The individual's ability to tolerate pressure is a crucial variable in understanding and describing work-related personality characteristics. Most people have a consistent and unique behavioral response to stress. The challenge facing the psychologist is to identify and describe this unique behavior pattern. The following questions are those asked in determining typical reactions to pressure. Does the candidate view the stress-causing problem as a challenge or insurmountable roadblock? Does it evoke a constructive response or withdrawal? Does the person remain calm or become emotional and disorganized? Does the individual procrastinate or meet the challenge head-on? Is more time spent complaining and looking for scapegoats than in planning, organizing, and implementing a solution?

The following excerpt is an example of the emotional organization section from a psychological assessment report:

Ms. V shares many of the characteristics of a Type A personality. That is, she is very much an aggressive go-getter with a bottom-line, results orientation. She is confident, assertive, and even driven at times. She has a great deal of enthusiasm, and in most situations will come on strong in a forceful manner. Her ambitiousness and strong will are manifested in her tendency to go directly to what she wants in life. She is more of a doer than a thinker and becomes frustrated when she cannot take direct action. She operates in a highly independent manner and has a great need to do things her own way. She likes to be in charge of people and things. She is also a restless person who becomes bored easily. She thrives on new experiences and feels frustrated in a routine. Because of this, she sometimes has trouble sustaining her concentration for extended periods of time. It is likely that she is occasionally erratic in her work. That is, she will work with tremendous energy, motivation, and dedication when she is spearheading a new and exciting project. However, she may have difficulty following through on half-completed projects that have lost their novelty. She is an emotionally expressive and temperamental woman who likes to think of herself as more stable, hardheaded and in control than she really is. She appears to be dissatisfied with some aspects of her job. She has an action orientation that pushes her to get things done quickly. She is impatient with delay and is not one to sit and deliberate for a long time before taking action. Because of this, others may see her as somewhat impulsive and unpredictable.

Human Relations Skill

This section of the psychological assessment report describes the quality of the candidate's relationships with people. The psychologist portrays how the person treats people during good and bad times, as well as specifies the interpersonal behaviors typical of the person. How the individual works in a group situation is a primary concern. Is the candidate cooperative or dominating, deferent or demanding, friendly or aloof, straightforward or devious? Is the individual able to persuade others to do a task a certain way? Or does the candidate simply try to force his or her will upon them? Does the candidate inspire trust and put people at ease?

The following excerpts from assessment reports focus on human relations skill:

Mr. J is an expressive person who can demonstrate much friendliness and humor when he wants to. He can be an enjoyable and charming person to be around. However, he is much more idea-oriented than people-oriented. He realizes that his people skills could be improved. He is not particularly comfortable in prolonged social situations. He is more at ease when operating on his own. Some people will feel threatened by his intellectual style and high degree of self-assurance. At his worst he will be perceived as arrogant and self-centered. In general, though, he likes to maintain a spirit of cordiality and good humor with his associates. It is clear, though, that he does not give the interpersonal areas as much attention as other areas in his life.

Mr. P tries to present himself in a low-key, nonaggressive, and accommodating manner so that others will approve of him. He is friendly and unobtrusive, and should fit in well in group situations where a high degree of cooperation is desired. He tends to misjudge how he comes across in significant ways. For example, he sees himself as being outgoing, witty, and gregarious. He feels that his interpersonal skills are his strong suit and that he immediately hits it off well with people. However, the interviewer saw him as being fearful, socially uncomfortable, and bland. It is highly likely that he responds to most new social situations in this manner. He might come across more similar to his self-description in the long-run when he has had a chance for repeated exposure to the same people.

Managerial and Administrative Style

This section of the assessment report discusses two basic areas: the candidate's approach to the management of people, and the style of managing the administrative aspects of the job. This section is contained in reports on managers or managerial candidates. A comparable section on "selling style" is found in the reports on salespeople or sales candidates.

The management of people, or leadership, can be viewed as a continuum. At one end is the autocratic, Theory X style manager. At the other end of the continuum is the participative, Theory Y manager. Most managerial candidates will lean toward one style or the other. Some managers will try to vary their approach to fit the particular situation or employees involved. Other managers will exhibit one style of leadership when the waters are calm, but will abruptly change modes when the sailing gets rough and they are under pressure. The candidate's preferred style is discussed in this section, as well as the conditions and situations under which changes are likely to occur.

The administrative style section contains information about the candidate's effectiveness in managing the day-to-day details of the job, as well as long-term planning. The questions that are addressed in this section are as follows. Does the candidate approach work in an organized and logical manner? Does the manager plan out the activities comprising a large project? Does the candidate prefer to work on one task at a time, or to move from one activity to another as the need or mood dictates? Does the candidate have a pattern of constantly being taken by surprise with "unexpected" work demands? Finally, does the candidate tend to get bogged down in details, or to keep the "big picture" in mind at all times?

The following is an example of the managerial and administrative style section from a psychological assessment report:

As a manager, Mr. B tends to take a hands-on, do-it-yourself approach. He is not comfortable delegating important responsibilities to subordinates, or letting them develop their own methods for accomplishing the objectives. He does not have a natural feel for the training and development of subordinates. He tends to be inconsistent in the task direction and feedback he gives to subordinates. Sometimes he is overinvolved in the nuts and bolts of someone's project, while at other times he is not involved enough in giving directions. He acknowledges that he could use some training in management skills.

Administratively, Mr. B may also be inconsistent. He works on what he is interested in and has difficulty completing routine and unexciting duties. He likes to get things started, but does not enjoy seeing them through to completion. He tends to get caught up in what he is doing at the moment and probably overlooks paperwork and deadlines. He is not a conforming company man and he likes to think of himself as different from other people. He is certainly bright enough to handle the intellectual demands of administrative work; it is his temperament that will keep him from excelling in this area.

Career Orientation

This section of the report is handled in one of two ways, depending on the amount of experience a candidate has in a specific occupation. For a young person with relatively little experience in any occupation, the career orientation section would present the candidate's views on the merits of various career directions. The candidate's perspective is followed by the psychologist's assessment of the candidate's "best bet" for an occupational direction. This assessment is based on career preference measures and the psychologist's experience in evaluating individuals from a variety of fields.

For a candidate or employee who has been established in an occupation for many years, the perspective is different. In this situation, the psychologist is more concerned about predicting the individual's potential for further advancement within the field. If the candidate is a general manager, the issue is one of how far up the management hierarchy within that company the manager could climb. Could the manager become an executive vice-president or president? If so, how long will it be before the manager is ready to assume these responsibilities? Also, what developmental experiences are needed to ensure progress up the hierarchy?

Two career summary excerpts are presented in the following paragraphs. The first is the career orientation section from a young candidate's psychological assessment report:

Mr. H appears to be trying to move away from those aspects of his current job that are not satisfying for him, rather than moving toward a new occupation that looks to be a good fit. Deep down he is not really sure what he wants to do with his life. He decided three years ago that his work as a media planner was unsatisfactory. However, he is just now doing something about making a change. This indicates that his motivation and drive are not strong. He is looking for something easy and will resist being pushed to achieve. He does not have a strong internal self-discipline. He does not like to work too hard and views a sales representative position as having more flexible hours with higher pay.

The second career assessment paragraph is from an experienced candidate's assessment report:

Mr. U has been with the Acme Company for 12 years. He began his career as a supervisor in the operations area, and has made slow but steady progress up the management ladder over the years. In his current position as vice-president of operations, he feels a need to broaden his exposure to other management areas within the company. He feels that he is stagnating in his current job, and that he can make no further advances without new experiences. He is willing to make a lateral or even somewhat "downward" move if it means that he will be learning a new management function. Over the past 12 years, he has earned an MBA degree at night, and feels capable of quickly mastering a financial or marketing area. His eyes are clearly on the future and he has mapped out his path to get there.

Summary

The summary section of the assessment report is more than a reiteration of information presented in previous sections. A good summary should paint a vivid portrait of the candidate in a brief paragraph. The most salient aspects of the individual will be listed as they relate to the position's key requirements. Some summaries include a hire/no hire recommendation based on those job-related dimensions that can be validly measured through the assessment.

The following excerpt from a psychological assessment report illustrates the summary section:

Mr. H's strengths are that he is enthusiastic and eager to please, enjoys being around people, likes to be helpful, communicates well both orally and in writing, and he has the desire to be somebody important. His limitations for a sales position include the following: He is below average in confidence, independence, assertiveness, take-charge ability, endurance, organization, and self-discipline. He is inexperienced in life and has not yet grappled with many everyday adult challenges. He does not have a clear picture of what sales work entails and, therefore, overestimates his ability to be successful. He will need formal training in the art of salesmanship. Most importantly, he is very dissimilar to successful sales people because of his low motivation level. He wants things to come easily to him and is not committed to going through the personal discomfort that usually accompanies personal growth and development. Overall, Mr. H is a below average candidate for this position.

Developmental Recommendations

In psychological assessments completed for developmental rather than selection purposes, an additional section is included. This section is written for both the employee's and company's eyes, though the previous sections might or might not be, depending on the policies of the client organization. The developmental recommendations section discusses specific weak spots in the employee's professional development. The discussion includes a listing of activities designed to improve the weaknesses.

The following excerpt is a brief developmental recommendations section from a psychological assessment report:

Given the above pattern of strengths and limitations, it is recommended that the company and Ms. V consider the following suggestions. If she is to continue her professional growth and move from her technical specialty to general management, she must begin broadening her work experiences. A progression of project assignments with increasing accountabilities in areas outside of her financial specialty would be desirable. These assignments should gradually increase her role as the project leader. Her progress should be monitored by an experienced manager who has made the transition from technician to general manager. Ms. V's confidence in dealing with nontechnical supervisory issues will grow if she gets supervised experience in these areas.

USES AND ABUSES OF PSYCHOLOGICAL ASSESSMENT REPORTS

Because the psychological assessment report is a permanent record documenting a psychologist's views on the intelligence, personality, and professional potential of an employee or employee-to-be, it is of critical importance that a system be set up to ensure the confidentiality of the report. Generally, the report is mailed, faxed, or given to the director of human resources, the hiring manager, or the company president, depending on the size of the company. The psychologist's intent is for the report to be seen by the appropriate authority. En route to the supervisor and subsequent to the person's review, however, the report may be handled by numerous personnel, including mail clerks, secretaries, subordinate managers, file clerks, and microfilm operators. This situation has the potential for creating problems. All it takes is one inquisitive employee and a photocopier to damage the effectiveness of a psychological assessment program.

A company using psychological assessments as part of its selection, promotion, or professional development programs must set up carefully thought out and monitored policies regarding the use of the information. The uses of the report should be in accord with state and federal legal guidelines, as well as in agreement with professional human resource management precepts. In general, the psychological assessment report should serve the positive needs of the company and the individual assessed. The following sections present some of the common abuses that can creep into the practices of companies using psychological assessments.

"Let's Fire Harry"

A common deficiency in the management practices of many companies is lack of documentation about an employee's performance problems. A situation may arise where the termination of an employee is being considered, but there is insufficient evidence in the employee's file to document a pattern of unacceptable performance. To bolster the case against the employee, some companies have retrieved the original psychological assessment, which might have been completed years earlier. Information on limitations is then excerpted from the report as further "evidence" of the employee's failings.

This practice is clearly a violation of good human resources policy. The psychological assessment results are meant to be comprehensively descriptive of a person at one point in time, as well as predictive of key performance areas in the future. The results cannot function as proof of poor performance, even when such performance was predicted. The psychological assessment report should not be used as a substitute for regular documentation of ongoing work performance.

"Should Harry Be Promoted?"

In cases where an assessment was completed as part of the hiring process, there is a temptation to pull out the report and review it when considering the same individual for a promotion a couple of years later. This is bad practice because the assessment report used was geared to the one purpose of selection. Over a two-year period, the employee might have changed significantly. If assessment information is to be used in the promotion decision, a second assessment at that time and for that purpose should be done. Most psychological consulting firms would agree and, in fact, many recommend, that old assessment reports be destroyed.

"Sorry, Harry, the Psychologist Said No"

A common management abuse of the psychological assessment that gives business psychologists a tarnished reputation is described in the following situation. A manager is at the stage in his tenure with the company when he should be considered for a promotion. However, the top executives do not like him and do not want him promoted. A psychologist is called in to do a promotion assessment of the man. If the resulting report is positive and recommends promotion, the executives ignore the information. However, if the results are equivocal or negative about the employee's prospects of success in a higher-level position, the executives pull out the negative aspects from the report and tell the manager that the psychologist ruled that he is not yet ready for a promotion.

This political tactic appears to shift the responsibility for denying the promotion onto the psychologist. While this is obviously not the case, many employees denied a promotion under these circumstances will come to believe this rationale. The outcome is that a culture of resentment toward the "meddling" of the outsider psychologist will evolve. The effectiveness of the psychological consultant in future assignments with this company will be reduced as employees refuse to fully participate.

"It All Depends on What the Psychologist Says, Harry"

As discussed in Chapter 1, some managers regard the observations and utterances of the psychologist as revealed truths above critique. These managers are opposite those in the previous scenario because they are naive rather than scheming. In practice, they defer to the psychologist in selection and promotion decisions. The assessment report becomes a fifth gospel to be repeatedly consulted for insight into the employee and guidance in managing the employee.

This approach to using the psychological assessment report is poor practice because the manager using the report in this manner is ignoring personal experiences over time in working with the employee in question. Even in the case of an outside candidate's assessment, the written report can be given too much weight and lead to the various management interviewers discounting any perceptions that contradict the report.

A PSYCHOLOGICAL ASSESSMENT REPORT ON AN "IDEAL CANDIDATE"

The following report was constructed to illustrate how an ideal candidate would be described. Because the hypothetical individual is ideal, some areas in the report are missing, such as an account of limitations for the position and developmental considerations for the future. Also, the structure of the report differs from that of the foregoing outline. For example, the personal impact and communication skills information is blended into the human relation skills section of the following report. The man who was assessed is a candidate for a sales representative position with a large consumer products company. The company was looking for a person with high intelligence, due to the technical nature of the products and contracts to be sold. Also, they wanted a person with a high degree of emotional maturity and interpersonal skill in order to successfully relate to the firm's clientele of top-level managers in *Fortune* 200 companies.

Intellectual Capabilities

Mr. Ideal's overall intellectual abilities are measured to be above average for individuals in management and professional sales positions. He is a bright man who is well-rounded in his education. He is alert and comfortable in dealing with numerous details, but maintains a primary focus on the practical goal of moving a project forward. He is able to visualize what needs to be done to successfully handle sales opportunities or problems.

He quickly and incisively probes regarding the needs and problems of a client in order to generate innovative solutions. He enjoys complex problems and tries to avoid routine and less effective solutions. He is a quick study. He is hungry for information and is constantly picking up new ideas. He is able to apply ideas in a practical manner. He is decisive, yet has the flexibility to modify his thinking to meet a client's needs.

Emotional Organization

Mr. Ideal has a very high degree of self-confidence. However, he knows the limits of his knowledge and is not afraid to ask for assistance when necessary. He profits from the constructive criticism of others, and he gives feedback in a helpful manner.

He has a very high energy level and amount of stamina. He is an early riser who is able to sustain long days and evenings of constant client involvement and decision-making. He is a self-starter who eagerly moves to the next responsibility.

Mr. Ideal is strongly driven by one of several forces. He is driven to master tasks and reach goals. He has an insatiable hunger to earn money and be recognized for his productivity. He is constantly running toward the next hurdle. He is competitive and likes to win. He thrives upon taking on challenges and succeeding. As such, he takes advantage of opportunities and does not give up. When he does fail at a task, he views it as a stimulus to try harder in the next situation. He is self-motivated and does not need the support or positive feedback of others. His awareness of his accomplishments and the symbols of his goal achievements are sufficient to motivate him from day-to-day.

He sets high, "stretch" goals that border what can and cannot be realistically accomplished. His personal goals are usually higher than those set by the company for him. He seeks to do better than his previous best. He needs to be the top salesperson.

Mr. Ideal prioritizes his time and organizes his day to maximize opportunities for sales. He is comfortable with himself and relaxes easily when the time is appropriate. He knows the limits of his energy, but is always able to call upon reserve energy. He recovers from fatigue and setbacks quickly. He maintains solid relationships with his family, co-workers, and clients. While he is intensely goal-oriented, he has a good sense of humor and is able to laugh at himself. He is energized by learning and being able to participate in life. He keeps himself in good health. He is open and honest with his emotions, but is tactful and controlled in how he expresses them. His emotions serve him well in helping to accomplish his goals.

Human Relation Skills

Mr. Ideal's dress and personal habits are professional and convey a sense of self-pride. His speech is clear and to the point. He is able to vary his language and style of presentation according to the needs of his clients. He listens well and asks probing questions that help elicit information without being intrusive. People feel comfortable with him and enjoy his enthusiasm and "can-do" attitude.

He enjoys people and is assertive and outgoing with them. He socializes easily. He has a quick and insightful understanding of the needs of people. He is able to provide support and help people explore their concerns. He comes across as straightforward and open. However, he is able to confront others and set clear limits in a nonthreatening manner when necessary. He leads and guides rather than directs. He invites participation while remaining in command of himself and the situation. He enjoys public visibility and seeks leadership roles in community and professional groups.

Sales Approach and Skills

He has an entrepreneurial spirit and relies on himself to make things happen. He is risk-oriented and opportunistic. He has a keen sense of timing and, while he is patient and persistent, has an urgency to move things forward. He thinks bottom-line. He is experienced in the industry and knowledgeable about the products. He is highly service-oriented and encourages diversity. He sells the decision-maker through the force of his personality and attractiveness of his service orientation. He is the opposite of an "order taker."

Summary

Mr. Ideal is an experienced and proven salesman of the highest caliber. He is confident, independent, outgoing, intelligent, dynamic, and persuasive. He presents himself very well and is highly articulate. His approach to selling is customer-centered, problem-solving, and service-oriented. In comparison to the requirements of this sales position, he is an excellent fit. It is predicted that he will do an outstanding job if hired.

CONCLUSION

As is evident from reading the foregoing report and the excerpts from a variety of reports, the psychological assessment report is not a literary work of art. Sentences usually begin with a pronoun and make a terse statement about an aspect of the person. The purpose of the report is to convey specific information about the assessee as clearly and concisely as possible. Excess words only create possible misunderstandings.

A good psychological assessment report describes a person in decisive terms. In other words, equivocal phrases, such as, "He is often confident but is sometimes unsure of himself," are avoided. A psychologist who "sits on the fence" in his reports is trying to be in the position of never being wrong. Like a horoscope, the equivocal statements seem to fit the candidate well. Unfortunately, they also fit just about everyone else.

A psychologist risks being wrong by making definitive statements in the report. Even the best psychologist will sometimes be wrong. Confounding the facts is that people can sometimes just be plain unpredictable in their behaviors. Also, their work environments and the nature of their jobs might change dramatically, which makes the psychologist's predictions less applicable. A manager should view the statements in a psychological assessment report as descriptions and predictions of how the assessee will behave *most of the time* and in *most situations*.

_____ **Part Three**

*Applications of
Psychological Assessment*

7

A Structured Screening System for the Assessment of First-Level Supervisors

John D. Arnold and Barbara Kruse

A BUSINESS SCENARIO

Three director-level managers at the Polk Life Insurance Company (Greg Washington, claims processing; Chris Brent, policy review; Juanita Gitano, management development) are discussing problems the company is having with its first-level supervisors.

Greg: I've got some real problems with the supervisors in my area. I know we've always had some problems at the supervisory level. Face it, it's a difficult job. They're just learning to manage. They're constantly fighting the fires started by the people above and below them. But our newer crop of supervisors seems to be having an even harder time than usual.

Chris: We've got the same problem over in policy review. I think a large part of it comes because we promote people who have the greatest tenure or who perform well in the entry-level positions. We get people who are technically good, but they don't know how to manage people.

Greg: I think that's our problem, too. But I don't know what to do about it. How do you know how good a person is going to be as a supervisor until you actually see him or her supervise?

Juanita: That's a good question and it applies at more levels than just supervisor. You don't really know how good a vice-president will be until he or she goes into that slot, either. At the vice-president level, we solved the problem largely by bringing in Dr. Grant. He performs individual assessments on department heads that we're considering for promotion to vice-president and identifies their strengths and weaknesses before they actually assume new jobs.

Chris: That sounds promising. Why don't we try that out at the supervisory level, also?

Juanita: I don't think we'd be able to do that. First, Dr. Grant is already pretty busy. Mostly, though, it's too expensive. We promote dozens of people to supervisor each year. And we'd have to assess multiple candidates for each supervisory slot.

Greg: I can see the problem. But it's also expensive not to do a better job selecting our supervisors. We're losing productivity because the supervisors don't know how to organize the work. Also, employee morale is very bad.

Juanita: I know what you're saying. But budgets are tight.

Epilogue

What should happen next is not clear, but several alternatives are possible. Juanita could push for budget expansion to allow for individual assessments before all supervisory selections. Things could just stay the way they are. Or— a third approach—the organization could develop a structured screening system that allows nonpsychologists to use standardized assessment tools to aid in selecting personnel for supervisory jobs.

STRUCTURED SCREENING SYSTEMS

Structured screening systems typically are designed by industrial-organizational psychologists who construct and validate the system; once constructed, the system can be implemented and maintained by nonpsychologists. Validation refers to a formal, systematic process to verify the job-relatedness and effectiveness of the screening system, and is required to satisfy legal concerns, as well as to ensure that the screening system operates as intended to provide top-quality employees. The system is designed to incorporate carefully-constructed procedures and decision-making rules that replicate the activities and judgments assessment professionals normally supply on a case-by-case basis.

The original investment required to set up the system is usually returned fairly quickly when the system is used to screen relatively large numbers of candidates. Thus, structured systems can be used rather extensively at low-to-middle levels in the organization (i.e., hourly and nonexempt employees up through middle managers). Another, equally important advantage of structured screening systems is their legal defensibility. Because they use well-defined, systematically-applied procedures, the documentation required to defend the system is developed and reviewed *in advance* of system implementation. Thus, all bases are covered in the event the system is challenged.

A structured screening system can be constructed for almost any job level.

Cost-benefit analyses are frequently conducted to analyze the return on investment expected from the use of this type of system compared to the use of more traditional resume review and interview-based systems. These studies consistently show that, even at the production worker level, the use of structured systems can yield thousands of dollars in savings a year through such things as increased productivity and improved quality for each employee selected through this type of system. The higher the level of employee, of course, the greater is the return on investment realized. Additionally, structured screening can target systems on specific employee characteristics that are especially important to the organization. Reliability, attention to detail, dexterity, and team-orientation characteristics, for example, are frequently targeted at nonexempt levels.

A number of structured screening systems are available that have proven successful in creating effective, legally defensible systems. This chapter describes one particular system, the ASSET (A Supervisory Selection Tool) supervisory selection system. ASSET was developed for use in the insurance and financial services industry by LOMA (the Life Office Management Association) in partnership with HRStrategies, Incorporated, a firm of industrial-organizational psychologists specializing in the construction of human resources systems for a variety of industries. ASSET provides an excellent example of how structured systems can supply assessment and developmental guidance functions that closely parallel those offered by individual assessment professionals.

Comparisons of the ASSET System and Psychological Assessment

The ASSET supervisory selection system incorporates an integrated set of procedures that structure the needs analysis, testing, and interview processes involved in screening candidates for first-level supervisory jobs. The procedures are designed to allow nonpsychologists to perform, in a limited fashion, the functions ordinarily performed by psychological assessment professionals. The components of the ASSET system parallel the key activities psychological assessors conduct.

The first step of the professional psychological assessment procedure is to complete a needs (or job) analysis of the position to be filled. With ASSET, supervisors and/or their managers responsible for the position are asked to complete a job analysis inventory, which lists responsibilities that are often found in supervisory jobs. Each respondent rates the importance of each responsibility. The responses are statistically summarized to identify the key demands of the supervisory job being studied.

The usual next step for an assessment professional doing a traditional psychological assessment is to identify and then administer appropriate tests or other evaluation procedures. Based upon the test scores, the assessment professional develops clinical judgments concerning the strengths and weaknesses of each individual relative to the demands of the job for which the candidate is being considered. The ASSET system uses a statistical approach to arrive at selection decisions. Job-related (valid), objectively-scored paper-and-pencil tests provide assessments of the basic capabilities of applicants for supervisory jobs. Scores on these tests are interpreted to reflect the candidate's likelihood of performing effectively on the job.

In addition to testing procedures, psychological assessments typically involve the use of assessment interviews. The assessment professional uses his or her knowledge of the job to determine the questions to ask in the interview and the conclusions to draw from the information obtained. Parallel to this method is the structured ASSET interview system. The system provides predefined skill dimensions that are widely required on supervisory jobs. A compendium of skill-related questions is available. Questions are chosen by the interviewer to elicit job-relevant information. Standardized evaluation approaches guide the nonpsychologist interviewer in assessing an individual's suitability for the job.

Finally, in traditional psychological assessment, the psychological consultant often will provide feedback to individuals being assessed. This feedback draws upon the consultant's professional judgment and ability to identify key areas requiring improvement. Conversely, the ASSET system uses statistical procedures to identify strengths and weaknesses. Using standard tables and a computer-generated interpretive profile, nonpsychologists can interpret the developmental data and provide feedback to candidates or to incumbents in supervisory jobs, if applicable. This feedback can then be used to construct developmental plans with applicants or incumbents.

Construction and Validation of a Structured Assessment System

ASSET was developed as a large-scale project in which more than 60 insurance and financial services companies across the United States and Canada cooperated. Psychologists were heavily involved in developing, structuring, and validating the system; thus, the need for employing experts to administer the system was minimized or eliminated. Following is a brief description of the stages involved in developing and validating the system:

Literature Review. An exhaustive review of the literature on the prediction of supervisory and managerial success was conducted. Of particular interest was the prediction of both *performance* as a supervisor or manager and *advancement* through managerial ranks. Exhibit 7–1 summarizes the findings from this literature review.

As Exhibit 7–1 indicates, professional assessment procedures were found to be quite effective in predicting both performance and advancement. The literature review also revealed that a number of objectively-scored procedures (such as statistically weighted background inventories, tests of reasoning skills, and situations tests) could be used without professional interpretation to predict success. Also of interest was the finding that somewhat different procedures are required

Exhibit 7-1
Prediction of Supervisory and Managerial Performance and Advancement

Type of Approach	Rank-Order Effectiveness in Predicting:	
	On-the-Job Performance	Advancement to Higher Levels
Professional Assessments	1	3
Statistically-Weighted Self-Reports of Background/Experience	2	5
Tests of Reasoning Skills	3	8
Tests of Quickness and Accuracy in Interpreting Information and Identifying Errors	4	6
Assessment Centers and Other Performance Simulations	5	1
Tests of Quantitative Reasoning Skills	6	4
Situations Tests (Involving How Candidate Would Handle Hypothetical Situations)	7	2
Unstructured Interview Procedures	8	7
Interest Inventories	9	9

to predict performance as a supervisor or manager versus the potential for advancement within the organization. However, the literature review showed that the procedures listed in Exhibit 7-1 were equally effective in predicting success as a supervisor and success as a manager. This means that the same procedures could be used at both levels, and that by using the procedures to select supervisors an organization is providing itself with a talented pool of individuals to select from as managerial jobs become available. The implication is that to predict both performance and advancement, the ASSET tests should contain a mix of tests.

Job Analysis. A structured job analysis inventory was constructed to measure the relative importance of a wide range of skills, abilities, and personal characteristics needed for effective supervisory performance. More than 2,000 supervisors and managers from more than 60 companies responded. The results were statistically summarized, and characteristics key to supervisory success—both across all supervisory jobs and to specialized families of supervisory jobs—were identified.

Test Validation. Sets of paper-and-pencil tests were constructed to measure the key skills and abilities identified by the job analysis. These tests include a mix of the types of tests revealed through the literature review to be successful in predicting performance and advancement. Once developed, the tests were administered to well over 1,000 supervisors across the United States and Canada. Performance appraisal information was gathered on each supervisor. The statistical relationship between test performance and on-the-job performance was studied to identify test batteries that would simultaneously optimize the prediction of incumbent success in supervisory jobs and the person's potential for advancement within the organization, as well as minimize or eliminate any adverse impact that might be associated with the testing program. The test batteries that were identified exhibited validities that would have placed them among the top-ranked procedures in Exhibit 7–1.

In addition to the validity data, utility data were gathered to help determine the net dollar benefit associated with using the ASSET tests. The utility analysis indicated that each supervisor hired with ASSET would be more productive than those hired without this tool. This performance improvement translates into a savings of $8,000 a year for each supervisor selected. If the supervisor remains at the company for ten years, the savings would reach $80,000.

Interview Construction. Job analysis results were reviewed to identify key supervisory job requirements that, while critical to success, are not measured as effectively as desired by paper-and-pencil tests. Sets of interview aids were constructed that would allow nonpsychologists to conduct an effective evaluation of candidates for supervisory jobs. The procedures were pilot-tested within a number of insurance companies. The interview program was then refined and prepared for use within other companies.

Developmental Scale Identification. Sets of items (scales) from the ASSET test battery were identified to aid in profiling candidates by their strengths and weaknesses. Procedures were constructed for using these profiles to provide feedback to candidates (or incumbent supervisors) on areas where developmental activities could lead to improved performance on the job.

Administrative System Development. Manuals and training procedures were developed to support the implementation of the ASSET system within a company.

Description of the ASSET Testing System

The two ASSET test batteries contain a total of four tests. The Decision Effectiveness Test, which measures reasoning, decision-making, and planning/ scheduling skills, and the Situation Management Test, which measures skills related to effectively operating within organizations, are contained in both batteries. The third test varies, depending upon whether the company wishes to use the tests for selection purposes only or to also obtain information used for developmental guidance. The ASSET Selection Battery contains the Information Verification Test (which measures attention to detail and the ability to identify errors in textual materials). The ASSET Selection and Development Battery contains the Background Information Inventory (a self-description of experiences and approaches to situations). Both batteries exhibit identical validities in predicting on-the-job performance. The Selection and Development Battery requires somewhat more time to administer and is more complex to score. As a result, companies interested in using the tests for selection purposes only will probably prefer the shorter and simpler Selection Battery. Exhibit 7–2 provides a full description of the four ASSET tests.

All tests in both batteries provide for objective scoring. The total score from all three tests can range from a low of 3 to a high of 27. LOMA provides tables to help the selecting person interpret an individual's total battery score in a variety of ways and as a guide in deciding whether to select an individual for a supervisory job. One set of tables, for example, indicates the expected level of performance on the job associated with each score level on the test batteries.

ASSET Interview System

The ASSET interview system is designed to allow interviewers to efficiently construct and conduct an effective, job-related interview. The interviewers do not have to be psychologists. In fact, the ASSET interview system provides professionally-developed aids that allow HR professionals and line managers to replicate the type of interview conducted by an industrial-organizational psychologist. Exhibit 7–3 provides a description of aids available through the ASSET system.

The ASSET interview system focuses on nontechnical supervisory skills. Exhibit 7–4 provides a list of 9 dimensions and 37 subdimensions that interviewers may evaluate using ASSET. An interviewer is guided through a systematic process to identify the key dimensions and subdimensions of the supervisory job for which a candidate is being considered. Focused interview questions are provided by the system for each dimension and subdimension of interest.

Two types of interview questions, *Past Approach* questions and *Situational* questions, are available to ASSET interviewers. These questions were structured to conform to current research on the best approach for assessing a candidate's skills during an interview. The Past Approach questions are structured to identify an occasion when the candidate used the skills to be assessed during the interview. The candidate's skill level is evaluated based on how the situation is handled. The Situational questions, on the other hand, allow the interviewer to present a hypothetical situation and ask how the candidate would respond to the situation. Follow-up questions allow the interviewer to examine why the candidate would handle the situation in such a way.

Both types of questions are effective for interviewers who are not trained psychologists. In general, interviewers find the Past Approach questions most useful for candidates who have extensive work experience and therefore a richer set of examples of actual performance from which to draw. Situational questions, on the other hand, are effective whether the candidate has work experience or not. In addition, Situational questions are much more useful than Past Approach questions for use with candidates who have relatively little work experience.

Exhibit 7-2
Tests in the ASSET Batteries

Type of Test	Selection Battery	Selection and Development Battery	Administration Time (Minutes)
Situation Management: Presents candidates with a series of situations involving: the formation of effective working relationships with subordinates, peers and superiors; dealing with problem employees; and balancing work priorities. Measures interpersonal skills, organizational savvy, and the ability to deal with situations in which the rules are not clear.	X	X	25
Decision Effectiveness: Presents candidates with situations that involve the application of policies and procedures. These situations include: interpreting a vacation policy; applying information about subordinate skill levels to effectively assign work; and scheduling subordinates according to work flow guidelines. Also, measures reasoning and decision skills by presenting problem situations in which enough information is available that only logic and reasoning are required to identify the best solution.	X	X	25
Information Verification: Presents candidates with a series of tables (for example; a productivity report, a time report summary, and a summary of pending work). Measures the candidate's ability both to correctly interpret quantitive information and to quickly and accurately verify the accuracy of information abstracted from tables.	X		8
Background Information Inventory: Presents candidates with a series of items that require them to: describe how they approach tasks; indicate whether they have participated in activities that develop skills related to successful supervision; and reveal the extent to which they have used leadership skills in the past. Measures how effectively a person approaches tasks and interacts with people.		X	30

Exhibit 7–3
ASSET Interview Aids

Interview Activity	Interview Aids

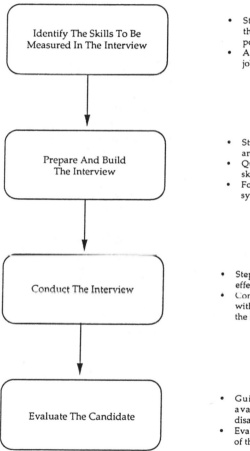

Identify The Skills To Be Measured In The Interview

- Straightforward instructions on how to identify the key skills required on a given supervisory position
- A listing of supervisory skills derived from a job analysis of over 1,000 supervisory jobs

Prepare And Build The Interview

- Straightforward instructions on how to build an interview
- Questions to use for assessing supervisory skills
- Forms that simplify the construction of a systematic, structured interview

Conduct The Interview

- Step-by-step guidance on how to conduct an effective interview
- Convenient note-taking forms that dovetail with the interview structure developed prior to the interview

Evaluate The Candidate

- Guidance on five evaluation methods available, and the advantages and disadvantages of each
- Evaluation and documentation forms for each of the evaluation methods

Exhibit 7–4
Nontechnical Job Skill Dimensions

Planning and Organizing

- Plans
- Schedules
- Manages Time
- Attentive To Detail

Personal Work Habits

- Initiative
- Flexibility
- Consistency
- Working Independently
- Stress Tolerance
- Follow-Through

Leadership

- Motivates
- Provides a Positive Role Model
- Influences Others
- Self-Confidence
- Corporate Loyalty and Support
- Willingness to Delegate Work
- Promotes Teamwork
- Personal Integrity

Personnel Administration

- Communicates Policies
- Maintains Required Personnel Records
- Follows Personnel Procedures
- Completes Performance Appraisals;
  Updates Job Descriptions

Dealing with Others

- Maintains Cooperative and Friendly Attitude
- Handles Conflict
- Acts Tactfully and Professionally
- Service Orientation

Problem Solving

- Identifies Problems
- Researches Problems
- Reasons
- Makes Decisions

Communicating

- Communicates Orally

Monitoring and Evaluating Activities

- Develops Monitoring Systems
- Maintains Progress Records
- Evaluates Activities (Against Goals and Budgets)

Guiding and Developing

- Coaches
- Provides Constructive Feedback
- Provides Training/Development

ASSET Developmental Guidance

Psychologists reviewed the ASSET tests to identify dimensions or item groupings that could be used to provide useful feedback to candidates about their strengths and weaknesses relative to key supervisory characteristics. The following eight feedback dimensions were identified:

- Problem Analysis
- Planning and Organizing
- Self-Confidence
- Interpersonal Contact
- Providing Guidance

- Monitoring Others
- Taking Responsibility
- Nontechnical Orientation

The items were then statistically analyzed to verify that scores derived from them would indeed provide valid and reliable measurements.

The ASSET Selection and Development Battery is scored by software that automatically produces a developmental profile for a candidate to be used by trained company personnel for counseling the candidate. An example of such a profile is provided as Exhibit 7–5. Those involved in providing feedback are advised to use the profile information as a starting point for discussing developmental activities directed toward improved performance. Combined with work history information, ASSET developmental profiles can be invaluable in developmental discussions. ASSET instruction materials emphasize, however, that test scores are not intended to be exclusively relied on. The developmental information from the ASSET tests, as with information provided by psychological assessment consultants, should be interpreted in combination with other available data and in collaboration with the individual receiving the feedback.

While this chapter emphasizes the use of the ASSET system for screening candidates for supervisory positions, it should also be noted that many companies routinely use the system to test incumbents and provide them with developmental guidance. Just as test scores can be a powerful mechanism for focusing developmental discussions with candidates, they can also serve a similar purpose for individuals already in supervisory jobs. In fact, an especially successful approach to facilitating developmental guidance for current supervisors is to combine the use of ASSET test results with performance information.

SUMMARY COMMENTS

The ASSET system provides a mechanism for evaluating a candidate's potential for success on a supervisory job; it does so without the use of relatively expensive psychological assessment processes. The system is structured such that the test information and the interview information can be used independently; used together, however, they provide a well-rounded view of a candidate.

The information that supports structured screening systems such as ASSET is compelling. First, the approaches used to construct the systems provide extensive information concerning the validity and, therefore, the legal defensibility of the system. Second, structured systems are administratively convenient to use. Third, they yield high dollar benefits through savings.

These structured systems can also effectively complement traditional psychological assessments made within companies. The assessments provided by a system such as ASSET can be used at lower organizational levels at which relatively large numbers of candidates are assessed, whereas more expensive

Exhibit 7–5
Feedback Report Example

PROBLEM ANALYSIS: Score in this area is high. Indicates the analytic skills required to successfully solve problems, schedule work, and reason through difficulties involving the application of policies and procedures are at a level that will allow the individual to be successful as a supervisor.

PLANNING AND ORGANIZING: Score in this area is high. Indicates that the orientation toward organizing own time and the work of others is at a level that will provide for success on the job.

SELF-CONFIDENCE: Score in this area is low. Responses indicate that when the individual takes on responsibilities there may be a concern that a failure will be the result. This lack of self-confidence may be communicated to others, leaving them to question the qualifications of the individual upon assuming a supervisory position.

INTERPERSONAL COMFORT: Score in this area is low. Responses indicate that the candidate may feel uncomfortable interacting with others and may be less effective in resolving conflict situations than would be expected of someone in a supervisory position.

PROVIDING GUIDANCE: Score in this area is average. This indicates that the candidate's ability to recognize appropriate ways to provide direction and performance feedback to others is at a level consistent with being an effective supervisor. The "average" score does, however, indicate that increased experience in this area might improve the candidate's ability to assume a supervisory position.

MOTIVATING OTHERS: Score is low in this area. Responses indicate that the candidate has less experience in attempting to motivate others and improve coworker morale than most supervisors prior to assuming supervisory positions. Additionally, responses indicate the candidate might feel unable to interpret others' motivations and to persuade them to act in desirable manners.

TAKING RESPONSIBILITY: The score is high in this area. Responses indicate that the candidate attributes success to factors such as ability and hard work rather than luck and external circumstances. As a result, the candidate is likely to assume personal responsibility for "making things happen" on the job.

NONTECHNICAL ORIENTATION: The score is low in this area. Responses indicate that the candidate may be more oriented toward the technical side of the jobs than toward the non-technical aspects, such as communicating with subordinates, providing motivation, and improving morale.

psychological assessments can be used for selecting at higher levels within the organization. An added advantage is that by using the structured systems at lower levels, companies can easily identify available candidates who have potential for advancing to higher-level positions.

CONCLUSION: BUSINESS SCENARIO REVISITED

As has been revealed in this chapter, the group overheard in the scenario at the beginning of the chapter does have some options. One is the option they discussed, the use of formal psychological assessment procedures. Another, less expensive approach, is the implementation of a structured screening system such as ASSET.

For insurance and financial services companies, ASSET is readily available for use with supervisory jobs. A job analysis process is used to link the company's jobs to the supervisory jobs included in the validation study. This allows the validity evidence developed in LOMA's 63-company consortium project to be transported to another user for purposes of legal defensibility.

For companies outside the insurance and financial services industry who are interested in obtaining a structured supervisory screening system, at least two approaches are viable. One option is that a company can participate in an industry consortium effort like the one used to develop and validate the ASSET system. More typically, though, targeted sets of procedures can be developed for an individual company by trained professionals. As with ASSET, the development screening systems require the services of trained professionals to construct them and document their validity. Once constructed, however, companies can continue to use such systems at a fraction of the cost of traditional psychological assessments.

8

The Psychological Assessment of Middle Managers

Kelley A. Conrad

"Middle management" is a term used often in business, but rarely defined clearly. Generally the term "executive" describes those managers at the highest levels of organizations whose function is to set broad policies, while middle- and lower-level managers implement those policies. "Supervisor" is the term describing the first level of management, those managers who direct employees. There can be several levels of responsibility between the top and bottom levels, but in this chapter, a middle manager is any manager (except the senior executive) whose function is to implement policies under the direction of other managers.

The task of psychological assessment in business is to describe competencies and characteristics that have a bearing on the individual's functioning as a manager or employee. The assessment provides a condensed behavioral description of the manager evaluating the fit between the person, the needs of the job, and the expectations of the organization. The focus is on the person's healthy responses to the demands of the managerial position.

Qualifications for middle management positions vary with the level of responsibility and the kind of people supervised. Through the years, Humber, Mundie & McClary has developed a standardized job specification of a middle manager's responsibilities. We use this as a general guide when conducting assessments. For each individual assessment, the standardized job description is changed to improve the match to the specific organization and position for which a person is being assessed. For example, a middle management accountant does not need to have the same degree of dynamic, tough-minded leadership normally required in an engineering plant manager. A middle management accountant in a fast-growing financial services business will need greater confidence, decisiveness, and nimble-mindedness than will a middle management accountant in an established, fairly mature manufacturing plant.

Through the years it has become evident that there are two sides to effective management: the leadership side and the administrative side. Recently, some management theorists (Kotter 1990) have elaborated on these two sides, defining them as two different and contrasting styles of manager. Most psychologists, however, see both as important dimensions essential to middle management performance. What varies is the degree to which a given dimension, or one of its component behaviors, is critical in performance on a particular managerial job. The ideal middle manager is a happy blend of both leadership and administrative abilities. The recipe for a successful blend is determined by the environment, the organization, the job, the people, and the manager. Some of the key elements that I look for (in varying degrees) in middle managers include:

Leadership abilities	Administrative abilities
Aggressiveness	High-level mental ability
Production-mindedness	Good verbal ability
Tough-mindedness	Good numerical ability
Self-confidence	Ability to think analytically and critically
Courage of convictions	Good judgment
Ability to take charge	Long-range planning ability
Ability to organize	Good cultural background
Decisiveness	Breadth and perspective
Ability to inspire others	Ability to see the big picture
Tact and social sensitivity	Nimble-mindedness

The categories used for reporting the psychologist's observations and impressions about the person being assessed have grown out of a combination of practical experience and scientific observation. In Chapter 1, Dr. Hansen presented a description of a typical business assessment interview, which included a brief summary of the categories often discussed. These were education, work experience, interpersonal orientation, family history, personal assessment and goals, activities and interests, and interest in the position. These are not, however, the topics that most business psychologists use to describe their observations and conclusions. The topical headings found in assessments usually include some variation of intellectual effectiveness, communications and impact, personality and emotional organization, interpersonal style and effectiveness, work planning and organization skills, leadership style, and goals and aspirations. Most assessments end with a general review of fit, potential, and a summary of the individual's assets and limitations.

MIDDLE MANAGEMENT ASSESSMENT AT HUMBER, MUNDIE & McCLARY

The process we use in assessments begins some time before a specific person is assessed. When we first start working with a client company we will spend time at the client's place of business getting to know them. Through informal conversations with several current managers and employees we develop a feeling for the organizational culture and the present climate. This includes understanding the organization's history, its statement and sense of mission, its operating philosophy, its management structure, and its prevailing management style.

Several years ago we reviewed and refined our standardized job description for middle managers using the Job Competence Assessment Model of Richard E. Boyatzis detailed in his book, *The Competent Manager: A Model for Effective Performance* (1982). More recently we have made revisions based on the assessment research reported by Ann Howard and Douglas W. Bray in their book, *Managerial Lives in Transition: Advancing Age and Changing Times* (1988). We also conduct periodic validity studies to evaluate our assessments and their predictive power. These, too, lead us to make certain changes in our procedures on an ongoing basis.

At the time of a specific assessment, I update my understanding of current expectations through a conversation with the hiring manager, the personnel manager, and sometimes the general manager or president. During these conversations I explore specific performance expectations: what, if any, concerns the manager has; what happened with the previous job holder; and any changes expected in the job or the reporting relationships affecting it. I review the job description and any supplementary specifications. For middle management positions I review the organization chart and might review past assessments on people who have a direct reporting relationship to the position. I often write specific questions to be addressed in the interview record form I use for documenting the interview.

The rest of this chapter describes each of the topical areas used in the assessment of middle managers. For each area I will outline the key knowledge, skills, and abilities that predict success, and how I measure these characteristics.

INTELLECTUAL EFFECTIVENESS

The focus here is on the manager's intellectual resources and how effectively those resources are used. While intelligence reflects the power of the manager's mind, a high level of intelligence does not guarantee effective thinking.

Intelligence is often described as general mental ability. It describes how able the person is in terms of the functions measured by various tests of intelligence, scholastic aptitude, and learning ability. Most managers have learned quite a bit about intelligence tests, having taken more than their fair share of them. If intelligence tests measured intelligence completely, most people would be satisfied with them. In fact, I find this not to be true. Most managers are more than a little frightened by the intelligence testing process. This could be the fault of the process or that the intelligence test does not really do what it purports to do. There are other characteristics involved in our thinking effectiveness. Most intelligence measures are precise instruments, so the problem would seem to lie elsewhere. Most managers think there is something beyond intelligence that is the key to thinking effectively. It is this portion of our thinking ability that we develop through use in our daily work and life.

One of our firm's founders, Dr. Paul Mundie, described intelligence in terms of two components: a vertical component representing general mental ability of the classic intelligence-test-measured variety, and a horizontal component representing the common-sense type of intelligence that enables us to do things, to live in a world of other people, and to be sensible. It is our common sense that enables us to act sharply and reasonably when faced with problems.

Lack of general mental ability (the vertical component) can limit a manager, but possession of a great deal of general mental ability does not assure success or excellence. As important, and possibly more important, is the manager's effectiveness in making practical use of general mental ability. To make these distinctions clear, our standardized job description for middle managers identifies the following dimensions.

General Mental Ability

This dimension describes the manager's power to understand and meet many situations. It reflects the person's skill in understanding the interrelationships of presented facts in such a way that they guide his or her action to a desired goal. It is measured by one or more traditional intelligence tests. Comparisons may be made to general population norms, college graduate norms, to appropriate managerial norms and, when available, to those from within the organization itself.

In my practice I most often use The Industrial Problems Test (a proprietary test), The Shipley Institute of Living Scale, tests from the Differential Aptitude Test Battery, or the Wechsler Adult Intelligence Scale-Revised to assess general mental abilities. The specific test I choose depends on the person and situation.

More descriptive detail about the manager's effective intelligence is detailed in statements about linguistic skills, quantitative skills, and specialized knowledge.

Linguistic Skill

The second dimension is the description of the manager's effectiveness in the use of language to communicate ideas and goals. Effective managers clearly express their ideas and routinely check that others have understood what was communicated. This skill is assessed directly by vocabulary strength and linguistic elements on the tests and by the manager's facility during the background interview and in the written exercises.

Quantitative Skill

The third dimension describes the manager's demonstrated facility working with numbers, computations, and interpretations when solving problems presented numerically as calculational problems, tables, or graphics. It also includes the person's skill in explaining numerical information to someone else when necessary. This skill is assessed directly by the quantitative elements on the tests and by the manager's ability to recall and explain an example of a task or assignment from a past performance in which the manager had to deal effectively with numerical information and analysis.

Specialized Knowledge

In this area I assess the manager's grasp of certain specific facts, principles, theories, frameworks, or modes that might be important or usable within the organization and job. While specialized knowledge is often related to a person's performance as a manager, research evidence does not show that "superior performance as a manager [is] related to the possession of more facts or concepts than average performance as a manager" (Boyatzis 1982, 183). When this issue is raised as a specific question by a client, I assess specialized knowledge using specific aptitude measures supplemented with focused interview questions.

The final part of the intellectual effectiveness section of the assessment report describes the manager's skill in making good practical use of his or her intelligence. This aspect of intellectual functioning is not easily measured in formal tests. I assess this component during the interview by looking for evidence of a range of interests, decision-making skills, and creativity.

Range of Interests

This dimension describes the manager's intellectual curiosity, range of interests, and knowledge beyond the person's special field. It includes interest in and curiosity about a variety of topics and activities such as science, politics, sports, music, and art. This skill is also reflected in the manager's efforts to keep informed about developments in the specialty field and to do broad-gauged thinking. I assess it through direct interview questions about hobbies and interests, reading habits, and personal goals.

Decision-Making Skills

This dimension describes the manager's skill in seeking out information: identifying or recognizing patterns from an assortment of information using a concept or system to interpret the events and make a decision. It includes an evaluation of how good those decisions are. I assess the manager's skills as a decision maker with the Kolb's Learning Style Indicator or the Watson-Glaser Critical Thinking test, and by having the manager talk through one or two key decisions in detail.

Creativity

This dimension describes the manager's skill in dealing inventively with situations by devising new approaches. Managers with high creativity are nimble-minded in their approach, are able to switch from one subject to another instantly, and exhibit the ability to think rapidly in unstructured situations. I assess this through the creativity and creative personality scales on the Adjective Check List (ACL), the manager's curiosity, innovative behavior, and past suggestions for improvement.

Sample Report Content

Typically, I will highlight in the report the dominant characteristics of the individual's thinking and problem-solving styles. For example, an individual might be described as high average in terms of learning capacity and general intellectual functioning, but somewhat rigid about applying formal logic. I also describe speed of problem-solving and whether an individual is strongly analytical in solving problems or tends to rely upon intuition. When making general statements about an individual's level of functioning, I include a phrase that indicates the norm group to which the person is being compared. I include descriptions of academic performance and range of interests when these add value or clarification with respect to the skills needed for the position. A sample paragraph describing intellectual functioning follows:

Mr. Jones's basic ability to think and learn is in the high average range when he is compared to individuals holding managerial positions. His conceptual skills are solid. He demonstrates an appropriate level of depth in his thinking. His verbal and quantitative skills are well-balanced. His vocabulary and verbal skills are above the average for managers. His ability to apply logic is stronger than for most managers, although his abstract thinking and numerical reasoning are slightly above the average for managers. In problem-solving he works at a quick pace but readily sacrifices accuracy for speed. Very rigid about his desire to have everything logically justified, he will delay decisions until he has a logical argument for them. Mr. Jones usually sees the big picture, but can gloss over some details. This can slow him down when he goes on to implement what he assumed would be a simple solution. He reads one book a week, with most of these being in his technical specialty. He reads little about management and has not taken any significant management or supervisory skills classes.

COMMUNICATIONS AND IMPACT

For many years Humber, Mundie & McClary included oral and written communications as a component in the intellectual effectiveness section of the assessment report. The skill to express oneself effectively was considered one aspect of the manager's intellectual effectiveness that was related to superior performance. The important relationship demonstrated between oral communications and superior performance as a manager in several studies (e.g., Boyatzis 1982) led us to begin treating communications and impact as a section on its own.

Three major dimensions are examined in communications and impact. These are use of oral presentations, written communications skills, and concern with impact.

Use of Oral Presentations

The section on oral presentations describes the manager's capability to say what is meant in terms easily understandable to the target audience. In one-on-one exchanges the manager will often summarize or restate what others have said or are trying to say. I assess this directly in the interview process by evaluating how effectively the manager describes personal nature and experiences. When this skill is particularly critical to success in a position, I supplement the interview observations with a brief exercise requiring the manager to analyze a small group of facts and then present and defend those judgments in a brief oral presentation.

Written Communications Skills

This dimension describes the manager's skill at composing an informative and grammatically correct letter or memo on a well-known subject. The intent is to predict how well-written the person's letters, memos, and reports are likely to be. I assess this area directly through several samples of the manager's writing completed during the assessment and from the manager's description of key examples of work behavior involving effective and noneffective past written communications.

Concern with Impact

The last dimension in communications and impact is the description of the manager's alertness to his or her impact on others, including the person's skill and willingness to use personal power to motivate and influence others. It also reflects the degree to which the manager feels personally important. I assess this through interview questions exploring how the person attracts attention to his or her ideas, how and when the manager takes a more assertive stand on issues, and on the person's need for power derived through the scoring of several picture story exercises adapted from the Thematic Apperception Test (TAT).

Sample Report Content

In the communications and impact paragraph the individual is described in terms of the ability to communicate in a clear and succinct fashion. Frequently I include comments regarding the manager's ability to elaborate upon complex ideas or to explain technical concepts in nontechnical language. Finally, I describe presentation skills and the overall impact of the person's communications. For example:

Mr. Smith has a strong vocabulary that he is able to use in effectively communicating his ideas and thinking to others. He typically prepares before committing himself publicly. He can lay out his thinking in a logical and easy to follow fashion. He is comfortable assuming a higher profiled role but does not typically seek out the spotlight. In many situations he is too quiet. He tends not to become more outspoken about his ideas unless he is particularly committed to them or unless he comes under attack. His written communications skills are quite good. His vocabulary is in the high range for experienced managers. He has the ability to present his thinking clearly and concisely in written form. People find his writing easy to read and understand. He is also quite good at developing and documenting more complicated procedures. His logical thinking and attention to detail ensure that the procedures are internally consistent and understandable.

PERSONALITY AND EMOTIONAL ORGANIZATION

Few people fail for lack of job knowledge. Failure on the job is more often related to personal inadequacy than to technical incapacity. I think of personality as a system through which a person organizes and interacts with his or her environment. A manager can interact with and use feedback in one way dealing with a supervisor and in an entirely different way with a manager who is a peer. That same manager can respond very differently to a challenge from another manager in the work environment than a challenge from that same manager in a sports event. Often people will get to know others quite well within a given environment or situation and believe they know what reactions to expect from that person. They can be surprised when they see that same person react very differently to a slightly different situation. A classic example is a person who performs well in his or her current job responsibilities, but who is overwhelmed by the new ones faced after a promotion. The former success now becomes a failure.

Many employment interviewers do very little to find out about the emotional behavior of the person they are interviewing as a prospective manager. In psychological assessments, observations about the individual's personality makeup include issues that reflect that person's emotional maturity and health. The description focuses on the effect of personality in the work environment. Even when evidence of serious personality disorders is found, I describe the impact on the job. In such situations I will encourage the person to seek continuing psychological counsel or support.

Although this area can include a wide range of personality-related information, I focus my observations on four major dimensions that have been shown to be predictive of middle management performance. These are self-confidence, independence, aggressiveness, and general adjustment.

Self-Confidence

The first element in the paragraph on personality and emotional organization is the description of the degree to which a manager demonstrates awareness of the capacity to perform well. It can be observed in statements of positive self-esteem and decisiveness. I assess this through the self-confidence scale on the ACL and impressions from the interview. Particularly, I listen and watch for the person to make clear and unequivocal statements about personal decisions, for evidence that the person acts in a forceful, unhesitating, and impressive fashion. In addition, I look for the manager's belief in his or her own success.

Independence

The dimension of independence describes the manager's comfort and willingness to act independently of the social values and expectations of others. Obversely, it is reflected in the degree to which the person shows a need for a superior's approval or peer approval. I assess independence by looking for above-average scores on the ACL scales for autonomy and favorable adjectives checked, and for low scores on the scales measuring needs for succorance, abasement, and deference. During the interview, independent managers will behave in an assertive fashion, will exhibit evidence of nonconformity, and will express some hostile or critical feelings directly. They may be a little condescending in their relations with others, but will, nonetheless, be sought out by others. They may also exhibit some cynicism, selfishness, and a subtle negativism.

Aggressiveness

Aggressiveness reflects the manager's comfort using personal assertiveness and position power to get compliance. An aggressive manager will demonstrate strongly direct interactions with subordinates and others to get them to go along with that manager's directions, wishes, comments, policies, and procedures. During the interview, I seek evidence that the person has given orders, commands, or directions and felt comfortable doing so based upon personal authority, and that it has been done so without the input of others. I also use an elevated profile score on the aggression scale of the ACL as a predictor.

General Adjustment

This dimension describes the manager's adjustment to life, including an understanding of others and of the situations they face. I also include the manager's acceptance and tolerance of self and others, and the willingness to help those in need. A well-adjusted manager has a positive attitude toward life, generally enjoys the company of others, and feels capable of starting activities and following through on them. I look for these characteristics in the interview and in an elevated score on the personal adjustment scale on the ACL.

Sample Report Content

In the written report, I make direct statements regarding the manager's levels of self-confidence, aggressiveness, independence, and personal adjustment as compared to other successful managers. I might point out, for example, that the individual is above average in self-confidence but below average in aggressiveness when compared to others in managerial assignments. I might qualify this statement, explaining that the individual is free of self-doubt to the point of being hostile. Finally, I emphasize the individual's goal orientation and general emotional adjustment, pointing out any indications of impulsiveness, restlessness, or anger that can affect the person's effectiveness or longevity on the job. For example:

There is a good deal of hostility within Ms. Johnson, which she has not, thus far, been able to channel effectively into worthwhile activities. She is quite opinionated and is critical of most people around her. She can also be negative in her attitudes. She is not aggressive or forceful in gaining her objectives. She is critical of most situations she does not understand. She must be careful that she is not demeaning to people who are threatening to her. While her stated intentions are good, she uses criticism as a defense against her own feeling of personal uncertainty. She puts pressure upon herself to perform well. She is quite dogged and determined in pursuing her goals. She is less satisfied with her life and career than is true for most managers with her experience.

INTERPERSONAL STYLE AND EFFECTIVENESS

A manager lives in a world of other people. In fact, the manager's job is defined as getting things done with and through other people. In this section of a psychological assessment, I describe evidence of the manager's style and flexibility when dealing with others. The section covers one-to-one relationships and one-to-group relationships. Unfortunately, the ability to get along with others is an art and not a science. It depends on one's personal adjustment. In other words, if I can learn to get along with myself, it is almost certain that I can learn to get along with other people.

We have tried for years to find the interpersonal hallmarks of good managers. We have been unable to find a single overt quality that will always mark the good manager. What we have found is that the marks of an effective or an ineffective manager are within the person. Many of these traits are more easily seen or described when they manifest themselves as problems. For example, does the manager demonstrate a feeling of insecurity? Is the manager able to control anger, envy, and jealousy? How does the person handle feelings of inferiority? For the most part, interpersonal effectiveness is not dependent upon techniques, although techniques and specific skills may help. Effective managers use psychological techniques to get hold of themselves psychologically. When they begin to measure their degree of insecurity and inferiority, recognize that their difficulties in communicating grow out of situations where their emotions take hold, and do not let their anger, envy, or jealousy control them, then those managers will get along with people.

Interpersonal style and effectiveness is difficult to assess objectively. One complication stems from the fact that in most psychological assessments we must rely on the manager's self-report of style and effectiveness. It is a common misconception that managers do not develop accurate perceptions of themselves. In practice, I do not find that to be true. Most managers can describe themselves very accurately. It is true, however, that they are reluctant to talk about themselves in depth. One reason for this defensive reaction is that they often simply do not know another way to react. They lack conscious alternatives to the reactions they currently use. Training for many managers proves effective when it gives them new alternatives.

While some formal measures can provide profiles of style (The Self-Referent Social Style Exercise, Wilson Learning Corporation; The Social Style Profile, TRACOM, Corp.; and the FIRO-B, Consulting Psychologists Press), all are essentially self-report devices. The most direct observation of interpersonal behavior during an assessment comes from the interaction with the psychologist and office staff during the interview. However, in this situation, most managers exhibit their "best behavior," which needs to be taken into account and contrasted with self-reported behavior in other situations. An example might be a report of how the manager has reacted to a recent situation in which anger was felt or expressed.

Examination of the manager's social self-concept, and of the psychological and social aspects of the manager's relationships to the surrounding world, is profiled in terms of social style, perceptual objectivity, accurate self-assessment, influence, skill in managing group process, and positive regard.

Social Style

By categorizing managers in terms of two major dimensions—their relative assertiveness in dealing with others, and their open or controlled emotional expression, it is possible to broadly classify the person in terms of four social styles. Each of these styles is characterized by identifiable patterns of response in the manager's interactions with people of same or contrasting styles. In my assessments, I develop my own hypothesis of the manager's style from the interactions during the interview and confirm it by the Social Style Profile instrument.

Perceptual Objectivity

This dimension describes the degree to which the manager is objective in view, and not limited by too much subjectivity, bias, prejudice, or distortion. Managers with good perceptual objectivity have a disposition to view an event from several perspectives simultaneously, and the skill to distance themselves from emotional involvement. In other words, they can view the event or situation with objectivity. Another term for this is "open-mindedness." I assess perceptual objectivity from the interview and from elevated scores on the intraception scale and low scores on the abasement Scale of the ACL.

Accurate Self-Assessment

This dimension describes the degree to which managers have a realistic, grounded view of themselves. I look for evidence that the person knows his or her limitations and strengths. I often ask the manager to outline both strengths and weaknesses. Often more important than what the manager lists is the elaboration of each strength or weakness, including specific examples of how the person has capitalized on strengths and worked to overcome weaknesses. Indirect evidence comes from the manager's ability to be an objective sounding board for others. In Boyatzis's study (1982), this dimension was found to be essential to performance as a manager but not causally related to superior job performance.

Influence

This dimension describes evidence that the manager uses personal or positional power, adapting it socially to build appropriate alliances, networks, coalitions, and teams. Effective managers will view themselves as members of the teams they have created. The effective manager will also view the relationship with a superior as important, even if it is not seen as completely successful. I assess this dimension from the interview, the control scores on the FIRO-B, and higher than average scores on the dominance, nurturance, and affiliation scales of the ACL.

Skill in Managing Group Process

Successful managers are skillful in stimulating others to work together effectively in groups toward task completion. Evidence that a manager can communicate ideas to a group, engendering and supporting cooperation in the process, comes from narrative descriptions of teams with which the person has worked.

I ask for examples of how the manager has created group identity, pride, and trust. Finally, I review the interview description of the manager's leadership or management style and look for an elevated dominance score on the ACL.

Positive Regard

This dimension reflects the degree to which the manager believes in others, and his or her willingness to communicate that belief to others. The Boyatzis study (1982) found that this dimension was important in the manager's day to day functioning but it did not predict long-term success. I assess it from the interview and from the affiliation, heterosexuality, critical parent, nurturing parent, and adult scales on the ACL.

Sample Report Content

In describing interpersonal style I highlight the manager's dominant social style and the degree to which the manager demonstrates flexibility in interactions with people of different styles and backgrounds. I look for the degree to which the manager demonstrates the ability to develop an appropriate understanding of the needs and motives of others using this understanding to assign tasks and motivate others. I also describe the manager's comfort level with a visible leadership role. Part of this is the person's ability to reward, criticize, and support direct reports. For example:

Mr. Allen can be very pleasant and friendly. An amiable driver in social style, he meets people in a friendly manner. In situations that are not competitive, he is kind to others. His insights, however, are not objective. He can appear artificial in certain aspects of his self-presentation. People have described him as being "artificially nice." He is so involved with his own needs it is difficult for him to genuinely accept and respond to the real needs of others. Strongly task-oriented, he will sacrifice the niceties of social convention when feeling pressure to perform. He can be particularly demanding in competitive situations. He can be stubborn and rigid when he does not get his own way. He would impress others as much more interesting and genuine if he would be more candid and forthright in stating his judgments and decisions.

WORK PLANNING AND ORGANIZATION SKILLS

At the core of every middle manager's job is the need to make things happen. The most effective managers do this consistently with a plan, often defining specific goals that provide milestones along the road to the successful achievement of that plan. This has been described by Kotter (1990) as the "management" role. To map out the plan and define appropriate goals, the manager must also be able to envision the desired outcomes. This vision proves to be motivating to successful managers—supplying the wellspring for their energetic pursuit of the goal. Given a clear vision of the future, the manager willingly takes acceptable risks, including initiating action as necessary. In Kotter's (1990) terms, this is the "leadership" role.

Successful middle managers who are effective in work planning and organization show competence in the dimensional areas of goal definition and orientation, proactivity, and efficiency orientation.

Goal Definition and Orientation

A successful middle manager seeks out information that will reveal patterns or deviations from patterns that provide an understanding of what is happening. This understanding is then communicated to others by defining and elaborating goals that break a given result down into unique steps that will lead the organization or the team to successful achievement of the goal. I assess this through statements made in the interview when the manager describes specific achievements, from the manager's use of personal goals, and from elevated scores on the need for achievement scale on the ACL.

Proactivity

The proactive middle manager is one who shows a disposition to get something accomplished. For successful managers the "something" is an organizational goal or a personal objective. Most successful middle managers also show a strong ability to prioritize their efforts, choosing to pursue proactively those goals that have high payoff potential. I assess this dimension in the interview, from the manager's descriptions of key work performance samples, from the person's score on the control scale of the FIRO-B, and from scores on the TAT picture stories.

Efficiency Orientation

This dimension reflects the degree to which a manager shows a concern for doing something better than it has been done in the past and doing it efficiently. Successful managers are seldom completely satisfied with past performance. They seek continuous improvement. They want to do things better than previously, better than those things have been done by someone else, or better against a defined target or standard of excellence. I assess this through the interview by looking for elevated need for achievement and order scales on the ACL, and by reviewing the manager's TAT picture stories and descriptions of key work performance samples.

Sample Report Content

In describing work planning and organizational skills, my reports focus on the manager's level of interest in and commitment to setting and achieving organizational goals. I include statements indicating whether or not the individual has difficulty articulating objectives or the steps needed to reach that goal. I describe the degree to which the individual is efficient and detail minded, the degree of priority sensitivity, and the degree to which he or she will initiate actions. For example:

Organizationally, Mr. Jones does a good job. He plans ahead and does not move until he has a good handle on the situation. He does a very good job of getting his arms around a complete situation. Able to step back from the immediacy of a situation, he sees problems with perspective and understanding. He is able to identify the essential issues and priorities in a situation. He does this in a manner that permits him to make accurate, nonbiased judgments. He is sharp, precisely correct, and on top of the problems in his area of responsibility. He is an efficient manager who communicates clear goals to his direct reports and maintains a proactive stance in the areas under his control.

LEADERSHIP

Leadership is another area that Humber, Mundie & McClary has begun to address as a separate topic in our assessments. Most clients ask specifically, "What type of leader will this person be?" In addition, there has been much emphasis in psychological research and management literature on leadership. It is also the most job-related category of the assessment for middle managers. This dimension describes the manager's skill in activating the available human resources. The successful manager can stimulate people. This is accomplished through a process of communicating goals, plans, and a rationale for the purpose of organizing and directing the human resources of the organization toward its goals. In Kotter's (1990) framework, this leadership dimension provides the charismatic, motivational, inspirational counterpoint to the more logical, routine, disciplined administrative management dimension.

Managerial leadership can be assessed by looking at the dimensions of leadership style and conceptualization.

Leadership Style

In a similar fashion as is true for social style, there have been several leadership styles defined through research. While no single leadership style is preferred for all situations, there is evidence that effective managers have developed the skill to use different styles in different situations (Clark 1990; Williamson 1981). The psychological assessment describes which styles the person uses most often and the flexibility the manager demonstrates adjusting style or adopting a different one when it is necessary to deal with different people and situations. I assess this dimension directly from discussion during the interview about critical incidents demonstrating the manager's style and flexibility dealing with subordinates and through the Managerial Style Questionnaire (McBer & Company, 1980).

Conceptualization

This dimension reflects the manager's skill in identifying structure within a set of facts. Successful managers develop conceptual explanations to interpret events and information. Such managers can identify a theme and communicate it to others. They can also break a concept apart. They may use metaphors or analogies to aid others in understanding a particular event or experience. I assess this dimension through the interview, often by asking the manager to describe a situation which was hard to explain and how he or she finally succeeded. I also look for high scores on the concrete experience and abstract conceptualization scales of the Learning Style Indicator (Kolb 1981).

Sample Report Content

In the paragraph on leadership, the focus is on the manager's comfort with responsibility and the person's style, assertiveness, and effectiveness as a leader of others. I describe the fit between the manager's style and that prevalent in the organization. I also describe how the manager handles tough situations where people do not respond to initial attempts to get something done. Finally, I look at the manager's commitment to the development and coaching of direct reports and the degree to which the manager has prepared someone to move into the manager's responsibilities when the manager is not on the scene. For example:

In structured situations where there is clear authority to match responsibilities, Ms. Parks can perform reasonably well as a leader of others. She works professionally more than persuasively in accomplishing the objectives that have been specified. She will insist quietly and persistently on quality performance. Her direct reports will know who is responsible for what and who has the authority to act. People who work closely with Ms. Parks will learn and prosper from her insights, knowledge, instruction, and coaching. At times, however, they will be surprised and hurt by her anger and criticism. She will occasionally undo a great deal of positive development with an angry remark made in the heat of the moment.

GOALS AND ASPIRATIONS

The next major section of the assessment reviews the manager's achievement motivation, work involvement, and personal goals for advancement and financial success. These dimensions are predictive of the manager's satisfaction, longevity, and personal development.

Achievement Motivation

The achievement-motivated manager will set challenging goals, stress improvements in work performance, and encourage high levels of goal attainment.

I assess this through interview comments, an elevated achievement score on the ACL, and scores from TAT picture stories.

Work Involvement

This dimension describes the extent to which managers find satisfaction in their work, and the extent to which they give it primacy in their life. I assess this dimension from the comments the person makes during the interview, and specifically in response to questions about personal goals and developmental plans.

Personal Goals

The last dimension examines the manager's personal goals to see if they are compatible with those of the organization. A successful manager who is likely to stay with an organization will exhibit a set of realistic expectations about the company, job, financial rewards, and promotional potential. These elements are important predictors of a manager's longevity. I assess this dimension primarily through the interview and, specifically, that part of the interview where the manager describes his or her goals and ambitions.

Sample Report Content

Mr. Black has typically defined objectives for himself and worked systematically to achieve those objectives. His personal planning is thorough. At least once each year he reviews his personal goals, revising old ones or adding new ones as appropriate. He maintains a diary of goals and records his progress toward them. He enjoys his work but feels he is more a technical expert than a manager. He enjoys the technical side more because he feels it is more concrete. He likes to be right about things. He feels some pressure in his present responsibilities and is not eager to expand his management role. Broader management responsibilities at this time would be difficult for him and would not be recommended. He can, however, continue to serve the company effectively in his present position or a related one.

CONCLUSIONS

The final section of the assessment report is a summary of the manager's key strengths and soft spots compared to the standards of the organization and the job requirements. The aim of this section is to bring into clear focus those psychological dimensions most likely to be critical to performance in the job. I also report the individual's perceptions of the position, including any reservations the person has.

Sample Report Content

It might be difficult for Ms. Gray to accept a horizontal move, but it appears to be the best way for the company to continue her development as a manager. She functions best in a fairly well-defined environment where there is a good deal of support and reinforcement. Within such a situation she can do a very solid job. She will take care of customers, give people good service, and be conscientious in her efforts. She is a proud person who is committed to doing the best work she can. If her pride is sustained and she can control her anger and occasional outbursts, she will continue to make a solid contribution.

SUMMARY

In our assessments we attempt to work in a way that our client's managers become progressively more knowledgeable regarding human behavior and that they use this knowledge in effective ethical ways. Our approach is personal and essentially clinical rather than psychometric or statistical. Yet it is objective and is soundly based in scientific evidence as we can make it. Underlying our strategy is the belief that most managers already possess more talent, more motivation, and more skill than they will ever fully effectively utilize. Our job as business psychologists is not so much to help them develop new capacities as to release those they already have. People who succeed in business all succeed in ways that are unique to their own experiences, opportunities, and personalities. Successful people do not all succeed in the same fashion. There is evidence, however, to indicate that many people fail for a common reason: they do not like something about themselves. One of our key goals in assessment is to identify such areas and to help the individual manager develop healthy self-perceptions. The assessment and interaction with the psychologist accomplishes this by:

- Helping the individual gain self-respect through increased insight into his or her own resources and aspirations.
- Creating and maintaining a healthy working environment that supports and rewards the efforts of people.
- Encouraging interpersonal cooperation and mutual support between all employees and managers.

We seek, through the assessment process, to create an effective behavioral environment supportive of the individual and realized in conjunction with that person's work with his or her employer.

REFERENCES

Bennett, G. K., Seashore, H. G., & Wesman, A. G. (1966, 1972). *Differential aptitude tests*. New York: The Psychological Corporation.

Boyatzis, R. E. (1982). *The competent manager: A model for effective performance*. New York: Wiley & Sons.

Briggs, K. C., & Myers, I. B. (1976). *Myers-Briggs type indicator*. Palo Alto, Calif.: Consulting Psychologists Press.

Clark, K. E., & Clark, M. B., eds. (1990). *Measures of leadership*. West Orange, N. J.: Leadership Library of America, Inc.

Gough, H. G., & Heilbrun, A. B., Jr. (1983). *The adjective check list manual*. Palo Alto, Calif.: Consulting Psychologists Press.

Grimsley, G., Ruch, F. L., Warren, N. D., & Ford, J. S. (1957). *Employee aptitude survey*. Los Angeles: Psychological Services, Inc.

Howard, A., & Bray, D. W. (1988). *Managerial lives in transition: Advancing age and changing times*. New York: Guilford Press.

Human Resources Development Corporation (1965). *Industrial problems test*. Milwaukee, Wis.: Author.

Kolb, D. A. (1981). *Learning-style inventory*. Boston: McBer & Company.

Kotter, J. P. (1990). *Force for change: How leadership differs from management*. New York: Free Press.

McBer & Company (1980). *Managerial style questionnaire*. Boston: Author.

McClelland, D. C. (1975). *Power: The inner experience*. New York: Irvington Publications, Inc. (Halstead Press/Wiley).

Merrill, D. W., & Reid, R. H. (1981). *Personal styles and effective performance*. Radnor, Penn.: Chilton Book Co.

Merrill, D. W., & Taylor, J. W. (1964, 1977). *The social style profile*. Denver: TRACOM, Personnel Predictions and Research.

Murray, H. A. (1943). *Thematic apperception test*. Cambridge, Mass.: Harvard University Press.

Shipley, W. C. (1939). *Shipley institute of living scale*. Los Angeles: Western Psychological Services.

Schutz, W. (1977). *Fundamental interpersonal relationship orientation-B*. Palo Alto, Calif.: Consulting Psychologists Press.

Watson, G., & Glaser, E. M. (1964). *Watson-Glaser critical thinking test*. New York: Harcourt, Brace & World, Inc.

Williamson, J. (1981). *The leader-manager*. Eden Prairie, Minn.: Wilson Learning Corp.

Winter, D. G. (1973). *The power motive*. New York: The Free Press.

Wechsler, D. (1981). *Wechsler adult intelligence scale-revised*. New York: The Psychological Corporation.

Wilson Learning, Inc. (1990). *The self-referent social style exercise*. Minneapolis: Author.

9

The Psychological Assessment of Top Executives: An Interview-Based Approach

RHR International

Few events in the life of an organization have the potential impact that replacing top executives has. Finding an individual to successfully fill the top one or two jobs in a company is a delicate process, fraught with danger. Leaders at this level have a tremendous effect on every other level in the organization. If an organizational system can be likened to a child's mobile, with all of its parts swinging in interdependent connectedness, then the chief executive officer and the executive vice-president represent the top beam of that mobile. The actions of these individuals set into motion reverberations that determine, in fundamental ways, what defines the organization and how it goes about its business. Inserting a new person into one of these roles results in different reverberations radiating out into the company, and such an event must be carefully planned and executed to ensure that these new reverberations create desirable results. Using a psychological assessment of potential candidates for a top executive job effectively maximizes the chances that the eventual selection will be a good one, furthering the growth and development of the organization and the individuals within it.

This chapter focuses exclusively on assessments at the chief executive officer (CEO) and executive or senior vice-president (EVP) levels. Assessing candidates for jobs at this level is different in fundamental ways from assessing candidates for jobs at lower levels in an organization. At the top of a company, the fit between the individual who fills the job and the other senior executives, the company culture, and the company's past and future is most critical. At lower levels, an assessment searches for requisite skills and experience to fill the performance demands of a job. Fit with other executives or managers and with the company culture is necessary, but not critical. At the top of an organization, skill and experience are assumed. How the person goes about employing this skill and experience is everything. The psychological assessment must be tailored to focus on this critical priority.

Psychological assessments (PAs) of top executives are usually done for one of two reasons. First, an individual might be needed to fill a top position that is currently vacant or will soon be vacant. The potential candidates may come from within the company or from outside. The task at hand is to identify the one person from the field of candidates who is most likely to successfully fill the position in question. Psychological assessments are also of value in succession planning and executive development. Existing vice-presidents might be assessed to determine their strengths and developmental needs in terms of the demands of the top jobs in the company. The results of these assessments are used to formulate development plans for targeted individuals that will prepare them to play top roles in the company in the future. The "buyer" of individual PAs for the top positions in a company might be either the board of directors or the CEO. A board of directors will most likely be interested in the selection of a new CEO, while a CEO might be interested in personal replacement, replacement of another key executive, or a succession planning and executive development process.

At the top of an organization, it is impossible to distinguish PAs done for selection purposes from PAs done for succession planning and executive development purposes. The processes are essentially identical and involve three general phases: pre-assessment, assessment, and feedback. These three phases characterize all RHR assessments, yet the unique performance demands of the positions of CEO and EVP drive numerous methodological details that differentiate PAs done for these positions from those done for positions at other levels in the organization. Other chapters in this book cover the general PA process. We will focus here on the customization of this process for selection and succession/development of these critical top jobs.

RESPONSIBILITIES OF A CEO

It will provide some context to first describe the unique performance demands that CEOs and EVPs face in the current business environment. For the sake of efficiency, we will focus on what CEOs are up against, yet much of what we cover applies to EVPs also.

CEOs of modern companies must be facile at dealing with a broad range of constituencies. They must work skillfully with their board of directors. They must deal with stockholders through formal presentations and informal small-group or one-on-one discussions. They must relate comfortably with lawyers, utilizing these experts to further the interests of the company. CEOs must also interact with numerous groups outside the organization, each of which has certain demands or interests. Some of these groups include government agencies and their elected or appointed officials, the press, and special interest groups like environmentalists and industry task forces. Working successfully with such broad constituencies requires strong interpersonal skills, a broad perspective on the business of business, and tremendous flexibility.

CEOs must play a key role in strategic planning. They must focus on the future of the company and help it prepare to meet this future successfully. In order to perform this vital function, CEOs must be able to discern both internal and external events and correctly interpret their meaning and implications. They must be good at developing hypotheses and putting these to appropriate tests. They must excel at doing fundamental analyses of both hard and soft data to extract meaning.

CEOs must be very knowledgeable about financial matters. An increased financial complexity characterizes the business world these days, and effective CEOs must be familiar enough with financial methods to oversee, influence, and participate in this complexity.

CEOs must be *willing* to make tough decisions, not just able to do so. This demand reflects personal courage and fiber. It separates those who analyze from those who analyze and then act. The volatility of the business world requires leaders of the second sort.

They must be able to anticipate and prevent problems, rather than just fixing them when they occur. Nowhere in the organization is this ability more critical than at the top. Only CEOs have the breadth of information and perspective that allows for the recognition of emerging trends and the development of interventions to head off problems or capitalize on opportunities. Effective CEOs know what information to attend to, what the information means, and what possibilities it suggests.

CEOs must be able to operate with good judgment under crisis. The world cannot be controlled. Crises will happen from time to time. Maintaining balance and a broader perspective allows the CEO to use reasoned decision-making while others are being buffeted around by their emotions and impulses. The impact of this stabilizing force on the organization is very strong, and it can go far to help turn crises into opportunities.

CEOs must be very good negotiators. One of their most important and yet critical responsibilities is to divide up scarce resources. They must be adept at stating their positions on issues forcefully and clearly without triggering a competitive "win/lose" response in others. They must be skilled at drawing others out, at facilitating listening, at stimulating creative, collaborative solutions to conflicts.

CEOs must be able to guide and develop the company's key people resources. Through their actions as well as their advice and counsel, they shape and train the leadership of the company. This is probably their most important responsibility, and it is one that requires considerable depth of insight, thoughtful planning, and strong interpersonal skills.

CEOs must fit with the company's past, present, and anticipated future, both in terms of basic values and style of leadership. CEOs' values determine the actions of their companies, and from these accumulated actions come the companies' operating norms and standards of behavior. A CEO's leadership style sets a model for how leaders in the company get work done and deal with others. The roles of the CEO as standard-setter and standard-bearer are inextricably joined and very powerful. Over time, these roles preserve what is essential in the company culture and change what must be changed.

From the foregoing, it is clear that the job of CEO (and, to a similar degree, EVP) is one that has unique and critical demands associated with it. Such demands dictate important modifications of the basic psychological assessment methods.

MODIFYING THE PSYCHOLOGICAL ASSESSMENT FOR CEOS

It is impossible to do a top executive assessment in a vacuum; an organization analysis is essential. Much time and energy must be spent in the pre-assessment phase of the process, gathering contextual information about the company, its leadership, its industry, and its marketplace. This fundamental information is gathered by interviewing the company executives and members of the board about each of these dimensions. The consulting psychologist uses this information to discover the unique demands of the target position. There is no laundry list of key leadership qualities that ensures their success across different situations. The very same traits or characteristics that make one CEO highly successful in one company at a given point in time will spell failure for another CEO in another company. The match between unique situational demands and organizational dynamics on the one hand and the skills, abilities, and operating style of the top executive on the other hand is what differentiates successful leadership from unsuccessful leadership.

This organization analysis is of tremendous value to the consulting psychologist, because it forms the foundation for the PA process. Just as important, however, are the insights gained by the individuals interviewed about their company, their leadership, and their methods of getting work done in the pursuit of their goals.

The next step in the PA process is for the consulting psychologist to condense the wealth of information from the organizational analysis into a working template summarizing the key performance demands of the position in question. This template is similar to a job description, though it is more dynamic and descriptive than is the typical job description. The template is then reviewed in detail with the representatives of the board or the CEO to solicit their feedback and buy-in. Once the template is hammered into final form, it becomes the benchmark against which individuals will be assessed. The following is an example of one such template:

- Thinks strategically and generates proactive solutions
- Enhances division credibility by providing accurate financial forecasts, business analyses, and sound thinking

- Communicates skillfully and with versatility, adapting to diverse audiences
- Operates effectively with summary information; broad-gauged thinker
- Learns quickly; shifts easily
- Motivates and energizes subordinates who have limited upward career mobility
- Leads change without generating resentment or resistance
- Takes positive and negative feedback in stride; is balanced and self-confident, with good sense of humor
- Acts as credible advisor and sounding board for peers; provides creative ideas that support how division executives can accomplish their goals within real constraints
- Boldly takes calculated risks
- Constructively challenges peers, superiors, and subordinates

The consulting psychologist designs the interview areas and specific lines of questioning so as to take the individual's measure on the key dimensions of a template such as this.

An additional step in the process is often useful at this point. This is the preparation of the company representatives (selection committee of the board or the CEO) for their interviews with the individuals to be assessed. It might be helpful to assist them in planning their interviews in some detail to increase the probability that they will obtain the information they need to make informed judgments. This planning should cover what judgments they want to make, what information about an individual might relate to these judgments, and what types of questions might solicit this information. Engaging in role-playing of questions touching on potentially troublesome or sensitive issues can be especially advantageous.

At this point, the consulting psychologist conducts the assessment interview with the targeted individual(s). The overall goal of the interview is to take a measure of the person relative to the key template dimensions identified in the pre-assessment phase. The individual's personal and work history are less important at this level. Rather, the interview concentrates on critical, strategic issues by exploring in some depth the person's actual or hypothetical responses to incidents similar to those that will likely be faced in the position in question. Examples of things the consulting psychologist might explore are the individual's ability to conceptualize, to think creatively, to elicit followership from others, to act decisively yet with sensitivity to likely reactions from others. Other things that might be discussed are how the person has handled or would likely handle events such as: failure, unexpected business downturns, a new competitor taking serious market share, wildly optimistic sales forecasts, the need for cost cutting, and the need for substantial staff reduction.

To take an example from the template presented previously, the seventh item was that the executive leads change without generating resentment or resistance. To explore an executive's ability in this area, the interviewer might say something like: "Tell me about a time in your current job when you championed a major change affecting a broad constituency. How did that situation go? How did others react? What forms of resistance did you encounter? What methods did you use to respond to this resistance? How did these tactics work? What lessons did you learn from this experience?"

Both the content of the person's responses to inquiries such as these and the way in which the executive engages the issues, and the interview itself, are grist for the consulting psychologist's judgments.

The style of the interview is substantially different with executives at the very top than it is with executives at other levels in an organization. The discussion is open and flexible rather than structured and regimented. The content focuses on strategically critical issues rather than comprehensively covering a multitude of facets of the person's life. It is much more of a targeted than a blanketing interview. Certain things about an executive are assumed to be in place at these levels; things such as a substantial amount of education, training, and experience. The valuable interview time is spent on exploring in depth those specific experiences, thoughts, feelings, beliefs, values, and operating style elements that are critical to the issue of fit with the salient demands of the position in question.

Following the interview, the consulting psychologist reviews and analyzes the information obtained. This is a complicated and painstaking process that combines both analytic and intuitive methods and is shaped by years of training and experience. From this work emerges the picture of the executive in question showing the matches and disconnects between the executive and the performance demand template that has guided the entire undertaking. At this point, the feedback phase of the work begins.

The post-assessment feedback portion of a top-level PA has several goals. The first of these is to enhance ownership of the decision-making process by the board or CEO. The accountability and responsibility for selection and succession decisions properly rests here and will be seen to do so by these people. The consulting psychologist seeks more than the formal execution of a corporate duty, however. The psychologist wants to engage the CEO or board in a process of examination and discourse that will trigger substantial emotional investment in the decision reached.

The second goal of the post-assessment feedback is to clarify what must be done by the board or CEO to make the selected individual successful and stimulate motivation to follow through on these actions. Rarely will the fit between the individual and the position be so perfect that matters can be allowed to run their course unguided. In almost every case, developmental issues will have surfaced due to the assessment process, and the top company executives must be engaged in addressing these in a planned and insightful fashion.

The final goal of the post-assessment feedback is to prepare the individual for success in the new position by stimulating interest in, and motivation toward, self-development in critical areas. It is unlikely that a top executive will modify key behavior patterns unless the difficulties these behaviors might cause in a new situation are clarified and the executive is helped to discover and understand what can be done to create the modifications needed. The feedback to the individual is designed to assist with this process.

With the board or CEO, the consulting psychologist facilitates a meeting to talk through the accumulated information from the people who interviewed the candidate(s). These observations, impressions, and judgments are examined with tremendous thoroughness, and they are critically compared to the dimensions of the performance demand template. The consulting psychologist assists the members of the board or the CEO to usefully interpret the available findings and identify those implications that are relevant to the position in question. The psychologist works diligently to create a vivid image of how the person will actually look, sound, and act in the target position. Through this highly interactive process, the areas of good fit and the areas of poor fit between the individual(s) and the position are clarified. As alluded to earlier, fit with the larger needs of the company is the context in which this discussion occurs.

Those areas of poor fit are examined in further detail. Shortcomings an individual has that can be remedied are less of an obstacle to success in the position than are shortcomings that are difficult or impossible to change. A board or CEO might do well to give pause to putting an individual in a position that requires a broad, overview perspective with a conceptual, strategic-thinking style when that person is by nature and prior experience pragmatic, ''hands-on,'' concrete, and reactive. On the other hand, installing an individual in a position that requires a great deal of ability to handle a diverse group of headstrong executives when the person in question has basically good interpersonal skills and insight but relatively little experience working with cantankerous subordinates might make sense. The consulting psychologist adds considerable value in this portion of the discussion because of broad expertise in human behavior and development.

Once the areas of poor fit between the individual(s) and the performance demands of the position are clarified and it is determined whether they are remediable, specific discussion occurs about what it will take to address the remediable shortfalls in a developmental way. Potentially useful developmental experiences such as temporary job assignments, additional duties, and involvement in task forces or project teams are explored, as are specific training and educational opportunities. Available coaching and mentoring relationships are also examined for their potential contribution to addressing the candidate's developmental needs.

At the top of an organization, the consulting psychologist is always working through this process with the individuals who are directly supervising the position in question. As such, part of the focus in this portion of the feedback must deal with ways in which the CEO or members of the board might have to modify their own behavior in order to help the person in question be successful. Although often touching on sensitive and highly defended material, these discussions are critical to the feedback process and ultimately to the success of the whole venture.

At this point, the board or CEO will be equipped to make a decision about the candidate's likely success in the target position. The feedback process has helped prepare them to do this. Incidentally, yet very purposefully, it has also bonded them on an emotional and psychological level to the decision they will make. They know what will be required of them to make the decision work, and they will be committed to doing what it takes.

The final piece of the PA process is the feedback to the individual assessed. This feedback is designed to aid in the preparation of the individual for successful performance of the job in question. The consulting psychologist meets with the person in a face-to-face discussion and reviews in considerable specific detail the inferences and judgments drawn about the person from the PA interview. The individual's strengths, operating style, and developmental needs are covered as these relate to the performance demands of the target position. Areas of good fit between the person and the position are discussed extensively to reinforce and strengthen these. Areas of poor fit are also discussed at length to help anchor in the executive's mind where the likely problems in successfully performing the job will occur and to facilitate an awareness of, and a motivation toward, the need to address these developmental issues in a direct fashion. Most executives at this level are heavily invested in being successful and readily embrace the need to take action to enhance their chances of success once this need is clarified. Those executives who are unwilling to recognize this need or who meet it with casual indifference even when they do recognize it require somewhat more work on the psychologist's part to stimulate the necessary seriousness of intent.

At this point, the consulting psychologist engages the individual in an exploratory discussion of various alternatives that are available for addressing the developmental needs identified. Those options are woven into the discussion, as are additional avenues for development known by the psychologist, based on training and experience in executive development. Ideas about potentially useful actions and experiences are actively solicited from the executive in order to create involvement in the process. When the stream of ideas slows, clarification and synthesis of the options is facilitated. Ultimately, the executive is asked to select which alternatives will be acted upon and to commit to doing so. In some cases, an action plan is formulated specifying what the executive will do, by when, and with what observable outcomes. Implementation of this action plan is typically monitored by the board or CEO and reviewed periodically with the executive. The consulting psychologist often plays an integral role in this review process.

The feedback discussion finishes with the consulting psychologist offering the executive the opportunity to ask any questions about the consultant's perspective on the position and the company, given that by this point in the process the consultant is quite knowledgeable about many facets of the organization. Such discussions often prove very valuable to the executive and, ultimately, to the company.

This completes the psychological assessment of the top executive. It is a process characterized by thoroughness, reasoned deliberation, extensive interaction, and focus. These elements seem most appropriate, however, given the stakes involved. Few events in an organization's life have the impact that replacing top executives has. Such replacements represent both a tremendous risk and a tremendous opportunity. Adding a professional psychological assessment to a company's existing repertoire of executive evaluation tools can effectively tip the balance from risk to opportunity and add substantial benefit, both foreseen and unforeseen.

The Psychological Assessment of Personnel by an In-House Psychologist

Robert J. Lueger and Susan A. Lueger

Most of the contributions in this book discuss individual psychological assessment from the perspectives of consultants who operate outside the business organizations they are servicing. In this chapter, we address the issues and processes of individual psychological assessment from the perspective of the in-house psychologist who is employed within the company or organization for which service is provided. The high-profile contributions of in-house individual assessments at AT&T in the 1950s, '60s, and '70s are a part of every industrial-organizational psychologist's educational training. The salience of these classic efforts might lead to the impression that in-house assessments are more frequent than externally contracted assessments. Instead, responses to a recent survey of industrial and organizational psychologists (Ryan & Sackett 1987) indicate that over two-thirds of psychologists conducting individual psychological assessments operate as outside consultants. Nevertheless, over one-fourth of the individual assessors are employees of the organizations to which they are providing the assessment results. It is the experience of this latter group that we now examine.

THE PERSPECTIVE OF THE COMPANY PSYCHOLOGIST

The in-house psychological assessor has a unique perspective as both *participant* and *observer*. As an organizational employee, the participant-psychologist shares with other employees in the ebb and flow of company fortunes. The psychologist owes a part of his or her career development opportunities to experiences within the organization. In turn, organizational commitment is always more complex, if not greater, for the in-house psychologist than the consultant.

Compensation, benefits, working conditions, peer relationships, and developmental opportunities all play a more direct and pervasive role in job satisfaction and dissatisfaction of the in-house psychological assessor. Also, the professional role of in-house psychologist as individual assessor might be more temporary in that the psychologist aspires to or is a candidate for managerial or executive roles in the same organization, roles that do not involve the practice of individual assessment skills.

As an in-house observer, the company psychologist enjoys an expert status that is underwritten by a line of authority described in the company's organizational chart. This ascribed status is often more than sufficient when servicing supervised employees or even middle-level managers. More importantly, the psychologist demonstrates a commitment to principles of professional practice and has gained the confidence of the users of the assessment services. The difficulties of gaining users' confidence, particularly at senior management levels, from an in-house assessor's role should not be underestimated. Just as the biblical prophet was not recognized in his own land, company psychologists are strapped by the familiarity between provider and user of psychological services because of their status as common employees of the same organization. The higher the object of the assessment in the organizational chart, the more important achieved status is in the effective provision of services.

On the other hand, the in-house assessor has opportunities to build an achieved-expert status that the outside consultant does not usually enjoy. For example, assessment recommendations can be fine-tuned to include developments within the organization of which the outside consultant is unaware. Also, informal conversations about assessed employees with, for example, division vice-presidents can enhance the value of the company psychologist as informant. The company psychologist often can gain access to sources of information among supervisees, supervisors, and customers that outside consultants are too obtrusive to ask.

PSYCHOLOGICAL ASSESSMENT VERSUS PSYCHOLOGICAL TESTING

Other chapters in this book have discussed psychological assessment as a practice, and have highlighted the varieties of psychological tests. It is important, though, to consider the import of assessment versus testing issues for the in-house psychologist. Joseph Matarazzo (1990) has addressed this issue cogently in the following passage:

The assessment of intelligence, personality, or type or level of impairment is a highly complex operation that involves extracting diagnostic meaning from an individual's personal history and objectively recorded test scores. Rather than being totally objective, assessment involves a subjective component.

Competent practitioners in psychology learn from . . . role models during apprenticeship training and from their own subsequent experiences that, objective psychological *testing* and . . . licensed psychological *assessment* are vastly different, even though assessment usually includes testing. Personnel technicians . . . monitoring group administration of [tests] . . . are involved in psychological *testing*, an activity that has little or no continuing relationship or legally defined responsibility between examinee and examiner. Psychological *assessment*, however, is engaged in . . . a one-to-one relationship and has statutorily defined or implied professional responsibilities. (Matarazzo 1990, 1,000)

This quote from Matarazzo, considered one of the deans of testing/assessment, is equally useful in distinguishing psychological assessment from psychological testing in the industrial context as it is in the clinical setting. The core of the assessment is a professional judgment based only in part on the collection of data from psychological tests. Anne Anastasi, another of the deans of testing/ assessment, also has addressed the importance of using judgment in the interpretation of test scores in the following quote:

The complexities we have encountered serve to illustrate the fact that personality tests— even more so than other types of tests—require a knowledgeable and psychologically sophisticated test user. Such tests cannot be employed routinely and automatically without serious danger of misinterpreting results. (Anastasi 1985, 15)

Rather than think of assessment as a process that emanates from psychological testing, it is more useful and more professionally relevant to think of testing as a subfunction of psychological assessment. The utility of tests in the assessment process is manifold: (1) Some tests have predictive validity for specific behaviors; other tests are rich sources for describing the current behavior and functioning of the assessee. (2) The use of tests can give respectability and professionalism to the psychological assessment process that interviews, simulations, and performance appraisal feedback do not. (3) High-achieving employees, especially those in middle and senior management ranks, have a history of doing well on tests; they are comfortable taking tests, expect to do well, and are eager to see their results. (4) Tests have confirmatory powers beyond the "opinion" of the assessor; thus, few assessees express surprise about test results, but are less sure about how they compare with others. Moreover, the general Barnum effect of test results carries with it other judgments within the assessment process. (5) Tests confirm the distinction between dimensions of assessment in the mind of the assessee; thus, dominance, extraversion, and responsiveness to customers can be separately discussed as valid components of one's job performance.

Assessment and testing are based in different philosophical perspectives about human behavior. As Exhibit 10–1 indicates, testing owes much in its heritage to faculty and structural theories that have sought to identify the elements of behavior and to organize those elements in distinct, hierarchial levels of analysis. Thus, identification of the *g* factor in cognitive abilities, the "big five" personality factors, and the six interest types are all efforts to exhaustively account for

Exhibit 10–1
Two Ancestral Lines of Individual Psychological Assessment

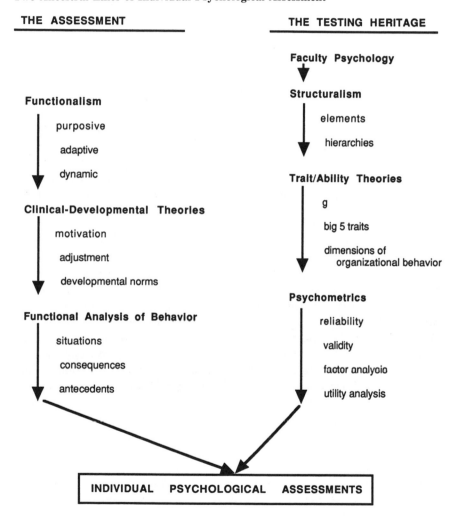

THE ASSESSMENT

THE TESTING HERITAGE

Faculty Psychology

Functionalism

   purposive

   adaptive

   dynamic

Structuralism

   elements

   hierarchies

Clinical-Developmental Theories

   motivation

   adjustment

   developmental norms

Trait/Ability Theories

   g

   big 5 traits

   dimensions of
      organizational behavior

Functional Analysis of Behavior

   situations

   consequences

   antecedents

Psychometrics

   reliability

   validity

   factor analysis

   utility analysis

INDIVIDUAL PSYCHOLOGICAL ASSESSMENTS

all elements of behavior at some level of analysis. Testing relies heavily on mathematical rules for establishing criteria of utility, and the sine qua non of the psychometric tradition is statistical significance.

In contrast, psychological assessment is rooted in the functional philosophical tradition. The process of change rather than the structure of elements is the object of study. Behavior can be understood only with reference to its developmental context. Behavior is hierarchially organized to reflect developmental maturation rather than levels of analysis. Moreover, behavior occurs within a context, called a "situation" by social learning theorists. Whether psychodynamically or behaviorally construed, the antecedent conditions, behaviors-cognitions, and affects-consequences are critical foci of the process of acquiring behaviors. Rather than the psychometric statistical criteria of the testing tradition, the assessment approach relies on a critical review of descriptive data that require judgments to discern their meaning. Thus, clinical significance is the litmus of the analysis of behavior.

Of course, the practice of individual personnel assessment reflects some melding of both the testing and the assessment traditions. The use of group-administered screening tests to facilitate the personnel selection process probably involves a minimum of judgment, and a large amount of statistical criterion validity. In contrast, the "standard" tests/techniques battery assessment of executives involves much description and judgment, but is less concerned with establishing criterion validity involving specific predictions.

The survey of assessment practices among industrial-organizational psychologists conducted by Ryan and Sackett (1987) revealed that consultants and company psychologists engage in assessment for generally the same reasons. Outside consultants conduct assessments for a broader range of reasons than in-house psychologists. Company psychologists are less likely to conduct assessments for development or selection purposes, but are slightly more likely to conduct preliminary employee screening. These differences would seem to indicate that company psychologists have placed somewhat greater emphasis on aspects of testing, whereas consultants emphasize the assessment tradition. This is congruent with the history of major psychological consulting firms who traditionally have been staffed by clinically trained psychologists.

A MODEL OF PSYCHOLOGICAL ASSESSMENT DECISIONS

N. D. Sundberg (1977) has provided a model of the psychological assessment process. We have modified elements of that model for use by company psychologists and have presented the model in Exhibit 10–2. The model begins by identifying the organization as the client. Consulting psychologists are reminded by the tangible retainer fee for their services that the organization is the object of their assessment work. Moreover, consultants who work with several business organizations can have a keener sense of extraorganizational sensitivity. Clienthood can be somewhat less apparent to the in-house psychological assessor

Exhibit 10–2
A Model of the Process of Conducting Individual Assessments for Personnel Decisions

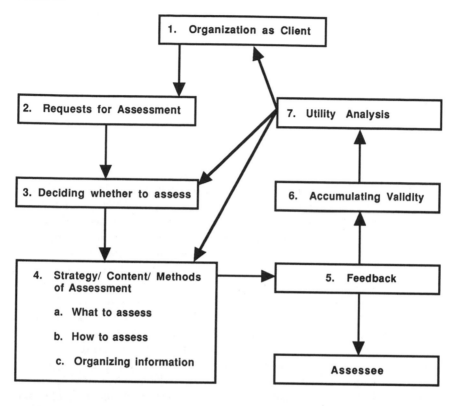

in that the source of the referral and the assessee are colleagues in the same organization. Thus, the process of assessment might be personalized as the in-house psychologist attempts to meet the needs of particular vice-presidents, managers, or supervisors, or tries to select, promote, or develop a worthy assessee. What is lost in extraorganizational sensitivity, though, is made up in intraorganizational sensitivity. If the challenge for the consulting assessor is to understand the nuances of the organization, the corresponding challenge for the in-house assessor is to see "the forest 'fore the trees." Although highly identified with the mission of the organization (organizational commitment), the company psychologist might not be privy to strategic organization plans.

A major issue for the company psychologist is whether to react to requests for assessment as they have been presented or to advocate along lines that meet broader and longer-term company goals. This dilemma is most salient when the organizational culture is changing rapidly, such as during a period of takeover activity or downsizing, and when the advancement of minorities and underrepresented groups is at issue. If the assessor treats the organization as the client, he or she most probably will have to engage in a heavy dose of advocacy, whether to modify the referral questions, the methods of assessment, or the nature of the feedback about the assessment. Alternatively, treating the referral source (for example, the division vice-president) as the client more probably will result in a more reactive assessment process.

THE PSYCHOLOGICAL ASSESSMENT CULTURE OF THE ORGANIZATION

The in-house assessor, more so than the consultant, must work within the organization culture regarding assessment of personnel. The history of bringing aboard professionals to conduct assessments, the quality of their work, and the range of personnel issues for which assessment has been used in the past all contribute to an organization culture that might or might not favor the conduct of assessments in the current tense. Highly political organizations, such as banks and legal firms, often pose more constraints on the scope, focus, and methods of the assessment process than do manufacturing, retail, and utilities, particularly when middle or senior management employees are the object of the assessment. The same constraints might not be evident for testing employees in entry-level positions without supervisory responsibilities. For example, personality tests may be used to ensure that responsivity to customers or sales skills are sufficiently present in prospective bank teller candidates. A similar exercise of expert opinion with empirically validated tests at the middle management ranks (for example, bank vice-presidents and assistant vice-presidents) may elicit power maneuvers aimed at isolating the assessment function and thus limiting its influence. In politically charged organizations, the exercise of judgment involving clinical significance can become too potent if anchored in test results, but might be more accepted if the data are obtained in less objective fashion, such as through interviews and performance appraisal reviews.

In general, the in-house assessor probably is more limited in the repertoire of techniques used, so that similar methods and a standard assessment approach regularly are used for each assessment function. That is, a battery of tests and performance data are used for promotion decisions, another battery is used for selection, and still another is used for developmental assessment. Certainly this reflects a stronger emphasis on criterion validity involving greater effort to predict behavior rather than describe personality.

Certainly the nature of the psychological assessment function can change as the corporate culture changes. The contributions of psychologists at AT&T within the Management Progress Study, mentioned earlier, are legendary in the in-house assessment for personnel decisions. The extensive use of assessment centers, which, of course, are very expensive in terms of personnel time (both assessors and assessees), performance data, and individual assessments at AT&T highlighted the usefulness of using intensive individual assessment for selection and promotion. At the same time, these efforts underscored the difficulties of establishing specific criterion validity for the dimensions being assessed.

The debate still wages on whether situational or dispositional variance best explains the differences in behavior observed on assessment center tasks. The establishment of more exacting legal requirements of validating selection/promotion systems has shifted the use of expensive and difficult-to-validate assessment systems. Where they continue in use, such systems often assess higher potential employees for developmental planning. The movement of AT&T to an unregulated, competitive organization resulted in different values being placed on the cost of obtaining extremely thorough assessment data. Again, the lesson is that corporate cultures can change, and that the in-house professional assessment culture might change as well.

The Role of Assessment in the Human Resources Function

The value of the in-house assessment is directly related to the potency of the human resources function within the business organization. If the human resources function is strongly represented in the personnel planning processes of the organization, in-house individual assessment has a greater chance of contributing to personnel decisions involving higher-level managerial employees. Thus, the use of assessment in succession planning and developing upper–middle-level managers is more likely with a strong human resources department. Also, a greater range of use of in-house assessments is likely, from preemployment screening to career planning.

Also important is the role of the psychological assessor in the personnel decision process within the human resources function. Two models are possible here. In the first, the psychological assessor is a source of expert opinion. That is, the assessment report contributes an important (often, the *most* important) recommendation regarding the disposition of the assessed candidate. In this model, the decision is possible without the assessor's opinion, but the decision process is so dependent on this expert conclusion, whether for confidence in the decision or to achieve thoroughness in the review, that the decision would not be rendered without the expert opinion of the assessor. Senior managers who are the recipients of the human resources function enact the resulting recommendation.

In the second model, the assessor not only provides expert opinion based on the assessment process, but also acts directly to implement the results of that assessment. Here, the assessor's expert status is used to persuade senior management to implement the report's recommendation. The assessment and the report are less salient than the persuasion and implementation initiated by the assessor. In this model, the assessor has a direct role in the decision-making chain, and, in a sense, is both judge and executioner. This role might be more useful in highly political organizations or in businesses that are staffed by highly educated, independently operating professionals, such as is found in brokerage houses and legal firms.

The Quality of the Organization's Human Resources

Individual assessment of personnel is an expensive process. Group administrations of psychological assessment, although cheaper than individual assessment, also is costly. As we will see later, these initial costs can be recovered over time, and a strong case can be made that an attractive return is realized when quality assessments are conducted. Nevertheless, the cost-benefit ratio of assessment can only be understood in the context of the quality of an organization's people.

The stability of the work force is a crucial variable. Group psychological assessments might be more feasible for high-turnover industries in which screening out unfavorable characteristics of a continually replenished supply of employees is the most challenging personnel issue. In contrast, for highly stable, low-turnover work forces, individual assessment might pay high dividends in a relatively short span of time. Here, issues of selection and promotion, development, and succession planning become more important as home-grown employees acquire experience and prepare for greater organizational challenges. In-house psychologists are more likely to be employed in the latter type of business organization or government force. Moreover, when in-house human resource psychologists conduct both group and individual assessments, there is likely to be a division of labor, so that some assessors address group assessment issues and others primarily assess individuals. Again, the testing model largely characterizes the work of high-turnover group assessments, whereas the assessment model is followed by the individual assessors.

The knowledge, skills, and abilities of the organization's work force are important determinants of the type of in-house assessments conducted. Likewise, the interview-to-selection ratio of selecting the existing group of employees must be taken into consideration. Highly trained, well-educated employees generally are perceived by senior management to have the greatest potential for managerial success (whether or not assessment results bear out such a prognosis). Thus, the study of promotion to middle managerial ranks that was conducted in AT&T's Management Progress Study (Howard & Bray 1988) indicated that having a college degree, regardless of the quality of initial supervisory work or of assessment results, was a dominant predictor of movement into middle management. Likewise, much has been written about the importance of separate career tracks for highly proficient technical professionals such as engineers, and professionals who also have high potential for managerial success.

The point here is that the qualities of the work force, far from presenting senior management with a "can't lose" choice (in the case of a highly talented work force) actually increase the saliency of the questions to be addressed and underscore the importance of highly professional individual assessments. This is one of the perhaps more infrequent cases when psychological science contradicts "common sense." The in-house assessor has the engaging challenge of persuading senior management that the "can't lose" choice can, indeed, be a loser, and that psychological assessments can have a more consistent result. Similarly, the use of a high false-negative criterion in the selection process for managerial positions can load that group with many talented employees aspiring to be the next CEO of the organization. This, perhaps, is most characteristic of organizations that have "high-potential" management trainees selected from outside the organization for their prospects as upper and senior managers. The nature of the assessment process changes with high-potential employees so that their development becomes primary and matches are made between strengths, weaknesses, and organizational challenges.

The rate of change of the business of the organization can greatly influence the viability and nature of in-house assessments. Change, of course, creates uncertainty, and uncertainty leads otherwise confident senior managers to turn to experts to reduce their uncertainty and increase their confidence. Thus, organizations with a high rate of change, whether in business climate, product development, or employee promotion, tend to place greater emphasis on expert opinion than do more staid organizations. In-house assessments are likely to be seen as sources of certainty or confidence only if the assessment function has demonstrated a prescient ability to anticipate such challenges. The readiness of senior managers in all organizations to turn to extraorganizational sources or benchmarks for the elusive certainty poses a ready liability for the in-house assessor. The allowed flexibility perceived by the assessor is some indication of the readiness of the in-house assessor to respond with confidence-providing information when such requests are rendered.

Another human resource variable that can influence the nature and extent of in-house assessments is the authoritarian nature of the organization. While all organizations have some degree of hierarchial layering of authority, those with more of it tend to create more complex bureaucracies where the assessment function is more circumscribed and particularized. Again, a testing model might be more useful here, because knowledge, skills, and abilities are specified by expertly conducted job analyses. In contrast, the hierarchically "flat" organization, in which the employees wield considerable autonomy in directing and developing their response to organizational challenges, might require more of a process model of assessment. The in-house assessor here is likely to be as much a participant as an observer in the assessment process. The in-house assessor gains credence by closely observing the actual work of the people assessed. At the least, the assessor spends considerable time in the workers' environment discussing what key people do. Here, job analysis is a first-hand, subjective process rather than an objective, categorizing process, as in the testing model.

THE CONTENT AND PROCESS OF THE IN-HOUSE ASSESSMENT

The reader might find it useful at this point to refer back to Exhibit 10–2 to review the process of conducting an in-house psychological assessment. It is not

Exhibit 10–3
Purposes for Which Individual Assessments Are Conducted

	Psychologists	
Purpose	*In-House*	*Consulting*
Selection (hiring)	82.9%	92.0%
Promotion	80.5%	81.3%
Development	68.3%	80.0%
Career counseling	63.4%	74.7%
Succession planning	58.5%	60.0%
Preliminary screening	48.8%	42.7%
Outplacement	10.8%	40.0%
Back-to-work evaluation	9.8%	5.3%
Other	4.9%	17.3%

Data taken from Ryan and Sacket (1987, 463).

our intention to contrast extraorganizational, consultant-provided assessments with those of in-house assessors in the structure of this model. In fact, there are as many, or perhaps even more, similarities than differences between the sources of the assessments. Rather, in a well-developed in-house assessment function, the elements of the structural model presented in Figure 10–2 become a part of the organization that the model serves. This underscores the dynamic nature of any in-house assessment function; not withstanding personnel turnover among assessors, the purpose, focus, manner, information yield, value, and utility are constantly changing.

Referral for Assessment: Routes and Requests

The primacy of the organization as client has been addressed already. We reiterate that point only as a jumping off point in the discussion of other elements of the in-house assessment model. First, consider the nature and source of requests for psychological assessment. Then, consider whether or not to assess.

The nature and source of referrals are closely intertwined. Exhibit 10–3, which has been derived from Ryan and Sackett's (1987) Table 2, lists the frequencies, expressed in percentages, of the purposes for which consultants and private organization psychologists conduct assessments. Company psychologists and consultants do not differ in the rank ordering of the frequencies of purposes for which they use assessments. Contributing to hiring decisions (selection), promotion, development, career counseling, and succession planning are the most frequent personnel decision issues addressed in assessments. In-house psychologists are somewhat less likely to conduct their assessments for hiring or development, and are significantly less likely to conduct assessments as part of an outplacement process. In-house psychologists conduct a somewhat larger proportion of their individual assessments with upper management assessees and with sales positions (probably a stronger testing orientation).

Referral sources within the organization usually determine the purpose of the assessment. A referral from the human resources planning group is likely an issue of succession planning, promotion, or development. A referral from the selection function is more likely to involve a "screen-in" than a "screen-out" strategy, although in a high-potential program with a high false-negative criterion, the screen-out strategy might be used to distinguish among equally skilled applicants. Assessment consults to individual senior managers might take any form; often, questions involving career planning, promotability, or development are at issue in such assessments. More clinical issues, such as the needs of a troubled employee, or an employee's capacity to return to work, are infrequently involved in assessments as the primary referral question.

The decision of whether or not to assess is not automatically incumbent upon receipt of a request for assessment. That is, a major function of the individual assessor is to determine whether an assessment is warranted under the present conditions, or whether additional clarification is needed before honoring the assessment referral. Referral questions often come to assessors either poorly focused or inadequately developed. Also, questions tend to take the form of previous questions rendered by a senior manager. In other words, if asked to assess the developmental needs of one subordinate, the assessor often gets a close variation of that same question for subsequent referrals. Some questions simply cannot be addressed, given the state of assessment technology. For example, if asked whether a subordinate middle-level manager has the potential for a CEO position in ten years, a wise assessor would ask for a reformulation of the question. Firstly, assessment technology is unlikely to give reliable predictive information for management behaviors ten years hence. Secondly, the referral agent's concept of CEO-like behavior might be vastly different from that of the actual needs of the organization.

Psychological assessments, however wise the assessors and valid the instruments, cannot predict the work-relevant behaviors of all assessees equally well. That is, assessees differ in the rate of change in their behavior. Some are slow developers, some "catch fire," and others seem to "trail off."

Assessment protocols are more vulnerable to some types of decisions, particularly those involving marginal candidates. Ann Howard (1990) has investigated predictive errors from the Management Progress Study and has identified groups of marginally performing assessees (that is, marginal choices on the basis of data from the assessment battery). Most of these groups experienced significant modifications in management abilities or motivation over time, whether for better or worse. Thus, before acquiescing to the assessment, it would be necessary to follow up a senior manager's referral such as the following: "This employee really seems to have caught fire in the last couple of months. I'm beginning to think of him as my next manager of. . . . " The assessor should ask what the nature of change was in the employee's behavior. What has been happening in the employee's nonwork life? What elements of the work expectations or supervision might have changed? Answers to such questions might reframe the referral question and keep the assessor from entering a difficult (impossible?) task of predicting performance on the basis of erratic past performance.

Choosing Assessment Strategies and Methods

The actual conducting of the assessment is highly salient for novice assessors, but for veteran assessors it becomes less important relative to the referral questions and feedback of information from the assessment. Whatever the emphasis, the choice of strategies and methods must address three questions: (1) What should be assessed? (2) How should it be assessed? and (3) How should the data be organized?

What to Assess. It almost goes without saying that the focus of the assessment (What to assess?) is closely related to the purpose of the assessment. Referral questions asking for promotability, managerial potential, or the development of executive skills will narrow the range of variables closely examined in the assessment. Typically, though, the referral questions are not framed in the constructs used by individual assessors. The relevant psychological constructs, whether traits or dispositions, dimensions, abilities, motives, values, or interests, figure prominently in the measurement, analysis, and reasoning activities of the assessor. Thus, a referral question involving managerial potential requires assessment of dominance or a similarly defined construct (such as power or leadership motivation pattern). Patterns of constructs (using the folk concepts that are the basis of the California Psychological Inventory) such as social presence, social awareness, and self-acceptance become useful in identifying the manner in which dominance is likely to be expressed in an interpersonal setting.

Assessors differ on the most relevant variables for predicting behavior in organizations. Some emphasize abilities, especially some aspect of g, or general intelligence; others emphasize interpersonal motives, such as dominance and social presence; still others focus on the values of the assessee, reasoning that knowledge of an employee's values is the best predictor of organizational behavior and future professional development (Graham, personal communication, 1987).

Whereas psychological constructs are indispensable to the assessor for reasoning about underlying psychological processes, more specifically defined business knowledge and skills are also the subject of assessment. For example, the relevant business knowledge and skills of any general banking officer are likely to include: (1) knowledge of commercial lending policies and procedures; (2)

credit analysis and risk identification skills; (3) sales skills; (4) familiarity with the local marketplace; (5) negotiating skills; and (6) skills in making lending decisions. Here, the in-house psychological assessor should have an advantage over the consultant. With a thorough knowledge of the organization's operations and the essence of its business, the in-house assessor can specify knowledge, skills, and abilities in a language that is comfortable for the recipients of the assessment report.

How to Assess. The issue here is the choice of tests, techniques, and assessment tasks. Psychologists report that they choose their instruments on the basis of published research data or in-house research data (Ryan & Sackett 1987). Interviews head the list, despite the issues of validity repeatedly raised by researchers (c.f., Arvey 1982). Personal history, ability tests, and personality tests are used by three-fourths of all individual assessors. Less frequently used are simulation exercises and projective techniques. Of those using simulations, over half use a variation of the in-basket exercise, a fifth use role-plays, and a sixth use group discussions. Sentence completion tests and Thematic Apperception Test–like tests are the most frequent projective techniques (Ryan & Sackett 1987).

For the in-house assessor, the development and validation of simulation techniques offer considerable organization-relevant data. Although the up-front costs are considerable, organization norms can be established and continually revised with the addition of data from ongoing assessments. Likewise, a behaviorally descriptive language can be developed that is immediately translatable to the report recipients. Role-play dilemmas with strong face validity can be construed around issues of managing employees in difficult and ambiguous circumstances. Not only is the actual choice of action interesting, but the reasoning for taking such action can be analyzed to provide further insight about the candidates' prospective managerial behaviors.

The use of employee performance appraisals is common in the assessment of a candidate. Again, the in-house assessor has an advantage here in being able to place the substance of such an appraisal in context. The meaning and value of performance appraisals have been the subject of much debate. Moreover, there are few consultant assessors who would take a performance review at its surface value, given the variability they have experienced in the meaning and quality of performance appraisals across organizations. However, the in-house psychologist has more of an opportunity to investigate the behavioral meaning of ratings on specific categories given by a certain manager in some division. Just as references are underutilized in the selection process because of the legwork necessary to get useful information, performance appraisals are probably too often dismissed as too global, political, or arbitrary to be of predictive value.

How to Organize the Information. Individual assessors are prone to using various descriptive categories to organize the contents of their assessment and to address the referral questions. See Paul Pruyser, 1979, written for the organization of data from a comprehensive clinical assessment but equally applicable to individuals' assessments in organizations. The senior author's own preference for organizing assessment data is presented in Exhibit 10–4. The format was chosen to be useful for a variety of referral purposes, including selection, promotion, succession planning, and career development. The categories reflect commonalities between descriptive clinical assessments and more specific personnel planning recommendations. The categories allow the assessor to retain psychological construct labels in the substance of a report, but also to include organization-relevant business knowledge, skills, and abilities.

FEEDBACK

The feedback process offers the in-house psychologist one of the greatest opportunities to influence the organization. The results of the assessment certainly have an impact on the assessee, have implications for the client organization, and contribute to the reputation of the assessment function. Many experienced assessors, including the authors, think that the feedback process is *the* most important facet of the assessment process. An appropriately focused, well-crafted, and well-conducted assessment goes for naught unless the results are communicated effectively and sold to critical managers in the organization. The goal of feedback is to persuade feedback recipients to begin to change their behaviors.

Feedback to Assessees

Given the opportunities to influence the organization, it might be surprising to know that surveyed in-house assessors were significantly less likely than consultants (66% versus 92%) to offer individual feedback to those assessed (Ryan & Sackett 1987). This discrepancy might be explained in part by the greater tendency of consultants to offer feedback to selection (hiring) candidates, whereas, in-house assessors often provide feedback to selection personnel, who in turn incorporate that information obtusely into the announcement of their selection decisions. Thus, in-house assessors are unlikely to have a follow-up visit with the assessed candidate.

Feedback to assessees typically includes: (1) suggestions for development; (2) descriptions and explanations of strengths and weaknesses; and (3) some interpretation of test scores. Feedback is usually provided orally, although about one-third of individual assessors allow assessees to read the assessment report. However the feedback is administered (and the experience of the authors is that there is no substitute for face-to-face delivery), the clarity of the content is critical. Being on the receiving end of assessment feedback is somewhat stressful for even the most well-adjusted. The importance of reducing the complexity of the feedback message cannot be emphasized strongly enough. The rule of ''three's'' is effective here: Three major points about the contents; three major recommendations regarding future directions. Moreover, expressing the feedback in con-

Exhibit 10-4
A Model for Organizing Assessment Data into a Psychological Report

I. *Cognitive Abilities/Skills*
   A. General intellectual ability
      1. Verbal fluency and oral communication skills
      2. Problem-solving skills
      3. Practical intelligence
   B. Cognitive style: global or specific
   C. Conceptual style: logical or valued
   D. Perceptual style: discrete or intuitive
   E. Judgment and decision-making

II. *Affective Functioning and Values*
   A. Predominant moods
   B. Affective flexibility, control
   C. Arousal threshold and need for stimulation
   D. Stress tolerance and coping patterns
   E. Predominant motive patterns
   F. Ideals, introjects of significant others
   G. Values

III. *Social Skills/Interpersonal Functioning*
   A. Self-perception on autonomy, engagement dimensions
   B. Self-awareness, self-acceptance
   C. Social presence, social awareness

IV. *Development*
   A. Expectations
      1. Next position
      2. Long-range
   B. Evaluation
      1. Strengths
      2. Weaknesses
      3. Availability
      4. Readiness
      5. Promotability

crete, readily observable organizational behaviors rather than psychological jargon is a necessity here to establish organizational credibility.

Feedback to the Client Organization

Feedback to the organization usually occurs through a face-to-face discussion or telephone conversation with the referral source. The contents of the feedback typically include strengths and weaknesses of the assessee, suggestions for development, a narrative description of the assessee, and, especially for hiring decisions, a specific recommendation. Important, too, are the likely conditions under which the best and worst performance of the candidate are likely to emerge. Often the role of the assessor is to clarify the options for senior management or the human resources planning function. Especially in succession planning, competing candidates are raised as additional possibilities. The expected performance of each under different organizational and business conditions can be highlighted to clarify the consequences of choosing the various candidates.

Human resources personnel often perform as advocates with the larger goals of the whole organization in mind. For example, technical managers often are interested in hiring more narrowly trained but technically skilled candidates who can make immediate contributions to the performance of the organizational unit. More broadly educated, less technically skilled employees with better long-term potential often must be sold to these technical managers. Likewise, in identifying potential successors, senior managers frequently demonstrate the all-too-human tendency to search for candidates who are mirror images of themselves. This ignores the organizational climate under which the incumbent managers achieved their measure of success. Still another tendency is for managers to reward protégés for their loyalty by elevating them to the top of the list of candidates in the succession plan. While the reward of loyalty is commendable, coming in this delayed fashion can obfuscate the true strengths and weaknesses of the protégé as revealed in the assessment process. Once again, managers must be persuaded of the value of the assessment information.

The assessor also is responsible for follow-up disbursement of assessment information within the human resources function. Where appropriate, the recommendations for development should be conveyed to other branches of the human resources function, such as the director of management training. Names of assessees who are candidates for training programs ought to make prospective lists, even if senior managers balk on implementing the training recommendations immediately. In this way, the assessor continues as an advocate for the assessee, the assessment function, and ultimately, the organization.

META-ASSESSMENT ISSUES FOR IN-HOUSE ASSESSMENTS

The individual assessment is formally completed with the provision of feedback and advocacy for the recommendations. However, three issues continue with the accumulation of subsequent assessments. These issues include: (1) the confidentiality of assessment records; (2) accumulating evidence for the validity of the assessment process; and (3) mounting evidence for the utility of the assessment function.

Confidentiality

Two questions can be raised regarding the confidentiality of assessment data: Who has access to assessment records, and how long is the data useful? Company personnel records, which are subject to review by the employee and often are available to more senior managers, usually contain some evidence that an assessment was conducted. The actual assessment report, however, is often kept in separate assessment files so that the presence of a trained assessor who can interpret the report can be guaranteed, should a review of those records be requested. Specific feedback data, such as strengths and weaknesses, planned development, and projected advancement in the company, are kept in confidential personnel files along with other pertinent succession-planning data.

The presence of this data within the organization poses some challenges not fully present when an outside consultant has access to the assessment data. First, there is turnover among in-house assessors, whether through job promotion or employment outside the organization. This means that the responsibility for the confidentiality of records is diffused among several assessment personnel. Second, there is always the possibility of accidental access by unqualified personnel. Although no set of safeguards is perfect, the presence of an in-house assessment function requires careful planning for information control and dissemination.

Most psychologists think that assessment data are useful for a period of three to four years. This is roughly consonant with research data on the stability of domains of behavior, and, thus, the predictive validity of assessment constructs. There is growing consensus that assessment data greatly loses its significance after about five years. Thus, in-house assessment functions would do well to transfer that data from active files to archival reservoirs that are kept to validate the assessment processes.

Accumulating Validity

Each assessment contributes to the evidence of assessment validity. In-house assessment functions often have the advantage of technical resources to study such data archives on a periodic basis as employee performance data accumulate. Any validity appraisal is the product of inductive and hypothetical-deductive reasoning processes. That is, validity reviewers are likely to observe trends or relationships that are pursued subsequently with more formal inquiry. Likewise, theory-based predictions about relationships guide the confirmation of hypotheses in ways that ensure more causal inferences to be supported or refuted. Finally, the conditions can be set for validity generalizations so that painstakingly obtained validity data on one set of employees do not have to be repeated completely on subsequent extensions to other employee groups.

Information from the accumulating validity process also has an impact on the decisions of whether or not to assess. Validity data might indicate that some questions are unanswerable given present technology; other questions can be shaped in a direction that does reflect the strength of organizational norms of assessment. Finally, the assessment strategy, methods, and processes can be modified on the basis of the accumulating validity data.

Utility Analysis

We have spoken repeatedly about the costs of assessment. Achieving greater confidence in making personnel decisions through assessment technology has a steep price. Identifying linkages to extraorganizational benchmarks is also expensive. In-house assessment functions increasingly need to justify such personnel costs in order to continue the function.

Wayne Cascio (1986), among others, has presented formulas for computing the cost-benefit ratios of making personnel selection decisions. John Hunter and Frank Schmidt (1982) have discussed the cost-benefit utility of using various cutoff points in the selection process. Similar analyses can and should be conducted with regard to other uses of individual assessments. The methods of conducting such analyses are available, and the results typically have made a strong case for the continued use of individual assessments.

SUMMARY AND FUTURE ISSUES

Test technologies have grown at a rapid pace. New test instruments appear each year, and computer-based scoring and interpretative systems promise to increase the volume of assessment. Consulting firms are continually experimenting with new products involving testing and assessment. Individual assessment has grown beyond its clinical origins so that industrial psychologists are openly discussing how to get proper training to conduct individual assessments. Assessment is as vital as an in-house function as it is among consultants.

Legal restrictions on the use of assessment data, and changing notions about the predictive validity of specific pieces of assessment data, both have provided challenges to the use of assessments by in-house psychologists. Already there are some indications that tests are being used less frequently for pre-employment screening because of these developments.

What further changes can be anticipated in the use of in-house assessments? One change already underway is the change of emphasis from selection to development. Descriptive data on an employee's strengths and weaknesses can be used to plan developmental experiences for individual employees. Likewise, the value of feedback from the assessment as an objective source is less threatening if the outcome is likely to lead to increased opportunities for personal growth and development. A second reason for this shift is the growing concern about the availability of qualified, prospective employees to staff business organizations. Selection standards based on entry-level skills might have to be eased in favor of selecting employees with potential for training and development.

We have tried to point out some of the issues of conducting individual assessments that are particularly germane to in-house psychologists. We have not attempted to be exhaustive of in-house assessment issues, but have tried to identify practical issues in the conduct of assessments. Just as we personally have experienced a growth in the use of assessments for career development and succession planning, we expect new applications of assessment to emerge from future challenges to identifying human resource qualities.

REFERENCES

Anastasi, A. (1985). The use of personal assessment in industry: Methodological and interpretive problems. In *Personality assessment in organizations*, ed. by H. J. Bernadin and D.A. Bownas. New York: Praeger, 1–20.

Arvey, R. D., & Campion, J. E. (1982). The employment interview: A summary and review of recent research. *Personnel Psychology* 35, 281–322.

Cascio, W. F. (1986). *Managing human resources*. New York: McGraw-Hill.

Howard, A. (1990). When does assessment *not* predict? *Proceedings of the 1989 National Assessment Conference*. Minneapolis: Personnel Decisions Inc., 59–63.

Howard, A., & Bray, D. W. (1988). *Managerial lives in transition: Advancing age and changing times*. New York: Guilford.

Hunter, J. E., & Schmidt, F. L. (1982). Fitting people to jobs: Impact of personnel selection on national productivity. In *Human performance and productivity, Vol. 1: Human capability assessment*, ed. by M. D. Dunnette and E. A. Fleishman. Hillsdale, N.J.: Lawrence Erlbaum Assoc.

Matarazzo, J. D. (1990). Psychological assessment versus psychological testing: Validation from Binet to the school, clinic, and courtroom. *American Psychologist* 45, 999–1017.

Pruyser, P. (1979). *The psychological examination*. New York: International Universities Press.

Ryan, A. M., & Sackett, P. R. (1987). A survey of individual assessment practices by I/O psychologists. *Personnel Psychology* 40, 455–88.

Sundberg, N. D. (1977). *Assessment of persons*. Englewood Cliffs, N.J.: Prentice-Hall.

The Psychological Assessment of Professional Sales Representatives

William P. Sullivan

INTRODUCTION: A CASE STUDY

It was my first week of doing professional assessments on my own, and I was orienting a young sales trainee prior to running him through an all-day testing session. The client company was a well-known *Fortune* 500 company. In the orientation session it was my job to put the young man at ease, to let him know how the day would go for him, and to inform him that he would get feedback at the end of the day. I was also to give him a better understanding of why he was going through the assessment and why it was important both to him and his company that he do so.

It was a very pleasant orientation session. The young man was at ease, he had good social skills and social confidence, and seemed to be looking forward to the testing session. He was a sales trainee, not a candidate. He was already hired and the client company was putting him through the assessment session to evaluate his strengths and weaknesses in order to plan for his future growth and development.

While this young man was just out of college, he knew how to handle himself socially and he had the "look" typical of the company's sales representatives. He was tall, good-looking, well-groomed, and dressed in the traditional Brooks Brothers style. He had recently graduated from a highly respected university, where he maintained a solid B average with an impressive array of extracurricular pursuits. It was easy to understand how this young man had survived the intense scrutiny of the company's sales and human resources professionals and was hired. As he prepared to go through a daylong assessment program, he seemed confident, and I was impressed. He looked like a sure thing.

THE ASSESSMENT PROCESS

Our assessment procedure for beginning sales representatives was a daylong testing session, followed by feedback to the candidate. The tests and questionnaires covered three general areas: (1) interests, values, and career goals; (2) personality and motivation; and (3) basic intellectual abilities. The various tests and measures in this case were specifically validated against sales performance for the company in question. The candidates' or trainees' test scores were compared directly to those of the company's own sales representatives. The assessment placed particular emphasis on those test scales and measures showing the strongest relationships with various criteria of sales performance.

The feedback session served several purposes. It was used, first of all, to review the candidate's background (i.e., education, training, or work experience) in order to reveal anything that might have an impact on the potential for later success on the job. Two, feedback sessions were used to give the candidates a clear understanding of how they performed on the tests and to ensure that their personality test profiles were accurate indicators of how they operated. It is during these feedback sessions that the professional assessment specialist begins to develop a clear picture of the candidate's assets and limitations for the job. On a personal level, the feedback interviews were also used to diffuse any anxiety that the candidates might have about the testing session and to make sure that they left the testing session better informed about themselves and with a positive attitude toward testing. Depending on the needs of the client company, the feedback sessions could also be used for guidance and counseling regarding the candidate's or trainee's future growth, development, and career planning.

Following the feedback sessions, written reports are prepared for the individual client companies on the candidates or trainees. The reports start with an account of the individuals' personal, educational, and work histories, followed by summaries of their specific test performances in the mental abilities, interests, and personality areas. The conclusions and recommendations section typically includes summaries of the candidates' or trainees' assets and limitations, followed by overall judgments of their potential for future success on the job.

APPLYING VALIDATION RESULTS TO ASSESSMENTS

The accuracy of an assessment process is a direct function of the strength of the validation studies backing it up. In the case study of the young sales trainee, several validation studies had been conducted in prior years relating to various predictors (mental abilities, personality and interest tests, and biographical information) with several criteria of on-the-job sales performance. The validation studies for the company in question also included a utility analysis that showed how the use of the total and various parts of the assessment process translated into potential dollars gained by the company.

The validation studies showed that the key factors for success in this job are high energy and strong work motivation. Assertiveness and sociability are also necessary for success. Poor personal relations, which in this case is defined as insensitivity, intolerance, and disregard for other people, and poor verbal ability were negative indicators of success for this company's field sales representatives. These results were not unusual; the same key factors were found to be related to success in field sales for other companies over a wide variety of products, industries, and sales situations.

In the case of this company, there were also validation data available showing which factors were critical for success in sales management. The studies indicate that many of the same factors important for high performance in field sales were also critical for success in sales management. The differences between the two job types were more of degree than of kind. For example, the sales managers seemed to require stronger intellectual abilities in the verbal and logical thinking areas. Energy was important, but extremely high energy was not critical for above-average success in management. Assertiveness, confidence, and sociability continued to be important in both areas, while personal relations was a more critical ingredient for success in management than in field sales.

RETURNING TO THE CASE STUDY: THE RESULTS OF THE ASSESSMENT

The sales trainee who passed through the stringent scrutiny of the company's own evaluation process when hired, and who looked like a sure success in the orientation interview, was then objectively and thoroughly examined in a validation-based assessment process. Since he was already hired, it would have been nice if the company's evaluation and the objective test-based assessment would have been in agreement. Unfortunately, this was not the case.

The test results showed that part of the young man's personality profile completely agreed with the image he projected. The personality tests correctly described him as being highly assertive and sociable. But the hidden part was that he was also very hostile. He described himself on the tests as being extremely critical, intolerant, and unsympathetic with people and their problems. During the feedback interview he agreed with this picture, and his smile faded as he admitted that he disliked and distrusted people. Also hidden was the fact that he was emotional and quite sensitive to criticism. The overall picture was of a man who was not likely to work well under pressure. While he could "dish out" criticism, he would have a difficult time receiving it. He seemed to be the type of person who had enough social skills and diplomacy to deal effectively with people in the short-term. However, over the long-term and under pressure, he could have considerable difficulty getting along with people. In his case, the people would be customers, superiors, co-workers, or subordinates.

An even more critical shortcoming that was also hidden was that this young man didn't have the strong drive, energy, and work motivation typical of the company's successful sales representatives. Also, his mental abilities were marginal for the position of sales representative for the company and "not in the ballpark" for sales management. He clearly was not the dynamic type of individual who usually becomes a superstar for the company.

WHY DO ASSESSMENTS?

Based on the objective assessment, this young sales trainee had very poor chances for future success in a sales career with that company. Aside from having poor sales potential, over the long run, he was at risk for eventually alienating the company's customers as well as his own superiors and co-workers. This young man had passed through the gauntlet of corporate evaluation by a company that is one of the best and most thorough in that regard. He was hired on the basis of the image he portrayed and not on the substantive inner qualities that determine whether he would have ultimately succeeded or not.

The lesson I learned from this, though not immediately, was that interviews are indeed fallible. With regard to any job there are deeper, more critical qualities, abilities, and characteristics that can only be evaluated accurately in a validation-based test assessment program.

In the case of sales and sales management, where communications skills, sociability, and appearance all have their place, interviews are important, but they should be restricted to evaluating those areas, and no more. Evaluations of the other critical areas should be left to objective assessment techniques.

Based on my years of experience in assessing sales candidates, it seems that the important areas of drive, energy, and work motivation tend to remain hidden from or are misinterpreted by the interviewers. Hyperactive, dynamic individuals who might become top sales representatives are often mistaken for being nervous and jumpy, while slow, low-energy people are often seen as being calm and self-assured. Hostility is often seen as assertiveness and psychopathic personalities are seen as being charming and likable. Only the objective assessment using psychological tests can tell you what you have for sure. In the end, both test data and interview evaluations should form a picture of the candidate's pluses and minuses for the job. Only the validation analyses can ascertain which of those pluses and minuses are critical for future success on the job.

To finish the story of the young sales trainee, he did not succeed with the company. He didn't even make it through the training program . . . something about having a fight with a senior executive. The company is now assessing candidates *prior* to hiring.

EMPIRICAL VALIDITY

What Does It Take to Be Successful in Sales?

If you compare criterion-related validity studies across various industries, companies, products, and sales situations, you will see some degree of variability in the findings, but also a surprising amount of consistency. For example, a sales representative's need for intellectual abilities can vary considerably across product lines, depending on the technical complexity of the products and technical sophistication of the customers. It is obviously going to take more know-how and technical ability to sell jet airplanes than to sell dishwasher detergent. Too, the valid personality test scales will vary considerably from "outside" sales (field sales) to "inside" sales (telephone sales). Motivational factors can also vary as the sales positions range from competitive, high-volume, commission-based selling to those that involve nothing more than telephone order-taking. However, within the broad contexts of industrial field sales, as well as inside sales and sales management, there seem to be consistent sets of qualities and characteristics relating to sales productivity and to varying levels of success on the job.

What Does It Take to Be a Successful Field Sales Representative?

In many validation studies on industrial field sales, the primary ingredient for success seems to be the simple factor of drive, energy, and work motivation. This factor is a combination of inborn physical energy and the ability to focus that energy on productive work. Of all the assessed characteristics of individuals, this factor is the only one that seems capable of standing alone as an excellent predictor of success. It is so critical that, despite whatever other strengths the candidate displays, if the person does not possess the ability to use that energy effectively, that person is unlikely to become a top sales representative. Low-energy candidates, if they don't fail completely, are not likely to be any better than average sales producers.

There are two other factors, high sociability and high confidence, that might also be related to success in industrial field sales. However, in the validation studies, those factors do not seem to differentiate between high producers in sales and those that are poor performers. It appears that all, or nearly all, field sales representatives have good social skills and social confidence and that they are also assertive and competitive. These seem to be constant factors across all sales representatives, whether they are high or low producers.

Energy and work motivation are different matters. Based on the numbers of average- and low-energy sales representatives who slip through the selection process, it appears that many industrial corporations are not doing a good job in assessing the energy and drive levels of prospective sales candidates using the usual interview-based evaluation process. Because energy is a key factor in sales success, and because it can be readily measured in an objective test assessment program, I recommend using a test assessment program as an integral part of any company's sales evaluation and selection program.

The validation evidence also indicates that there are several other critical areas that can be assessed in a testing program, but might be difficult to evaluate in an interview. Personal relations is one of those factors. Personal relations, in this case, refers to an individual's feelings toward other people. Aside from one's social skills, social confidence, and ability to use tact and diplomacy, it is the inner feelings that people have toward one another that determines if they are able to get along well with those around them. In sales work, it determines whether they are able to get along well with their co-workers and superiors, and whether they are able to maintain long-term positive relationships with customers. According to almost all of PSP's validation studies covering many industries, companies, sales situations, and products, those people who tend to be critical, intolerant, unsympathetic with, or hostile toward people are more likely to be rated as poor or marginal sales performers. While personal relations can be reliably measured in an assessment process, it apparently escapes detection in many companies' interview-based evaluation procedures.

The reason for this is that interviewees are on their best behavior during the interview. Most interviewers do not typically place candidates in situations that would evoke their hostilities.

They are not under the same conditions that, on the job, might break down their controls and cause negative reactions. Even for the trained interviewer, it becomes a difficult task to differentiate between the positive qualities of assertiveness and confidence and the negative qualities of hostility and aggression. Furthermore, from validation studies of sales management, it appears that good personal relations is an even more critical element for success as one moves up into sales management.

A third area important for success in field sales jobs is the individual's system of values—those motivation generators that drive our behavior and give us the push to succeed. The validation evidence clearly shows that successful sales representatives usually place a high degree of importance on making a good financial return for their efforts. Top sales performers generally have a strong desire for competition and an even greater need to win.

What Does It Take to Be a Successful Inside Sales Representative?

The validation evidence on inside sales work shows that it takes a different type of person to be successful in this environment than to be successful in outside sales. Both jobs require good communications and social skills; however, they also require different levels of energy and drive. Inside sales jobs that tend to be confined and deskbound presumably require less energy than outside sales, where the best performers are out and about and always on the go. While paperwork is certainly a necessary part to an outside sales career, it is the primary focus of inside sales work. In sum, the primary goal of an outside sales representative is to sell goods, products, and services, but the primary goal of the inside sales representative is to take and record orders and to do so completely, accurately, and efficiently.

In view of this distinction, it is not surprising that personal factors of energy and drive do not predict inside sales performance, while these same factors are the key ingredients for success in outside sales. Personal characteristics related to success in inside sales are those that describe individuals as being planful, careful, organized, and conscientious in their approach to work. Individuals who are impulsive, happy-go-lucky, not detail-oriented, or hyperactive are most likely to fail in inside sales.

Other major differences between employees proficient at inside and outside sales are the person's work interests. Field sales representatives tend to have interest patterns showing strong interests in dealing with other people, while their interests in computational and clerical pursuits are often limited. Inside sales representatives, while they should show an interest in working with and dealing with people, also have an interest in doing the computational/clerical activities that are critical parts of their jobs. While there are differences between these two occupations, it is not surprising that successful inside sales representatives and top field sales representatives also share a number of personal characteristics related to their relationships with people.

Characteristics that validate for both inside sales and outside sales are sociability, social skills, social confidence, and oral communications skills. It seems that all sales representatives, whether inside or outside, need to be able to deal with and communicate with people effectively. It certainly helps, both in dealing with customers and getting along with their own sales team, that these salespeople have positive personal feelings and regard for other people. Sales representatives who are hostile, intolerant, and unsympathetic with other people seem to do poorly in sales productivity, whether they are dealing with customers face-to-face or over the telephone.

Similar to outside sales, the intellectual and technical requirements of inside sales are likely to vary considerably, depending on the products and services involved, and are likely to vary somewhat, depending on the company and industry. There does seem to be one major difference between inside and outside sales that frequently arises in the validation analyses. While measures of verbal ability often predict success for both inside and outside sales, mathematics and basic arithmetic skills seldom, if ever, are shown to be significant factors for success in outside sales. On the other hand, mathematics skills and computational interests often validate for inside sales positions.

What Does It Take to Be a Successful Sales Manager?

The validation studies on sales managers show that many of the same factors that are critical for success in outside sales are also important for success in sales management. The differences are based more on the required levels of abilities and personal qualities than on the kind of factors that seem to be important. This being the case, it is not surprising that moves from outside sales to sales management are often easier and smoother than similar moves in engineering, computer science, and the technical fields.

A primary example of the differences in field sales and sales management is the variation in intellectual abilities required for success in each field. According to the validation evidence, low verbal ability and low logical thinking ability are both negative predictors of success in outside sales, but neither verbal ability nor logical thinking ability show linear relationships with sales productivity beyond a modest level of ability. Sales representatives with superior verbal ability or logical thinking ability do not outperform those with moderate levels of the same abilities. In fact, in some studies, salespeople with superior mental abilities are less productive. It may be that the dynamic, hyperenergetic people who are superior sales performers do not have the patience to sit for extended periods reading and studying. Superenergetic people are always on the go, they tend not to have high literary and academic interests, and they might very well be no better than average students.

On the other hand, good verbal ability and logical thinking ability do predict success in sales management. Strong communications skills, high verbal ability, and sound logical thinking ability are prerequisites for success in sales management and for progression to higher levels of management. PSP Human Resource Development's study of company presidents (Sullivan 1983) shows that they had very strong verbal and logical thinking abilities, while only a few presidents were ranked in the average range.

In terms of personality, both sales representatives and sales managers tend to be high in sociability, social confidence, social skills, and assertiveness. Although success in outside sales seems to be a direct function of energy and work motivation, this does not seem to be the case for sales managers. While good energy, drive, and work motivation are important for success in sales management, high-energy sales managers may not perform any better than those of average levels of drive and energy.

The same type of effect, though in an inverse direction, seems to be the case in the area of personal relations. Good personal relations is an important asset for success in both field sales and inside sales, but it seems to be a critical ingredient for success in sales management. The validation evidence shows that successful sales managers tend to be very high in personal relations. More than just being able to get along with people, they are described as understanding, sympathetic to other people's problems, uncritical, and accepting of other people.

Exhibit 11–1
Summary of Important (*) and Critical (**) Factors Related to Success in Inside Sales, Outside Sales, and Sales Management

ABILITIES

	INSIDE SALES	OUTSIDE SALES	SALES MANAGER
Verbal Ability	*	*	**
Computational Ability	**		
Logical Thinking Ability	*	*	**

INTERESTS

	INSIDE SALES	OUTSIDE SALES	SALES MANAGER
Social/Persuasive Interests	*	**	**
Computational/ Clerical Interests	**		

PERSONALITY

	INSIDE SALES	OUTSIDE SALES	SALES MANAGER
Physical Energy/ Drive		**	*
Planful, Careful, Detail Oriented	**		
Social Skills & Social Confidence	*	**	**
Personal Relations	*	*	**

Successful sales managers have a positive attitude toward others that is deeper than just surface friendliness and diplomacy.

SUMMARY

Exhibit 11-1 summarizes the degree of importance that each of the major abilities, interest areas, and temperament factors has been shown to have on success in inside sales, outside sales, and sales management. While these same factors may vary slightly from industry to industry and company to company, they are very consistent and widely replicated in a variety of sales and sales management validation studies conducted by PSP Human Resource Development.

In Exhibit 11–1, a double asterisk indicates that the particular trait, factor, or ability is of critical importance, while one asterisk denotes that the factor is important. A blank space indicates that there is little empirical evidence that the factor predicts success in the various sales job families.

REFERENCE

Sullivan, W. P. (April 1983). Have you got what it takes to get to the top? *Management Review* 72 , 8–11.

12

Issues in the Selection and Development of Professional Salespeople

Curtiss P. Hansen and Kelley A. Conrad

Chapter 11 presented an overview of how psychological assessment can improve the selection of salespeople. William Sullivan discussed how the interview can be combined with psychological tests to arrive at an overall estimate of a candidate's sales potential. Generally, he focused on a description of the characteristics common to a broad variety of good salespeople.

This chapter will extend the discussion begun in Chapter 11 by describing an applied research study in which psychological assessment was used to select salespeople for a specific industry. This will be followed by a description of how market, geographic, and cultural differences within the United States can affect the success of a salesperson, and how these differences must be accounted for in the assessment process. Finally, an analysis of issues pertinent to the use of psychological assessment in the selection, placement, promotion, and development of salespeople will be presented.

THE PSYCHOLOGICAL ASSESSMENT OF INSURANCE SALES CANDIDATES

This chapter's co-author, Curtiss P. Hansen, recently conducted an investigation of the characteristics associated with success as a salesperson in the group health insurance industry. While there have been many previous studies demonstrating a strong relationship between various personality characteristics as measured by psychological tests and sales performance (e.g., Dunnette & Kirchner 1960; Greenberg & Mayer 1964; Harrell 1960; Kirchner, Dunnette & Mousley, 1961; Lamont & Lundstrom, 1977; Merenda & Clarke, 1959; Miner

1962; Sager & Ferris 1986; Wallace & Clarke 1956), little has been done in the research arena to integrate those personal traits identified by tests with results from the personal interview, just as it is done in a psychological assessment. Hansen's (1990) applied study accomplished that objective.

Background of the Hansen Study

Hansen's validation study determined which personality traits distinguished high-performing from average-performing salespeople within the large insurance company so that a comprehensive psychological assessment process could be developed and instituted. Forty-one group health insurance salespeople were administered the Adjective Check List (ACL), a self-report personality description profile. Salespeople with at least three years' experience were selected, representing all areas of the United States. Each salesperson was rated by one of two regional managers as being average or above average in meeting the company's performance expectations for the position. Performance was evaluated as percent of quota achieved, total volume of sales, new customers gained, and percent of customer attrition.

Dr. Hansen analyzed the job of group health insurance sales agent. Information was gained from incumbents and from job description documents. From this job analysis several personal characteristics emerged that were judged to underlie successful performance on job tasks. These salesperson attributes are listed in Exhibit 12–1.

The administration of the ACL to current sales representatives served the purpose of validating both the ACL and many of the characteristics listed in Exhibit 12–1. It was expected that many traits measured by the ACL would correlate highly with the measure of sales performance, and that those ACL traits would correspond to several of the characteristics on the following list.

Results of the Validation Study

The responses of the 41 salespeople on the ACL were statistically analyzed. The results showed that about half (12) of the ACL scales significantly correlated with sales performance. This meant that on these 12 scales, the best salespeople described themselves using the adjectives in ways that were significantly different from the average for all salespeople. Many validity coefficients for these scales were quite high, with some in the .50 and .60 ranges (see Hansen 1990 for a technical discussion of the study and the statistical results). The following is a narrative interpretation of the validity coefficients.

Profile of the High-Rated Salesperson Group. In terms of personality traits, the high-rated salespeople differ from those rated average in the following ways. The top performers are more independent and self-directed. They exhibit a strident confidence, assertiveness, and aggressive competitiveness. They are also extraverted and outgoing, though not in a particularly sensitive or supportive

Exhibit 12–1
Personal Characteristics from Job Analysis of Group Health Sales Positions

- Oral communication skill
- Listening skill
- Written communication skill
- Ability to quickly establish rapport with people
- Interpersonal perceptiveness
- Persuasiveness and ability to influence people
- Social poise, maturity, and comfort
- Ability to deal with and resolve conflict
- Problem-solving ability
- Ability to plan and organize
- Ability to handle multiple demands effectively
- Achievement motivation, ambition, and initiative
- Self-confidence
- Assertiveness
- Ability and desire to work independently
- Endurance, perseverence, and stress tolerance
- Aggressiveness in pursuing opportunities and achieving goals
- Ability to think effectively "on the spot"
- Ability to develop and maintain personal credibility

manner. Rather, they are highly egotistical and concerned about achieving their own goals. These are dominant people who need to be in highly visible, status positions. They are less satisfied with themselves and life than the average-rated performers, and are driven to excel.

Profile of the Average-Rated Salesperson Group. The salespeople rated as average are more moderate in their personalities and dispositions. Compared to people in general, they have many positive traits. They are more similar to high-performing lower and middle managers than they are to high-performing professional salespeople. Compared to the high-rated group health salespeople, they are more self-disciplined and organized. They are concerned about their image and how they affect people. They are likely to be more tactful, controlled, and willing to follow the rules. They need more time to think and plan before acting than do the top salespeople. They are similar to top salespeople in being extraverted and outgoing, but average salespeople exhibit more genuine sociability and concern for others.

Comparison to the Job Analysis Findings

The results of the ACL study described in the preceding section overlap considerably with the results of the original job analysis. It appears that several

Exhibit 12–2
Candidate Rating Scale

Employee Benefits Sales Representative

The following scale is for use in evaluating a candidate's personal interview. Refer to
definitions (Exhibit 12-3) for clarification of the characteristics being rated. Candidates
should be compared to a typical or average applicant for the above position. Circle the
item corresponding to your rating. Leave blank any dimensions that you could not assess
in the interview.

CHARACTERISTIC	Above Average		Average		Below Average
1. Oral Communication	5	4	3	2	1
2. Listening Skill	5	4	3	2	1
3. Interpersonal Skill	5	4	3	2	1
4. Problem Solving Ability	5	4	3	2	1
5. Planning and Organization	5	4	3	2	1
6. Achievement Motivation	5	4	3	2	1
7. Self Confidence	5	4	3	2	1
8. Personal Independence	5	4	3	2	1
9. Assertiveness	5	4	3	2	1
10. Self Discipline & Endurance	5	4	3	2	1
11. Aggressiveness	5	4	3	2	1
12. Sales Producer Potential	5	4	3	2	1

personal characteristics are not only required to function at a minimal level of
job competence, but also are needed to perform at an outstanding level. These
traits are independence, motivation, self-confidence, assertiveness, and interpersonal extraversion.

The next step in the study was to combine the results of the job analysis with
the results of the test validation to create a comprehensive profile of characteristics
needed for success as a group health sales representative. This profile is essentially the one derived from the job analysis and presented in Exhibit 12–1.
However, the characteristics derived from the job analysis that were similar to
the test-validated personality traits were given more weight when used in the
selection process.

The result of the study was the creation of a candidate rating scale, shown in
Exhibit 12–2, and the introduction of psychological assessment into the sales
selection process. The rating scale lists the 11 most important personal char-

acteristics, or dimensions, for success in the job as identified from the previous analyses. When selecting new candidates for group health insurance sales positions, ratings of each dimension are completed by each manager who interviews the candidate. Each rater has the list of dimension definitions shown in Exhibit 12–3. One of the company psychologists (Dr. Hansen) concurrently conducts a brief psychological assessment on the candidate and completes the same rating form. The psychologist also writes a brief assessment report on the person. This report is a narrative elaboration of the psychologist's ratings with a detailed description of how well the candidate's job-related personal characteristics compare to those shown in the job analysis and test validation. All the ratings from the managers and the psychologist are then reviewed by the hiring manager, who makes the final decision based on this information. Discrepancies are usually discussed with the psychologist.

ASSESSING SALES CANDIDATES FOR SPECIFIC MARKETS

The use of psychological assessment as a tool to help select salespeople has been discussed in general terms so far. Chapter 11 looked at traits possessed by all successful salespeople, while this chapter has presented the success traits for salespeople in the insurance industry. There is another factor to be considered when assessing salespeople. That factor is the type of market in which sales will be made. The market could be based on geography, or could simply refer to different sociocultural groups within one geographic area.

The following material is based on a study conducted by a Humber, Mundie & McClary psychologist (HM&M Technical Report, no. 19-4). The study attempted to identify all the personal characteristics that would help a salesperson be successful selling mechanical parts in southern California. The job information that formed the basis for the study's conclusions was gathered from interviews with job incumbents and sales managers, and from reading job descriptions, product brochures, and other company literature.

Results of the Study

Surprisingly, most of the personal characteristics needed for success in selling industrial parts in the southern California market were not unique to this area of the country. The successful salesperson was described as being:

- Good in communication and presentation skills
- Able to develop credibility quickly
- Emotionally mature
- Confident and motivated
- Independent in work habits
- People-oriented and friendly

Exhibit 12–3
Definitions of Sales Position Characteristics

1. *Oral Communication.* Ability to express ideas and information effectively in a face-to-face meeting. Includes completeness, clarity and conciseness of expression. Also, skill in presenting one's viewpoints persuasively without creating defensiveness and resistance.

2. *Listening Skill.* Ability to focus on the other person and understand the ideas and information presented. Includes skill in "reading between the lines" in perceiving the speaker's viewpoints and the implications of the speaker's words. Also includes the listener's ability to convey his or her level of understanding to the speaker.

3. *Interpersonal Skill.* Ability to develop rapport with others. Includes the level of comfort the candidate establishes in a meeting. Reflects an awareness of the position and needs of the other person as demonstrated by appropriate behaviors. In short, is the candidate able to get the other person to like and accept him or her?

4. *Problem-Solving Ability.* Ability to quickly assimilate information and generate viable solutions to deal with a problem situation.

5. *Planning and Organization.* Ability to foresee future work needs and situations, and to take appropriate actions in the present so that the future can be most effectively dealt with. This should be reflected in a noticeable economy of effort in achieving current objectives.

6. *Achievement Motivation.* The drive to undertake and succeed in challenging life activities. The need to be recognized for outstanding accomplishments. A strong internal motivation to do well in all things.

7. *Self-Confidence.* The belief that one can accomplish what one sets out to do, even when the parameters and components of the activity are not familiar. An observable sense of self-assurance and control over one's world.

8. *Personal Independence.* The need to make one's own decisions and carry out work activities according to one's own plans. A strong dislike of close supervision. Doing things based on one's convictions rather than the desire to please others.

9. *Assertiveness.* Ability to get what one wants in life by presenting one's needs in a direct and straightforward manner. Comfort in defending one's position when challenged.

10. *Self-Discipline and Endurance.* Ability to undertake work on one's own initiative and to stay with a task until it is completed. Includes stress tolerance and ability to remain focused on the objective in the face of distractions and competing demands. A strong work ethic.

11. *Aggressiveness.* Competitiveness and the desire to win. The need to do better than other people, including co-workers. A hard-charging, flamboyant approach to work.

12. *Sales Producer Potential.* Overall estimate of the candidate's capacity for success on the job.

- Understanding with the customer
- Organized and responsible
- Energetic and competitive

These characteristics are similar to those found in other studies of successful salespeople, regardless of the market. Evidently, these traits are common in good salespeople.

However, there were a handful of characteristics that appeared to be unique to the Los Angeles market. Some traits might also be needed for sales success in large cities. These personal attributes are listed as follows:

- Street smarts and common sense
- Flexibility of thinking and willingness to improvise
- Healthy, robust appearance
- Social poise
- Knowledge of how to sell self and product
- Adaptability to surprises
- Willingness to devote long hours to work
- Past sales experience
- A resident of the Los Angeles area or other large, urban area
- Temperament to deal with crowded freeways and long commutes to customers

ISSUES IN THE SELECTION, PLACEMENT, PROMOTION, AND DEVELOPMENT OF SALESPEOPLE

Although the selection of salespeople has long been a topic of interest, a recent workshop (Adler 1990) concluded that much of the "accepted wisdom" is based on limited research support. Seymour Adler's review of the validity literature found 226 studies between 1918 and the present dealing with the selection of salespeople. However, many studies were old, based on simple predictive models, and examined only one type of predictor. There were few comparisons using the same predictors for different sales jobs. This makes generalization of the available research an uncertain, risky endeavor. In his review of the various sources of measurement used in the psychological assessment of salespeople, Adler examined research evidence on mental abilities tests, personality tests, biodata, interviews, and simulations.

Mental Abilities Tests

A major study that examined validity studies published for various occupational groups (Schmitt, Gooding, Noe & Kirsch 1984) found that the average validity for mental ability tests used in the prediction of later job success was the lowest for sales jobs in comparison with five other occupational groups. There was evidence, however, that mental ability tests did a better job of predicting the performance of salespeople on licensing or registration exams. When specific mental abilities were identified by a job analysis, tests of those abilities were found by various studies to be valid predictors of sales performance in the job on which the analysis was completed (Ford, Walker, Churchill & Hartley 1986). Ford et al. also found that the predictive validities for mental abilities were higher for more complex sales positions. Adler's conclusion was that mental abilities tests are easy to administer and have potential validity for specific sales jobs (often more complex ones). He cautioned about possible adverse impact with protected groups and the tendency to set the acceptability level or pass rate for such tests higher than justified by the job requirements alone.

Personality Tests

Schmitt, Gooding, Noe and Kirsch (1984) reported low average predictions of job success and personality measures. Adler's (1990) review found little evidence for a solid theoretical basis guiding the selection of personality dimensions for measurement. He did, however, find some evidence showing that the personality dimensions for sociability and responsibility were valid predictors of sales performance in several studies. He concluded that while personality tests are highly descriptive of the individuals who are tested and have a high level of management credibility and acceptance, the results are vulnerable to faking, they create defensiveness in candidates, and they are rarely valid as stand-alone predictors. Personality tests were seen as having potential, but need to be based on job-relevant dispositions (such as style, consistency, and adaptation). Adler encouraged the use of behavioral measures of personality attributes. He believed that the greatest potential use of personality tests is in extending our understanding of the sales job. Two key areas where personality results can help are developing our knowledge of impression management and perseverance as components of sales success.

Biodata

The use of biographical information (biodata) as a predictor of sales success is the second most popular approach found in the published research (Schmitt, Gooding, Noe & Kirsch 1984). It has a long history of use in the insurance industry and a strong record of low but significant validity (Brown, Stout, Dalessio, & Crosby 1988; Hunter, Schmidt & Judiesch 1990). This area of measurement, however, is more affected by differences in the sales environment. Specific environments that demonstrate some validity are individual customer sales and services sales. Like tests of mental abilities, biodata information is easy to collect. With reference and background checking, much of the data can be verified. Thorough job descriptions and empirical keying of biographical factors with job performance lead to the most valid results. Difficulties with biodata include the legal constraints that eliminate some areas of questioning, the ease with which a candidate can fake the information, and the fact so much biodata is very situation and time specific.

Interviews

Virtually every selection of a new salesperson involves an interview. When the interview is carefully done, the results can be valid (for instance, see Arvey, Miller, Gould, & Burch 1987). Unfortunately, many interviews ignore the principles of good practice—they are less structured, specific, and controlled than they need to be. The way most interviews are conducted, they are highly subject to bias. Interviews as part of a psychological assessment prove more valid as predictors when they are based on a thorough knowledge of the organization and the specific sales job for which the person is being selected. Comer and Dubinsky (1985) have found clear differences between positions for consumer products and services, industrial products and services, insurance, and retail sales. For example, full-time salespeople selling to business and industry will typically:

- Meet rejection by influential executives many times a week
- Work independently, away from direct supervision, for long periods
- Work alone, away from the community of people
- Function at a high energy level all day, every day
- Make quick assessments of many new business situations and people regularly
- Appreciate and be sensitive to personal and organizational needs of others
- Seem larger than life in order to sell to the customer, and make a positive, lasting impression
- Balance the needs of a demanding customer with the sometimes-unresponsive nature of a company

(Doyle & Shapiro 1980)

Although less researched, it appears that success with different customer types calls for differences in the salespeople as well. Demands vary when the salesperson works with manufacturers, direct consumers, organizations, or distributors and other resellers.

Recently, the dynamics of customer relationships have become the focus of much research (Jackson 1985). This research has developed two contrasting basic types of marketing relationships with customers. *Relationship* marketing is oriented toward establishing strong, lasting relationships with separate accounts. In contrast, *transaction* marketing stresses the individual sale. This research has shown confusion and mistakes between salespeople in relationship marketing and transaction marketing situations. Salespeople sometimes want to develop a relationship so badly that they ignore signs that their target customers are transaction-oriented and unlikely to develop the desired relationship. Such mismatches can be very costly.

Simulations

As an outgrowth of the recent popularity of assessment centers for the selection of salespeople and sales managers, simulations have become popular measures of sales success. When directly tied to the assessment of specific skills identified in the job analysis, simulations provide observations strongly predictive of sales success (Adler 1987). While this method of measurement has considerable potential, it has been used only rarely in psychological assessments. Its use, however, is growing. Effective simulations are direct models of job situations the salesperson will probably meet on the job. When properly designed, simulations are very credible to the applicants and managers using them, and provide realistic job previews for applicants. They can be costly to prepare, time-consuming, and difficult to administer. Many are situation-specific. It does appear, however, that their use will grow because of their usefulness.

IMPROVING PSYCHOLOGICAL ASSESSMENT OF SALESPEOPLE

As with other types of psychological assessment, the greatest accuracy in prediction occurs when the psychologist begins by developing a thorough understanding of the hiring organization. This should include a knowledge of the products and services sold, the specific activities and duties of the organization's salespeople, the characteristics of and relationships with clients or prospects, and the knowledge, skills, abilities, and other characteristics necessary for job performance. Some key psychological dimensions include:

- The degree to which the sales position calls for the incumbent to be active or reactive to customers
- The primary mode of interaction (e.g., in person, by phone)
- The social challenges to be faced when meeting and working with clients (e.g., similarity of backgrounds of clients and salespeople)
- The complexity of the sale
- The risks involved for the salesperson or the customer
- The time frame within which most sales happen
- The technical knowledge and skill required of the salesperson

Most assessments will at least include information on the following dimensions, which appear to be common requirements for many sales positions:

- Communication
- Social adeptness
- Persistence
- Fact finding
- Problem-solving
- Adaptability
- Responsiblity

Future work on the effectiveness of salespeople will also need to use measures of sales performance that reflect all aspects of effective job performance. As Landy and Farr (1983) have shown, "There are two distinct categories of sales measurement: outcome measures and behavioral measures. The outcome measures are the traditional ones—sales volume, type of sale, sale renewal, etc. The behavioral measures deal more with what the sales representative does and to a lesser degree with the result of those behaviors" (44–45).

More and more psychological assessments of salespeople are including simulations and job samples in the traditional assessment batteries composed of mental ability tests, personality measures, biodata, and interview observations. The cost of training a salesperson runs $5,000 to $10,000 on average. When added to the costs associated with the three to six months of orientation and training needed to bring a salesperson to full productivity (Bragg 1988), the cost of turnover in the sales force can be considerable. Even small reductions in turnover or gains in productivity pay for the costs of the psychological assessments of the candidates.

REFERENCES

Adler, S. A. (1987). Toward the more efficient use of assessment center technology in personnel selection. *Journal of Business and Psychology* 2 (1): 74–93.

———. (1990). *Strategies and techniques for selecting and managing a salesforce.* Workshop presented at the 5th Annual Society Conference of the Society for Industrial and Organizational Psychology, Miami Beach, Fla.

Arvey, R. D., Miller, H. E., Gould, R., & Burch, P. (1987). Interview validity for selecting sales clerks. *Personnel Psychology* 40 (1): 1–12.

Bragg, A. (1988). Are good salespeople born or made? *Sales and Marketing Management*, September, 74–78.

Brown, S. H., Stout, J. D., Dalessio, A. T., & Crosby, M. M. (1988). Stability of validity indices through test score ranges. *Journal of Applied Psychology* 73 (4): 736–42.

Comer, J. M., & Dubinsky, A. J. (1985). *Managing the successful sales force.* Lexington, Mass.: D. C. Heath.

Doyle, S. X., & Shapiro, B. P. (1980). What counts most in motivating your sales force? *Harvard Business Review* (May-June): 133–40.

Dunnette, M. D., & Kirchner, W. K. (1960). Psychological test differences between industrial salesmen and retail salesmen. *Journal of Applied Psychology* 44: 121–25.

Ford, N. M., Walker, O. C., Churchill, G. A., & Hartley, S. W. (1986). Selecting successful salespeople: A meta-analysis of biographical and psychological selection criteria. University of Wisconsin–Madison, Graduate School of Business Working Paper 3-86-9.

Greenberg, H., & Mayer, D. (1964). A new approach to the scientific selection of successful salesmen. *Journal of Psychology* 57, 113–23.

Hansen, C. P. (1990). *Personality correlates of success in insurance sales*. Paper presented at the 98th Annual Convention of the American Psychological Association, Boston, Mass.

Harrell, T. W. (1960). The relation of test scores to sales criteria. *Personnel Psychology* 13: 65–69.

Humber, Mundie & McClary (1985). Technical Report No. 19-4. Milwaukee, Wis.

Hunter, J. E., Schmidt, F. L., & Judiesch, M. K. (1990). Individual differences in output variability as a function of job complexity. *Journal of Applied Psychology* 75: 28–42.

Jackson, B. B. (1985). *Winning and keeping industrial customers*. Lexington, Mass.: Lexington Books.

Kirchner, W. K., Dunnette, M. D., & Mousley, N. (1961). Use of the Edwards Personal Preference Profile in the selection of salesmen. *Personnel Psychology* 14: 421–24.

Lamont, L. M., & Lundstrom, W. J. (1977). Identifying successful industrial salesmen by personality and personal characteristics. *Journal of Marketing Research* 14: 517–29.

Landy, F. J., & Farr, J. L. (1983). *The measurement of work performance: Methods, theory, and applications*. New York: Academic Press.

Merenda, P. F., & Clarke, W. V. (1959). Predictive efficiency of temperament characteristics and personal history variables in determining success of life insurance agents. *Journal of Applied Psychology* 43: 360–66.

Miner, J. B. (1962). Personality and ability factors in sales performance. *Journal of Applied Psychology* 46: 6–13.

Sager, J. K., & Ferris, G. R. (1986). Personality and salesforce selection in the pharmaceutical industry. *Industrial Marketing Management* 15: 319–24.

Schmitt, N., Gooding, R. Z., Noe, R. D., & Kirsch, M. (1984). Meta-analyses of validity studies published between 1964 and 1982 and the investigation of study characteristics. *Personnel Psychology* 37: 407–22.

Wallace, S. R., Dry, R., & Clarke, W. V. (1956). The Activity Vector Analysis as a selector of life insurance salesmen. *Personnel Psychology* 9: 337–45.

13

The Psychological Assessment of Technical Personnel

Patrick R. Powaser and Kelley A. Conrad

Beth felt very confident when she graduated with top honors with her degree in engineering. She was heavily recruited and had her pick of where she wanted to work. But things aren't so perfect now. Beth has trouble coming up with innovative solutions to the company's problems. She has so many things to do that nothing gets done as quickly and efficiently as it should. Beth also has trouble dealing with other people. She likes to work alone, prefers doing the work herself to delegating it, and finds criticism in others' suggestions. Technically, Beth is very bright and well-educated. But being passed over for the last promotion in her department has shown her that it takes more than that to be a good engineer in today's world.

The preceding scenario illustrates some of the difficulties in selecting qualified people for technical positions. While an applicant's technical skills may appear exceptional, there are other important characteristics that cannot be evaluated based on transcripts, degrees, or resumes. A psychological assessment can help determine whether a job candidate has all the skills necessary to be a good performer in all aspects of the job.

Assessments for technical positions will often involve the use of special tests, inventories, simulations, and interviewing skills to investigate the job applicant's strengths and weaknesses. The best technical assessments are based on careful job analyses and a thorough understanding of the organization, its climate, and its needs. In the assessment, the psychologist gathers information on the candidate's skills, abilities, and experiences, summarizing them clearly with respect to critical job dimensions and behaviors. These assessments help identify individuals who have a high probability of working out well on the job. This chapter provides several illustrations of the benefits of psychological assessment in the selection of technical personnel. Specific positions considered are: information services professionals, accountants, engineers, firefighters, and police officers.

INFORMATION SERVICES

One field particularly exemplifies the challenges of selection and placement in technical occupations. That field is information services. In many organizations, this function has been in existence a relatively short period of time. Even the most progressive companies have only had specialists in this field for 30 to 40 years. Originally, the position was often part of the accounting function or the production scheduling function. As the activities and involvement of professionals in this role grew, the functions themselves expanded. To represent the broader focus of concern with data from all corners of the organization, the field began to be called data processing (DP). Continued rapid proliferation of technology and the massive office and factory automation effects that the "information age" has created have significantly impacted professionals in this area. Today the field is referred to as information sciences (IS), and it is at the center of the critical competitive and survival issues of organizations.

The IS professional has become less the technical expert of 20 years ago and much more a participative consultant who needs strong business knowledge and a client-centered perspective. This is clearly reflected in the following job description developed to specifically address the changing roles of IS professionals. Individuals who will be successful as IS professionals will need to be able to:

- Use information to help set corporate and department priorities and goals
- Design information systems consistent with corporate and department information needs and strategy
- Provide support for end-user computing; act as an information consultant
- Develop technical solutions to operations issues
- Facilitate redistribution of information as appropriate
- Promote collaborative process management; link work groups together
- Use hardware to monitor work in process and manage projects more efficiently

(Ferreira & Harris 1986)

Entry-Level Information Services Personnel

In psychological assessments of IS individuals, the primary focus is on personal style and abilities rather than technical knowledge and proficiency. The psychologist will usually expect the company to have carefully screened a candidate in the technical areas such as databases, operating systems, operating software, computer operations, and telecommunications. For entry-level IS professionals, key behavioral dimensions include the person's team participation, basic inter-personal skills, oral and written communications skills, time management skills, ability to work with and understand systems, ability to learn, ability to adapt to changes, and ability to think. Many of these individuals are highly creative with very strong technical interests. One unique problem in selecting programmers and systems people is that, while their skill is knowledge-based, it is also a creative art. Some of the best performers will expect an open, supportive en-vironment, and will need clear recognition and acknowledgment of their con-tributions from someone who understands what they have accomplished. A technical expert with "controlled creativity" is more likely to be successful in the typical business environment than one who has moved further in the direction of "unrestrained creativity."

As an example, an entry-level computer programmer entering an IS department might be asked, "Think about a time when you avoided making a mistake as a result of carefully checking a program you had written. Describe the steps you went through in checking the program. What problems were avoided as a result of finding the error?" This and similar questions would give the psychologist an understanding of the person's approach and care in writing programs.

To explore both interpersonal relations and oral communications capabilities, the person could be asked, "Many end-users come to the IS department asking for a program, but are unable to clearly describe what they want. Tell me about a time when you have been able to help such an end-user define his or her needs in a way that you were able to write a program to fill those needs."

Mid-Level IS Managers

At the next level of responsibility, selection and development criteria broaden to include:

- Supervisory abilities
- Project management skill
- Problem-solving skill
- Personal persuasion and impact
- Alertness to human-factor considerations in systems design
- Sophisticated interpersonal skill

An example here would be interviewing a candidate for a systems analyst position. In doing so, the psychologist would be interested in the person's ability to discuss plans with end-users and supervisors. This would include keeping interested parties informed of plans and progress. A good way to explore this area would be to ask the person about a project that did not develop according to original plans. For example, "Tell me about a project that caused you difficulties. What was your original plan? How was it agreed to and communicated? What went wrong? What extra efforts were required from you to correct the problems? How long did it take to get back on schedule? What did you learn from this experience that you have used in your thinking and planning since then?''

Top-Level IS Managers

At the highest level of responsibility, the focus shifts again, this time to the management, mentoring, consulting, teaching, team-building, and strategic planning skills or abilities needed to provide senior-level direction to an IS department. A particularly key component is the ability to provide leadership through the identification and communication of the goals and objectives for the department as an integrated part of the organization and of the information services field. Questions that would assist the psychologist in developing this perspective often deal with key decisions the person has made. For example, ''Tell me about the last major decision you made about an IS operations area where the conditions were uncertain but where you had the authority to act. Describe the situation. Why was it uncertain? Describe your decision-making process. Was any information particularly critical to your decision? How certain were you of your decision? How did you know that?''

Some organizations have defined dual career tracks for IS professionals. One track is a traditional one, emphasizing increasing responsibilities for the manager who has authority over expanding operational areas, including both people and projects. The other track is the professional one, providing for growth in responsibilities and salary with increasing technological expertise. The top rung of this ladder is filled by the super scientists and technological gurus who become the idea generators that lead information services technology.

The information described above provides some examples of knowledge, skills, and abilities specifically related to performance at different levels of IS responsibility. These aspects would be covered in addition to the more traditional sections on general potential, leadership skill, administrative skill, and personal skill that are normal parts of most psychological assessments (see Chapters 1, 6, 8, and 9).

ACCOUNTING PROFESSIONALS

The next technical profession we will consider is that of accounting. Traditionally, the focus in selection of accounting professionals has been in finding people who were extremely well-organized, systematic about record keeping, able to tie together important account details, and quick and accurate in working with numbers. These remain key checkpoints for bookkeepers and many accounting support personnel. For accountants themselves, however, the assessment is much more complicated.

Entry- and Mid-Level Accounting

Accounting, like other professions, has been changing. An accountant today is also part systems analyst, part manager, and part counselor. In psychological assessments of accountants, it is now common to explore the degree to which the individual:

- Counsels clients, providing patient and considerate professional advice
- Seeks out appropriate information and guidance in order to provide clients with well-informed advice
- Acts as a business counselor, offering effective suggestions for improving the organization's profitability and effectiveness
- Takes initiative to go beyond specific job requirements offering management and systems advice
- Stays on top of emerging trends and new regulations affecting the accounting field

There are many similarities in the knowledge, skills, and abilities required of accountants in different levels of responsibility. The actual level of each characteristic changes in accordance with the specific organization and assignment. Entry-level positions place less demand on the accountant's intellectual abilities and more demand on carefulness, orderliness, clerical speed, accuracy, and attention to details. Mid-level accounting positions increase the demand on mental abilities, verbal abilities, judgment, and the ability to plan and organize. At mid-level, psychologists also begin to look for abilities that mark potential for success at senior levels of responsibility. Skills and abilities particularly important at top levels include: high-level mental and numerical abilities, good verbal and clerical abilities, the ability to see the big picture, and the ability to think analytically and critically.

Many accountants have been assigned auditing sometime during their professional career. Auditing work is a good area from which the psychologist can obtain direct behavioral descriptions of past performance to understand the person's approach and effectiveness. An example of a set of questions follows: "Think of a recent audit task you completed. Describe the task and situation for me. How did you organize your time to work effectively on this particular task? What support was provided for you? Describe any difficulties you encountered. What went well for you in completing this audit? If you were doing it over again, what might you do differently? Why?"

Chief Financial Officers

At the level of chief financial officer, the focus of psychological assessment shifts from technical to primarily management skills. Chief financial officers need to be able to handle complex systems. They are usually the financial planners for their organizations. The chief financial officer must be a senior manager, a systems manager, and an accountant. In many organizations, there will be holding companies, centralized systems, and distributed manufacturing or service locations with which to deal. In some smaller and medium-sized companies the chief financial officer can be responsible for the computer or information services (IS) area, which can include developing a marketing concept and IS team, developing hardware and software support, and controlling access to and scheduling for the computer.

From the psychological viewpoint, the role of the chief financial officer has changed dramatically. The person must be a "heavyweight." This means having excellent technical training and keeping up to date. It also means that breadth of managerial exposure and experience is important. Chief financial officers are usually required to manage relatively large groups of people. In the psychological assessment of chief financial officers, the psychologist is looking for individuals who are intellectually capable, well-educated, up to date in knowledge, broadly experienced in multifunction management, computers, and information management, and good communicators. They must have a sense of timeliness and urgency, be able to handle stress and pressure, and respond to a variety of people and problems. Full effectiveness at the top level of management also requires demonstrated qualities of leadership, a concept of self that supports peer relationships with other senior executives and board members, planning and facilitating ability, and considerable resourcefulness and awareness of state of the art accounting and management information systems. Chief financial officers must be able to keep their fingers on the financial pulses of entire organizations.

ENGINEERS

Selecting engineers has typically involved evaluating applicants on a narrowly defined set of qualifications. Characteristically, a potential employer would look at an applicant's degree, college or university, grade point average, relevant course work, experience, and letters of recommendation. All these elements are concerned with very technical aspects of an applicant's education. Today, many employers look for more than just exceptional engineering training.

Good interpersonal and communication skills are important. Engineers must be able to interact with their colleagues and support staff to effectively complete job assignments. Written and oral communication skills are essential to success in most jobs. The engineering field has started recognizing that engineers need training in these areas as well as in the areas of traditional technical training.

Today's dynamic, complex world demands innovative solutions to technical problems. New materials, designs, and processes are needed to meet these demands. Organizations now specifically look for engineers with highly developed creative skills who can implement innovative solutions to these complex problems. Creativity and innovation are difficult to assess from a job candidate's

application materials. It is in this arena that the psychological assessment can
provide extra insights helpful to the organization. There are a number of psychological measures of creativity that, when combined with the structured interview that is part of the typical psychological assessment, provide information
on an applicant's ability to develop abstract, innovative solutions.

Creative Engineers

Creative engineers exhibit distinct characteristics and behavioral dimensions
that significantly differentiate them from other engineers. Some of the key behavioral dimensions for which the psychologist looks include:

- Constantly seeking and finding challenging problems
- Fluency and flexibility when dealing with change in the engineering
  environment
- Intense curiosity about almost everything
- An expectant and responsive attitude toward life
- Originality in thinking and openness toward other's original thoughts
- High self-confidence, including not being afraid to make mistakes
- High energy level, including more impulsivity and responsiveness than is
  evident in many engineers
- Ability to tolerate ambiguity and complexity in contrast to engineering's
  more typical order and predictability
- Ability to analyze and synthesize fundamentals of the problem and appro-
  priately select those most critical to progress
- Creative memory capabilities, combining data whether obviously related or
  not
- Ability to toy with ideas
- Unusual persistence

(Raudsepp 1976)

Because many engineers feel uncomfortable with informal social conversation,
the interviewing psychologist will often have them talk about their work as a
way of getting necessary information. Examples of questions that can get engineers talking include the following: "Keeping up with new developments is
a challenge; give me an example of how you have learned and applied new
techniques in your field. Describe for me any original research you have conducted. How did you report the results? Describe for me your most innovative
project. What was personally most satisfying about this project? What aspects
of your job do you like best; why? Which do you like least; why?"

Finding an engineer who has many of these characteristics is not easy. One company that is very selective about the engineers it hires recently decided to add creativity to the criteria in the hopes of bolstering the innovation of its design engineers. Its experience has been that the addition of this behavioral dimension has significantly reduced the number of attractive candidates. To date, they have found that only about 7 percent of their otherwise qualified engineers meet the criteria to be considered creative. In spite of the difficulty it is experiencing in finding creative engineers, the company thinks the effort will be of sufficient value to the organization, and it is continuing its efforts.

Project Managers

Hiring companies are also increasingly looking for engineers with project management skills. The typical engineer is involved not only in the technical aspects of a project, but might also need to coordinate the efforts of numerous other engineers and support people. While, technically, the engineer is able to solve the problem, many times the engineer is unable to see the project through from start to finish. Some projects will be too large and complex to remain fully the responsibility of one person. When either situation develops, the engineer moves out of the purely technical role and assumes management or coordination roles as well. The project manager requires greater communication and inter-personal skills than does the engineering specialist. A critical behavioral di-mension contributing to effective performance in this role is the engineer's ability to communicate specific time and resource objectives during the delegation of tasks. This will include stating goals that are tied to the organization's mission, following up to provide feedback on task accomplishment, recognizing and rewarding performance of team members, and supporting people through a clearly demonstrated concern for fair treatment.

The business psychologist who is interviewing prospective project managers will gain the most valuable insights in this area by having the engineer describe projects he or she has managed or coordinated. A typical questioning approach might include the following: "Think back to your most recent project. Think about the details of how you structured it in order to be successful. How did you set up and manage the communications process? How did you select the individuals to whom you delegated key tasks? What written communications did you use as part of your process? How were they effective or ineffective? How did you monitor progress? Were there any problems? How did you solve them? Were any of the team members confused about their responsibilities? If so, how did you help clarify the situation?"

Overall, the results of psychological assessments help the hiring organization identify the key communication, interpersonal, creative, and project management skills that are required of engineers in assignments that extend beyond the tech-nical specialist role. While a business psychologist will use the candidate's application materials and test information as a starting point, more critical in-formation will come from the clinical interview. This interview explores the key behavioral dimensions that exemplify the special performance needs and the candidate's fit to the organization.

DANGEROUS PUBLIC SERVICE POSITIONS

Firefighters

Selecting firefighters is usually approached from one of two major directions: some fire departments only seek applicants who have previous firefighting training (usually obtained in vocational or technical school), while other departments accept untrained candidates. For the former departments, there will be some information available from the applicant's experience on whether or not the person can actually fight fires. The other fire departments, who do not require any previous exposure to methods or principles of firefighting, have a more difficult task. These departments must provide all the necessary training.

Entry-Level Firefighters. Most fire departments will request information on the applicant's education (usually requiring at least a high school degree) and any previous relevant experience (for example, military service). Many require background checks and personal interviews. While providing useful information, these techniques might not assess other equally important aspects of an applicant's qualifications. Firefighters must possess certain skills and abilities that ensure their safety as well as the safety of fellow firefighters. A psychological assessment can determine whether or not an applicant has these necessary skills and abilities.

Firefighters need good mechanical and spatial abilities to operate equipment and navigate through smoke-filled buildings. Written and oral communication is a daily part of a firefighter's life. The firefighter must be able to understand spoken direction and information from superiors and fellow firefighters, whether at the scene of a fire or while working around the firehouse. Firefighters are often called upon to present fire safety training to school children. Here the firefighter must be clear and articulate and must be able to communicate on an appropriate level with the audience. Technical reports on new firefighting techniques or reports of a firefighter's administrative activities require a firefighter to possess good written communication and reading skills. A psychological assessment helps identify applicants with the strong communications skills needed for success in this challenging profession.

Questions that help the psychologist evaluate the degree to which candidates demonstrate the abilities necessary for success include: "Describe the kind of firefighters who seem to build up morale and lend spirit and professionalism to the fire service. If you had a question about the procedures involved in using a complex piece of equipment, how would you find the answer? How are you at fixing things that do not work? What is your approach when you teach someone basic fire prevention? Have you ever lost your temper to the extent that it got you into trouble? Describe what happened. What do you feel are the critical aspects of a firefighter's performance? What has been the most dangerous situation you have had to face? Describe how you handled that situation. Describe why you became (or want to become) a firefighter.''

Firefighters typically live in close quarters with their co-workers and must, therefore, possess suitable interpersonal skills. These cannot be assessed by looking at most application materials. Psychological assessment provides both interview and test opportunities for an applicant to exhibit interpersonal skills appropriate for the living conditions and stresses experienced by firefighters. This is also true for the ability to learn—which is critical for those departments that do not require any previous firefighting training or experience.

Firefighting Officers. For officer-level positions, the psychological assessment is broadened to include behavioral dimensions such as technical knowledge, leadership, organization skills, planning effectiveness, decision-making speed and accuracy, decisiveness, stress tolerance, communication skills, and general interpersonal skills. As the level of responsibility increases, the dimensions dealing with management and leadership become more critical while those dealing with technical knowledge become less critical. The lower-ranked officers are, for the most part, field officers who are on the scene at fires and who need to address the emergencies quickly. This can include calling for assistance, taking action to save lives, and confining and extinguishing fires. These officers need to be good at giving clear verbal orders. They also have day-to-day responsibilities to work with firefighters on personal problems that can affect on-the-job performance.

Some departments also extend the specific behavioral competencies into attitudinal areas. These departments are looking for spirit of service, sincerity of purpose, devotion to duty, determination to improve, favorable attitudes toward progress, and sense of fair play. In the psychological assessment, the psychologist investigates these areas when judging the candidate's fit to the ''personality'' of the department and the community.

Fire Chiefs. Chiefs are a special challenge because of their dual role as administrative-operational manager for the force and community-political spokesperson. In a recent selection for its fire chief, a major metropolitan city identified the following mix of competencies as representative of its chief's job: public relations (20%), administration (20%), supervision (20%), judgment and decision-making (20%), written or oral communication (10%), and leadership (10%).

Questions that help the psychologist assess candidates at this level include: ''Describe a situation that was difficult or challenging from a public relations point of view. How did you handle that situation? How would you present your department's budget in order to win support for it? How would you handle a conflict with the mayor? How do you ensure that important tasks you delegate to others are actually completed? Describe a situation where you have had to discipline a firefighter or officer. How did you handle that situation? What was the result? How satisfied were you? What is the most difficult decision you have had to make as an officer? What do you find to be the most challenging part of being an officer?''

In addition to these questions, the assessment of fire chiefs often includes short simulations of job tasks. The following paragraphs are from the problem statement for a writing and analysis exercise given as a part of the assessment of fire chief candidates in a major metropolitan city.

Fact-finding Interview Instructions. In this exercise you will be presented with a problem situation. Your task is to gather as much additional information as you need to make specific recommendations as to the best way to handle the problem. The purpose of this exercise is to help determine your ability to gather information, to make decisions based on that information, and to present your decisions.

Fact-finding Interview Problem. The chief is out of town and you, as deputy chief, have been contacted by the mayor concerning a newspaper article very critical of the city's fire department. The article states that the Emergency Medical System is in jeopardy because of city and fire department mismanagement. Apparently, the critical information came from within the department and a couple of members are "quoted."

The mayor wants to know what is going on. All press releases are supposed to clear his office. He wants you to find out what happened, what the underlying problem is, and what needs to be done to solve this problem. You are to take corrective measures and report back to the mayor.

In this selection situation, the psychological assessment is included as one step in the selection process. A typical process could include the following steps:

1. All applications received by closing date are reviewed and evaluated by the fire commission.
2. The commission accepts or rejects candidates through initial review of applications.
3. Invited candidates are orally interviewed by the commission.
4. Selected candidates undergo psychological assessments.
5. The commission reviews the assessment results with the psychologist.
6. Selected candidates undergo medical and physical examinations.
7. Selected candidates undergo background investigation.
8. The commission makes its final selection.

Police Officers

The police officer of today has diverse duties and responsibilities. Like other technical experts, officers were originally selected primarily on the basis of their technical abilities to perform the basic duties of law enforcement. More recently, communities have begun to understand that not every person who is willing to try will necessarily make a good officer once hired and trained. A specific, definable set of personal characteristics and behavioral dimensions are common in successful officers. In addition, there are some distinct personal preference differences between individuals who will make good police officers and those who will make good firefighters. Police officers are more social service–oriented than firefighters. Police enjoy working with people more directly, and are more involved in community activities. Firefighters, on the other hand, are more practical in nature, enjoy hands-on work, and are more frequently involved in some kind of outside business. Police officers place more emphasis upon intellectual pursuits and often convey a more professional image. Firefighters are more rugged, and often have a handyman type of background.

Entry-Level Police Officers. Behavioral dimensions that indicate individuals who are likely to be good police officers include:

- Ability to communicate well with a wide variety of individuals
- Good judgment and decisiveness when a situation calls for it
- High achievement motivation—getting things done and willing to work hard to be successful
- Willingness to persist in efforts
- Ability to function appropriately under high stress
- Ability to understand and analyze the feelings and behavior of others
- Comfort with being the center of attention
- Willingness to dominate others if a situation calls for it (this is typically accomplished without the officer becoming directly aggressive)
- Motivated by a clear and defined ambition to serve the public through objective enforcement of the law

(Bauman & Graf 1986, 1987)

Hiring mistakes by police departments can be costly and embarrassing. Police officers are charged with the stressful job of protecting life and property. Entrusting such responsibilities to a person must be done with care. The psychological assessment might reveal whether or not an applicant has the emotional stability, intelligence, and motivation to be a successful police officer. Police assessments will often follow the standard psychological assessment format, while adding special instrumentation to examine personality and motivations. It is also common practice to add small job simulations. These are brief scenarios of typical on-the-job situations an officer may have to address. Applicants read the scenarios and then describe their responses and actions. They may also be queried about the reasons for taking particular actions.

Police Chiefs. Behavioral dimensions that are most critical for performance as senior police officers include:

- Ability to express self clearly and effectively, particularly when speaking before groups and to persons of diverse backgrounds
- Good problem-solving ability, including gathering information, identifying problems, and making logical decisions
- Ability to talk and correspond effectively with people without arousing antagonism
- Ability to make people feel at ease in one's presence
- Ability to write original and required reports, instructions, and correspondence of intradepartmental and interdepartmental nature
- Impartiality in conducting investigations involving possible violations of the law, complaints against officers, citizens, or environmental conditions
- Ability to decide on appropriate courses of action
- Skill in supervising uniformed and nonuniformed members of the department
- Effectiveness as the public relations official spokesperson for the department

While many of the questions used in the assessment of police chiefs are similar to those described elsewhere in this book as appropriate for top-level managers and executives, we have found a few questions to have particular merit. These include: "How would you describe your responsibilities as chief? Describe two specific incidents with respect to your present responsibilities: One in which you performed very well and one when you weren't so successful. How do you feel your experience in police work has affected your values? How do you feel your education has prepared you for the jobs you have held and the career you want? Describe the role of chief. What do you feel your biggest challenges will be as chief? What needs to be done? What are the highest priorities? What are your objectives for the future as chief of the department? Have you ever had what you would consider a really tough problem in human relations? Describe the problem and your solution. How do your subordinates feel about you? Are there particular things that irk you when you are trying to get something done and the people or the group doesn't seem to cooperate? How do you handle your own pressures and tensions?"

SUMMARY

Technical jobs spread over a wide range of job content. At one end of the scale are straightforward jobs of a practical nature. In these jobs the technical component involves understanding the special knowledge that is unique to the position and the practical application of that knowledge to the problems met on the job. Many entry-level technical jobs have such requirements. Examples discussed in this chapter included entry-level IS personnel, firefighters, police officers, and accountants. On the other extreme are jobs that have highly sophisticated technical content, the need for top-level mental abilities, and that require skill in management. Examples discussed in this chapter include top-level IS managers, creative project managers, fire chiefs, police chiefs, and chief financial officers.

Many technical jobs require the job holder to take full advantage of educational opportunities in order to develop the tremendous body of knowledge and skills needed on the job. The challenge to the psychologist completing assessments of technical people is to be clear about characteristics that are assets or liabilities to effective performance. To interview people for technical jobs, the psychologist needs a thorough knowledge of the jobs. This begins with the psychologist spending time in the job setting, becoming familiar with the working conditions, physical demands, occupational hazards, and other factors in the work setting. Next, the psychologist will talk with the manager or supervisor to understand his or her views on what is important for success in the job. The job study will often extend to job holders and to research reported in business and professional publications. All this concludes with a job specification that describes the traits and abilities that appear most important for successful performance on the job. Careful attention to this process enables the psychologist to complete accurate assessments for a number of diverse technical positions.

REFERENCES

Bauman, R. C., & Graf, J. M. (Nov.-Dec. 1986). Current parameters and techniques in the selection of police officers: Part I. *The Wisconsin Police Chief*, 8–10.

———. (Jan.-Feb. 1987). Current parameters and techniques in the selection of police officers: Part II. *The Wisconsin Police Chief*, 8–10.

Ferreira, J., & Harris, P. R. (1986). The changing roles of MIS professionals. In *Handbook of MIS management*, ed. by R. E. Unbaugh. Boston: Auerbauch Publishers, Inc., 216–29.

Hurley, K., Wong, R., & Joiner, D. A. (1982). Description of the San Francisco police captain assessment center. *Journal of Assessment Center Technology* 5 (1): 23–28.

Magaldi, R. J., Mendoza, R. H., Jr., Stafford, G. T., & Frank, F. D. (1984). Police promotional level assessment center: The metro-Dade police department experience—focus on race, sex, and assessment center cycle. *Journal of Assessment Center Technology* 7 (2): 9–16.

Raudsepp, E. (Jan. 1976). What makes an engineer creative? *Chemical Engineering*, 147–52.

14

The Psychological Assessment of Advertising and Marketing Professionals

**Deborah L. Parker and
Kelley A. Conrad**

The advertising industry is an environment that presents any manager with unique challenges in managing human resources and facilitating work. The coordination of a number of inherently different tasks is further complicated by the symphony of forceful personalities usually present. Creative, nonroutine work must be processed efficiently in an environment full of deadlines and dynamic, sometimes arbitrary, demands.

The purpose of this chapter is to highlight some important considerations that bear on the selection of executives and managers in both the creative and non-creative areas of advertising agencies. A brief description of broader executive and managerial positions is followed by a discussion of considerations that are especially important when consulting in the advertising industry. These descriptions are followed by the specific factors that we address during the psychological assessment process for the different positions.

Advertising agencies are generally quite unique organizations. Creatively focused agencies and operationally focused agencies have very different organizational goals and structures. Within the operationally focused agency, we will discuss the account service and account executive positions. Within the creatively focused agency, we will discuss the standard creative position and the creative director position. The general responsibilities that we describe are likely to be dispersed differently in different agencies. Our intention is to highlight key differences in skills and responsibilities at both the executive and nonexecutive levels.

TOTAL AGENCY CONSIDERATIONS

It is important to consider a number of agency-specific factors while conducting assessments for the selection of advertising executives. A clear understanding of the environment in which an individual will be performing is critical in matching individual skills, personal characteristics, and expectations to agency needs.

Organizational Culture

Understanding the predominant values and beliefs that underlie the agency operations is critical when identifying individuals whose personal characteristics are well-suited to the organization. Understanding elements such as leadership style, communication patterns, and the public image of an agency support the psychologist in the identification of individuals who will fit well.

A predominant issue to consider is whether the agency is creatively driven or operationally driven. For example, it is a risk to hire a creative director who is accustomed to giving creative needs first priority for a position at a strongly pragmatic and account management–driven organization.

Organizational Structure

Understanding organizational structure is important base knowledge. For example, some agencies require strategic thinking at the level of account service. They call the personnel responsible for daily client interaction ''account executives.'' It is critical to know how responsibilities are divided throughout an organization so that individual skills and experiences are well matched to the position.

Occupational Stress

The advertising industry is one of the most stressful businesses with which we have worked. Individuals must have tremendous flexibility because of changing demands, multiple deadlines, frequent overnight travel, and late night project work. Stamina, resilience, and emotional stability are critical when dealing with that level of stress.

Turnover

Another area of importance, and an additional stressor within advertising jobs, is the low job security. This is often referred to as the ''throw-away mentality'' of the advertising industry. Frequently, individuals are terminated as the result of one failure, even after a long history of successful performance. Contributing to this is the fact that many skilled, effective performers can be laid off or terminated when an agency loses a major account. Job security remains low regardless of one's abilities. Movement back and forth between various agencies is high, and severance packages are limited.

Merging and Coordinating Highly Diverse Tasks

Coordinating creative with administrative tasks and project management is like trying to blend oil and water. This requires the advertising executive to skillfully respond to both administrative and interpersonal needs. The executive must be able to bring out the best in people, yet allow for their creative needs and expression.

Forceful Personalities

Creative personnel are asked, by virtue of their roles, to draw products from within themselves. The dynamic and stressful environment of the advertising industry, combined with the creative requirements of the work, require strongly self-confident, energetic, forceful, and resilient individuals. Such individuals are a challenge to manage and are not easily motivated by simplistic or authoritarian approaches. The advertising executive must develop keen insights into individual values and priorities and must use these insights when assigning tasks, developing subordinates, exercising discipline, and maintaining momentum and timely production.

TAILORING THE ASSESSMENT PROCESS

When conducting psychological assessments for the selection of key personnel for an advertising agency, the main focus of the psychologist is on matching individual skills, needs, and values with organizational processes, requirements, and other characteristics. During the assessment process, the psychologist emphasizes obtaining samples of behavior appropriate for the position and agency under consideration.

ASSESSING ACCOUNT SERVICE PERSONNEL

Description of Position

Account service personnel could also be called account supervisors or coordinators. They direct the overall services provided to designated clients and serve as the key connecting points between the client and the agency. They assume responsibility for strategies, programs, communications plans, and budgets that are developed and presented to clients. They fulfill the role of coordinator and leader, but rarely receive a lot of recognition or operate in the limelight. They must motivate, discipline, and sell the creative personnel on completing assignments on time, within budget, and following the agreed-upon plan.

Vital skills that are critical to account service personnel are the following:

- Excellent planning and organizational skills
- Ability to track progress and maintain momentum
- Flexibility in managing interpersonal relationships
- Ability to identify key decision makers
- Excellent listening skills
- Ability to identify business and marketing needs
- Ability to manage client structure
- Sensitivity to different individuals and perspectives
- Ability to be proactive in raising ideas
- Excellent writing skills
- Excellent presentation skills

Evaluating Account Service Personnel

When assessing candidates for positions such as those in account servicing, we focus on skills most similar to those of a strong middle manager (see Chapter 8). Strong administrative skills combined with interpersonal flexibility and sensitivity are central to success in the advertising industry. Communication skills and personal impact are also important factors that influence an individual's ability to develop influential relationships with clients at various levels of management.

There are additional factors, however, that are particularly important to target during our assessments.

Leadership. A unique style of leadership is required of the account service person. This position requires an individual who is comfortable in a liaison role, with heavy responsibilities for coordination and project management. At the same time, however, this individual operates with low visibility and receives little public recognition.

During the interview, we ask candidates to describe past leadership experiences and focus on discussion of how the individual facilitates work and articulates action plans. We look for a solid comfort level with leadership responsibilities, both in the interview and on paper-and-pencil tests. Additionally, we assess whether or not the individual has a strong need for recognition and visibility.

Expectations. For any of the administrative positions in advertising agencies, it is important to evaluate the candidate's expectations regarding the responsibilities of the position. A candidate's expectations in regard to workload or other job characteristics can indicate whether or not that person has a realistic view of the position. One way to clarify that is to ask exactly what the candidate did in previous jobs. Of course, it is vital for the psychologist to have a clear understanding of the organization's expectations for the position.

Stress Tolerance and Stamina. Energy level and indicated adaptability in the interview and in test profiles are considered in determining the degree to which an individual will be comfortable responding to the demands of the position. Descriptions of general work patterns and habits also support conclusions drawn in this area.

Communication Skills. In the advertising industry, the oral and written communication skills that are needed are generally above the average range, even for successful middle managers. Strong listening skills, the ability to be succinct, and skill in organization are all factors that we look for in writing samples and during the interview. Excellent presentation skills are so critical that we often request candidates complete a brief exercise demonstrating their presentation skills.

Interpersonal Skills. The account service area demands that an individual have a broad repertoire of skills in the interpersonal arena. The individual must be assertive enough to raise and press issues without appearing to be taking decision-making authority from clients or superiors. Diplomacy and the ability to appreciate other points of view are skills that support the individual in liaison and coordination activities.

During the interview we ask the candidate to provide some examples of situations that have required some interpersonal finesse. We also ask the candidate to describe projects, and how he or she went about motivating and coordinating the people involved in order to complete the task successfully. Strong candidates will demonstrate characteristics such as the ability to include appropriate people in meetings, check progress without pressuring people in a negative fashion, and track the budget.

Emotional Resiliency. For all four of the key positions in agencies, individuals adapt most successfully if they have the ability to manage stress, rejection, and substantial conflict. A number of personal characteristics and skills can support an individual in such an environment. High levels of self-confidence, self-satisfaction, and assertiveness all provide such support. The ability to accept and learn from constructive criticism is also a key factor.

In assessing emotional resiliency, it is important to look beyond test profiles. During the interview we discuss past experiences, such as transitions and other stressful circumstances. We note the relative ease with which the individual manages such situations. Adaptability, comfort with uncertainty, and the ability to learn from mistakes without feeling defeated are factors that support an individual in a turbulent environment.

The skills listed above are critical for success in most positions of operational responsibility in an advertising agency. As positions change, additional and, in some cases, distinctly different skills become appropriate.

ASSESSING ACCOUNT EXECUTIVES

Description of Position

Account executives need to have all of the skills of the account service personnel, and in addition, must have broader general management skills. Frequently, account executives are responsible for long-term marketing strategies for groups of key accounts. They are responsible for coordinating the manpower necessary to keep individual projects on target and on time.

Evaluating Account Executives

The account executive shifts focus from serving clients as a project manager to serving the agency as an internal facilitator and the client as a strategic planner. The account executive must interface effectively with creative and noncreative groups. They also need to be able to envision and develop broad client marketing strategies.

Another critical skill for the account executive is the ability to train and develop subordinates. Account executives must hire, conduct performance reviews, and also have the courage to terminate individuals who are not performing.

Account executives are also frequently responsible for developing agency systems and procedures, as well as project fee development. They support service personnel in searching out and recommending areas where the client might be served better, and ensure that the client receives more than requested in service, creativity, and consultation.

Two critical skill areas are added at the account executive level of functioning.

Ability to Think and to Plan Strategically. At the level of account executive, the individual must be able to think well beyond one creative ''spot'' or project. He or she must be able to identify business opportunities and develop long-term marketing strategies. In this area we look for examples where the candidate used industry knowledge and a long-term focus in developing and selling advertising strategies to clients. We are sensitive to the fit between the individual's approaches and those of the client organization.

Human Resources Management Skills. Another task of the account executive is the hiring, training, managing, and, if necessary, terminating of employees. Account executives need to have a genuine interest in people and their ongoing professional development. They need to guard against adopting a strongly task-focused approach to management in the agency's turbulent environment.

We look for examples that demonstrate the ability to clearly articulate action plans and to coordinate multiple groups and activities. A candidate with high potential will use knowledge about individual strengths, weaknesses, and preferred activities in making task assignments.

Summary

It is evident that there is overlap in the skills necessary for success in the operational responsibilities for an advertising agency. Planning and organization skills, client interface, persuasiveness, presentation skills, and interpersonal skills are all critical. The account executive must adopt a broader business perspective while actively managing enormous amounts of work through other people. In the key operational positions, it is critical for the individual to be able to articulate client needs and abstract ideas to creative contributors. Hence, communication skills and social adaptability are baseline requirements.

ASSESSING CREATIVE CONTRIBUTORS

Description of Position

The creative contributors are individuals whose primary purpose is to produce the actual artistic products that compose advertising campaigns. In many cases, they are simply referred to as "creatives." Copywriters and graphic artists are examples of creative positions. Employees in creative roles are responsible for generating compelling ideas that are unique, but which remain strictly related to selling the product.

A major challenge to the creative contributor in advertising is that the individual is faced with producing creative material against a number of constraints and deadlines. Hence, the creative contributor must be able to address detail and work in an organized fashion. Some key skills are the following:

- The ability to produce unusually creative work while meeting a concrete business objective
- The ability to attend to production details and track progress
- The ability to maintain a realistic focus
- The ability to stay within budget
- The ability to interact effectively with people

Many of the skills described earlier are also critical for creative contributors. Advertising agencies constantly face the challenge of identifying creative people who can also plan, prioritize, and organize effectively. The successful person must be able to communicate and present ideas effectively. A key consideration during the assessment of creative personnel is that of fit between the organizational needs and the candidate's work style and expectations.

This includes defining exactly the level and style of creative work needed by the organization. It is critical to match the expectations of both parties. For example, an individual who is accustomed to working with large budgets in a highly modern facility and working with complex tasks might not be a good fit to a position that is responsible for accounts that have small budget allowances and the use of a limited number of expressive modalities.

Evaluating Creative Contributors

We frequently spend extensive time in the assessment process with creative contributors. It is important to allow them to express what they feel is important. Occasionally, we allow candidates to walk through their portfolios. Candidates are well accustomed to selling themselves, operating as they do in sales-oriented situations. The psychologist must exert significant effort toward maintaining objectivity as opposed to being "sold" by a savvy candidate.

The advertising industry places demands upon the clinical skills brought to the assessment process by the psychologist. The psychologist must be sensitive to subtle indicators of emotional instability or a temperament that would be incompatible with the needs and demands of the position. For example, creative contributors must be able to maintain a realistic focus and accept constructive criticism. The psychologist is alert to subtle cues that indicate issues with authority, inappropriate sensitivity, or difficulty managing stress.

Creativity. Standard intellectual indices do not necessarily apply to the creative contributor. A walk through the portfolio is one of the most straightforward ways to evaluate the suitability of the candidate's creative work with the needs of the position. We construct questions to learn how the creative person believes he or she generates material and how the person produces material as deadlines approach, or when stuck for ideas.

The Rorschach Ink Blot Test is often a useful tool for evaluating creativity and problem-solving style. We track the number of ideas that are generated in response to each card, as well as the novelty of the ideas. We also look for indications that the individual views things from different perspectives and expands on ideas. A systematic pattern of examination can indicate analytical and, to some degree, organizational skills.

ASSESSING FOR CREATIVE DIRECTOR

Description of Position

At the executive level, the creative director is responsible for the leadership and administration of current departments. The creative director handles the evaluation and upgrading of creative products, as well as interviewing, hiring, and supervising creative department personnel. The director provides guidance throughout the department by carrying out administrative functions, monitoring workloads, making creative team assignments, and shifting accounts when necessary. The creative director must maintain familiarity with all jobs in development in order to address any problems. A summary of the key skills for a creative director is provided in David Ogilvy's (1983) book, *On Advertising*. The creative director must:

- Set high standards
- Command strong administrative skills
- Be capable of "positioning" and strategic thinking
- Be comfortable with research and analysis
- Be comfortable with television and print
- Be well-versed in graphics and topology
- Work hard and fast
- Share credit and accept responsibility
- Command diplomacy
- Command excellent communication and presentation skills
- Be a good teacher and recruiter
- Command charisma

Assessing the Creative Director

Creative directors are responsible for judging, as opposed to developing, creative product. They must determine whether or not a given idea supports the marketing objective of the client's campaign. They must merge marketing research with broad concepts and long-term themes when envisioning creative strategies.

In general, creative contributors must balance the generation of creative ideas with a realistic focus on business objectives. They must be able to attend to production details and command the interpersonal skills necessary to operate on project teams. In regular creative positions there is less emphasis placed upon logical, analytical, and organizational skills. Responsibilities as creative director, however, present challenges requiring far more than creative skills.

Many agencies promote the most "creative" artistic contributor in the organization to the position of creative director. This is frequently a mismatch, because the creative director needs many of the same operational, strategic thinking, and human resources management responsibilities that the account executive has.

Creative directors must be able to develop long-term strategies, operating more as a judge of creative work than as a producer of creative material. Broad thinking and the ability to give and take within client negotiations are critical. One of the areas that we emphasize during the assessment of the creative director is the description of what the candidate has done in the past. From this we can evaluate comfort level with managerial activities.

Creative directors also face high demands in the area of interpersonal skills. They must extend themselves socially with clients and exercise a keen understanding of others' perspectives, needs, and motives. These characteristics are often hard to find in candidates who have been primarily individual contributors in the past.

Supporting, training, and judging the work of others is another key area of responsibility for the creative director. It is important to assess the expectations of the candidate regarding supervisory responsibilities and their comfort level with a leadership role, as opposed to a strictly creative role. The ability to resolve conflict and manage interpersonal as well as task-related stress is critical. Again, the psychologist uses clinical interviewing skills along with test profiles to determine the degree of fit between the candidate and the organizational needs.

SUMMARY

Four key positions of responsibility in the advertising industry were described and special considerations that bear on the selection of advertising managers were presented. The demands of the advertising industry are unusual in that individuals must frequently possess administrative and interpersonal skills as well as creative capacity.

In assessing candidates for key positions in advertising, the psychologist must command a clear understanding of unique characteristics of the client organization. Assessments focus upon identifying the relative degree of fit between the candidate and the needs of the organization. Assessments for advertising are typically lengthy and require the psychologist to use clinical skills in the interview.

REFERENCES

Ogilvy, D. (1983). *Ogilvy on advertising*. New York: Vintage Books.
Schein, E. G. (1985). *Organizational culture and leadership*. San Francisco, Calif.: Jossey-Bass Publishers.

15

Psychological Assessment in International Business

RHR International

[T]he more we consider our views and experiences to be absolute and universal, the less prepared we are to deal with people who have different backgrounds, experiences, culture and therefore different views of the universe.

(Szalay, 1981)

In today's competitive business environment, with the globalization of trade and internationalization of corporations, transnational career assignments are vital to the organization's and the employee's vitality and future growth. Indeed, to survive locally, an organization needs to think and act globally. Competing only in your home market is a blueprint for decline. The agility required to shift from a domestic to an international focus pays off—in innovation, improved quality, greater competitiveness, and increased profits—even for smaller firms.

The key to success is to make sure you have the right people, in the right positions, in the right locations to capitalize on the international opportunities. Usually such assignment decisions are made on the basis of a person's availability, professional accomplishments, and technical expertise. However, because of the unique adaptation demands of such assignments, success in the position is not guaranteed by professional credentials; personal characteristics weigh heavily in the equation. This chapter addresses how a thorough understanding of the placement context and the individual under consideration will help you make better assignment decisions. Further, it will explain the processes involved if you should decide that psychological assessment, provided by an outside consultant, can assist you in these decisions.

THE IMPORTANCE OF GOOD ASSIGNMENT DECISIONS IN INTERNATIONAL BUSINESS

International assignment decisions have high importance in overall corporate strategy. These decisions play on a world stage. Operating on a worldwide basis increases organizational complexity. Selecting the right people for international positions is of critical importance because of the need to work with these people to coordinate the efforts of the two entities and overcome the barriers of distance, time, language, and culture brought on by far-flung operations. Also, the person in the subsidiary is functioning as your firm's representative to that country. Your reputation rides on the employee's performance.

The economic consequences of international assignment decisions are high for both the employee and the organization. A poor assignment decision has extremely high economic consequences—hard and soft—in international situations. The immediate hard costs are easily seen. It has been estimated that between 20 and 50 percent of the personnel sent abroad return prematurely from their overseas assignments; the average hard cost to the parent company of each failure ranges between $55,000 and $150,000 (Mendenhall, Dunbar, and Oddou 1987). However, these figures do not begin to measure the true cost of the error to the organization; they are easily corrected with a fixed amount of money. Harder to see, but even more costly to the organization, is the intangible, ongoing damage done by the poor selection. It diminishes the company's worldwide reputation, which has ramifications in markets beyond those of the particular affiliate. It affects the morale of all employees (not just the selected person) in both parties. It negatively affects the relationship between the two entities. And, most destructively of all: It inhibits the organization's growth. It prevents the company from seizing opportunities. One company estimated the difference to its profits caused by hiring an average versus a superior performer to oversee its international operations to be in the ballpark of a million dollars a year (Canadian Manager 1989). Given these types of numbers, the effort put into superior international assignment decisions is a very sound investment.

What makes international assignment decisions difficult is the fact that the ground rules one takes for granted when operating in one's home environment are not the same across different environments. When functioning in an international climate, the organization is faced with the task of managing, or coordinating with, people from other cultures. Systematic thought of how best to manage the issues this creates is just in its infancy. What we do know for sure is that applying current, "country-specific" human resource management techniques to an international context is inadequate. Just as there is no manager who is perfect for every situation, there is no management style that is perfect for every culture.

Management occurs within a context. In order to manage well, it is necessary to understand the management context. Americans, in particular, have been slow to understand and accept the impact of national cultural differences on organizational cultures and the consequences for the management of employees. American bias is toward individual initiative, free will, and the concept of an ethnic melting pot. As such, Americans have tended to think that basically people are the same and that good management is the same in Jakarta as it is in Pittsburgh. Recently, this attitude has been changing.

THE INTERNATIONALIZATION OF TRADE

The recent economic events of European integration, the free-trade pact between the United States and Canada and the potential free-trade pact with Mexico, and the opening up of Eastern Europe and the Soviet Union to market forces set the stage for accelerating the increase in international trade flows. Between 1950 and 1985, international trade flows increased over 500 percent (*The Economist* September 22, 1990). There has been a globalization of sourcing, markets, and financing. Every company, no matter how large or small, is affected by this globalization of commerce.

A case in point is a U.S.-based food supplier of preservatives. The CEO received a telephone call from a major customer that indicated that in order to maintain the company's status as a primary supplier, it must organize its own operations along the same lines as the customer. In order to do this, they have had to commit resources to dedicated facilities overseas, as well as create organizational structures that align with those of the customer. These moves have forced top management to reconsider not only the way the organization is structured, but also the type of management talent needed to cross organizational lines and international boundaries in order to meet customer needs.

In today's environment of shortened product life cycles, innovation is a critical competitive element. Exposure to different environments with their different learning opportunities gives international corporations a significant potential advantage over their nationally constrained competitors. The inevitable result of these trends has been more multinational cooperative ventures and the internationalization of corporations. More and more, companies are finding themselves involved in international relationships. In order to deal effectively with these new international relationships, executives must have a good understanding of the people involved, the new people they may need, how to use their current employees most effectively, and how to develop their people to be successful internationally.

The success of Japanese companies has opened American eyes to the world of international competition and different ways of managing. This trend has intensified because Japanese transplants in the United States have shown that the same pool of workers selected and managed differently often can outperform their traditional U.S. counterparts. Japanese companies offer a good example in another way. They too have had to (sometimes grudgingly) adapt their styles to meet the norms and values of American employees. Further, with the economic growth that Europe and East Asia have experienced over the past two decades,

American businesses have realized that to be the top players in their industries, they have to be actively involved in these two markets. Once involved in these markets, they soon realize that the ways to success are rarely exactly the same as back home in North America. They also quickly realize that it is even more difficult to select managers who will be successful in international assignments than it already is to select successful managers within their home organization.

Different companies—basing their strategies on their unique mix of product and market—have used different types of corporate structures to deal with this increased internationalization. Each type of structure has direct consequences for what is needed in their people. Expanding on the work of Bartlett and Ghoshal (1989), the following describes the four major types of corporate structures that have been used to manage internationalization, as well as the consequences of each for the people component. Up to this point we have used such terms as global, international, and transnational interchangeably. Bartlett and Ghoshal (1989) attach these terms to particular types of corporate structures.

Global

The global organization's structure is characterized by a high degree of centralization. The home office views the foreign operations as distribution centers. Bartlett and Ghoshal (1989) use the phrase "centralized hub" to describe this type of organization. The person in the managerial role in the affiliate could be seen by the home office as either part of or not part of the executive team. If the latter, then the ability of the person to function as an independent distributor fully integrated into that market would be at a premium. If the former, then the manager's ability to maintain his corporate identity while simultaneously immersing himself in the marketing characteristics of the affiliate's culture would be at a premium.

International

The international organization's structure is characterized by multiple entities revolving around a centralized hub. The home office views the foreign operations as conduits for its expertise, as well as sources of information. Bartlett and Ghoshal (1989) use the phrase "coordinated federation" to describe this type of organization. Turning to the ramifications for the people component of such a structure, a manager's ability to coordinate between the two entities (i.e., home office and affiliate) would be at a premium. Consequently, you would look at all the elements that go into an executive who can function as both a leader and a team player—plus; the plus being that the person needs to not only balance his loyalties across the two entities but also must balance his being a part of two different cultures without alienating either.

Multinational

The multinational organization's structure is characterized by multiple entities, each with a high degree of autonomy, loosely connected across national boundaries. Within this type of organization, the home office views its affiliates as a collection of related, but independent businesses. Bartlett and Ghoshal (1989) use the phrase "decentralized federation" to describe this type of organization. There are many ramifications of such an organizational set-up for the management of human resources. At the leadership level, when choosing a head for an affiliate, the person's psychological ability to assume the responsibility necessary to serve as the head of an independent business with a minimum of home office supervision would be at a premium. In essence, you are selecting the CEO of a company, and all the psychological elements that go into the selection of top-level executives should be employed here—plus; the plus here being the ability to evaluate the person's ability to function in the other culture.

Transnational

The transnational organization is driven simultaneously by the demands of global efficiency, national responsiveness, worldwide learning, and transference of knowledge. Its structure is characterized by a complex configuration of reciprocal interdependencies that optimizes the distribution of capabilities and resources. Bartlett and Ghoshal (1989) use the phrase "integrated network" to characterize this type of organization. The building of organizational capabilities rather than a specific organizational structure is its guiding principle. The type of manager required will depend on the characteristics of the market the affiliate is serving. Hence, this can be a variant of any of the roles discussed above. However, for top-level management within this type of organization, personal features such as flexibility and adaptability, as well as the ability to obtain the individual commitment of each employee to a shared vision, the ability to coordinate the efforts of the management members, the ability to view situations from a systems perspective, and the ability to take a broad view of competitive challenges are a must.

Firms are currently giving much thought as to how to best structure their corporations to meet the demands of globalization. The same energy and thought need to be devoted to the task of how to best integrate their human resources for their worldwide efforts. A starting point would be to integrate human resource efforts around this rallying point. Firms often have a good amount of information about their people and the demands of their different corporate cultures. The problem is that this information is not used constructively. Assignment mistakes get made that in retrospect could have been avoided if information had been used proactively.

International strategies require capable managers who have—or can develop—an international perspective. However, this type of manager is the most scarce of all resources. The firms that have these people are going to be the most successful in the '90s. Given that globalization is already happening, firms are being confronted with international assignment decisions now (and, indeed, some firms have been facing this issue for a long time). Decisions are being made. Because adequate information is lacking, these decisions usually are made by trial and error.

International assignment decisions are high-risk, and high-reward, decisions. When top-level management makes a decision that contains both high risk and high reward, they seek out the best information and counsel they can find. They often bring in an expert to facilitate the decision. The purpose is to help control risk and exploit opportunities, to handle certain steps of the decision process or to orchestrate the process itself. The assessment of individuals for international assignments can help to control the risk and maximize gain in the selection, placement, and development of these personnel.

Psychological assessment in international business is a specialty. To do it well, you need to know all the types of information about psychological assessment covered in this book and more. You need to consider the relevant cultural elements that will affect the assessment, evaluation, and development of candidates. To sum up, when you find yourself asking the following two questions, then it is important to do an international psychological assessment: (1) Can the person do the job in the other environment? (2) Can the person successfully coordinate—at the required level—his or her efforts with me?

The Relationship Between the Consultant and the Organization

The assessment, placement, and development procedure is a process that involves active interplay and cooperation between the consultant and the organization. It requires openness on both sides, clear expectations, and definite goals. However, a consultant in international assignment assessments is a specialist. The consultant is trained to understand management capability in relation to, for instance, what leadership means in a particular culture.

In the beginning of the working relationship, the consultant needs easy access to the management member who has the responsibility for the international assignment. Both persons will have to exchange information frequently. This flow of information enables both parties to develop an in-depth understanding of the context for the assessment. At the start, the consultant must study the position in question with top management to understand how it fits into the structure of the across-the-border entity. A new job description might be needed. The consultant must interview top management in order to understand the parent organization's corporate culture. The consultant also interviews the managers who will work with the prospective candidate in order to develop an understanding of the type of management style that will be needed to be effective. Finally, if practical, visits to the cross-border company would be useful to develop a better appreciation of its organizational climate.

Complexities of Psychological Assessment in Cross-National Situations

In order to help find the best match between person and position in cases of international, or more aptly, cross-national assignments, the assessor needs to consider the interrelationship between the organization's overall structure, the culture of the two relevant divisions of the organization, the country culture that each division is operating in, and the considered individual's background, management beliefs, personality, and family situation. The starting point is the company's international structure. Once the organization's overall structure is known, we begin to understand the relationship that exists between the home office and the affiliate and the consequences of this particular type of relationship for the people component of the assignment decision.

As has been discussed in a preceding section, the international structure of the organization determines the general dimensions of the management style that is required. Additionally, one needs to be aware of the interplay between the organization's overriding structure and the type of assignment decision. In other words: (1) whether the organization is structured along global, international, multinational, or transnational lines; and (2) whether the particular assignment decision is one that involves (a) sending a person from the home office to the affiliate; (b) bringing a person from the affiliate to the home office; (c) transferring a person from one affiliate to another; or (d) including the home office in selecting a person for the affiliate from the affiliate's home base. Taking the time to understand the history of the relationship between the home office and the affiliate can be an easy way to prevent repeating mistakes.

The next step for fully understanding the position involves an understanding of the corporate culture in both divisions of the company. As will be detailed later, it is erroneous to assume that because it is one organization it has only one corporate culture that has been cloned onto each of its parts. Each division develops its own unique culture, and since each will—to a lesser or greater degree—influence the effectiveness of the selected candidate, it is important to have a basic understanding of the two corporate cultural contexts. Yet to truly understand each corporate culture, one must be aware of the surrounding national cultural context in which each entity operates. The country culture exerts a powerful influence on the corporate culture, sets the expectations for appropriate managerial/leadership behavior, and shapes each individual's style of interpersonal interaction.

Individual behavioral characteristics that are influenced by the national culture, in turn, influence the company's corporate culture, as well as the way the company leans toward organizing itself. As an illustration of how these factors can interact, consider that the Japanese emphasis on interpersonal harmony and group cohesiveness, which gives special importance to face-to-face encounters, works naturally toward a more centralized organizational structure. Consequently, this has been one factor that has led Japanese companies to be highly centralized in their internal organization, and global (in Bartlett & Ghoshal's terminology) in their international structure. Further, through defining the role that the affiliate plays, it also has implications for the person-position match. American egalitarianism and individual competition also have implications for structure.

Once the assessor has this basic understanding of the context of the position, the assessment can be refined to meet the particular needs of the situation. Further, by developing an understanding of the characteristics that are more likely to bring success in the situation, the consultant can evaluate candidates with an eye toward helping the organization make better assignment decisions. Therefore, the assessment will pay particular attention to those elements that are important for cross-cultural assignment. The assessment of the individual will include an understanding of the person's development or background, management style or management beliefs, personality, and family situation.

The assessment approach is a contextual one. While one's understanding of each of these elements will never be perfect, the better one understands each of these elements, the more successful the corporation will be in its decisions concerning which person, for which position, in which location. Since it will be rare to find a candidate who is the perfect match for the unique demands of the position, this type of thorough assessment allows the company and the individual to put together plans for addressing those areas in need of continued development. A pictorial representation of this contextual approach, which gives an overview of the process of psychological assessment in international (or cross-national) business, is given in Exhibit 15–1. The details of the process will be developed in the remainder of the chapter.

PSYCHOLOGICAL ASSESSMENT IN CROSS-NATIONAL SELECTION DECISIONS

While the idea behind "knowing your organization" might seem abstract, the management actions that flow from this knowledge are very concrete. One of the more visible actions is building the people organization. The best companies know that the best talent comes from a worldwide recruiting effort. Building a world-class organization begins with assembling world-class talent. There is a need to recruit people who are able to have an international perspective. Psychological assessment provides important information to guide your selection decisions. While in domestic selection and placement decisions you might feel capable of making good decisions through experience and sensitivity, in the international arena the use of an outside expert can prove invaluable.

There are differences in cultural expectations regarding effective management techniques and style that are not eliminated by a strong corporate cultural en-

Exhibit 15–1
Matrix of Factors Used in Psychological Assessment for International Business

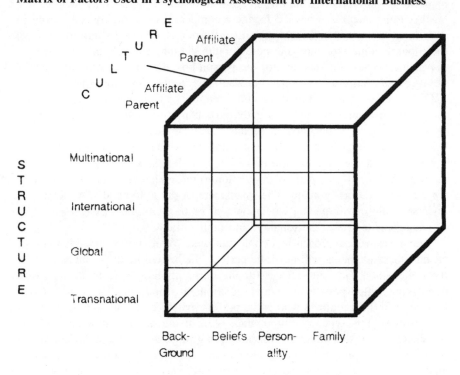

INDIVIDUAL

vironment. Laurent's (1986) research within a large U.S. multinational company demonstrates this point. Laurent found that native managers (managers functioning in their home countries) across the multinational's various European affiliates showed no convergence in their views on management, even though they were working for the same firm. These findings were similar to what he had found working with managers in nonrelated firms. Together, these findings lead to the conclusion that an individual's assumptions about the nature of management are much more strongly shaped by the person's national culture than by his or her experiences working within the culture of a particular corporation.

Laurent looked at the firm's affiliates in Britain, Holland, Germany, France, and the United States. These are some of the differences he found between the cultures as to what characteristics are considered necessary to be an effective manager. The German managers held a rational view of management and placed an emphasis on professional knowledge and competence. For French managers, the key to being a successful manager was the ability to handle the social aspects of the organization. Therefore, they placed particular emphasis on the ability to negotiate the power relationships inherent in the organizational hierarchy. The British managers viewed managing in terms of influencing others. Consequently, they emphasized conveying the proper image and being good at communicating and negotiating.

Considering these findings, it would be difficult to view candidate selection as simply matching a candidate's qualities against a single model of an effective manager that could be used in all cultural contexts. Using Laurent's phase, there is no "Management with a capital M." There are variants of effective management, and effective managerial characteristics, based on cultural and corporate expectations. As a consequence, human resource management, which starts with effective candidate selection, is one of the most challenging tasks for companies that function across national and cultural boundaries. Consider the following situation:

The Far Eastern subsidiary of an American manufacturing company is based in Japan. After an initial period of rapid growth throughout the 1970s and early 1980s, sales started flattening out. The company's major competitor in the Far East began gaining market share in the latter half of the 1980s, even though their products offered no substantive price or quality advantage. The vice-president of international operations in the United States attributed this loss of market share to the lack of aggressiveness on the part of the general manager of the affiliate. He vowed that the next president of this affiliate would be a take-charge, highly aggressive, turnaround specialist who would shake up the affiliate and regain the momentum that had been lost.

Once the consultant psychologist and the company's president and vice-president of international operations discussed the position in detail, the consultant was able to point out that while the affiliate needed forceful turnaround management, the person needed to be able to do this within a Japanese (and not American) context. The selected person would have to be aggressive and directive, but within a patient, consensus-driven mode that would be respected by the Japanese staff. Too unidimensional a manager in either direction would fail.

Candidates from Inside the Organization

In selecting from your own people, motivation is a primary requisite—does the person really want to work in another country? The person must have more than an interest in foreign travel. The person must have a cultural awareness— a willingness to probe for the reasons why people in other cultures behave the way they do—as well as openness to accepting others. Look for a person who can be a leader in another country rather than within the familiar, home, corporate culture. International assignment often involves both a transfer and a promotion. What are the political consequences in both the parent and the subsidiary? Each firm needs to consider how its corporate culture perceives international assignment. Is it desirable to take an international transfer? How does it fit with the individual's overall development plan?

Candidates from Outside the Organization

Each candidate brings individual idiosyncratic conceptions of effective management, based on their cultural predispositions and personal experiences, into the new situation. The selection fit then becomes a matter of evaluating candidates by taking into account the needed characteristics dictated by the parent organization's structure and culture, as well as the distinct needs of the affiliate, based on its own structure and culture.

Placement Decisions

Assuming that the assessment findings are positive about such factors as the candidate's attitudes, personality, and management skills, there is still the question of putting the right person in the right place in the organization. Cultural adaptation, language skill, and the level of the position in the country's cultural hierarchy also have to be considered. In internationally based companies, transfer of employees between parts of the organization based in different countries creates cross-fertilization and a truly international perspective. Through such transfers the organization develops an in-house pool of managers with international experience and perspective.

Development

Beyond the selection decision, the psychological assessment should also give guidance to management about how to facilitate the new person's transition into the new setting. Plans for helping the person translate his strengths, as well as strategies for remedying the person's areas of relative weakness, should be in place before the candidate starts the new position. The best way to begin such a process is for the consultant to review the findings of the assessment interview first with the individual, then with the person's supervisor, and then jointly with the both of them. Issues important for early development, such as studying the new country's financial system, fortifying language skill, or extending human resource skill in a new culture, need to be given priority.

Organizational Change

The psychological assessment of key personnel again becomes a necessity when the organization is in a structural and cultural transition, such as moving from a global to a transnational structure. In this example, you will need people who can shift from functioning in a centrally controlled organization to one where reciprocal interdependence is emphasized. Further, you will need to know what areas your people will need to develop in order to maximally contribute to the effectiveness of the new structure. Understanding the mix of cultures in a transition is one of the key issues.

An example is a U.S. headquartered electronics company with significant affiliates in its European markets. Historically, the technology and the know-how had originally come from Europe. However, with the growth of the U.S. market, the company had moved its home office to the United States. Each of the European affiliates remained powerful within their respective countries and each functioned independently. Recently, for strategic and efficiency reasons, the CEO decided to go from a geographical and functional structure to a business unit, matrix structure (i.e., from a multinational to an international structure). This change had dramatic impact on the affiliates, because corporate research and development and marketing programs took away decision-making power from the local general managers. Without proper selection of the people put into position to implement these changes (as well as clear enunciation of the strategic vision), heated conflicts arose between the local and corporate managers.

INFORMATION TO BE CONSIDERED IN A CROSS-NATIONAL ASSIGNMENT ASSESSMENT

Personal Presentation and Communication Issues

Misunderstandings between managers from different cultures can happen right from the start. Managers often evaluate candidates or employees as much on the way they answer the questions as on what they say. If cultural differences are not taken into consideration, a poor conclusion can result. *The Economist* (November 24, 1990) provided a wonderful illustration of this issue: When asked a question, Americans expect a trustworthy person to respond quickly and with confidence. If the person pauses too long after the question is posed, the American manager assumes that the person is making up an answer that he thinks the manager wants to hear. For the Japanese, the situation is exactly the opposite. The Japanese are suspicious of quick, fluid answers. They instinctively associate such a style with untruthfulness. They place more confidence in people who give careful thought to a question before replying.

Language

Organizations use language as a carrier of the organizational culture, purposes, and strategies. The international assessment explores the usable language skills in a particular cultural setting. Managers are needed who can communicate to both the parent and the subsidiary.

In certain countries, the language of commerce is often the language of a foreign country; for example, French in North and West Africa, English in the Netherlands. However, English is increasingly the international language of business. A few managers, without the local language, surmount the barrier through leadership skill, clear goals, and a winning personality. Even then, they may be at the mercy of those people who know the nuances of language and culture and have their own ulterior motives. On the other hand, the aim for your organization is to find competent leaders and managers—in the particular cultural context you want—rather than competent linguists. In earlier days, North American companies all too often were charmed by well-spoken English and good manners and forgot management capability.

National Culture

Culture can be defined as a shared set of implicit assumptions, expectations, and rules for appropriate behavior. The international assessment deals with the interface between company and country cultures in order to make good decisions about selection, placement, and development. Values are shaped by an individual's particular culture. The assessor's goal is to find a reasonable fit between the individual's values and expectations and the values and expectations of the organization. Cultural issues have relevance for such areas as the appropriate exercise of authority, the definition of fiscal responsibility, and worker participation in the decision-making process.

Some organizations build strong internal cultures that try to override country cultures. Their people stick together, sometimes immune to local issues and the local people. Within a strongly centralized organization, particularly one that places its people in local postings for relatively short periods of time, such an arrangement might succeed in its objectives. However, by isolating its people, the organization loses the insights such people could provide into the local culture, politics, and markets. Further, since it would be highly unlikely that the organization would choose to staff the affiliate entirely with its own people (this would be economically, not to mention politically, unwise), at some level there is going to be an interface between the two cultures. With the meeting of these two sets of cultural norms, there inevitably are going to be differences of opinion on the proper handling of such issues as fiscal responsibility, legal guidelines, managerial authority, and worker participation. The better prepared the managers are for potential conflicts in these areas, the more likely they will be to handle them well.

Legal

The company needs to be aware of the human rights and labor laws in both countries. In the United States, the Japanese find themselves in a number of U.S. court cases because policies made in their headquarters regarding the promotion of women conflicted with customary U.S. employment practices. The consultant can be expected to provide an understanding of how such laws impact on the assessment of candidates. For example, in the Netherlands, professional rules of conduct concerning the right of privacy mean that an external candidate for a company position always has to receive a copy of the assessment report and has the right to block the filing of this report by the future employer. An internal candidate has access to the report and is entitled to feedback. When the candidate does not agree with the content of the report, the person can request that it is not made available to the employer.

Job Analysis/Role Expectations

The company and the consultant both need to be aware of the actual job responsibilities, in addition to those listed in the formal job description, of the person in the affiliate organization. In other words, what will this manager be doing in this company in that culture? To do this, the consultant needs to include job information from supervisor(s), peers, and subordinates. On the surface, two jobs might appear to be the same—and even have the same title—yet, because of historical and cultural differences in the two entities (resulting from the interplay between national cultural and each entity's own developmental history), the expectations for the person in the position might be different. This is particularly important when the affiliate is acquired rather than built by the parent organization. Consider the following vignette:

Herr Richten is director of internal communications of a German division of a recently merged international company that provides products to the construction industry. As director, he has responsibility for internal publications, telephone systems, forms, and related duties for a regional network of nine construction companies. After the merger, he came to the United States to meet his counterparts and to see if there were any systems or processes that could be used in Germany.

In the Midwest division, he asked to meet the director of internal communications. He was pointed to a wizened old man pushing a mail cart. He inferred that the local employees were giving him a hard time, possibly as a way of expressing some anger about the takeover. He decided to play along, however. Upon talking with the old man, he discovered that this gentleman had been with the company over 40 years. Though not terribly bright, he was enthusiastic and loyal. He conveyed immense pride in the fact that his important title had been awarded to him in person by the founding family of the Midwest company.

It is very important that before the person is selected for the position, the expectations for how the position will function in relation to both the affiliate and the home office are clearly spelled out. The consultant will need this information to help with the evaluation of candidates. The candidates will need this information to help them make informed decisions about whether or not they are interested in the position. Over time, the expectations for the position and its relationship with the home office will evolve. It is important that the person in the position be kept well-informed about any changes in expectations for the functioning of the position.

WHAT IS ASSESSED IN CROSS-NATIONAL ASSIGNMENT DECISIONS

The actual assessment of candidates for cross-national assignment involves an expansion and refinement of the procedures used for domestic selection and development decisions. Areas such as the candidates' native intelligence, how they use their intelligence, emotional stability, motivation, their insight into themselves and others, the impressions they make on others, interpersonal relationships, leadership abilities, management skills, the situations they function best in, and how they are best supervised are examined. However, for the international assignment assessment, all these factors will be looked at not only from the home cultural frame but also within the frame of the culture in which the person will be expected to function.

The same behaviors can mean different things in different cultures. Managerial behaviors that might be seen as supportive guidance in one culture might be viewed as authoritarian control in another. Further, in different cultures, within different corporate settings, either one may be effective. The key is obtaining an understanding of not only what type of management is called for in the affiliate but also what types of behaviors the person will need to exhibit to demonstrate this type of management style. Also, the personal qualities that appear to correspond to international assignment success will need to be evaluated. Though not superseding the particular contextual elements of the specific assignment decision, the following additional areas need to be evaluated in the candidate: social awareness, flexibility, openness to new experiences, adaptability, tolerance for ambiguity, sincerity, integrity, patience, and perseverance. Of course, consideration of these psychological factors assumes that the person already has demonstrated superb professional and technical abilities.

Since in cross-national assignments the company will be moving the entire family into the new country and culture, an assessment of the family's circumstances must be included. While no definitive numbers exist for the percentage of failed international assignments that are due to family difficulties, it is our impression that they are the cause of the majority of early termination of these assignments. As the following vignette illustrates, in many ways, the international assignment is more demanding on the spouse than on the employee. The employee has work to keep him or her busy and to provide an immediate social group. The spouse has neither, and either must have this provided for in other ways, or be the type of person who can readily create such an environment. If not, the spouse can become increasingly isolated, lonely, and frustrated, thereby setting the stage for the family deciding to leave the assignment.

Jim and Carol have three young children, all under the age of eight. Jim works for a large international corporation, while Carol has developed her own business, which has taken a great deal of her personal time. The family appears to be fairly well-adjusted and family members have close working relationships with one another. Both Jim and Carol, however, are very strong-willed, driven adults, who have clear ideas as to the way things ought to be. They often respect one another more for having separate views than for being in agreement in every situation. Jim is much more experienced in travel than is Carol and has traveled rather extensively. Carol has lived most of her life in the city in which she was raised, not far from her parents and other family members. The family has spent considerable time with her side of the family and are concerned about leaving her family and her business. On the other hand, both are excited about the career possibilities this assignment would offer Jim and the educational opportunities it would provide the children. While health issues are not of concern to the family, there is an underlying concern expressed primarily by Carol as to whether such an assignment might be more appropriate later in Jim's career rather than now. Carol appears to be dealing more honestly with conflicting feelings than Jim, who is basically very optimistic and assumes that everything will work out.

The consultant's recommendation to the corporation was that the timing of this particular move was not the best, despite the fact that Jim would be a good candidate for the position in question. The corporation had already begun the transfer process and, despite the consultant's input, decided to go ahead with the move. The consultant then strongly recommended that additional sessions with both husband alone, and husband and wife together be used in order to help bridge the gap, in addition to psychological counseling services for the family once they arrived at their new assignment. Due to logistical problems, the company felt it could not arrange the latter.

During the first six months after the move, Jim became very involved in his work and spent long hours away from the home. Carol—not speaking the local language and being culturally cut off from her environment—found herself with plenty of time on her hands, not knowing what to do despite her involvement with her children. She became increasingly irritable as the time passed. In the sixth month, the family received an emergency phone call from Carol's sister indicating that their father had had a severe coronary attack. The entire family sped back to their native home. After the initial emergency passed, Jim went back alone but found that he was not able to devote his entire energies to his work because he kept finding himself thinking about his family.

In the tenth month, Carol and the children returned to Jim's posting. Jim and Carol reached the decision that they would stick out Jim's mandate but then return back home. After Carol rejoined him, Jim once again resumed his excellent performance. However, with the shroud of these difficulties hanging over him, his advancement in his corporation was seriously compromised.

This case highlights the role family dynamics play in the employee's adaptation to a cross-national assignment, the rationale for doing the assessment early in the assignment process, the need to give consideration to the person's extended family, and the importance of actively planning for the difficulties that might arise once the employee is in the assignment. When assessing families for cross-national assignment, the following six areas need to be considered: (1) family stability; (2) family flexibility; (3) family self-sufficiency; (4) family mobility; (5) family health; and (6) family motivation.

THE ASSESSOR AND THE ASSESSMENT INTERVIEW

It would be virtually impossible for the consultant to be an expert in all the areas that have been touched on in this chapter. You won't find a trilingual assessor who is an expert on Korean controllers working in Malaysia for a Japanese affiliate of an American-owned international organization. However, even if you were to find this person, your situation would be further complicated when, after having developed a relationship with this consultant, you then wanted to use the consultant to assess a different situation in your organization, one that has nothing to do with Korean controllers but instead deals with placing an American in the VP marketing position in your Japanese affiliate.

So what characteristics must consultants have to be effective assessors in international assignment decisions? First and foremost, consultants must respect cultural differences. They must be able to maintain an inter-cultural egalitarianism. Every culture has its strengths and weaknesses, its good and less good features, that have developed over time in relation to each other. Consultants must be able to understand this interconnectedness while also maintaining healthy respect for the nonnative culture. Second, they must appreciate the international perspective and be able to maintain a nonparochial world view. Third, they must understand the international nature of business and be able to understand your organization's corporate culture and its variants in your affiliates around the world. Fourth, they must understand the indigenous management style of the placement country. Last, consultants must understand how language and cultural issues can affect the assessment process and the impression the candidates make on them.

Often in such assessments the interview will take place in the consultant's native language but the candidate's second. Since there are no totally "culture-free" assessment instruments, nor is there an interviewing style or process that can completely remove cultural confounds, the consultant needs to keep in mind how this might bias the results or conclusions. The consultant needs to be aware of the culture and language in which the person will be functioning. Sometimes, even though the person is assessed in an English language cultural setting, the work setting will actually be in the person's native language and culture. As the following example illustrates, many cultural and language issues can be examined in detail by having two assessors involved in the interview—one who is part of the parent organization's corporate and national culture and one who is knowledgeable about the affiliate's national culture and the language.

A U.S.-based auto parts manufacturer acquired another company that had a major plant based in southwestern Puerto Rico. Soon after the acquisition, the general manager of the Puerto Rican plant decided to retire. As his replacement, he recommended Gilberto, the director of operations at the plant. As a standard part of their internal selection process, they had Gilberto travel to their Midwest home office to attend a two-day assessment center. The results of this assessment rated Gilberto as too low in ability to be promoted to plant manager.

Upon being appraised of the situation by the company's human resources department, the consultant psychologist suggested further assessment, including both English and Spanish instruments. It quickly became clear that while Gilberto performed poorly in English, he did extremely well in Spanish. Given that the work force at the plant was Spanish-speaking, Gilberto's language difficulties were not currently a problem. He was therefore promoted into the position and a developmental plan was laid out that included English language lessons to prepare Gilberto for further advancement opportunities within the company.

Finally, the assessment must be in the right setting and the correct place. The worst option is in a hotel room in a city in which neither the assessor nor the candidate speak the local language. But this is often the case. A better option is to use the parent company's headquarters where the parent's company and country culture can serve as the backdrop. In this situation, visiting managers from other cross-border entities could take part in phases of the total assessment process. The best option would be to do the assessment within the corporate and country cultural setting where the candidate will actually be performing. This will present a clearer picture of what the person will be like functioning in the work situation.

SUMMARY

Help is available to organizations faced with complex decisions about selecting, placing, and developing individuals for cross-national assignments.

Psychological assessment in cross-national assignment decisions involves understanding how the organizational structure, corporate, and national culture will interrelate with the candidate's individual characteristics to affect the person's success in the particular position.

Assessments need to be custom-tailored to the organization because of the unique complexities of country, location, communication, and culture.

With cross-national moves, psychological assessment of the individual as a person as well as a professional is a vital part of an executive's development. As such, family factors need to be given careful consideration.

The management of cultural issues that come out of the cross-national assessment is key to the success of the individual and the organization.

Psychological assessment in international business is a time-consuming procedure, but a very economical one. The information it provides helps the firm to meet the challenges posed by globalization more successfully.

The value of the assessment ultimately is determined by whether or not it leads to better assignment decisions.

REFERENCES

Bartlett, C. A. & Ghoshal, S. (1989). *Managing across borders: The transnational solution*. Boston: Harvard Business School Press.

Corporate hiring and executive search will dramatically change in the 1990's. (Fall, 1989). *Canadian Manager/Manager Canadien*: 21.

Laurent, A. (1986). The cross-cultural puzzle of international human resource management. *Human Resource Management* 25: 91–102.

Management in America: Do it my way. (Nov. 24, 1990). *The Economist* 317: 74–76.

Mendenhall, M. E., Dunbar, E. & Oddou, G. R. (1987). Expatriate selection, training, & career-pathing: A review and critique. *Human Resource Management* 26: 331–45.

Survey of world trade: Jousting for advantage. (Sept. 22, 1990). *The Economist* 317, special section.

Szalay, L. B. (1981). Intercultural communication—a process model. *International Journal of Intercultural Relations* 5: 133–46.

16

Psychological Assessment in a Developmental Context

John B. Miner

Psychological assessment is typically conducted by companies for one of two reasons—either the person is a candidate for a new position, such as being hired from the outside or being considered for promotion, or the person is experiencing some type of performance problem that requires attention. There are also cases where the assessment is carried out strictly for guidance or career development purposes. In these instances, no specific problem need be manifest initially. Usually, however, a problem does appear as the assessment process unfolds; the difference is that the problem is in the mind of the person being assessed rather than being a current organizational concern. This chapter deals with situations where some type of problem exists. Either the person's performance is currently suffering or there is a likelihood that it will suffer later if the problem is not solved. In addition, special attention is given to using feedback sessions, where the results of the psychological assessment are discussed with a person, as a method of dealing with problems.

TYPES OF PROBLEMS

Performance problems are rarely all-encompassing. Even when they are, if a person is a total failure, psychological assessment is unlikely to be brought to bear; the person is simply dismissed. Where psychological assessment makes most sense is the situation involving certain clear positive contributions combined with some pronounced deficiencies in specific areas. An example is an extremely technically competent young manager who moved up rapidly in his company because he was able to solve engineering problems that others could not. As a result, he contributed substantially to both product sales and production efficiency. Yet he had a disturbing propensity to go off on his own and do things, including making commitments to customers, without telling other members of the top management team what he was doing. There was a real risk that this lack of communication might ultimately put the company in serious danger because of an overcommitment of resources.

This particular problem involved a lack of needed cooperation with other managers. A manager might also have a negative impact on subordinates, failing to provide a clear picture of what needs to be done, for instance, or being so punitive that subordinates are constantly leaving. Other problems include failure to make decisions and get things done on time so that productivity suffers, and insufficient concern with training and quality control so that errors occur frequently. These are the kinds of problems that one sees often in doing psychological assessment. The closer a manager is to the top of the company, the more likely the performance decrement is to appear not just in the manager's individual performance, but in the company's performance as well. At the managerial level, excessive absenteeism is rarely a factor that brings a person to psychological assessment. However, turnover is often an issue; there is a prospect that the company might very well lose a person that it can ill afford to lose.

THE DIAGNOSTIC PROCESS IN PSYCHOLOGICAL ASSESSMENT

Once a problem is identified, a need for diagnosis arises. Solutions cannot be applied unless information is available regarding the causal factors that operated to produce the problem in the first place. The situation is essentially the same as exists in medicine, only the causal factors are quite different. Psychological assessment is a method of identifying the causes operating to produce problems so that appropriate solutions can be applied, thus serving to remove the causes. Basically what is involved in this diagnostic process is that a series of hypotheses is formulated regarding possible causes. Each hypothesis is then checked against the existing data and either accepted or rejected. The result is a list of contributory causes that have combined to create the problem and that can guide the selection of solutions in the form of treatments or corrective actions.

We know from research on attribution theory that there is an enormous potential for bias among both individuals with problems and their superiors in this whole process. These biases are particularly acute at the point of diagnosis, although they can emerge in the selection of corrective solutions as well. Superiors are predisposed to attribute an individual's problems entirely to that individual, no matter what outside environmental forces may be operating. The individual, on the other hand, tends to overstress outside factors. The value of psychological assessment under these circumstances is that it introduces a more objective process into this attributional quagmire. Tests, questionnaires, and focused data collection can serve to construct a picture of what is really happening. That is no guarantee, however, that interested parties will, in fact, accept the reconstruction that emerges from psychological appraisal.

Intensive study of individual cases where performance problems have occurred has resulted in the development of several schemata covering the various causes that should be considered in making a diagnosis (Miner and Brewer 1976; Miner 1985). Exhibit 16–1 presents the schema that I have developed from the cases I have handled. The number of confirmed hypotheses or causal factors that will emerge from the diagnostic process varies considerably from case to case. On the average, I find about 4 of the 34 factors noted in Exhibit 16–1 to be involved. In some situations there will be only 1 cause, while at the other extreme there are situations that involve 7 or 8. Typically, problems arise because people with their own particular pattern of abilities, skills, and personality characteristics become enmeshed in a specific constellation of circumstances. The need is to spell out which among these individual and environmental factors have in fact played a causal role. Following Exhibit 16–1, I consider the potential causes in the order of individual, group, and organizational/contextual. More extended discussions of these factors are available in Miner and Brewer (1976), in Miner (1963, 1966, 1975, 1985, and 1992), and in Ginzberg, Miner, Anderson, Ginsburg, and Herma (1959).

Individual Causes of Performance Problems

Diagnosis involving individual causes is where psychological assessment has traditionally concentrated. With the exception of physical illness or handicap, all of the factors noted under this heading are of a psychological nature. In fact, many psychological assessments concentrate entirely on cognitive and personality aspects of the individual. Although the schema set forth in Exhibit 16–1 clearly deals with much more, assessing individual knowledge, skills, and abilities (often referred to as KSAs), along with personality factors (the motivational and emotional factors in the exhibit), is at the core of psychological assessment.

My preferred strategy in selecting assessment instruments is to develop a test battery that focuses primarily on personal characteristics found in the past to have a relationship to performance in the job under consideration. I also incorporate measures associated with performance in closely related or overlapping jobs. If at all possible, I find multiple measures of each personal characteristic. This means a good deal of searching around for appropriate questionnaires, scales, and tests before starting an assessment.

I can illustrate what I have in mind with reference to a battery constructed to assess entrepreneurs who either head up their own firms or head major new ventures within a larger corporate context. The battery includes four measures of achievement motivation, two measures of locus of control (that is, the belief that you have control over what happens to you), two measures of risk taking/ risk avoidance, two measures of Type A personality, three measures of cognitive style, and a sociological index of both entrepreneur type and firm type. There

Exhibit 16–1
Schema for Carrying Out Diagnoses in Psychological Assessment

Individual Causes

    Intelligence and Job Knowledge
        Insufficient Verbal Ability
        Insufficient Special Ability (Numerical, Mechanical, etc.)
        Insufficient Job Knowledge
        Defect of Judgment or Memory

    Individual Motivation
        Strong Motives Frustrated at Work
        Strong Motives Satisfied Through Means Not Job-integrated
        Excessively Low Personal Work Standards
        Generalized Low Work Motivation

    Emotions and Emotional Illness
        Frequent Disruptive Emotions (Anxiety, Depression, Anger, etc.)
        Psychosis
        Personality Disorders
        Alcohol and Drug Problems

    Physical Characteristics and Disorders
        Physical Illness or Handicap
        Physical Disorders of Emotional Origin
        Inappropriate (to the Job) Physical Characteristics
        Insufficient Muscular or Sensory Ability or Skill

Group Causes

    The Groups at Work
        Negative Consequences Associated with Group Cohesion
        Ineffective Management
        Inappropriate (to the Job) Managerial Standards and Criteria

    Family Ties
        Family Crises (Divorce, Death, etc.)
        Separation from a Family
        Predominance of Family Considerations Over Work Demands

Organizational/Contextual Causes

    The Organization
        Insufficient Organizational Action
        Placement Error
        Inappropriate (to the Job) Organizational Style (Overpermissive, Excessive Training, etc.)
        Excessive Span of Control
        Inappropriate (to the Job) Organizational Standards and Criteria

Exhibit 16–1 (continued)

The Societal Context
    Application of Legal Sanctions
    Application of Societal Values
    Conflict Between Job Demands and Societal Values (Morality, Fair Play, etc.)

The Work Context
    Negative Consequences of Economic Forces (Competition, Recession, etc.)
    Negative Consequences of Geographic Location (Climate, Population, etc.)
    Detrimental Conditions in the Work Setting (Noise, Illumination, etc.)

Excessive Danger (Real and Phobic)

are also two measures of managerial motivation, a measure of professional motivation, and two measures of intelligence. Finally, there is an instrument designed to confirm that the individual does in fact operate in an entrepreneurial context. This latter instrument is completed a second time with instructions to describe the person's ideal organizational context. All in all, there are 18 separate instruments which take about three-and-a-half hours on the average to complete.

For any kind of managerial or professional position I always use three instruments that I have developed. All are sentence completion scales (Miner 1964, 1981, 1986). The personal motivation patterns tapped by these three measures are given in Exhibit 16–2. Examples of the clinical use of these measures as well as information on their theoretical derivations and psychometric properties are contained in Miner (1991). My impression is that most psychologists who do many assessments like to use a basic core of instruments with which they are thoroughly familiar, and in which they have considerable confidence. The three sentence completion scales are my core instruments. Nevertheless, I believe it is undesirable to use a standard battery for all assessments. What is built around the core should vary, depending on the nature of the job, the situation, and the problem under investigation.

Group Causes of Performance Problems

We have a wealth of psychological measures for getting at individual causes. In contrast, group causes have not been the subject of nearly as much attention, at least from a measurement viewpoint. There are various sociometric and communication network approaches that can be applied to work units. They can be useful. However, my preferred approach to getting at information related to group cohesion, clique formation, ostracism, problems with a superior, and the like is to utilize multiple interviews.

The chief advantage of the interview for this purpose is that it can be structured to varying degrees to obtain answers in specific problem areas and still remain flexible enough to follow up leads that emerge during discussions. Standardized questions can be used to verify answers across respondents. I prepare an interview

Exhibit 16–2
The Miner Sentence Completion Scales and Their Components

Miner Sentence Completion Scale—Form H (managerial motivation)

Favorable attitudes to superiors

Desire to compete

Desire to exercise power

Desire to assert oneself

Desire to be distinct and different

Desire to perform routine duties responsibly

Miner Sentence Completion Scale—Form P (professional motivation)

Desire to learn and acquire knowledge

Desire to exhibit independence

Desire to acquire status

Desire to help others

Value-based identification with the profession

Miner Sentence Completion Scale—Form T (entrepreneurial motivation)

Desire to achieve through one's own efforts

Desire to avoid risk

Desire for feedback on performance

Desire to introduce innovative solutions

Desire to plan and establish goals

guide covering the things I want to get at prior to starting the interviews. It should be emphasized that this type of interview is completely diagnostic in nature. It should not be confused with a feedback interview which should be conducted separately from the diagnostic process.

Diagnostic interviews need not be, and typically are not, restricted to the collection of information related to group causes of performance problems. Yet this is one of their primary functions. It is desirable to conduct these interviews with the manager undergoing the assessment, with at least a sample of the employees reporting to the manager, with the manager's superior, and with at least a sample of the other managers reporting to the superior. Thus, all work group relationships are investigated. In one recent instance involving the assessment of a vice-president of human resources, information on group causes was collected from interviews with the vice-president, his superior, and the president. Information was also collected from eight other managers who reported with the vice-president to the president, thus constituting the top management team. Finally, interviews were conducted with ten managers in the human resource department, most of whom reported directly to the vice-president. This is a somewhat more comprehensive effort than is usually required, but because the replacement of the vice-president was at issue, it was deemed necessary.

Obtaining information related to family factors that might be at the root of problems is sometimes easy, but more often very difficult. Again, a wide-ranging interview effort is more likely to turn up important leads. Ideally, one would interview family members directly, yet this is rarely possible. The one instance where it might be feasible is where an individual is a candidate for foreign assignment. Other than this, intrusion into the family context is generally considered out-of-bounds in the United States, although in other countries of the world such as Japan, it may well be entirely legitimate. Yet, in spite of the problems, it seems that many family problems do emerge in interviews with the person assessed and those associated with the assessee. In spite of the barriers, family causes tend to be recognized as legitimate concerns for a psychologist conducting an assessment, and consequently they often come to the surface.

Organizational/Contextual Causes

This is an area in which psychological assessment has often been at a loss. For whatever reason, psychologists tend to obtain much less information about the organization, its culture, and the wider environmental context in which the work occurs than is needed for a comprehensive diagnosis of individual performance problems. In part, this is a consequence of psychological training that tends to focus on the individual and, at most, the group levels. But also, companies are often loath to provide the kind of detailed information needed in this area. Thus, at one time I carried out an extensive evaluation of the assessments made by outside psychologists on candidates for employment by a major consulting firm (Miner 1970). It was evident that the recommendations resulting from psychological assessments had little relationship to the career success of those who were hired; in short, the assessments did not work. The reason appears to be that the psychologists did not really understand the firm and the demands of consulting work, as distinct from the managerial work with which they were used to dealing. This lack of understanding might have been because the psychologists did not make the necessary inquiries, but it is also entirely possible that the consulting firm did not wish to reveal its internal workings.

In any event, a full, comprehensive psychological assessment requires information on organizational/contextual causes of performance problems just as much as on individual and group causes. Interviews are one of the most useful methods of obtaining this information. Diagnostic interviews that provide data on group causes can often be extended to the organizational/contextual causes as well. Where I have been concerned with problems at the top-management level, I often interview not only other members of the top-management team, but board members also. The emphasis is on identifying factors within the company and in its environment that might account for the problems in evidence.

A somewhat different approach has been used in our work with entrepreneurs.

As part of a formal development program for entrepreneurs, the participants each present their own companies through written handouts and a two-hour oral workshop discussion with other participants in the program and to a panel of three or four reactors. The latter are either faculty members with relevant knowledge or highly experienced business people; they are selected for their capacity to provide useful advice bearing on the particular problems the company faces. The reactors critique the presentation, providing suggestions for company improvement and growth. There is considerable give-and-take between those making the presentations and their audiences, centering on the company's (and implicitly the entrepreneur's) problems. Although the information unearthed through this process may relate to individual or group causes, by far the greatest proportion relates to organizational/contextual causes. I take detailed notes throughout the discussions. Using these notes and the materials prepared by the entrepreneurs, I am able to construct a reasonably accurate picture of the various companies and the environments in which they operate.

There are other approaches that may be used as well. For instance, I have frequently attended board, executive committee, or unit meetings convened for troubleshooting purposes. The point is that doing a comprehensive psychological assessment requires much more than simply administering tests to an individual. Not infrequently, in fact, I administer my core sentence-completion scale battery to a number of people who work with the focal individual to get a better picture of the context within which the person functions.

SOLUTIONS AND CORRECTIVE ACTION

The diagnostic processes described result in the identification of a set of problem causes. An analysis of these causes then serves to determine what might be done to solve the problem; what causes can meaningfully be eliminated, and what ones cannot. Exhibit 16–3 contains a listing of some of the things that can be done, depending on the specific nature of the causes operating. Each corrective action considered needs to be evaluated against the following criteria.

1. What will the corrective action cost and who will pay for it? Is it too costly?

2. How long will it take before the corrective action takes hold and has an effect? Will it take too long?

3. Are suitable replacements readily available to take over should the position be vacated?

4. What are the probabilities that the corrective action will succeed or fail?

Let us take, as an example, a young retail store manager recently promoted to his present position whose store has experienced excessive turnover and losses,

Exhibit 16–3
Possible Corrective Actions

Job redesign and changed role prescriptions

Promotion, transfer, or demotion

Management development and training

Changes in supervision (either the style of the existing supervision or the person holding the position)

Changes in method or amount of compensation

Personnel policy modifications (or exceptions to policy)

Threats and disciplinary action

Alcoholics Anonymous and other such group procedures

Medical treatment

Psychotherapy Counseling (including assessment feedback)

Employee assistance program

in part due to his volatile moods and poor judgment. The diagnostic process revealed the following causes:

A. Individual Causes

    1. Intelligence and Job Knowledge

        —Defect of Judgment (due to emotions)

    2. Individual Motivation

        —Strong Motive Frustrated at Work (strong competitive need)

    3. Emotions and Emotional Illness

        —Personality Disorder (intense depression and guilt)

B. Organizational/Contextual Causes

    1. The Organization

        —Placement Error (job too likely to defeat competitive need)

    2. The Work Context

        —Negative Consequences of Economic Forces (depressed local economy and intense competitor price-cutting)

The diagnosis indicated that the young manager overreacted to the economic pressures in the situation, out of his intense competitive need, and ended up depressed and guilt-ridden to a point where he could not function effectively under any circumstances. Putting him in such a situation reflects a failure of the firm's placement processes. There is reason to believe that the young man was caught up in competitive striving in relation to his father, who was a senior official in the same firm.

Looking at the individual causes, one has to conclude that psychotherapy is the appropriate solution. Under the duress of circumstances, the young manager has become seriously emotionally disturbed. He needs to work through the underlying emotional problems and understand the dynamics behind his unrealistic competitive striving. The use of anti-depressant drugs might well alleviate the present problem to a degree, but they would not reduce vulnerability to similar problems in the future.

Yet from an organizational viewpoint, psychotherapy does not emerge as quite as appropriate a solution. There are suitable replacements for the store manager available, psychotherapy is a costly process, it does not always succeed, and in any event, psychotherapy takes time. The company needs to correct the situation in the store as soon as possible to cut its losses. The net of all this is that the young manager should be relieved of his duties as soon as possible and a replacement should be brought in. What happens then is a function of the firm's assessment of the young manager's long-term potential and the possibilities for alternative assignment. Ideally, psychotherapy would be initiated and an appropriate, less stressful position would be located. In all this it should be recognized that there is no way in which the economic forces that actually set off the problem can be reversed by some type of company action (for further information on this example see the case of Store Manager Edward Kaplan in Miner 1975, 207–10, and the analysis in Miner 1975a, 95–99).

THE FEEDBACK PROCESS

In Exhibit 16–3, assessment feedback was noted as an aspect of counseling and as a type of corrective action. It is, in fact, a very important approach under certain circumstances. It applies most frequently where personality factors (motivational or emotional) are operative. It can serve to develop individuals by focusing motives and emotions on desired objectives. It is most effective where the individual is unencumbered by severe defensive reactions and thus can accept some negative feedback. Where real emotional disturbances are present, something more than assessment feedback is needed, and, in fact, feedback can have negative consequences. These and other considerations lead to the conclusion that assessment feedback should not be attempted under all circumstances. If job changes are envisaged, for instance, there is little point in getting into assessment feedback. But if the goal is a developmental one, to stimulate certain types of motives or redirect motives into desired channels, then feedback can be very useful.

Feedback is a regular part of our program for entrepreneurs, and an understanding of what I do there may prove helpful. The first step is to analyze all the tests and questionnaires and relate the resulting data to what is known about the company. The objective is to identify and understand company strengths and weaknesses that might have their roots in the psychology of the entrepreneur. This analysis is then fed back to the entrepreneur, forming a basis for discussion of how the problems facing the firm might be overcome and how growth might be achieved. These sessions last from an hour-and-a-half to three hours. They tend to be very candid. I find relatively little defensiveness in this group.

The feedback session starts with a review of problems faced by the individual and the firm. I try to get agreement on a list of problems that we need to address. My initial list might be altered during this discussion. Some problems have disappeared since the entrepreneur's clinic presentation, and others may not have come out there. Then I go through the results from the test battery. I do not deal with test scores, only characteristics. Thus, we talk about intellectual capabilities, locus of control, managerial motivation, and so on. The data from different measures of the same construct are pooled in some manner with emphasis on what I believe are the better measures. I try to get agreement on my interpretations. If I do not understand a given test result in the context of the other findings, I say so, and ask for assistance. Often the individual will come up with a reconciliation, where I could not. My general approach in presenting these results is positive; I play up strengths. But I do not ignore weaknesses. If the individual does become defensive I avoid getting into an argument. I listen, and go on to the next point.

The final part of the feedback session represents an attempt to apply the findings from the tests and other sources to the problems originally considered. We try to understand how these problems could have arisen, and what might be done about them. Often the test data are very helpful in providing explanations. Yet there are also instances in which the individual starts to look at problems in new ways and actually creates new solutions on the spot; I am simply a catalyst. I have had people develop entirely new approaches to their careers, and even new careers, in these sessions. Insofar as possible, I encourage setting specific and difficult goals. This problem-solving part of the feedback session can extend over considerable time. Once people get going on ideas of this kind they want to continue, and it is productive for them to do so. I try to arrange my schedule so that the session does not have to be terminated at a specific time.

With the entrepreneurs, the problems tend to revolve around the survival and growth of their firms. In other contexts, with other problems, the feedback discussions might take a different course. In any event, I believe it is important to sketch out in advance what problems, results, and solutions one wishes to cover. The discussion might wander so that it is necessary to pull the subject matter back to what was originally envisaged. Notes made in advance are thus important to the success of a feedback session; you need to know where you are going. However, I do not make these notes available to others, and I do not provide written feedback. If people know that they will receive a written version of what is being discussed they tend to concentrate less during the session. Sometimes a person will want to take notes and I do not discourage this. However, it is rare for the note-taking to continue beyond the first half hour. As people become enmeshed in the discussion, it is simply too time-consuming to continue, and they put their pads aside.

CONCLUSION

The approach to assessment that I have outlined here differs from many presented in the literature and considered in this book. It is unusually comprehensive, it takes considerable time, and it is costly. In recent years as the approach has continued to evolve, I find that I am using it primarily with individuals at the very top levels of their organizations. This is not a necessary condition, but it may justify the cost. Also I believe that having over thirty years of experience makes a difference in carrying out this kind of assessment. Certainly it contributes to one's legitimacy, but it is also true that I pick things up now that I almost surely would have missed in the early days. In the end, psychological assessment is problem solving, and the more extensively one can search in one's experience, the more likely it is that the problem will be solved.

REFERENCES

Ginzberg, E., Miner, J. B., Anderson, J. K., Ginsburg, S. W., & Herma, J. L. (1959). *The ineffective soldier: Volume II. Breakdown and recovery*. New York: Columbia University Press.

Miner, J. B. (1963). *The management of ineffective performance*. New York: McGraw-Hill.

———. (1964). *Scoring guide for the Miner Sentence-Completion Scale*. Buffalo, N.Y.: Organizational Measurement Systems Press.

———. (1966). *Introduction to industrial clinical psychology*. New York: McGraw-Hill.

———. (1970). Psychological evaluations as predictors of consulting success. *Personnel Psychology* 23: 393–405.

———. (1975). *The challenge of managing*. Philadelphia, Penn.: W. B. Saunders.

———. (1975a). *Case analysis and description of managerial role motivation training*. Philadelphia, Penn.: W. B. Saunders.

———. (1981). *Scoring guide for the Miner Sentence-Completion Scale—Form P*. Buffalo, N.Y.: Organizational Measurement Systems Press.

———. (1985). *People problems: The executive answer book*. New York: McGraw-Hill.

———. (1986). *Scoring Guide for the Miner Sentence-Completion Scale—Form T*. Buffalo, N.Y.: Organizational Measurement Systems Press.

———. (1991). *Role motivation theories*. London: Unwin Hyman.

———. (1992). *Industrial-Organizational Psychology*. New York: McGraw-Hill.

Miner, J. B., & Brewer, J. F. (1976). The management of ineffective performance. In *Handbook of Industrial and Organizational Psychology*, ed. by M. D. Dunnette. Chicago: Rand McNally, 995–1029.

17

Psychological Assessment in Career Development

Richard J. Brunkan

THREE SCENARIOS

Bart has recently taken a job in the cleaning room at ABC Foundry. He went to school because he was required to and barely made it through high school. When he did graduate, he realized he needed money. The way to get it was to find a job. Not having any specific skills or education to fall back on, he checked the want ads and found the position in the foundry. If we ask him where he will be going from here, he very likely will shrug his shoulders and say he doesn't know, but will be quick to add that he does not want to spend the rest of his life in the cleaning room.

Downtown at XYZ Insurance Company, Cindy has just been promoted to a position as supervisor in claims. She is a bright young woman who liked school and graduated from college with a 3.5 grade point average in anthropology. When she graduated, she needed a job but soon realized that she was not likely to find one in anthropology. Therefore, she took a position paying claims at the insurance company. Because she was capable and had developed skills in dealing with people, she was promoted to supervisor after six months. Ask her where she will go from here and she also is likely to say she doesn't know, although she would like to advance.

In the executive suite of XYZ Company, Stacy, the vice-president of operations, is wondering about her next career move. She knows opportunities are limited, but also knows she would like to advance. She has advanced rapidly without much career planning, but now is wondering what she can do to better her chances for further promotions.

Situations like these are common with both younger and older employees.

This is part of the reason why companies are placing more focus on career development. Their companies also would like Bart, Cindy, and Stacy to advance and, in fact, need them to advance. The growth of any organization depends on its employees being able to assume the additional responsibilities of higher-level positions in the future.

WHAT IS CAREER PLANNING?

How much time do most people spend on career planning? Many spend more time planning for Christmas or a birthday than they do planning their careers.

Career Plan as Part of Life Plans

Ideally, every person should have a life plan, a major segment of which is a career plan. The life plan includes a clearly identified purpose for one's life, specific goals one wants to achieve, and strategies or action plans for achieving those goals. The career side of a person's life plan is considered to be a vocation or general calling. We may be most familiar with this term as applied to the religious life but it can just as appropriately be applied to a vocation to heal people, to entertain, or to engage in the world of commerce. Just how one fulfills that vocation is called a career. So a career might be to become a doctor, a singer, or a CPA.

Career Development

What, then, is career development in the business world? It is essentially the process of helping individuals clarify a purpose and vocation, develop career plans, set goals, and outline steps for reaching those goals. A typical career plan includes the identification of a career path, and the skills and abilities needed to progress along that path. Career development involves assessment, planning, goal setting, and strategizing to gain the skills and abilities required to implement the plan. The process can be supported by coaching and counseling from a psychologist, or from the managers and human resources specialists within a company.

The exact nature of career development can differ considerably depending upon individual circumstances. For example, Bart at the foundry will need help in identifying his basic skills and talents, and in determining what types of positions might therefore be available to him.

Cindy, on the other hand, went through career counseling at her university and found that she really did like anthropology. However, the job market has caused her to go back to the drawing board to reassess and look for other ways to use her talents. She always took her people and leadership skills for granted as being "part of her," even as she developed them further in extracurricular activities. Now she finds supervising challenging and satisfying. She is beginning to think of a career path that will use her leadership skills as well as her organizing ability. Her career development is certain to include learning supervisory and management skills, as well as identifying specific technical interests. Her career path might eventually point to an executive position.

Stacy is also thinking about career development because she does not want to remain a vice-president to the end of her career. She realizes there are not many positions farther up in the organization, and that she needs to carefully assess what she has to offer and how to increase her chances of gaining a top spot. For all three people, a systematic approach to career planning and development can pay dividends. The first step in that approach is a careful career-oriented assessment.

WHY DO CAREER DEVELOPMENT PLANNING?

Before we focus specifically on the assessment, let's take a few moments to consider why career development is important. The purpose of career development is to establish goals and to focus energies clearly on the attainment of those goals.

Importance to the Individual

Career development is important for the individual because it means continued personal and occupational growth. It increases the chances of finding the success that the individual wants and thus the chances of gaining satisfaction in day-to-day activities. The person is likely to feel more motivated and more complete as an individual.

Value to the Company

Career development is important for the company because the modern day competitive business environment places a premium on productive and motivated employees. Companies are also becoming aware of the need and the value of "growing their own." Any process that increases the capabilities and potential of employees has long-term value. Add to this the increasing limitations of the labor pool, as well as the ever-increasing costs and difficulties of hiring and firing, and it is not difficult to see why companies want to help employees advance in their careers.

Often people conceptualize career development as mapping a plan or path to lead one from the present to the time of retirement. In reality, this is usually not the case, because it is difficult for most people to look that far into the future with any degree of certainty about what will be important to them. Thus, frequently the career development process will focus on just one or two steps beyond the current position because these are close enough to see and feel. In essence, the development process becomes a procedure that may be repeated a number of times by an individual throughout a career. As one step is achieved, the plan is pushed out another step. This step-wise process also enables people to reassess their desires and the probability of moving on to the next position.

PSYCHOLOGICAL ASSESSMENT IN CAREER DEVELOPMENT

How does the psychological assessment enter into career development? As mentioned earlier, almost any planning process begins with a thorough assessment of one's current status. Career development is no exception. A critical first step is a thorough assessment, similar to the psychological assessment discussed in earlier chapters. It includes an in-depth interview as well as the use of a number of psychological tests and inventories. However, the *focus* of the interview—the tests and inventories—is often different in several ways. Specifically, the career development assessment differs from the standard psychological assessment in the following ways.

Broader Focus

The assessment for career development will generally take a broader focus than the assessment of a candidate for a specific position within a company. It is likely to focus on all aspects of the person's life rather than on just those that are work-related since a successful career is an integration of all aspects of one's life. It is an opportunity to reexamine where one has come from and where one might be going.

More Exploration

Part of the process of career assessment is to find as many clues and bits of information as possible to fit together into a total plan. Thus the assessment process is likely to involve exploring a variety of avenues to find those elements that make a significant contribution to the person's overall life satisfaction, rather than exploring factors critical to a specific position.

More Focus on Values, General Interests, and Lifestyle

In a career assessment these factors are important, along with items such as abilities and work experience, because they strongly impact long-term satisfaction and motivation. People will tolerate discomfort and incongruities for a short time but not for a lifetime. This, again, is part of the broader focus and the need to develop an overall picture.

More of a "Working Together" Process

In the assessment of a candidate for a position, the focus of the psychologist is on determining and measuring those success factors that are critical to the position. In career assessments, the psychologist and the individual are likely to engage in a joint process of searching and exploring. In this give-and-take, they develop as much information as possible and consider it all as part of the planning process. Continuing feedback to the individual is definitely a part of working together. It provides additional data to the individual to aid his or her thinking, and frequently results in additional ideas and routes to explore as the assessment continues.

On-going Process

As mentioned previously, career planning or career development only covers one or two steps beyond the person's current position because it is too difficult to look clearly beyond that point. Thus, as a person advances, career plans will probably need updating. This can involve a reassessment, review, and a new plan. There might also be intermittent follow-up conferences with the psychologist to check on progress and determine whether adjustments need to be made in the plan.

THE CAREER ASSESSMENT PROCESS

What is the process of psychological assessment in career development, and how does it differ from the process of other psychological assessments? The tools used are relatively similar to other assessments, including the interview, tests, and inventories as described in chapters 1, 4, and 5. The process is to use these tools to gain a broad range of knowledge in four major areas: abilities, interests, personal traits, and values. Each area will be discussed separately.

Abilities

This part of the assessment considers general ability or overall intellectual capacity, as well as special skills, talents, and capabilities. Overall intellectual capacity is generally considered a measure of the complexity and difficulty levels an individual can successfully handle. Thus, it gives a rough indication of the position level at which the person will be comfortable. Of equal importance is the manner in which people use their abilities. For example, some people are systematic and logical while others are intuitive and random. Some are concrete, practical thinkers, and others are abstract and theoretical. Some people are quantitative, while others are verbal. These are only a few of the dimensions that can be considered in assessing intellectual capacity. All relevant areas need to be interpreted carefully in terms of overall strength and the implication for a person's career.

The importance of general intellectual ability often depends on the capabilities of the individual. A person who falls within the average ability range will have limitations on the number of choices available. On the other hand, people who are superior or very superior in intelligence can likely handle almost any intellectual challenge. The preferences of the latter group dictate the types of activities to which they like to apply their minds. Two people might be equally bright, but one might enjoy the abstract world of nuclear physics, whereas the other person enjoys the practical world of running a business.

Special talents or abilities such as mechanical, musical, sports, writing, and speaking also vary among people. In assessing for career development, as many of these talents and abilities as possible need to be identified so that all relevant opportunities are explored. For Bart in the foundry, the focus is more likely to be on technical skills such as mechanical or electrical ability, or on physical strength and coordination. For Cindy in the insurance company, the focus is more likely to be on intellectual know-how, and a range of technical and interpersonal skills. In career development, we want to know as much as possible about the special talents on which the individual can draw.

Interests

Interests are frequently not as clear-cut and defined as abilities and, therefore, not as directly measurable. However, as with abilities, the desire is to approach interests with a broad focus, identifying as many factors as possible for consideration as part of the career plan. After the key interests are identified, they need to be integrated with other available information into an approach that fits both individual and company needs.

In this area, the focus is primarily on career or occupational interests, because the concern is the person's career. However, personal preferences, hobbies, and special outside pursuits can also have significance. Someone with a strong interest in writing or photography can bring those talents into the job directly by working as a technical writer or a photo offset, or indirectly, by being a company photographer or a writer for the newsletter. An interest in planning and organizing could result in leadership responsibilities, while an interest in working with volunteers could lead one to be part of a company's community service efforts.

The major focus, however, is on career or work-related interests that are explored in the interview and assessed with written interest measures such as the Strong Vocational Interest Blank, the Career Assessment Inventory, or the Kuder Preference Record. The goal is to both reaffirm current interests and to identify hidden interests that could influence career satisfaction and effectiveness. Since the inventories cover only a limited number of occupations, it is often necessary to extrapolate to families or groups of occupations.

The strength and clarity of career interests can vary considerably from individual to individual. The Career Adjustment and Development Inventory and the Career Maturity Inventory by Dr. John Crites are used in determining the level of a person's career development and maturity and, thus, the extent to which interests are likely to develop or change. Some people have strong and clear interests that have existed from a relatively young age, adding to their motivation throughout their lives. This is more likely to be true of a person who has chosen a technical or professional field such as carpentry, tool and die making, nursing, or law. Many individuals who pursue careers in business do not have a single strong interest area. They are often more motivated by competitiveness, variety, responsibility, and decision-making authority than by specific interests.

Occasionally, the assessment process will bring to light an interest suppressed because parents rejected the associated career. Examples of this are careers in one of the arts, or in an occupation considered dangerous, such as law enforcement. When such interests are identified later in a person's life, the individual might no longer be able to pursue that career due to lack of training, background, or opportunity. However, the interests involved can sometimes be incorporated into a current career and add another dimension that is motivating. For example, an interest in law enforcement might be applied to a job as a fraud investigator for an insurance company.

Personality Traits

Personality and personal traits are significant in career planning because they need to match the career path being contemplated. If the path is in sales or management, one group of traits is important; if it is a path with a technical or research focus, a different set of traits is needed. Personal traits that fit the job contribute to personal satisfaction and to effectiveness in the job. This is a very broad area that could be the subject of a book by itself. Therefore, this treatment will, of necessity, be a brief overview.

When considering personal traits in career development, the desire is to gain an overview of the individual's strengths and shortcomings, assessing these with respect to appropriateness to specific career interests and goals. For example, Bart in the foundry will need a certain amount of toughness as well as considerable patience and persistence if he is going to earn additional opportunities. Likewise, Cindy definitely needs to be effective in communicating, leading, organizing, and problem-solving in addition to her innate strength in being sensitive to people if she is to advance in management. Stacy will need all of these as well as many others, such as conceptual thinking, creativity, vision, and long-range planning skills in order to move into the higher ranks of management.

A wide variety of inventories and measures are available to identify the strength of specific personal traits. Some of these are clinical and psychological, while others are more practical and applied in nature, as indicated in chapters 1 and 5. The primary interest in career assessment is in traits that contribute to a person's work effectiveness, career satisfaction, and advancement potential. These include such traits as confidence, organization, motivation, and assertiveness. In addition, ''people skills'' such as communication, insight, and ability to work as part of a team are important at the management level. At the executive level, an important capacity is the ability to think conceptually and multidimensionally, and to see the long range as well as the short term. Measures such as the California Psychological Inventory and the Adjective Check List provide information on a variety of traits in nonclinical terminology. A skilled practitioner is able to interpret the results of measures of this sort to gain a wealth of information about an individual's traits and how they would impact the workplace.

Values

This is probably the most nebulous of the four areas, and therefore the one to which we might give less attention because it is difficult to pin down. However, values, beliefs, and personal standards become significant as an individual assumes major responsibility in a company. There should be a close match between the individual's values and those of the company if the manager is to thrive. Most paper-and-pencil techniques available for assessing values, such as the Allport Vernon Lindzey Study of Values or the Work Values Inventory by Dr. Donald Super, measure general values such as economics, aesthetics, and achievement. In order to pinpoint specifics for the individual, it is important to listen carefully in discussions for value statements and to ask the individual to identify the key factors that govern the person's life and actions. Usually value statements are prefaced by "I believe" or "I think." Examples of value statements are: "I believe a company should share all of the information it has with its employees"; "Whatever you can get away with is okay"; "I believe a company should be people-oriented, which means that the good of the individual always comes first"; "I can't stand a boss who is always looking over my shoulder"; "I wouldn't live in North Dakota for all the money in the world."

Getting a handle on a person's values is important because it is frequently these values that influence long-term goals and decisions. Many people can tolerate almost anything for a short period of time. But when faced with the prospect of doing something distasteful as part of a long-term career with one company, they are less likely to be tolerant. In such situations, the individual's value system becomes much more important in decision-making.

Ed, for example, moved his family from Minneapolis to rural Georgia to take a promising position as plant manager. However, after a year he found the culture of the plant and the community to be very different than his previous experiences. Also, the work ethic was less strong and the school system was below his expectations. He soon updated his resume and began a search for a position back in the North. What he found in Georgia did not fit his values.

THE PROCESS OF CAREER DEVELOPMENT PLANNING

This process is essentially one of looking at where people are now compared to where they want to be. From this comparison, development activities necessary to reach the goals are determined. As stated earlier, while it might be useful to outline a general career path that covers a lifetime or at least a significant period of years, it is advisable to limit the development plan to the next position on the path or, at most, to the next two positions on the path. Planning specific needs and activities many years in advance is particularly difficult for the technical aspect of a person's development because technology is changing quickly today and will continue to do so in the future. However, the past ten years have also shown that management function can change rapidly and require quite a different set of skills.

Because of the limited time focus for developmental planning, the process becomes an ongoing activity. For best results, the plan should be reviewed and updated annually. This keeps developmental needs current and facilitates the addition of new resources that become available. One approach that is becoming more popular is to combine the career development plan with the performance review system so the process involves both looking back and looking ahead, while setting new goals and directions.

Different techniques are used in the planning process. All are essentially aimed at the same objective—to identify developmental needs and ways of meeting those needs. The basic approach is to identify career steps, list the developmental needs that will enable the person to reach each step, and determine action plans that will result in successful development.

A way of putting this plan on paper is to use a set of T-charts as illustrated in Exhibit 17–1 which is a plan for Cindy's growth to claims manager. A separate chart is used for each position or level of responsibility along the individual's career path. The left section of each chart itemizes the development needs that will enable the person to reach that position, while the right side of each grid identifies developmental activities and action plans that will fulfill the developmental needs. By adding a general cover sheet (Exhibit 17–2) and an explanation of the development plan (Exhibit 17–3), the career plan becomes a booklet for continuing review and reference for the individual. Additional career-related information can easily be added.

Exhibit 17–2 outlines the steps involved in one approach to career development. The following steps are included:

1. A thorough career assessment with the psychologist.

2. A second meeting with the psychologist to review the assessment and develop a preliminary career plan.

3. A planning session with the psychologist, the individual's manager, and a representative from human resources. In this session, the preliminary plan is reviewed and firmed up. Planning charts are completed. By the end of the session, the individual should know what his or her goals are, what the developmental needs are, the types of activities and action plans that should be pursued in order to reach those goals, and what the time frame is for each.

Exhibit 17–1
T-Chart for Development Plan

CINDY PLAT
XYZ Insurance
September 12, 1990

Development Plan for Claims Manager

Development Need	*Action Plans*	*Timeline*
A. Group presentation skills	A.1) Enroll in Toastmasters	November
	2) Ask manager for opportunity to make presentation to the department	Conference on Friday
	3) Join PTA and ask for chance to present information at a meeting	Monday night
B. Knowledge of budgeting	B.1) Take course "Accounting for Non-Accounting Managers"	Check dates with AMA
	2) Ask Jeff in Accounting to review company forms and procedures	after completing course noted in B(1)
C. Improve leadership skills	C.1) Ask manager for feedback on day-to-day approach	
	2) Take "Leader Effectiveness Training" course	February 1991
	3) Read *The Leader-Manager*	

4. An annual review and update, both to assess progress and to extend the plan when appropriate.

Some psychologists will take a slightly different approach, focusing only on the individual. In place of the meeting with the person's manager and a human resources representative, they will provide a developmental letter to the individual and let the individual decide how to use it. Some individuals review the plan outlined in the letter with their manager, while others do not, depending on the strength of the relationship and the culture of the company. (There are still some managers who are threatened by a subordinate who aspires to the manager's job.)

There are variations to these approaches, but the goal remains basically the same. That is, to provide the individual with a written plan that can be used as a guide in career development and can be updated periodically as advancement takes place.

Exhibit 17–2
Cover Sheet for Development Program

Development Plan

The following pages contain your development plan, which was compiled with the assistance of your manager, a human resources professional, and the psychologist. It contains separate sections focusing on your development in your current position, and on your development for future positions. We suggest that you use this plan as a working document in your personal and career development efforts. Review it periodically and add your own progress notes and additional ideas as you progress. An annual review with your supervisor is also suggested.

There are a variety of developmental activities that are beneficial. Some possibilities are:

- Courses, seminars and workshops
- Committee memberships
- Community involvement
- A planned reading program (a reading list is attached)
- Feedback and coaching from your supervisor or others in the company

The last, feedback and coaching, is frequently overlooked in the planning process. The recommended approach is to ask your supervisor or manager for frequent feedback regarding a developmental area on which you are working. People usually are willing to do this if they know you are interested. It is an ongoing process that helps your progress and also helps build solid working relationships. With certain traits and skills it is frequently beneficial to confer with the company psychologist.

In future review sessions, your plan will be updated and extended. Development is an ongoing rather than a static activity. The implementation of certain action plans might extend through a significant portion of your life.

Career development planning might also be done by a human resources professional within the company, especially if the candidate is an hourly employee or a first-level supervisor. People who go through a structured apprenticeship program have a partial career path laid out for them as long as they remain in the trade. However, if they move beyond the technical focus into supervision or management, they will be in need of an additional career plan to prepare them for those responsibilities.

Returning now to Bart, Cindy, and Stacy, we find Bart developing a plan that includes both vertical and horizontal moves within the foundry so that he can develop a breadth of skills while taking on additional responsibility. His plan has a technical focus that could change if he decided he wanted to be a supervisor. Cindy's plan involves only two positions beyond her current job. She feels that two positions is as far as she can plan clearly. She also feels she has a lot to learn, development-wise, since she just moved into her current position. Her plan involves focusing more on people skills than technical skills, since the

Exhibit 17–3
Explanation of Development Plan

Your Development Program

This booklet is for your use in recording and summarizing the results of your personal and career assessment. We hope that the experience and the summary will help you to understand yourself better and to become more effective in your personal life and your career.

Successful companies recognize that the human element is a primary resource and an organization is only as competent as the people who work within it. Thus, they are focusing extra time and effort on developing their human resources.

As a nation we are becoming more aware of the impact that appropriate career choice and development has on both personal satisfaction and occupational effectiveness. We are also recognizing that career planning is an important factor in reaching one's goals.

Our first goal as professional psychologists is to provide you with as much accurate information as is available. Our second goal is to assist you in understanding and using that information to increase your personal and career effectiveness.

Our approach involves several steps:

- An assessment to assist you in becoming more aware of your strengths and limitations by reviewing your abilities, interests, personal traits, and values.

- A conference with the psychologist to review the assessment, establish a preliminary career plan, and set preliminary development goals.

- A conference with the psychologist and your manager to review, modify, and firm up the career path and development goals, and to focus on action plans that can be implemented to assist in reaching those goals.

- A periodic review and update of the career path and development plan, usually on an annual basis.

former will be more critical for her long-range growth. Stacy has developed a plan that focuses on gaining experience in areas where she has limited background. She too has bettered her chances to achieve her objectives.

Bart's plan was developed with the help of his manager and the human resources manager from his company. Cindy's and Stacy's were developed with the help of their manager, a human resources representative, and the company's consulting psychologist. All are pleased with the direction they have set for themselves. They see their career plans as challenges rather than struggles. All realize that there might be some sidetracks along the way, but also realize that if they hadn't set plans and goals they likely would do a lot more floundering and not advance as rapidly as they should now.

Finally, all three employees realize there are no guarantees and that positions can disappear even after one has reached them. There is a need to continually update and refocus in order to stay abreast in the changing world.

18

Psychological Assessment of a Group: The Management Audit

**Deborah L. Parker and
Kelley A. Conrad**

It frequently becomes appropriate for the psychological consultant to gain more than an informal feeling for an organization's culture and present climate. It is often valuable to understand an organization from the perspective of operating philosophy, prevailing management style, specific group characteristics, and individual idiosyncrasies. When initiating a relationship with an organization, complete assessments of all the top managers can provide a critical body of information. This can be especially helpful when the psychologist is to be involved in development or personal change programs. A complete audit of the management group develops a comprehensive view of the strengths and weaknesses of the management team. Upper management is an appropriate place to focus initially because the characteristics of this group have tremendous impact on the style and effectiveness of management throughout the organization. The nature of top management also affects the probability of success of organizational development efforts.

AUDIT FOR ORGANIZATIONAL DIAGNOSES

Ideally, the psychologist completes a standard psychological assessment of the president or CEO during the initial stages of the consulting relationship. Psychological assessments are standard when they include a clinical interview combined with paper-and-pencil testing to evaluate the individual and predict future managerial performance. Individual assessment procedures have been described in depth in chapters 1, 4, and 5. When a management audit is to be conducted, the assessment of all members of the upper management team follows promptly after the assessment of the CEO. This maintains the momentum of the process and helps manage potential resistance and anxiety. It is important that individuals enter the assessment and audit with an understanding of the nature and purpose of both. Alleviating anxiety and focusing on a positive, developmental perspective enhances the likelihood that individuals will cooperate and contribute valuable information and perspectives to the audit. This is made more critical by the fact that the degree to which communications regarding the management process can be open and positive is sometimes constrained by the purpose for which the audit is planned. For example, if serious restructuring is taking place and there is a clear need to eliminate some positions or individuals, it is difficult to alleviate anxiety. Proper positioning ensures that individuals understand not only the impartiality and objectivity of the audit, but also that regardless of the outcome, they will receive beneficial developmental feedback and support.

Importance of CEO's Support

The support of the CEO during the management audit is critical. Successful audits are dependent upon the strength of the relationship that has been established between the CEO and the psychologist. Participating in an assessment allows the CEO to gain first-hand experience with the process, considerably enhancing the CEO's ability to communicate accurately to subordinates about the process. The credibility of the process from the perspective of subordinates is also enhanced when the CEO completes the assessment first. Most importantly, however, experiencing a complete assessment allows the CEO to judge the accuracy and usefulness of the process. This judgment contributes to the confidence that the CEO has in the psychologist and the audit results.

Conceptual Models

The assessment process during an audit is similar to that described in chapters 1 and 6. During the interview, however, questions are asked that allow the psychologist to evaluate each individual's perspectives regarding the strengths and weaknesses of the organization and its operating philosophy. Many psychologists follow a conceptual model of some sort to structure the inquiry. Detailed information is collected about important organizational processes in each functional area of the organization.

Open Systems Model. A number of firms, including a prominent management consulting group that specializes in organizational development, follow an open systems model in diagnosing organizational processes (Nadler & Tushman 1988). This model accesses information that falls into the three major categories: (1) Organizational Inputs, (2) Transformation Processes, and (3) Organizational Outputs.

Some examples of organizational inputs are environmental factors (such as the influence of the government and markets), resources (such as people and raw materials), and history. Transformation processes are activities that take place within the organization in order to convert or process inputs. They are the activities that lead to results or outputs. Transformation processes can include informal as well as formal management processes, organizational structure, tasks, and individual skills. Organizational outputs include things such as organizational goal attainment, group or unit productivity, and individual task performance.

Opportunity Mapping Model. A second prominent model used to direct audit questions is the opportunity mapping model (Wilson Learning 1986). This model identifies selected key aspects of organizational functioning. Specific questions explore performance areas in detail. In the audit, individuals are asked to indicate the levels of excellence and importance for each item using a five-point scale. Following each numerical rating, the manager is asked to briefly explain his or her rating. The psychologist is able to conduct opportunity mapping on the basis of the numerical data generated and add specific details from content analyses of the managers' supportive comments. The main concern is with areas of high importance but poor performance, or those with high importance and solid performance. The former areas indicate possible weaknesses in managerial performance, or the whole organization's performance in that particular area. Identifying these is useful in determining developmental needs for both the individual managers and the organization. Items that are rated high in importance and performance indicate key managerial or organizational strengths. The audit we use at Humber, Mundie and McClary assesses the following twelve areas:

1. Communications: upward, downward, and lateral
2. Image to employees, customers, and community
3. Planning and goals, long-range and short-range
4. Responsibility and authority: clarity and empowerment
5. Reporting relationships: clarity and definition
6. Performance standards: clarity, performance management, and feedback
7. Staffing and management of human resources
8. Organizational culture and morale
9. Problem detection and solution implementation
10. Effectiveness
11. Readiness to adapt
12. Quality orientation

ANALYZING THE MANAGEMENT AUDIT

The focus during a management audit is on each individual's perceptions of the key challenges facing the organization, including how each person would prioritize these challenges. This focus allows the psychologist to identify the underlying values and beliefs that contribute to successful as well as unsuccessful managerial actions throughout the organization. Once all the audit-related psychological assessments are complete, there are several different approaches the psychologist can use to analyze the information obtained.

Examining Individual Assessments

At the individual level, the psychologist can review each report and identify developmental needs that indicate appropriate training. If some of these needs appear consistently across the group, the psychologist makes recommendations regarding appropriate group seminars and other possible training interventions.

Generating Group Information

Group Profile. To generate group-level information, the psychologist examines average scores and consistency obtained across tests indicating cognitive functioning or personality characteristics, such as achievement motivation and assertiveness. This information is appropriate for group feedback sessions where the purpose is to describe a group profile of characteristics that are consistent among group members. Patterns of intellectual capacities are examined to identify the degree to which the abilities of current managers support or work against successful performance in each position.

Social Style. A second major area of analysis focuses on the interplay among different personality characteristics and social styles of group members (Merrill & Reid 1981). Social style is a popular concept that helps individuals understand interpersonal problems that come from differences in personal preferences. The basic idea is that we all become comfortable with a certain pattern of behavior through our experiences. Behavior that is comfortable for people is usually predictable. A person's social style represents the person's comfort zone—the way the person will be seen by others as most frequently and comfortably behaving. The identification of a person's style comes by combining assessments of how assertive the person is when attempting to influence the thoughts and actions of others and how responsive he or she is when expressing feelings in relations with others.

Potentially difficult relationships can be identified where the dominant social style of an individual in the group is incompatible with those of others. The interplay among the personalities of individuals in key roles has important implications for patterns of communication, leadership style, and decision-making throughout the organization. Useful information in identifying such patterns of interaction and operation can also be obtained from personality measures such as the Adjective Check List (1983) or the Myers-Briggs Type Indicator (1976).

A scoring system can be developed where sections of the report are rated and weighted according to their criticality in contributing to successful performance within the group. Scores can be examined in order to compare individuals or groups on different dimensions or on sections of the report, indicating some of the strengths and weaknesses of the group as a whole.

The focus on key management activities during audit interviews reveals critical information about organizational strengths and weaknesses, and the level of consensus among management regarding organizational priorities. Either the open systems approach to inquiry or the opportunity mapping approach allows the psychologist to quickly identify potential problems.

Partial Example of Audit Results

Audit Results for Key Areas. Eight of the twelve management process areas were judged to be high in importance. The three areas judged most important were organizational morale, organizational staffing, and responsibility and authority. In decreasing level of rated importance, after the top three, were organizational communications, performance standards, organizational planning and goals, problem detection and solution, effectiveness, organizational image, organizational relationships, readiness to adapt, and quality orientation.

The overall excellence ratings of the management processes at the company were seen as more average in level. Five of the areas of management process were rated as having excellence high in the average range, four were rated as straight average or slightly below average, and three were rated below average. The five areas with the highest excellence ratings were organizational morale, readiness to adapt, organizational image, performance standards, and organizational communications. The process areas rated in the average range were quality orientation, problem detection and solution, organizational relationships, and effectiveness. Areas rated as below the average were organizational planning and goals, and responsibility and authority.

Three management process audit areas demonstrated significant differences between the importance and excellence ratings. These were organizational planning and goals, managerial responsibility and authority, and managerial performance standards. For all three of these managerial processes, the rated difference between excellence and importance exceeded one full point on the average rating level.

Organizational Planning and Goals. The key managers and supervisors who participated in the audit indicated that while this remains an area of concern, the company has taken significant steps in the last six months to improve in this area. Most were optimistic that the new planning process will be productive and worthwhile. A few individuals lower in the management chain of command indicated that while they know that the process had started, they had yet to see any direct impact on their own areas.

The greatest concern showed up in the area of long-term goals and seemed to reflect the comments just mentioned. While people know that the process has been implemented, many have yet to see any direct effects. While many people are excited by the knowledge that the strategic thinking is taking place, many indicate a direct need to know more about the strategic goals that have been defined.

In the short-range planning area, excellence was rated at the average area. Some concerns were expressed that it is hard to understand how some of the short range actions and activities relate to the professed longer-term goals. Many made comments about crisis-type interventions made by various managers that are highly situationally specific and often counterproductive when viewed against the longer-term goals. There was also some concern that some of the first-level managers and supervisors were not given enough responsibility to make decisions. One person commented, "We make some plans, but organizing, monitoring, and carrying them out in a systematic way is often a joke."

Recommendations. Overall, it appears that it would be beneficial for the company to make systematic efforts to communicate its long-range plans and goals to all key-level managers and supervisors. It is not unusual for a communications gap to occur between the top managers and the main core of middle managers in an organization. This seems to have happened here. Because of this, it is important for the division heads to make a special effort to translate the company's strategic goals and objectives into divisional goals making special efforts to ensure these are then communicated to all their managers. It is also important that all managers know what is expected of them. The whole performance goal-setting and appraisal process becomes quite crucial in organizations such as this one where the managers are bright, achievement-oriented, and well-educated. While many managers in the company fit this description, their goal-setting and appraisals with their reporting managers have not reflected the sophistication that is required to maintain job satisfaction in those junior-level managers. Finally, it would be wise for all managers to review the manner in which they feedback specific concerns to those who report to them. Care needs to be exercised to avoid disturbing major long-term priorities by issuing too many incidental and nonrelated orders.

Review of Results

Once the audit is complete, the results are reviewed with the CEO. Feedback sessions are then conducted in private with each manager. It is important that each individual receive feedback regarding the findings of that person's psychological assessment. Regardless of the purpose of the management audit, individuals benefit from the assessment feedback and developmental suggestions. The feedback sessions allow managers to judge the accuracy of the report from their own perspectives. Afterwards the senior operating group meets for feedback on the management team and its effectiveness. This can be followed by meetings that provide the CEO and each manager an opportunity to discuss audit results and develop a plan for improvement.

It is critical to maintain individual confidentiality throughout the audit process, where information is shared only during selective, prearranged meetings. The management audit can easily become a sensitive procedure. Assessments and audits can present a threat to long-standing perceptions based on personal loyalty and close associations. The psychologist and the CEO must protect people from their natural human curiosity and, in some cases, competitiveness.

PAYOFF FOR MANAGERS

When a management audit is conducted, it provides managers with measures of managerial effectiveness that give an overall feeling about the organization and that allow comparisons of departments. The audit also provides early identification of problems and establishes a base for the development of workable solutions. When conducted on a regular schedule every few years, the management audit provides managers with a way of monitoring progress in the key areas of management functioning. Trend data can be used to check progress from year to year. A typical company program conducts a management audit on an ongoing basis, every other year. On the alternate years a general employee attitude survey is conducted involving all employees and managers. It is a valuable tool available to management for "taking the temperature" of its management team. The data obtained assists in developing and maintaining an able, productive, and effective work force. Organizational needs change continuously as a company progresses through different periods of establishment, growth, and decline (Greiner 1972). The audit process assists an organization in tracking its effectiveness as a management team responding to such ongoing change.

APPLICATIONS OF THE MANAGEMENT AUDIT

Quick Familiarization with a Management Team

A completed management audit provides an information base that is applicable to numerous needs and interventions. One of the most obvious reasons to complete an audit is to quickly familiarize a CEO with the capabilities and potential of key members of the management team (DuBrin 1972, 29). This focus is frequently the case in situations of merger, acquisition, or the introduction of a new CEO. This information allows the CEO to make realistic human resource plans that best match individuals with different responsibilities in the organization. Individual assessments also provide critical information for succession-planning activities, addressing organizational needs against a background of appropriate individual skills, abilities, and personal characteristics.

Improving Selection

Information from the management audit also contributes significantly to the selection process in the organization. Understanding the dominant characteristics and the needs of upper management provides a solid base for selecting individuals who will be compatible with the rest of the group and who will add strength in needed areas. The audit can also help to refine the selection assessment process for the whole organization by identifying skills and characteristics that match organizational needs and culture.

Improving Interactions

Group-level feedback from the audit is a powerful team-building tool. Such feedback, delivered in team-building sessions, promotes mutual understanding of the skills and personal characteristics of each individual in the group so that more effective means of interactions and task assignments are accomplished.

Identifying Problem Areas

One of the primary reasons for the management audit is to identify key problem areas throughout the organization. For example, communication barriers or conflicting priorities that inhibit cross-functional team efforts can be identified and addressed. Broad-based training needs can be identified, or a basis for strategic human resources planning can be established.

Facilitating Change

An audit enhances the ability of the psychologist to be a strong facilitator of almost any change in the organization. The audit is particularly helpful in terms of identifying discrepancies in perceptions, visions, expectations, or priorities between different individuals or levels of management. This enables the psychologist to work with groups and individuals throughout the organization in such a way as to increase consensus regarding the operating philosophy and priorities for action.

Team-Building

The audit supports the psychologist as facilitator in another respect by acting as a thought or action starter involving employees in the analysis and solution of problems. This can contribute to employees' personal and professional growth while increasing their involvement, participation, and commitment to the solutions. In this way, the audit serves to enhance communications both upward and downward in the organization, and often results in increased morale and motivation for managers and employees.

SUMMARY

The management audit provides both top management and the business psychologist with a critical body of information. Having this information increases the effectiveness of efforts to facilitate or improve many processes and relation-ships in the organization. Audit results are particularly useful in facilitating change within the organization through formal programs such as quality pro-grams, or through more subtle efforts such as those designed to create cultural change. Potential barriers to developmental efforts can be identified and man-agement consensus regarding priorities can be increased. A management audit is a powerful tool in conducting organizational diagnosis, and can be administered to upper management, any target subgroup, or to the entire organization.

REFERENCES

Briggs, K. C., & Myers, I. B. (1976). *Myers-Briggs type indicator*. Palo Alto, Calif.: Consulting Psychologists Press.

DuBrin, A. J. (1972). *The practice of managerial psychology*. New York: Pergamon Press.

Gough, H. G., & Heilbrun, A. B., Jr. (1983). *The adjective check list manual*. Palo Alto, Calif.: Consulting Psychologists Press.

Greiner, L. E. (1972). Evolution and revolution as organizations grow. *Harvard Business Review*, July-Aug.

Merrill, D. W., & Reid, R. H. (1981). *Personal styles and effective performance*. Radnor, Penn.: Chilton Book Co.

Nadler, D. A., & Tushman, M. G. (1988). A congruence model for organizational problem solving. In *Organizational analysis series/analysis*. New York: The Delta Consulting Group. Inc.

Wilson Learning, Inc. (1986). *The Innovator family of group creative thinking tools*. Minneapolis: Wilson Learning, Inc.

_____ **Part Four**

*Providers of
Psychological Assessments*

19

RHR International and Psychological Assessment

RHR International

This chapter presents a brief history of RHR International's (formerly Rohrer, Hibler & Replogle) approach to psychological assessment. We will focus mainly on our Personal Development Guide, which is both a product and a process. How we assess candidates external to a company, as well as internal professionals, will also be included, with emphasis on the primary outcome we attempt to impact: Management development in support of a company's desired business strategies and outcomes. Our discussion is intended to be a straightforward description of RHR's history with the psychological assessment, or Personal Development Guide process, the nature of the process, and its benefits to our clients.

When Perry Rohrer, Francis Hibler, Fred Replogle, Charles Flory and other psychologists decided to become partners in corporate psychology, they began by structuring an assessment approach. Their first attempts centered on assembling a battery of test instruments that would most effectively differentiate successful from unsuccessful candidates. However, they found the test instrument approach to be a dead end. Although they discovered test batteries to be useful in selecting hourly and office workers, psychometrics alone yielded an incomplete picture of managers and executives. Moreover, they could not satisfy themselves that any combination of tests would reliably differentiate among candidates across the wide array of their client's work environments.

RHR International's founders' unsuccessful search for the ideal candidate assessment test battery led instead to the following fundamental beliefs that still guide our firm's work today. First and foremost, they determined that the complexities of manager selection and assessment require the synthesis of both objective and subjective information about people. This conclusion places our work within the realms of art and science, and places the primary responsibility on the assessor's professional judgment rather than on the assessment tools employed. Without the assurance of scientific certainty, we are dedicated to collecting a thorough base of subjective data so that we can provide our clients with the most valid and professionally honest conclusion available.

Fully understanding the business professional requires face-to-face conversation about those key work and life issues that the professional finds most significant in making the person what he or she is today. Also, there are critical job and company-specific success factors that can only be identified through a thorough understanding of the work environment (i.e., the company's history, current culture, and employees). The psychologist must gain knowledge of both the individual undergoing assessment and the specific context within which the professional will work to determine the goodness of person-job fit.

The most reliable and accurate "instruments" for assessing person-job fit are corporate psychologists. They are uniquely qualified through education in behavioral science, professional training by RHR, and generalist experience in a wide range of businesses and industries. With the average cost of a bad top-executive hire approaching $250,000, RHR helps protect clients' bottom lines by increasing our clients' "hit rate" with new hires and by helping to develop current managers.

RHR PERSONAL DEVELOPMENT GUIDE

In terms of the RHR Personal Development Guide (PDG) as a product, we provide to the client a report with our professional interpretation of the interviewee's psychological characteristics. For each professional interviewed, we also provide a practical plan to maximize that person's strengths and to meet opportunities for professional development. The report is a confidential and stand-alone document written with minimal psychological jargon. We record our observations in five core categories essential to a thorough understanding of a manager: intellectual functioning, emotional maturity, interpersonal skills, insight into one's self and others, and organizational skills. Each of these categories includes a number of specific issues designed to capture the interviewee's capabilities within a specific work environment.

Most of the interview process consists of an open-ended conversation between the psychologist and interviewee. Major topics covered during the interview include the interviewee's personal background and education, with a primary focus on job history and career ambitions. Leisure activities and family relationships are also explored to ensure a multidimensional view of the individual. In many ways, the psychologist is less concerned about the actual details of the conversation than how they are expressed and the central themes derived from the details.

Intellectual Functioning

Within this category are included thinking style, decision-making and problem-solving abilities, and quality of the individual's professional judgment. Problem-solving ability is assessed using the RHR copyrighted Personnel Problems Test. This twelve-minute exercise is often the only paper-and-pencil test used in the assessment. However, raw intelligence is only one part of the equation. It is essential to determine how well the person applies problem-solving skill in business and other life situations. This can be assessed during the interview discussion. How quickly and thoroughly the interviewee responds to questions and how logically the person reviews his or her life history, as well as how much flexibility, curiosity, reflectiveness, and results orientation the person shows, all contribute to the psychologist's conclusions in this area.

Emotional Maturity

Included in this cluster is not only the person's level of emotional stability and control, but also the interviewee's values, motivations, energy, ambition, and stress-coping ability. Conclusions in this area are derived from both the person's interview behavior and self-description. How one deals with life crises, major successes, and day-to-day stresses indicate emotional strengths and limitations.

As in all categories of the PDG, the interaction of the work environment with the interviewee's personality must be considered. For example, an emotionally controlled, low-key, yet self-confident executive might work extremely well in a setting where infrequent but targeted expressions of enthusiasm are valued. However, in a work culture that demands outward displays of commitment on a frequent basis, as in some sales environments, a more effervescent style might need to be learned.

Interpersonal Skills

This category deals with human relations and runs the gamut from the first impression the interviewee makes to the impact on people over time. Critical social issues include how effectively one communicates, persuades, and handles conflict. The kind and strength of individual relationships a person builds can suggest the level of organizational support the person can build. Openness, honesty, and integrity are also addressed in this section.

A sizable challenge in this area is to give appropriate weight to what is often the interviewee's best or worst behavior during the interview in terms of how the individual operates in other situations. Although some level of artificiality is expected in the interview, it is amazing how well interview behavior can predict social behavior at work.

Insight into Self and Others

This category is often the most difficult but rewarding for the psychologist to pursue. One's level of insight into self and others is often a covert and guarded area, but one with profound consequences if not adequately assessed. How well one develops insights about oneself can indicate personal flexibility and, ultimately, how well the person will respond to professional development efforts. A professional with a substantially inaccurate self-image builds on a faulty foundation. Likewise, one's objectivity and quality of insights about people can suggest the level of skill at mentoring and providing useful feedback to future subordinates.

Characteristics addressed in this section include one's understanding of personal motivations, whether there is an understanding of personal strengths and limitations, interests in self-development, and how realistically and accurately the interviewee can describe himself or herself. Insights about others encompass a person's intuitive and analytic skills at reading other's motives, needs, strengths, and weaknesses.

Organizational Skills

An area that clearly distinguishes the report of an RHR corporate psychologist is the organizational skills category. Because of the psychologist's grounding in a variety of business environments and understanding of the particular organizational context, the psychologist is uniquely qualified to make observations about a manager's administrative style, ability to organize and direct, performance as a manager, colleague, and subordinate, and skill at planning and initiating. Even as new technologies and organizations evolve, RHR has found the same behavioral categories described in the previous sections to be applicable in assessing managers and other personnel, as they were in the organizations of almost a half-century ago, when RHR began its business.

THE HIRING RECOMMENDATION

For candidates outside the company, RHR makes one of the following recommendations in the Personal Development Guide: "We recommend (or do not recommend) Ms. Smith for the position of vice-president of manufacturing, insofar as her psychological characteristics are concerned."

RHR includes the hiring recommendation paragraph because the client is not only asking for a description of the candidate, but also our synthesis of that data into a specific conclusion. We make it clear to the candidate and the client, however, that our job is to contribute to the decision-making process, but the client is the final decision maker. In any event, the inclusion of a hiring recommendation shows that we are willing to be held accountable for the outcome of our professional judgment.

From a different perspective, the inclusion of a specific recommendation encourages the professional discipline and development of the RHR psychologist. For each candidate assessed, we commit ourselves to not only apply our skills at describing human behavior, but to make a professional judgment about whether the candidate will succeed in that particular organization.

For internal promotion candidates, a hiring recommendation is not included in the PDG. It is our belief that a professional already on the job will have proven to the employer how effectively he or she can function. Instead, we state in our developmental recommendations section the steps the employee must take to successfully assume additional responsibilities.

DEVELOPMENTAL RECOMMENDATIONS

The idea of including developmental recommendations represents an historical shift by RHR. Forty-five years ago, RHR called the Personal Development Guide an "evaluation." This title was apt because our early clients needed the description of the interviewee along with a hire or do not hire recommendation. During the 1960s, we realized that the evaluation neglected a key facet of human behavior—that people do change and can grow with proper guidance. It was at this point that developmental recommendations were added to the evaluation, and the result was called the Management Planning Guide (MPG). This hybrid document also represented the management trend of its time. With U.S. management practice still modeled upon the autocratic military style, the MPG focused on what management's parental role and duties should be in developing employees. In the past ten to fifteen years, as management philosophies have become more participative and empowering, the Personal Development Guide was designed to keep pace. The PDG is written with the assumption that the individual and the organization will both take responsibility for the person's professional development.

Two sets of developmental recommendations are prepared for feedback: one for the interviewee and one for management. The psychologist prepares recommendations for professional development from the personal characteristics described in the five PDG categories, in light of the organizational context.

Recommendations vary as widely as the range of candidates and internal employees we have interviewed. Yet, most areas for improvement cluster around a few key professional survival skills: managing others, problem-solving, and developing trust within the organization. Moreover, dealing effectively with people to achieve desired business results is the foundation for nearly all of our recommendations.

FEEDBACK

Feedback to the interviewer and management turns the PDG product into a value-added process. Informing all involved parties of the PDG results and action plan through the facilitation of the corporate psychologist elevates the PDG from a static diagnostic report to a dynamic developmental intervention. The richness of the document and its value to the client are optimized by input from the psychologist who conducted the interview. The psychologist can build on the documentation by participating in "what if" scenarios with the client. The psychologist can also clarify and expand on the PDG document to help the interviewee understand and act upon the developmental recommendations.

In a selection interview, the psychologist provides feedback first to the client, along with a hiring recommendation. The candidate is also offered feedback, whether hired or not. As psychologists, we feel an ethical responsibility to the interviewee to provide responses to the questions raised during the PDG discussion. It is normally positioned with the candidate that, if hired, we will see him shortly after being hired for the feedback session. If the candidate is not hired, we leave the responsibility with the individual to contact us for a feedback session at no charge. Feedback is a natural consequence of an employee PDG because assessment and development cannot be separated. Assessment feedback is the vehicle for professional development.

Introducing the Feedback Process

After the interview and the PDG report are completed, the psychologist is prepared to share personal observations and recommendations with the client and interviewee. One copy of the report is often provided to whomever is responsible for professional development in the client organization. This person is usually the top human resources professional. Photocopying the report is prohibited to prevent abuse of the confidential information. The interviewee is encouraged to take notes during the psychologist's presentation of the information, but is discouraged from acquiring a personal copy of the report.

The psychologist begins the feedback session with an explanation of the five PDG categories, as well as the limitations of the interview process. Because the PDG conclusions are drawn primarily from interview information, they are subjective. For this reason, and to ensure that the interviewee is actively involved in the feedback session, the interviewee is encouraged to agree or disagree as he or she feels is appropriate. By having the opportunity to explore the observations and conclusions in this manner, the psychologist often learns even more about the interviewee and client during the feedback session than in the PDG interview. The psychologist's observations and recommendations provide a forum to clarify insights and intuition, and to encourage the interviewee to commit to professional growth.

In the feedback session, the psychologist presents a view of the interviewee's characteristics in terms of the five PDG dimensions without valuing them as good or bad. However, the psychologist does contract with the interviewee to explore the "so what" of each characteristic within the context of the work situation to determine its significance. The psychologist does not attempt to make fundamental personality changes in the interviewee to force fit the person into the organization. The feedback is instead tailored to capitalize on the interviewee's strengths, and is designed to demonstrate mutual benefits to the organization and individual. A key issue is often that of how big of a change can realistically be expected of the interviewee, and how motivated the person is to make this change.

PDG REPORT: STORAGE AND SHELF LIFE

The cover page of the PDG document states that the PDG should be kept in a file separate from the individual's personnel records. This procedure helps ensure that the PDG is used only as a tool for professional development and not for future performance evaluation. Moreover, the PDG should also be viewed as a temporary product. Because people are dynamic, they grow and change. The relevance of the PDG is therefore time-limited. We recommend to our clients that they dispose of the document after three years and that we update the report with their employees at this time.

SUMMARY

The RHR International PDG represents both a product and a process. The PDG report is a product designed to reflect the individual's core characteristics that will most impact work performance. The PDG also provides recommendations to maximize strengths within the work environment. The interview and feedback session are designed to develop a psychological contract between client and interviewee to commit to the process of ongoing professional development.

RHR International's consulting philosophy stresses our commitment to facilitating our clients' desired business outcomes through the professional growth of their employees. We believe that using our services is a visible statement of our clients' commitment to human resource development as a strategic advantage.

20

Humber, Mundie & McClary

M. Gordon Pederson

VALUE TO EXECUTIVE MANAGEMENT

At 3:00 A.M. fretful chief executive officer finds sleep difficult because he foresees upcoming problems in a successful company experiencing explosive growth. As the company expands, an increase in the number of operating decision errors is occurring. The CEO made some hiring mistakes that now impact the company in a negative fashion. The vice-presidents are acting territorial, reluctant to share information relevant to other departments. Some people have a hard time coping with their jobs and suffer from emotional burnout because of what they think the company expects them to do. The company is experiencing a loss of cooperative spirit among the staff. In many respects, the organizational structure seems unwieldy, with the operational and administrative divisions not working together effectively. The CEO might be able to sort out the solutions to the above problems over a period of time, but this is a situation in which a business psychologist could be of value to the executive.

Humber, Mundie & McClary business psychologists are hired to help identify the salient problems and make recommendations to help a company function more successfully as a team. This supports the organization in achieving the present and future goals of the chief executive officer. The consultant works together with management to implement ideas to improve the well-being of the company. The business psychologist's expertise runs the gamut from offering ideas on assessing the talent of employees to helping the CEO deal with cultural changes. The consultant often gathers survey data of the attitudes of the employees, handles situational counseling sessions, recommends outplacement when necessary, and develops or recommends relevant training programs to help the organization cope with the changing business environment.

As an outsider who desires to see the company function more effectively, the Humber, Mundie & McClary business psychologist offers a fresh pair of eyes to examine management problems dispassionately. The consultant calls upon past experiences in assisting other clients to overcome similar problems, making objective observations and recommendations. The business psychologist often challenges the status quo. The consultant helps in planning for and assessing new opportunities, makes relevant judgments about people to be brought into the organization, and provides supportive encouragement to the chief executive officer to deal with some of the tough business decisions that need to be made for the ongoing health of the organization.

HISTORY

In November 1953, Drs. Wilbur J. Humber, Paul J. Mundie, and John D. McClary formed a partnership that became the basis for the firm of Humber, Mundie & McClary. The firm originally had 40 firms as clients in the Milwaukee area. Our original operating principle was to start with the study of top management in a process called a "management audit," wherein all levels, beginning with the president, were studied. The top-level managers were reviewed to determine how well-suited they were to their jobs, how well they were functioning, and whether they might be better-suited to another type of work within the company.

Originally, assessments covered only five major areas. First, the person's ability to assimilate new ideas and put them to work. Second, the individual's emotional maturity and reactions to different situations that might arise. Third, the ability to get along with people in the organization. Fourth, the person's work habits, and fifth, the person's motivation, persistence, and what the person considered a satisfying level of success.

The firm has continued to grow through the years, and currently contains seven full-time psychologists working in assessment and consulting. The firm also supports a growing training and development function. The primary client base centers in the Midwest. However, the firm has grown to provide business psychological consultation on a national and international basis.

MISSION

Humber, Mundie & McClary has identified the following mission:

- As business psychologists, we are dedicated to providing significant psychological leadership in the business community.
- We help people and organizations achieve personal, organizational, and leadership goals to meet current and future challenges.

- We believe that people want to contribute and are the building blocks of an organization.

- We also believe the success of an organization depends upon the success of individuals and the success of individuals depends upon an environment deliberately designed for growth.

- By providing psychological principles at the highest professional standard, we help our clients identify and implement key strategies to create an effective organization.

THE HUMBER, MUNDIE & MCCLARY APPROACH

Individuals who are responsible for organizations today have many of the same broad objectives that their counterparts have had through time; that is, leading the organization to the fulfillment of its mission. Humber, Mundie & McClary psychologists aid corporate leaders in achieving the vision they have for their organizations. The psychological assessment remains our best-known service and product. However, each psychologist attracts and holds client organizations according to the psychologist's own talents and professional style. Most of our clients are of moderate size, enabling a psychologist to understand many of the key people in the firm.

Philosophically, Humber, Mundie & McClary views organizations as systems that are orchestrated by the chief executive officer. Successful organizations have a clearly defined mission. This focus is translated into objectives that move the organization forward. The consulting psychologist's role in accomplishing this is to assist the organization in the creation of the milieu within which its people can prosper, achieving personal goals and growth while realizing the organizational objectives. The psychologist helps management build healthy and productive environments that are supportive of the human effort necessary to accomplish business goals.

Humber, Mundie & McClary remains convinced that working directly with the CEO is a key factor in successful consultation. The organization's healthy mental attitude begins with the president. Often the life and success of the corporation is a direct reflection of the philosophy and style of the chief executive officer. The president will consciously and unconsciously communicate personal desires to the entire organization. If despair, indecision, and obscure goals are communicated, these quickly become apparent in the daily operations of the company. If the message is one of hope, leadership, and clearly defined goals and objectives, these aspirations likewise will be reflected in the attitudes and feelings of company personnel.

A new consulting relationship is initiated by exploring the management style and personal aspirations of the chief executive officer and the top management team. Often this begins with a psychological assessment of the chief executive. The top management team is included in the next round of discussions. This often includes psychological assessments of the top management team. An important addition, however, is the inclusion of management audit questions that assist the psychologist in developing a clear, consistent definition of the corporate objectives. Once completed, this audit is reviewed with the president and the top management team. The audit information provides a basis for defining the goals desired as an outcome from the psychologist. These goals are then extended and elaborated into an organizational consulting plan and strategy. In a typical, ongoing relationship, this strategy and plan will be revised every few years in order to make sure it is appropriately targeted.

Our primary approach to consulting centers is the psychological assessment of people. The firm has a variety of psychological assessment programs tailor-made to clients' needs. All assessments are made after getting a thorough understanding of the job specifications, job responsibilities, and job expectations. Emphasis is placed upon learning about the special technical and managerial skills required for success in a position. It is also important to determine the psychological weaknesses the client is willing to live with and which psychological weaknesses the firm finds unacceptable in employees. The psychological assessments are conducted when executive management plans to bring people into the organization, upgrade a current employee through promotion, or provide career development for valued employees.

VARIETIES OF ASSESSMENTS

Executive Assessments

Humber, Mundie & McClary executive assessments are unique developmental experiences for middle- and top-level managers. They are designed to provide in-depth understanding of the dimensions of managerial performance related to the successful accomplishment of important tasks or responsibilities. They provide detailed feedback and developmental guidance. Based on assessment center technology, these executive assessments utilize a number of sample job situations to evaluate performance against dimensions selected on the basis of organizational importance.

After a candidate completes the executive assessment, a thorough review of the results helps management develop a clear picture of the candidate's performance. The follow-up discussion with the Humber, Mundie & McClary business psychologist helps the candidate consider changes in techniques and tactics. The discussion helps the person plan developmental experiences that will result in greater effectiveness.

Selection and Promotion Assessments

The main purpose of selection assessments is to determine if a person coming into the company can perform the tasks required by his or her responsibilities.

The business psychologist is also concerned with how successfully an outside person responds to the culture of the organization, and whether or not the individual can consistently bring value-added ideas that benefit the organization. When an employee is being promoted to a different position, the emphasis is on whether the position is a good fit for the individual and whether it maximizes the person's opportunity to succeed in the new job role.

In all selection and promotion assessments, judgments are made concerning the managerial style of the person and how this can affect others working in the particular department or area that will be that person's responsibility. Other judgments are made about the intellect of the individual and how the person approaches problem-solving. Thought is given to how skillfully the person communicates thoughts, orally and in writing, and the impact the person makes on other people. Key aspects of personality and the emotional stability of the person are described. The person's human relation skills and how they impact the immediate work group and the organization are profiled. It is also pertinent to focus upon the work ethic and personal motivations of the person. The assessment includes a description of the person's administrative skills and approach to managing others. The report concludes with a description of the person's career goals and the degree to which the goals are compatible with those of the organization.

Developmental Assessments

Humber, Mundie & McClary business psychologists believe strongly in the continuing growth of a person. In our judgment, it is important to have a written report of developmental assessments. Often in letter form, the report is addressed to the individual manager with a copy to executive management. The letter provides a basis for specific planning involving the individual and the manager. The employee can then use the developmental strategies as a key road map for personal self-development.

In the developmental assessment, the written report of the business psychologist focuses upon the following areas:

- Intelligence and problem-solving skills
- Impact and communication skills
- Emotional organization
- Human relation skills
- Work motivation
- Administrative and managerial skills
- Career orientation
- Overall summary
- Developmental strategies

The report concludes with a summary section in which the psychologist highlights specific strengths and notable liabilities on which the individual and executive management should focus attention. The focus is upon educational progress that can be relevant, such as university course work, work on a specific degree program, or seminars. Often a list of books or tapes is suggested. In addition, some special projects might be suggested or specific work experiences designated to help the employee.

The developmental assessment takes about a half day. Review of the developmental assessment takes from one to two hours. The time is used to brainstorm together how a person can work upon individual growth. Over the years, we have found it is helpful for the business psychologist to talk with the employee's supervisor. This conference alerts the supervisor as to how the developmental strategies might be made a part of the ongoing performance appraisal of the employee.

MANAGEMENT AUDIT

The management audit consists of coordinated psychological assessments and career counseling for all members of the management team conducted in a short time frame. The audit differs from assessments conducted one at a time in that executive meetings are held to discuss succession planning, organizational structure, potential of key people, and often team-building programs to enhance communication among the management team upon which the audit was focused.

Humber, Mundie & McClary recommends a management audit every three to five years as a regular check on managerial effectiveness. This provides an opportunity for the business psychologist to observe whether or not individuals are growing professionally.

Mergers and acquisitions are another area where the use of comprehensive management audits can help executive management determine which managers to keep, what efforts need to be made to retain key people, and which individuals are perhaps not an appropriate fit for the acquiring company.

CAREER COUNSELING

The career counseling process combines a psychological assessment with an extensive feedback interview to formulate a comprehensive developmental plan, tailor-made to the individual needs of the employee. Following the career counseling meeting, a developmental letter is sent to the individual, pinpointing the information shared in the report.

SUMMARY

Humber, Mundie & McClary's fundamental objective is to provide our clients with the expert knowledge and special techniques of the behavioral sciences, and of psychology in particular, to the end that our client organizations may become better managed and more effective in achieving their business objectives. We also seek to create and maintain a consulting organization of professional equals, wherein each of us can realize maximum opportunities for personal and professional development, satisfaction, stimulation, and association. We seek to provide our services and conduct ourselves in accordance with the highest standards and ethics of professional behavior, providing services in accordance with our clients' needs and our own competence. We accomplish this by:

- Developing an understanding with the client concerning the limitations as well as the value of our psychological judgments, predictions, and recommendations.

- Offering our services in areas where the client has clearly demonstrated need for such services, and terminating services when it becomes reasonably clear that the client is not benefiting from them.

- Limiting our services to areas where we have clearly demonstrated our competence, while at the same time broadening and deepening our knowledge and skill through a continual program of education and individual development.

- Assisting our clients in obtaining professional help for all important aspects of their problems that fall outside the boundaries of our competence.

- Maintaining a client relationship that is long-lasting. Our goal is to be a partner with the client. By having a long-term historical relationship with the client, we provide better insights to the current managers in coping with present and future change.

- Making recommendations that, at times, challenge the status quo. We make recommendations that fit the organizational structure and culture of the company.

We also seek to protect the dignity of the individuals with whom we work and to safeguard the confidential nature of the information we obtained. We do this by:

- Explaining to each individual we evaluate the purpose of our interviewing and testing and the ways in which the obtained information may be used.

- Revealing obtained information only to such responsible parties as have a legitimate concern with it, with special attention to appropriate controls on all written material, including the evaluation report.

- Defining the nature and direction of our own loyalties and primary responsibility, which is normally to the client or the organization rather than to any individual related to it.

Finally, we seek to ensure the high standards of scientific accuracy in our work and to contribute in the greatest extent possible to our profession. We achieve this objective by:

- Validating our work with our clients through scientific research.
- Participating actively in psychological associations with other professional groups.
- Publishing and in other ways sharing with our colleagues the results of our research and experience.

PSP Human Resource Development

Stephen L. Guinn

PSP is a human resource consulting firm that applies the principles of behavioral science to solving problems in the workplace. Its professional staff consists of experienced doctoral-level, licensed psychologists whose training and interest is in applying psychology to human resource issues to increase organizational effectiveness and productivity.

PIONEERING PSYCHOLOGY TO BUSINESS

Psychological Services of Pittsburgh (PSP) first opened its doors in 1946 to provide hiring and career counseling services to individuals and companies in western Pennsylvania. Before long, however, the work grew beyond the local area, as PSP began to work with national and international corporations. Following World War II, PSP quickly began to assist America's growing business community in the selection and effective placement of people returning from the armed services to civilian jobs. What began as a specialized consulting firm grew into a professional service group offering a variety of human resource consulting services to businesses, both large and small. PSP's recognition also grew nationally, due to the publication of its research findings on studies involving employee attitudes and motivation. PSP's professional services have kept pace with the changing needs of business, and now include the following:

- Employee selection
- Succession planning
- Career development

- Employee opinion surveys
- Organizational development
- Training
- Validation studies
- Outplacement counseling

In its 44-year history, PSP has worked with more than 500 companies of every size and product line and has provided employment assessment services for more than 70,000 people for the purpose of employee selection, succession planning, and career development. PSP recently changed its name to PSP Human Resource Development to better describe its business activities.

RESEARCH ENHANCES SERVICES

While there were many psychological consulting firms that emerged after World War II, PSP was unique in its early commitment to conducting research as a means of enhancing the delivery and effectiveness of its professional services. PSP, for example, was conducting validation studies on the effectiveness of its selection methods in the 1950s, long before there was a Civil Rights Act or an Equal Employment Opportunity Commission with government guidelines for industry to follow. PSP has always provided employee assessment services that adhere to the highest professional and scientific standards for reliability and validity. Thus, the information provided to businesses is more accurate, and, thereby, of greater benefit to both employer and employee. When employment testing came under government scrutiny in the 1970s, PSP had for many years been meeting the selection guidelines that were eventually established in 1978. During this period, representatives from PSP even visited Washington, D.C., and provided expert testimony to the federal government on the creation of the *Uniform Guidelines for Employee Selection Procedures*.

LINKING MOTIVATION TO PRODUCTIVITY

Helping companies meet their employment needs through effective employee selection, career development, and succession planning led PSP to devote significant resources to the study of employee motivation. The result is the historical Bi-Factor Theory of Motivation, by Frederick Herzberg, who conducted the research during his tenure as PSP's director of industrial research. The theory states that factors leading to job satisfaction are not simply the opposite of those that cause job dissatisfaction. Job satisfaction accrues from those considerations directly related to the job itself, while job dissatisfaction is influenced by conditions that surround the job. In 1959, the Bi-Factor Theory was presented in Herzberg's book *The Motivation to Work*, which has become a classic in its field.

PSP went on to conduct further studies on motivation that resulted in an extended framework for the Bi-Factor Theory that was reported by another PSP researcher, Ray Hackman, in his 1969 book titled *The Motivated Working Adult*. Hackman went on to discover, through objective, quantitative, and systematic analysis, that individuals had work motivation patterns that could be recognized and measured for effective job placement. The research conducted by Herzberg and Hackman has held up well over time and PSP still utilizes the results of their work for analyzing employee motivational characteristics.

Having tackled adult motivation patterns, PSP began a major study in the early 1970s on youth motivation. The idea was to determine when adult motivation patterns begin to develop within the individual and what environmental conditions might accompany this development. PSP's research studies concluded that at the high school level, only about one-fifth of the boys and girls had achieved comparable adult motivation patterns. Further, it was found that motivational growth was impeded by poor reading skills, negative teacher attitudes, and poor outside job experience. Motivational growth among high school students was found to be enhanced by opportunities to meet and form positive relationships with adults. Those students who showed adult motivation patterns demonstrated stronger identification with working parents and reported greater encouragement from home to read and excel in school.

ADAPTING TO CHANGING HUMAN RESOURCE PATTERNS

Recognizing changing work force patterns beginning in the 1970s, PSP also conducted a pioneer study of female middle managers and how they compared to successful middle managers who were male. This female executive study included interviews and psychological management assessments of successful female and male mid-level managers in twelve major corporations located in major metropolitan areas throughout the Midwest and Northeast. This research study received substantial attention from the national media and showed that successful women in management roles were not substantially different from successful men who occupied those same positions. While today this appears to be self-evident, in the early 70s female executives were considered ''different,'' mainly because there were very few of them. PSP's research scientifically identified that successful middle managers demonstrate the same high motivational patterns, able intellectual skills, and positive personal characteristics, regardless of whether they are male or female.

In the 1980s, PSP continued its research studies of the changing work force by conducting a study of dual career couples who were employed in business management positions. It was PSP's purpose to look at the changing social and family patterns emerging in the work force and to understand the resulting implications for human resource planning and development. PSP found that changing family relationships required more flexible human resource planning for successfully managing an increasingly diverse work force.

EMPLOYEE SURVEYS FOSTER ORGANIZATIONAL CHANGE

Another research area where PSP has performed pioneering work has been in the assessment of employees' opinions and attitudes. PSP's first publication on the subject came in 1957 with *Job Attitudes: A Review of Research and Opinion* by F. Herzberg, B. Mausner, Richard O. Peterson, and Dora F. Capwell. Throughout its history, PSP has devoted resources toward achieving accurate employee survey results through scientific measurement. It has been in the fore-front of utilizing computer and scanner technology for the successful gathering of employee response for analyzing information objectively and accurately. PSP's emphasis, however, has always been on more than just research. It has championed participatory employee surveys and the sharing of survey results to all employees to foster more effective communications and build greater trust. PSP's organizational development consulting also assists companies with appropriate follow-up in response to the information gathered in employee opinion surveys, thereby enabling companies to achieve effective organizational change.

SERVICES LINKED TO BUSINESS STRATEGIES

Throughout its 44-year history, PSP's emphasis has always been the practical utilization of scientific methods for helping organizations and individuals implement effective and workable strategies for obtaining results objectives. While offering specific techniques, PSP takes a broad prospective and insists that techniques not be an end in themselves, but be utilized for achieving results that foster a company's overall business strategy. Whether it be succession planning, employee selection, performance management, employee opinion surveys, or outplacement services, it is important to tie the delivery of such programs into the overall strategic approach of the company. PSP takes pride in making good companies even more efficient, responsive, and competitive in the marketplace and helping them tie their human resource development to their business planning strategies.

PSP's long history places it in a position to assist organizations and individuals in the 1990s to effectively deal with the rapid change in all economic, political, and social sectors. Our programs are aimed at effectively dealing with the changing work force, global competition, and the management leadership characteristics needed to address the changing competitive economic factors that will continue to challenge business into the next century.

_____ **Part Five**

Users of Psychological Assessments

22

Lincoln National Corporation

Richard J. Vicars

COMPANY PROFILE

Lincoln National Corporation (LNC) is the seventh largest publicly held, multiline insurance holding company in the United States. In 1989, our total revenue was over 8 billion dollars with net income of 269 million dollars on over 25 billion dollars in assets. Lincoln National has almost 17,000 employees worldwide. We have five primary business segments: property-casualty, employee life-health benefits, individual life, life-health reinsurance, and investment products. Lincoln National is headquartered in Fort Wayne, Indiana, and owns affiliate companies throughout the United States and England.

Lincoln National's property-casualty segment is led by American States Insurance Companies. This line of business generated one-third of our revenue in 1989. In the employee life-health benefits area, we are leading the way into the next century with our state-of-the-art automated systems and our focus on managed care. We have over five million lives under management. Our affiliate company, Employers Health Insurance, covers primarily small employee groups.

In the competitive individual life segment, Lincoln National has maintained profitability through careful underwriting and management in its many affiliate companies, as well as its core company, Lincoln National Life. Lincoln National's reinsurance segment is the leading life-health reinsurer in North America, and is a major participant in the world reinsurance market. Similar to our individual life area, we have provided reinsurance for more than 75 years.

Lincoln National's investment products segment is comprised of two main business units. The annuities unit focuses on savings vehicles for individual investors, while the corporate pensions unit gears its business to corporate pension-plan sponsors. Our investment segment has grown greatly in recent years. It accounted for 12 percent of total corporate revenue in 1989.

LINCOLN NATIONAL'S PHILOSOPHY OF MANAGEMENT

Lincoln National Corporation has a clearly articulated approach to the management of its human resources. We call this approach Total Management. This philosophy of management has six components. Each component relates to people management in a rapidly changing business environment. The principles taught to each new manager are those that we believe will help that manager succeed. Likewise, when current managers and managerial candidates go through psychological assessments, we are interested in knowing how each person compares to the ideals set forth in our Total Management approach.

Leadership

The first characteristic of the total manager is leadership. Lincoln National defines leadership as providing vision, goals, and direction for employees. It means being a guide, identifying a path to follow, being the first to take that path, and inspiring others to follow. Many leaders might be good managers, but only a few managers are good leaders. A leader has the ability to get others committed to the course of action the leader wants them to take.

Sensitivity to People

Another component of the total manager is sensitivity to people. By sensitivity, we mean the ability to understand the needs of individual employees, knowing what motivates them, and how best to develop their talents. Sensitivity in this context is not being wishy-washy; it is both understanding the feelings and concerns of employees, and taking a stand on their behalf as a result of that understanding.

Delegation

The third part of Lincoln National's Total Management approach is delegation. In other words, learning to let go. Effective delegation is the key to several desirable outcomes. One, it allows managers to accomplish more than if they tried to do everything themselves. Two, it enables employees to develop new skills and greater confidence as they take on more responsibilities.

Accountability

For delegation to succeed, a manager must instill a sense of task ownership in employees. We call this ownership "accountability," and it is the fourth part of Total Management. Being accountable does not mean demanding that others do what you want them to do. Instead, it means that we expect nothing less from ourselves than we expect from our employees. Accountability is one aspect of leadership, and it is also communicated by setting an example for employees to emulate and from which to learn.

Planning

The fifth component of Lincoln National's Total Management is planning. Effective planning today requires highly developed skills in strategic thinking and problem-solving. Effective planning involves anticipating events that can't be known until they occur. A good planner must be flexible, creative, intelligent, analytical, and adaptable. The total manager thinks about the individual activities comprising projects and ongoing work in terms of plan phases, rather than as separate tasks in and of themselves.

Communication

The glue holding all of the above components of Total Management together is communication, the final aspect of Lincoln National's approach to management. We have a strong belief in open communication. This policy is endorsed from the executive suite on down. Any employee can send a memo or brief note to the president and CEO of Lincoln National. Unlike many executives who give lip service to an open communication policy, our president will read and respond to all legitimate employee questions or concerns. Although it is time-consuming, he does this because he wants to set an example for all his managers to do likewise.

The total manager welcomes the opportunity to not only receive information from employees, but also to give it. The average manager fears giving out too much information, as if employees' awareness of certain details would be a personal threat. The truth is usually quite the opposite. Good communication reduces rumors. In most instances, a rumor is a distorted version of a grain of truth that has "leaked out." The best policy is to tell the truth before the rumor mill starts grinding. That way, our managers can control the communications, rather than leaving communications to the whims of the grapevine.

PSYCHOLOGICAL ASSESSMENTS AT LINCOLN NATIONAL CORPORATION

It is necessary to understand the Total Management philosophy described in the previous section to understand the use of psychological assessments at Lincoln National. The psychologists who provide this service have been working with our company for many years. They understand many aspects of our business, and are familiar with the individuals on our management team. Most importantly, they are aware of where we are trying to go in getting closer to the goals expressed in our Total Management approach. The psychologists are adept at assessing leadership capacity and potential, sensitivity to employee diversity issues, and whether or not a manager is a good communicator, as well as the more traditional "hard" management skills such as delegation, planning, and accountability.

The Types of Psychological Assessment Used at Lincoln National

At Lincoln National, we use psychological assessments for both selection and development. Different divisions within the company use assessments in ways that meet their needs. As a whole, though, assessments are used more in developmental contexts than for selection. When Lincoln National first started using psychological assessments about 35 years ago, they were used almost exclusively to provide input into selection decisions. In recent years, we have moved away from that usage, becoming more focused on developmental assessments.

Who Gets Assessed and Why

Lincoln National puts all candidates for key positions through a psychological assessment. Key positions are vice-president, senior vice-president, group vice-president, executive vice-president, and president. Occasionally, candidates for a position lower in the hierarchy will be assessed if that position is in a critical or sensitive area. The information that is gained from these selection assessments is carefully reviewed and discussed among the senior managers involved in the hire or promotion.

The rules are less formal when we are assessing employees for developmental purposes. In this case, employees who are thought to be of high potential are referred for assessment. We determine who these individuals are through our "round table" process. During the round table, all managers at a given level in a department meet to discuss the performance and developmental progress of each of their subordinates. Through these discussions, certain employees are recognized as current outstanding performers, as well as possessing characteristics that would seem to indicate high future potential. By referring them for a full psychological assessment, we receive corroboration (and sometimes disagreement) of our perceptions. This feedback helps the responsible managers become more skilled at the day-to-day evaluation of employees' capabilities.

How Selection Assessment Results Are Used

Lincoln National does a good job on its own of interviewing managerial candidates and sizing up their potential effectiveness with our company. We like to have the psychologist's input for several reasons. One, the psychologist, as an outsider, is more objective. Psychologists can tell the emperor about the emperor's lack of clothing because they are not involved in the managerial politics that are a part of all corporations. Two, the psychologists we use are experts in evaluating individuals for business-related purposes. They do this type of work every day, while our managers may do candidate interviews only once or twice each year. The psychologist's lack of intimate knowledge about the insurance and financial services industries is more than offset by the comprehensive understanding of what it takes to be an effective manager.

We use psychological assessments for both selection from the outside and for promotions. These two situations are handled somewhat differently. For external candidates, more weight is placed on the assessment results than for the internal promotion candidates. This is because we know very little about the external candidate. For this person, we would also spend much more time in intensive interviews of our own. Many executives would be involved in the interviewing of a top-level managerial candidate. At this level, it is difficult to determine who will be an outstanding performer. All the candidates who have made it through our initial screening look good. The psychologist's input helps us to frame the issue more clearly. Occasionally, the executives working on the hire will meet with the psychologist to review his report on the candidate, and to discuss areas of disagreement. By the end of the process, though, the choice to be made is usually clear.

When considering a current employee for a promotion, the focus is somewhat different. For one thing, we have a track record on the candidate. We know how well the individual has performed in the current job and in past positions with the company. We are aware of the individual's strengths and weaknesses. However, we still need the psychologist's input. Our familiarity with the employee is a two-edged sword. We recognize that we may let situation-specific behaviors overly influence our conclusions about the person's capabilities. For instance, an employee in a first-level supervisory role might be judged as too dependent on formal rules and regulations to ever function well as an independent decision-maker. In this case, it is the nature of first-level supervision that could be creating the conclusion about the employee, rather than the employee's inherent personal qualities.

Another difference between external and internal selection assessments concerns the feedback of results. After the selection decision has been made, the psychologist will eventually meet with all internal candidates for the position to discuss their assessment results. The focus of this discussion will not only be on why they were or were not chosen for the position, but also on what their weaker areas are, and what they can do to improve for future promotional considerations. The meeting with the successful candidate focuses on awareness of personal areas most likely to cause difficulty when performing on the new job. For non-selected external candidates, feedback of this nature is rarely requested, and so is rarely given.

How Developmental Assessment Results Are Used

As previously mentioned, the bulk of the psychological assessments conducted at Lincoln National are completed on current employees for developmental purposes. In this case, selected employees are asked to meet with the psychologist as a part of their development plans. Most employees are eager to do this because it signifies that top management might be considering them for promotions. There are two purposes in conducting developmental assessments at Lincoln National. One is to obtain information useful to management in planning for the future. Combined with the conclusions and observations from our round table process, the psychologist's assessment report and in-person remarks help us to slot each assessee in our overall succession planning.

The second purpose in using psychological assessments is to provide feedback to employees. Even the best employees with the highest potential have a few rough edges. Our goal is to make all assessed individuals aware of their current limitations so that they can begin to make improvements. That way, when we are ready to fill an open position, we will have someone waiting who has already begun to address areas of limitation.

The mechanics of the process are as follows. The psychologist meets with an employee, usually a manager, for the in-depth interview and, possibly, psychological testing. After the report is written and the top management is briefed, the psychologist reconvenes with the employee to review the assessment results. The focus in this meeting is on problem-solving. Strengths and weaknesses are identified, and plans to remediate the weaker areas are agreed upon. Developmental assignments may also be specified at this point.

For some employees, the psychologist might hold follow-up meetings to facilitate developmental progress. For other employees, a follow-up assessment session will be held several years later. In this latter meeting, the initial assessment will be reviewed, with activities and accomplishments during the interim analyzed. Further developmental recommendations will result from this second assessment meeting.

CONCLUSION

Psychological assessment has proven to be a useful addition to Lincoln National's selection and development systems. During the many years we have used assessments, the candidates with the best assessment ratings have done well in our company. In almost all cases, there is agreement by the psychologist and interviewing managers as to the overall recommendation of the candidate. However, the hiring manager can override the psychologist's recommendation. This would be an unusual case, though, because of the preselection of assessed candidates.

The psychologist's opinions are by no means infallible, however valuable they might be in most cases. I have vetoed the psychologist's recommendation on appropriate occasions. In these instances, the hired or promoted candidate worked out just fine. In almost all cases, though, there are no disagreements about the bottom-line conclusion. We may deliberate over specific points made about the candidate, such as the person's ''social polish.'' All in all, though, we feel that the use of psychological assessments has helped to make Lincoln National a better company.

23

McDonald Davis & Associates

Richard McDonald

MCDONALD DAVIS & ASSOCIATES

In the 27 years since McDonald Davis & Associates (MDA) was founded, it has grown in both traditional and unique ways. The resulting diversification of accounts is responsible for the company's accelerated growth.

In the mid–1970s, MDA moved into marketing strategic planning. Goals were set for development and expansion of services beyond what was being offered by traditional advertising agencies. In addition to traditional advertising and public relations services, our firm began offering marketing/strategic planning/market research, a more sophisticated approach to media planning and buying, and the integration of marketing and media into the whole creative strategy and planning process, thus establishing a true "team" approach to marketing and marketing communications. This team concept, represented by all disciplines in our firm, contributed to our growth in the business-to-business, financial, consumer service industry, and retail fields. It also enabled us to expand our service base and pioneer marketing programs in the legal fields, and propelled us into a leadership position in the healthcare field, which we had entered as pioneers in the late 1960s.

As one of the largest firms of our profession in Wisconsin, we serve 60+ clients in 24 states and employ more than 100 professional people. The last four years have been the most successful in the company's history. McDonald Davis's headquarters are in Milwaukee, with offices in Houston, Los Angeles, and Honolulu.

OUR INSURANCE POLICY IN HIRING AND PROMOTION

I see psychological assessments as an extremely valuable advisory component in our hiring process. Assessments are our insurance policy, saving the agency time, pain, and dollars. Considering the cost of hiring a new professional and moving that person to Milwaukee, the cost of the assessment validating our impression that the person will fit into our culture and prove to be a productive employee is a fraction of what is at risk.

Unique Requirements of Service Firms

It is very important for us to work closely with our psychologist so we can clearly communicate what we need. As a service organization, we are keenly aware of the differences between people who will be successful in our environment and those who will be successful in a manufacturing environment. Our employees must be much more externally directed. They must be, or learn to be, customer-oriented. They must stay focused in their areas of expertise. This distinction is often a critical element in determining who will be successful in our culture.

Pre-promotion Assessments

Another key area where psychological assessments provide insurance is in the area of pre-promotion reviews. By using assessments prior to promotion decisions, we avoid falling prey to the Peter Principle of promoting people to their level of incompetence. Developmental assessments conducted prior to promotions assist us in working with individuals to hone their skills. We seek to reduce the weight of our weaknesses while freeing our positive potential.

Making "Style Moves"

For the insurance to be effective, the psychologist must know the agency and its culture. When this is true, we are able to reach out for "style moves" that are designed to impact our agency culture in very specific areas and ways. For example, when we identify a need to find someone with a specific style or talent, we might decide to hire a candidate who is very different from the people who are presently in the target department or area. Another place where an intimate knowledge of our culture is of assistance is when we are at an impasse with a client. In these situations, we might use our psychologist as a sounding board. We explain our problem and how we feel stuck. Our psychologist will often say, "Have you thought about doing it this way?" or "Have you tried approaching them from this perspective?" Often these questions and insights help us break through the barriers that were impeding our progress.

Developing Trust in the Psychologist

In many ways I see our psychologist in a role that is parallel to that of my internist. I trust the psychologist's judgments because of his or her training, experience, and intimate knowledge of McDonald Davis & Associates. The psychologist has taken the time to get to know us. That time investment has helped our people come to trust the psychologist a good deal. When our psychologist is not available, he or she will refer us to someone else in the office. At other times, the psychologist might refer us to a specialist who addresses a unique problem. In these situations, we accept these other psychologists based on the trust already established.

WHO WE HAVE ASSESSED

We have assessments completed on all our people above the level of our support staff. This includes all our professional people, whether artists, media, or account people. We are looking at each person and their incorporation into our agency culture. We are very protective of that culture; it is what makes us unique as an agency and something we have spent a lot of time and energy building and maintaining. When we are considering someone new, we need assurance that the person will fit into the team we have built. Can that person be a star player making significant personal contributions and at the same time be active as a cooperative member of the team?

We also use assessments to evaluate the reality of someone being able to move up to greater responsibility within MDA. For example, we had a secretary from a blue-collar family background who, after a number of years here, wanted to move into a professional role. We built a program to help her develop the knowledge and skills that she needed to accomplish this goal. Assessment in such situations makes sure that we do not make the person false promises. We want them to be working toward a career goal that they can reasonably be expected to accomplish.

In situations where we are considering promoting someone, the psychological assessment helps us avoid promoting a person for the wrong reasons. I feel most organizations make the mistake of promoting someone simply because that person has been around for a while. This results in many people being promoted to jobs that they are not right for. In a recent MDA promotion, we had a person who was going to be required to work alone. This person was used to being part of a team, so we had concerns. These were confirmed by the assessment. Working with our psychologist, the individual mapped out and completed a program of development to prepare for the promotion. This included five or six sessions with the psychologist, reading assignments, and special thinking and planning efforts. In the end, she was promoted. The move has been a successful one. The new manager has commented a number of times since then how valuable the work with the psychologist was in supporting her move.

HANDLING REPORTS

We handle the reports as we do much important, confidential client information. The written report is given to the executive doing the hiring. If the
candidate will be assigned to a supervisor or department head, that person sees
the report as well. I see all the reports. Once we are finished with the reports,
we keep them in a locked, confidential file. Access to this file is controlled by
our office manager.

FEEDBACK

Everyone gets an oral feedback session with the psychologist who completed
the report. In special cases, when that person is not our regular account psychologist, we often arrange for an additional review with the account psychologist. We have instructed our psychologist to take the initiative to contact the
supervisor and schedule the meeting with the new employee 90 days after the
person is hired. We also encourage the psychologist to discuss suggestions with
the person's supervisor. It is not unusual for our psychologist to suggest that a
supervisor meet with an employee to discuss some specific aspect of the assessment. If someone asks to see the report, we show it to the person. It is not
a big no-no.

EXPLAINING ASSESSMENT

When we first mention assessment, about half of our candidates demonstrate
some tightness. I always use the term "business psychologists" to describe our
consultant. I will kid with the person a bit. I say something like, "Let me tell
you what it isn't and what it is." I emphasize that it is absolutely career-oriented.
I'm selling the idea that, as an agency, we do not want round pegs in square
holes. I'll often comment on how sad it would be for someone to uproot themselves, move to Milwaukee, and not have it work out. I emphasize that the
assessment is advisory only. We make the decision; the assessment is only part
of the process we go through. Finally, I will cite some examples. I use one
describing a time when we were ready to make an offer, but decided not to after
the assessment. In retrospect, this proved to be a good decision for the individual
and for the agency. A second example I use is a situation where we had decided
not to hire the person, but where the assessment convinced us to reconsider and
hire someone who became a top performer. Most candidates see the psychologist
as simply one more person interviewing them as a part of our typical round-
robin hiring process. We also promise people feedback, regardless of the decision. When the person is from out of town, this is done on the phone. With
this as an explanation of our procedure, I often see people visibly relax.

We started doing assessments six years ago. At this point so many people have come back and said it was a fantastic, positive experience that people who were already in the agency before that time now ask for assessment.

ACCURACY

I don't know how I would quantify the accuracy of assessments. We have missed on a few. These misses occur when we have not done a good job of preparing the psychologist by explaining what we feel we need. Sometimes we, or our psychologist, have had a busy day or week and have shifted into "rote." Sometimes we did not prepare candidates right and they were not comfortable enough to be candid about themselves. Sometimes we think the psychologist simply listened to what the candidate said and regurgitated it to us in the report. We wonder whether the psychologist probed enough to really understand what the person was like. A few times it seemed that both the agency and the psychologist got duped. We believe that psychologists should not be fooled; they should be able to get at the underlying nature of people. We count on our psychologist to be our safety net.

We do not do anything quantitative to evaluate assessments. When we make mistakes, we go back to the psychologist who did the assessment and examine the situation in order to figure out how this person got by us. Both the agency and our psychologist work to become better in assessment. We don't expect that our batting average will be 100 percent.

In several situations, agency people making the decision disregarded what the assessment said. This occurs when we simply do not want to hear the concerns. An example is a creative writer we hired even though the psychological assessment warned us that the person had very poor interpersonal skills and often experienced difficulties working with others. Our department head, however, loved his writing. We wound up with a great writer who was a problem employee. The person stayed with the agency several years, creating substantial pain, frustration, and problems.

Assessments are most accurate in the description of the person's intelligence. I personally find the style section valuable, and would like more information in this area. It is very helpful. When we have made mistakes, it is less likely that we have hired an unskilled or ineffective person than that we have a personal style contrast that is causing the problem. This can have impact inside the agency or in our associations with our clients. It is important for us to communicate to the psychologist the predominant styles of the people with whom the candidate will have to work. Some clients are very task-oriented and aggressive, while others are more people-oriented and service motivated. I find the summary conclusions good. As a succinct summary, they are an easy way to get to the heart of the psychologist's impressions.

SUMMARY

For McDonald Davis and Associates, the psychological assessment provides our best insurance that we hire, develop, and promote those individuals with the best fit to our culture and the strongest potential to be significant individual and team contributors. With the direct and indirect costs of making errors as high as they are, we consider the assessment a small investment for a safety net. Our culture is critical to us. It is also fragile in nature. It does not take many mistakes when hiring or promoting people to seriously damage the culture. When that starts to happen, the agency is in serious jeopardy. The psychological assessment provides a key management tool that keeps us on track.

24

Time Insurance Company

Lesley S. Keegan

PROFILE OF TIME INSURANCE

Time Insurance is a nationally licensed health and life insurer, operating in 47 states and the District of Columbia. The company provides individual and group coverage through a network of close to 15,000 independent agencies. As a company, it has one of the most comprehensive medical portfolios in the country and is a recognized innovator in designing health and life products. The company is organized into three strategic business divisions representing the three major lines of insurance sold. The three divisions are: individual medical; multiple employer trust, which markets its products to groups with 2 to 19 people; and life, disability, and annuity. Each division is headed by a senior officer and supported by its own actuarial, marketing, underwriting, claims, and data processing functions. The divisions operate to develop new products for their specific market niches.

Time Insurance is a strong believer in corporate philosophy. Its statement of commitment is regularly communicated to employees and customers. Four key elements of the Time commitment are the following: (1) The commitment to customers, the independent agents to whom it offers highly marketable insurance products backed by a commitment of quality service. (2) Commitment to Time's policyholders to whom it offers products that meet the needs for financial security at prices they can afford. (3) Commitment to Time's employees, who are responsible for putting everything together, and for whom Time offers the opportunity to experience success and growth. (4) Commitment to the community by offering financial support (through the Time Foundation) and employee participation (through volunteerism) in community activities.

TIME'S GUIDING PHILOSOPHY: THE DIFFERENCE BETWEEN MANAGEMENT AND LEADERSHIP

A key example of where the psychological assessment provides added insights that are hard to obtain elsewhere is in distinguishing between managers and leaders. In the operational need area of creating an agenda, strong management provides planning and budgeting primarily through detailed steps and timetables and careful allocation of resources. In contrast, strong leadership establishes direction by developing a vision of the future and broad strategies for producing change.

In the operational area of developing a human network for achieving a given agenda, management provides direction through organization and staffing, the development of policies and procedures, or the creation of methods and systems to guide people. Leadership, in contrast, achieves this objective by aligning people using communication and influence to create teams and coalitions that understand and are motivated by the leader's visions and strategies.

In the operational area of strategy execution, management provides control and problem solution, monitors results against a plan, identifies deviations, and plans to solve problems. In contrast, leadership achieves execution through motivation and inspiration, energizing people to overcome major resource barriers by satisfying basic but unfulfilled human needs.

In terms of operational outcomes, management produces a degree of predictability and order with the potential to consistently produce key results in areas of being on time, being on budget, delivering a regular quarterly dividend, and so forth. On the other hand, leadership as an outcome often produces change to a dramatic degree. It has the potential of producing extremely useful change, such as new products or new approaches that can help make the firm more competitive or even change the firm's entire direction.

Achieving a balance between leadership and management within the organization is critical. The result when either leadership or management is strong and the other weak is a variety of undesirable consequences. John Kotter, in his book *Force for Change, How Leadership Differs from Management* summarizes the consequences of strong leadership and weak management as follows:

- Strong long-term vision without short-term planning and budgeting.
- An almost cult-like culture without much specialization, structure, and rules.
- Inspired people who tend not to use control systems and problem-solving discipline.

In some organizations, this problem leads to a situation that eventually gets out of control, with critical deadlines, budgets, and promises not met. It can threaten the very existence of the organization. In contrast, Kotter outlines the consequences of strong management with weak leadership as follows:

- A strong emphasis on short time frames, details, elimination of risk, and scrupulous rationality, with little focus on the long-term, the big picture, strategies that take calculated risks, and "people" values.

- A strong focus on specialization, fitting people to jobs, and compliance to rules, with little focus on integration, alignment and commitment.

- A strong focus on containment, control, and predictability, with little emphasis on expansion, empowerment, and inspiration.

The end result is a firm that is rigid, not innovative, and thus incapable of dealing with changes in its markets, its competitors, or the technologies used. Its performance will typically deteriorate slowly as long as the firm is in a strong market position, but quickly if it is not.

In reviewing Time's selection of candidates for key management responsibilities, we recognized that it was somewhat easier for interviewers and managers to identify strong managers than strong leaders. The reason for this is that management typically consists of a set of very specific skills. These skills are readily identified in the concrete evidence that can be accumulated in a typical employment interview. It is not hard to get a sense of a manager's skill in organizing and decision-making by having that manager talk about specific examples of problems they have solved or decisions they have made. With only a small amount of probing, a good interviewer is able to accumulate specific examples of key behaviors that allow an accurate assessment of a candidate's managerial skills and approach.

On the other hand, when Time began asking itself the question, "Do people have the skills that will lead us in the future, even when we cannot clearly define what that future may be?" a different conclusion was reached. We made the decision to broaden our use of the psychological assessment to specifically address skills we felt indicated leadership or leadership potential. In doing so, we did not abandon the key management skills important in placement fit, but added the second dimension of leadership.

Along with Kotter, Time believes that the skills necessary for success in management and leadership can be developed. This belief adds another component to the results Time looks for in psychological assessments. That is, we rely heavily on the assessment to tell us, "Do the individuals that we are hiring have the potential to develop into leaders?" Specifically, we are looking for the level of intellect, ability, openness, open-mindedness, and willingness to think and learn that will be the key to the employee's growth and success within our organization. We are truly looking for people who believe that there is still more learning that they can do, for people who recognize that things keep changing and that to stay abreast they must change.

During the five years since Time began implementing this new vision of itself and its people, the psychological assessment has become increasingly important in helping us assess the leadership potential of our employees and external candidates. Key components of leadership potential include the person's potential and ability to grow, how intellectually capable the person is, and how well the person handles abstract conceptualization. We want people who, no matter how well developed they are, will have the courage and conviction to make changes tomorrow when such changes are appropriate and in the best interests of the organization and themselves.

USE OF PSYCHOLOGICAL ASSESSMENTS

Time Insurance has a fairly long history of using psychological assessments. Over the years the company has had consulting relationships with two major psychological consulting firms involving several psychologists from both firms. Affectionately known as "psychs," the assessments are seen as positive personal and developmental experiences for anyone selected for the process.

Within Time Insurance there are three primary areas where psychological assessment is used. These are: assessment for broader organizational development; assessment of placement fit, internal and external; and assessment for specific developmental planning. These three areas are discussed in detail in the remainder of this chapter.

ASSESSMENT FOR ORGANIZATIONAL DEVELOPMENT

The selection of the three areas for the application of psychological assessment is strategically driven. In 1985, Time completed a thorough analysis of its culture, identifying a number of key areas that the company wanted to actively influence and change. One key aspect was to identify and develop more opportunities for innovation and to ensure that innovative quality improvement was a regular part of the ongoing strategic planning process. As this effort has matured, Time has become aware that much of its success relies on people, and particularly on senior management. Therefore, Time has begun to use the "psychs" as a mechanism for recognizing and bringing into the company people with the skills, abilities, and characteristics to help the company lead and prepare its culture for the future. The psychological assessment is seen as a vital element because some of the skills, abilities, and characteristics that Time needs are not easy to identify in the usual employment interview process.

ASSESSMENT FOR PLACEMENT FIT (INTERNAL OR EXTERNAL)

The fit of an individual to the needs and demands of a given position at Time is a key element in determining the employee's success. It is in this area that Time Insurance has long used psychological assessments to provide basic input. Like most companies, Time is keenly aware of the cost of placement. It is not unusual for Time to process a number of applicants to find one who truly fills the needs of key positions. A mistake in hiring can be costly. When this happens, it takes several years before the problems associated with lack of fit lead us to part company with the poor hire.

An important aspect of Time's vision of the future and its commitment to employees is that we recognize that no matter how careful we are, we will still make mistakes. On a philosophical level, we have accepted that reality, and have consciously chosen to take "the high road" in such situations. When someone is not working out as expected, we communicate the problem to the person early and clearly so that the employee has opportunities to make changes. If that approach fails, we are willing to bite the bullet and inform the employee of the need for termination. In so doing, we offer the person a generous severance package, outplacement, and additional support as necessary to help the person find a position that will be more satisfying and productive. The decision allows us to find someone who more accurately fits our needs.

For some hiring managers, a mistake or two on the part of previously hired employees can cause the managers to be gun-shy. When reading a psychological assessment report on a candidate, they may be overly concerned about small problem areas. Our approach at Time is to try to remain aware that we could look for a perfect candidate forever, though we would probably never find that person. We need to balance the desire for the best fit possible with the opportunity costs of leaving a position unfilled for a long time. When reading psychological assessment reports, our managers are encouraged to look at areas that may be problematic and try to assess the chances of "fixing" it for the person's and company's benefit. It is not unusual for the manager to talk with the psychologist who completed the assessment in order to get a more accurate handle on a person's immediate performance and development potential.

PSYCHOLOGICAL ASSESSMENT FOR DEVELOPMENTAL PLANNING

The third major area for which Time Insurance uses psychological assessments is developmental planning. From what I have described earlier, it should be clear that the developmental issues and focus are present in every assessment situation. As a company, Time is concerned about identifying issues that surface in the assessment that should be included in an employee's or candidate's developmental plan. The difficulty is determining the difference between developmental areas and other problem areas that indicate a clear lack of fit to our needs and expectations. The subtlety of this difference makes it hard to differentiate the two in a traditional employment interview.

The psychological assessment can often make the difference in identifying the "one little thing" that a person doggedly will not master, even though learning it should be a small task. This small "failure" might seem inconsequential at first, but might become the person's Achilles' heel and result in a failure to achieve the kind of success we hope to develop in all of our people.

Another developmental focus is Time's shift from looking only at the job in question, to broadly recognizing the competencies of the person with respect to future responsibilities. Like many organizations, we are doing more planned career pathing with employees. This includes lateral moves at high levels of management in order to broaden our key people and their perspectives. It also includes recruiting people with different and more diverse perspectives for our sales force. Because of the importance of career pathing, we look for more evidence in the psychological assessments of open-mindedness to other cultures and a willingness to learn and to explore and effectively manage employee diversity.

To ensure that developmental planning proceeds systematically, we appoint mentors for all of our professional trainees. The process begins with the psychological assessment on new professional trainees. Shortly after the person receives the new employee orientation to Time Insurance and has developed some awareness of the job responsibilities, a meeting with the mentor and the psychologist who completed the assessment occurs. In this three-way conversation, the assessment results are reviewed and explained. The discussion then focuses on the specific areas the professional trainee can address that will initiate personal development. Contracting occurs between the trainee and mentor regarding the key issues discussed and agreed upon. The psychologist provides suggestions that might be included in this agreement.

The developmental focus has also become more important for first-level supervisors. We have come to recognize that Time's corporate culture is communicated by an employee's supervisor. For most of our employees, this person is the first-level supervisor. These managers have the biggest impact on our quality and productivity. Unfortunately, they are often poorly prepared to be effective managers. In recognizing this, we are trying to encourage and support their development in a number of ways. The psychological assessments provide us with key guide points in thinking about and planning how to extend a supervisor's capabilities.

We have worked to define the role of supervisor in a broader fashion, and to encourage supervisors to make decisions and participate actively in problem-solving. As a part of this effort, we have changed our handbook so that it functions as an employee guide. We have worked to define general policies that emphasize to our supervisors the importance of thinking about and making decisions with respect to the specifics of the situation and individual involved. We are trying to move our supervisors away from rigid views of supervision, and from operating in a rule-driven environment. In support of this goal, we have, on occasion, used the psychological assessments within established teams to help supervisors recognize friction points and to do problem-solving relationship building. Within senior management ranks, we have also done joint reviews with senior managers and their direct reports. In this case, each party discusses aspects of his or her psychological assessment that impacted the relationship with the other person. Throughout the organization, we have a commitment to build relationships between and within teams, and have found the psychological assessment helpful in team-building situations.

PROBLEMS TO AVOID WHEN USING ASSESSMENTS

As with any powerful procedure, there is always the potential for abuse. At Time Insurance, we have found it is important to use the psychological assessment only as one component of the hiring or promotion decision-making process. We do not expect that the psychologist completing the assessment will be able to make the decision for us about whether to hire or promote a person. Occasionally, we will have a supervisor or manager succumb to the temptation to rely solely on the psychologist's bottom-line assessment. We try to stay alert to this situation so that it does not become the psychologist who makes the hiring decisions. One way we avoid this is to encourage more communication between the psychologist and the manager. We also recognize that there are some situations where the psychological assessment will raise a number of warning flags because an individual's fit to our organization might not be good. In this case, we might see talent and potential that we can use, and are willing to pay the price of ruffled feathers or other organizational difficulties. In those situations, we might hire the person against the advice of the psychologist but turn right around and ask the psychologist to help us make sure the person will succeed.

In summary, Time Insurance believes that when a company decides to use psychological assessments it is very important to sit down with the managers and supervisors who will be reading and using the assessment reports to explain what the psychological assessment is and is not. Before managers begin using assessments, we want to ask them how and why they want to use it in order to ascertain that they understand Time's philosophy of use. As an organization, we do not believe the psychological assessment should make life simpler. In fact, we believe just the opposite: Assessments should make the issue more complicated. If that is the case, then why should we use assessments? We believe that assessments lead to better and more information about individuals, help us deal with people in a comprehensive and effective fashion, and help us achieve our goals as an organization. Finally, it provides information critical to identifying and developing both the leadership and management skills Time needs as a company to be successful.

REFERENCE

Kotter, J. P. (1990). *Force for change: How leadership differs from management.* New York: Free Press.

25

Aqua Chem, Inc.

Charles A. Zwerg

PROFILE OF AQUA CHEM, INC.

Aqua Chem, Inc. is a world leader in the manufacture of water desalting systems and packaged boilers. Aqua Chem, Inc. traces its origin to 1931, when John Cleaver and Raymond Brooks joined forces to be the first to supply packaged boilers to industry. Since then, Aqua Chem has become a multidivisional corporation serving international markets. Our growth continues and is enhanced by our association with our parent company, Lyonnaise des Eaux of France. Lyonnaise is a multibillion dollar worldwide group specializing in products and services for water supply, waste control, and energy management. Aqua Chem, Inc. has three divisions.

Cleaver-Brooks is the largest division of Aqua Chem. It is a worldwide leader in providing products, systems, and services to solve energy and environmental problems involving combustion, heat transfer, incineration, and steam generation technologies. Cleaver-Brooks is headquartered in Milwaukee, Wisconsin, with three manufacturing plants in Lebanon, Pennsylvania, Greenville, Mississippi, and Stratford, Ontario. Cleaver-Brooks also has a service unit in Elk Grove Village, Illinois, other service units serving the southeast and California markets, and a subsidiary operation in Mexico.

The Water Technologies division is a multiproduct organization producing water desalting systems, fluid conservation systems, product recovery and pollution control for chemical and process industries. Water Technologies is headquartered in Milwaukee, and has manufacturing facilities in Milwaukee and Knoxville, Tennessee, and ship overhaul businesses in Norfolk, Virginia, and San Diego, California.

Our Industrial Combustion division is a leading manufacturer and innovator of forced-draft gas and oil burners packaged for easy installation for the retrofit and original equipment manufacturer markets.

RELATIONSHIP BETWEEN MANAGEMENT AND THE PSYCHOLOGIST

The relationship that exists between management and the psychological consultant should be absolutely straightforward and bottom-line in nature. The consultant should be as trusted and involved as if he or she were a member of the top management team. In fact, to be truly effective the psychologist must be an extension of management. The consultant must understand the unique characteristics of the business as well as the characteristics of the top management team. To develop and maintain this depth of understanding, the communications between the psychologist and the management team have to be very open, straightforward, and deep. Relationships of this depth and quality have to be nurtured over time. In my experience, it will usually take a number of years working together before the trust level is created to really make the relationship work. This relationship is so important that any management team considering using psychological assessments should not make the decision lightly.

The team should realize it is making a long-term commitment. They are, in fact, forming a partnership. It can be a beneficial partnership; but, in order to pay off, it needs to be as close and, in some respects, closer, than most business partnerships. There are many aspects of the organization and its operations that are confidential, but the trust in the psychologist must be high enough that there is no hesitation about including the consultant in any discussion. It is only through absolutely open communication that the psychologist will remain well enough informed about the organization to be able to provide meaningful counsel to senior operating management about succession planning, developmental planning, stress management, or any of the many other areas where the psychologist can be an objective sounding board for management.

USE OF PSYCHOLOGICAL ASSESSMENTS

At Aqua Chem we use psychological assessment in a number of ways to support management decision-making. There are, however, two essential applications that characterize the bulk of the assessments we conduct. These are the selection of new employees in key professional/technical/managerial positions and the promotion of individuals from within.

Selection of New Employees

In the selection of new employees for key responsibilities, the role of the psychologist is to support line management and their assessment of candidates for employment. At Aqua Chem, the company goes through its normal process to identify and select talent. Once one candidate or a select group has been identified, these individuals are assessed by the psychologist. This assessment provides an objective confirmation of the company's selection process by verifying that we have done an accurate job in identifying someone who will fit in with the existing team and perform well in the job responsibilities. This confirmation becomes more critical the higher the level of the position being filled. It is also critical in positions where the person becomes the voice of the company to those outside—for example, customer service or sales.

Our company is dedicated to the principle of advancement from within, so the assessment of a candidate's overall potential for career advancement and growth is another important consideration in this process.

Promotion of Existing Employees

The psychologist's role in assessing existing employees for promotion is often more complicated than for the selection of new employees. It begins with the same need to act as an objective confirmation of management's selection process. In many cases, however, it becomes necessary for the psychologist to persuade a candidate's department head to let the employee transfer to a new department. This means the psychologist must be able to make a case that the promotion will be in the best interests of the company, as well as important in the career development of the candidate. Many department heads are not easily convinced that it is in their interests to release a good performer. The psychologist can act as an arbiter to help managers make decisions that are in the best interests of the company and support them in their search for appropriate replacements.

When the company has two or three internal candidates, it is often difficult to choose the single person to be promoted. In these cases, the psychologist can provide an objective third-party opinion of who should be promoted and why. The psychologist's deeper insights and broader organizational view can be extremely valuable in such cases. The role of the psychologist must, however, remain that of advisor. It is always management's responsibility to make the final decision. It is important for management to make the best decisions possible and to use the best tools available to guide and support those decisions. The psychological assessment supports management promotion decisions by reassuring the responsible manager that there are not any hidden things that might have been overlooked that could be of critical importance.

CANDIDATES FOR ASSESSMENT

I used to believe that assessment was so valuable that I had a company policy requiring every exempt employee be assessed. My thinking has changed, however, because of changes in the stability of our work force. Many new exempt employees are not thinking about a career with Aqua Chem when they apply to the company for a job. Our current rates of turnover make it impossible to cost justify the assessment of every new exempt employee. I do remain convinced that assessment is justified for all candidates for supervision, highly specialized positions (such as research and development), areas dealing with critical proprietary knowledge, and special products or market areas.

Ideally, I would return to the assessment of all exempt employees if it was affordable and justified by lower turnover. A big reason for this feeling comes from the value of the assessment in the career development of employees. I believe that this aspect of the assessment process is extremely important. The insights developed by the assessment can help people begin serious career planning early in their tenures with Aqua Chem. In addition, assessment helps new employees see the importance of taking personal responsibility for the planning and management of their careers. This leads to the development of the skills and abilities needed to be successful. The initiation of such personal career management can be worth many times the cost of the assessment in speeding the development of the individual.

WHO SEES ASSESSMENT REPORTS

At Aqua Chem we feel strongly that access to psychological assessment reports has to be controlled internally. Over the years, I have become more guarded in the release of written reports. I now believe that if the company does not have someone in-house with psychological background and training, there should be no written reports maintained in-house. Even when there is an appropriate and knowledgeable control person, I believe access to the psychologist's written reports should be limited to very high-level managers. By this I mean the chief executive and his or her operating team. I do not think that the employing supervisor or manager should see the written report. A better procedure is to have the psychologist meet with the employing supervisor and manager to discuss the report and relevant decisions. I have come to this conclusion because I have seen too many situations during my pre–Aqua Chem days where inexperienced supervisors and managers have read and interpreted assessments incorrectly. I have also seen a few instances where specific information from an assessment was used out of context to inappropriately criticize the person who was assessed. There have also been situations where unauthorized copies were made that later found their way into inappropriate hands.

There should be a written report for the one or two people who can use it properly. Otherwise, most feedback should be verbally presented one-on-one. The appropriate focus for these reviews is the key areas of qualification for the job and the development of knowledge, skills, and ability to perform well. The reviews can also discuss danger signs and specific areas for follow-up by the supervisor. This can be important as a way of ensuring that the supervisor or manager works with the individual in ways that support the counsel given by the psychologist. In the most effective reviews it is clear what the psychologist will talk about, what the supervisor will be focused on, and where the individual will be expected to take responsibility for his or her own development.

When someone leaves or retires from Aqua Chem, we shred the reports or return them to the psychologist. We are very disciplined in controlling the reports within the company and allow absolutely no copies to be made. This requires careful personal control of the assessment reports. An appropriate control person is the individual who is responsible for the management succession and development plan. At Aqua Chem, this control is my responsibility as vice-president of human resources. We control the information in much the same manner as we control medical reports from the executive physical program. Only information that could affect the company is released to senior management.

ASSESSEE FEEDBACK

Feedback of the assessments is critical to their effective use. More benefit is derived from good feedback than any other use of the information. It is critical that this feedback be open and complete. This is particularly true for new hires. This gives them the full benefit of the process early enough in their careers for the information to have maximum impact. When there are serious concerns about an aspect of a candidate, but the company decides to hire the person anyway, it is very important that the candidate be made aware of our concerns. The feedback provides the opportunity to communicate our concerns in an objective way and begin the positive process of planning to overcome the problem areas. Often, this can be done in a positive manner that structures the situation to maximize the chances of job success.

ATTITUDES OF ASSESSEES

With 30 years of experience scheduling hundreds of people for assessment, I can think of only a handful of people who had a negative attitude going in and coming out of the assessment. Many people who have not gone through the process previously feel trepidations when hearing that psychological assessment is part of our hiring and promotional procedure. When the assessment process is explained to these people, their fears are greatly reduced. People are mainly interested in why the process is used and how confidentially the information will be treated. Our position is to reassure people that the assessment will be a very positive experience. We explain that the assessment is a tool and that in the future they can request consideration for reassessment if and when they desire one. It is also important that individuals realize the psychologist does not make our selection or promotion decisions. The assessment is supplementary, objective information that management uses to guide and confirm its decisions. Whether someone is selected or advanced is always a management decision.

EVIDENCE FOR ACCURACY AND VALUE

We have clear evidence that assessment assists management in making better selection and promotion decisions. That evidence comes from on-the-job performance measures, improvements in turnover ratios, and the increased ability to promote people from within the organization. I have clear empirical evidence within Aqua Chem and from my experience with my previous employers supporting both the practicality and the benefit of our ongoing program of assessment.

In addition, like many organizations who are right-sizing their management ranks, we are moving toward broadening the scope of our managers' control and responsibilities. Doing this makes it more critical that we do not gamble when we put a person in a position of significant responsibility for Aqua Chem. If we can prevent even one serious mistake every three years, the whole effort is worthwhile and cost-justified. One bad apple in a key position can have a devastating impact.

The value of assessments is directly tied to the costs of turnover and relocation. An easy way to determine the value of assessment is to add the average $18,000 cost of turnover (losing one employee, recruiting, hiring, and training a replacement) to the average $40,000 cost of relocating an employee. With $58,000 at stake with most middle management promotions that involve a relocation, you want to be right. Often, this cost is more than the manager's salary for a year.

The accuracy and value of assessment is easily demonstrated by examining job performance and growth within the organization and comparing these to the descriptions and predictions of the assessment. We expect and are not concerned to find that many people perform somewhat better than was predicted. In fact, this is one of the key reasons why we use assessment. The psychologist's role is often one of coach and counselor, with the intent of guiding and supporting employees as they develop greater effectiveness and proficiency.

WHERE ASSESSMENT IS MOST IMPORTANT

Assessment provides many valuable insights. I find that some content areas of the assessment, however, are particularly critical to supporting and guiding the management decision-making process. These are:

- Ability to communicate
- Ability to take responsibility
- Ability to make things happen—to accomplish objectives
- Basic intellect
- Problem-solving effectiveness
- Effectiveness of management style

- Ability to be a leader
- Ability to involve others in a participative fashion
- Skill in team-building

This list is different than one I would have made ten years ago. There are fewer roles or opportunities for an autocratic manager in today's globally competitive world. Leadership skills have become critical to managerial success. Today we need managers who can direct people through a vision of accomplishment, expecting high performance and profitability, but achieving the objectives through teamwork and individual commitment. Finding managers who can accomplish this is a challenge. The person's track record is a valuable guide when the person has a job history. Careful reference-checking and probing can identify some of the person's potential. A prime source of information, however, is from the psychological assessment. When the psychologist knows the organization, has developed the trusting relationship, and is kept truly informed on where the firm is going, then that psychologist is in the position to offer advice on selection and promotion that will support the company developing the management talent it needs to be successful. We have found psychological assessments to be very accurate and valuable in support of our selection and advancement decisions. The more definitive the psychologist is in predicting the person's performance and potential, the more value the assessment has to management.

_____ **Part Six**

*The Future of
Psychological Assessment*

26

Legal and Ethical Issues in Psychological Assessment

Pierre Jacques

As with many business procedures, the implementation of a new selection or assessment method must meet specific guidelines, both professional and legal. This chapter examines several steps in the development of a psychological assessment method for employee selection, and reviews the standards and guidelines written by professionals in the fields of selection and testing. These guidelines, set forth in the *Standards for Educational and Psychological Testing* (1985) and the *Principles for the Validation and Use of Personnel Selection Procedures* (1987), are not legally binding, but are often used for support in legal decisions. The purpose of this chapter is to familiarize the managers responsible for selection decisions with the laws and professional standards. When a selection method is implemented, the company is held liable for any decisions based on that method. A manager who knows the relevant laws and guidelines will be better prepared to avoid legal problems or defend against a claim of discrimination.

OVERVIEW

The first two sections examined in this chapter are the selection of a trained psychologist to develop the assessment method, and the selection of tests for assessment. The second section details how the psychologist would choose a test to fit the needs of the organization or develop a test when one is not available. Ethical guidelines that must be followed by the psychologist are included to familiarize the manager with rules of standard practice. These are taken from the *Casebook on Ethics and Standards for the Practice of Psychology in Organizations* (1985).

The third section describes proper use of the test. This includes administration of the test, and the retention of information crucial for future legal defense of the test as a selection tool. Also discussed in this section is the proper reporting of test scores. Reporting test scores includes issues of confidentiality and liability. This section closes with a brief overview of possible discrimination from the use of tests. The assessment interview, although considered a test by many, will be discussed separately because of the subjective nature of many interview techniques. Legal issues especially pertinent to the interview will be presented. In the final section of this chapter, specific legal issues, legislation, and court cases will be presented. This includes a review of the Civil Rights Act of 1964, and the *Uniform Guidelines on Employee Selection Procedures* (1978).

SELECTING A PSYCHOLOGIST

When a human resource problem has been identified that requires the use of a psychological assessment, most likely the manager's first step will be to engage the assistance of an industrial-organizational (I/O) psychologist or other psychologist trained in human resources, the use of psychological tests, and one-on-one interviewing. If such a person exists within the company, the manager's job is that much easier. However, if the manager must hire an outside consultant, great care must be taken. It is not enough to go by titles such as "personnel consultant," or even "psychologist." Often, people without the proper background and training will use a title to persuade managers that they are qualified to do the job.

It is unethical for psychologists to provide services and use techniques that are beyond their training and experience. Similarly, psychologists should accurately represent their competence, education, training, and experience in their resumes. A licensed psychologist is not always better than a nonlicensed psychologist. In fact, generally, only clinical and counseling psychologists are required to be licensed. I/O psychologists, who are specially trained for business testing, are not usually licensed. These facts should be considered when selecting a consultant. Do not be afraid to question the abilities and experience of anyone considered. A qualified psychological consultant will be happy to discuss credentials.

As with any work performed by an outside firm, a contract should be drawn up between the manager and the psychologist. The contract should address the type of work to be performed, along with the costs of the project. The contract should also state who has access to the data collected, how long the data will be retained, who has proprietary rights to reports generated, and what the manager's obligations are. Many of these issues are not considered when psychologists are first hired and later cause serious conflicts between the two parties.

SELECTING A TEST

Assuming the manager has selected a consultant, the next step in psychological assessment is deciding which tests to use in the assessment. This function falls primarily under the duties of the consulting psychologist.

Job Analysis

The first step is to determine the personal characteristics the manager would like to assess in candidates, and ensure those characteristics are job-related. This is the most important step. Most legal issues of testing and selection revolve around the relevance of the test to the job. If the test does not address characteristics that are shown to be important for success on the job, the test should not be used for selection or promotion decisions.

There are several ways to determine what is important for success on the job. The most common method is called job analysis. Job analysis is the backbone of almost every type of work done in human resources, including compensation, selection, and performance appraisal. Through the use of questionnaires and interviews of job incumbents and their supervisors, psychologists identify the most important behaviors required for success on the job. The incumbents interviewed are those who have been successful on the job. Success is determined by examining performance scores or productivity rates. The psychologist should also look at the specific knowledge, skills, and abilities (KSAs) required for success on the job.

A minimum job analysis should examine the job descriptions of the positions for which testing is done. The job descriptions should be based on a job analysis previously conducted for the job. It is important that the job descriptions be as current as possible so that an accurate picture of the position can be obtained.

Test items are then used (or developed) that measure the behaviors and KSAs deemed important for success on the job. However, it cannot be stated for certain that the test items actually measure these behaviors and KSAs. That is an assumption that must be tested. To do this, the test must be demonstrated to be a valid measure of behaviors and skills, or be a direct predictor of future performance.

Test Validation

Validation is the acquisition of evidence, through research, to support the assumptions of the test. The psychologist makes inferences about the relationship between the test, personal characteristics and important job behaviors. For example, a common inference to make is that the higher someone scores on an IQ-type test, the better they will perform on the job. Or, a candidate with a higher level of assertiveness will be a more successful salesperson. To use the test these inferences are based on, the truth of the inferences must be demonstrated. This is the process of test validation, although it is actually the inferences from the test that are being validated. Validation of selection tools is an important aspect of selection, and is crucial for legal defense and proper use of tests. If a test is shown to be valid, it can be said that the test accurately measures what it is said to measure, or that it accurately predicts what it is said to predict.

Construct Validation. There are several ways to conduct research for determining validity. Construct validation, which is rather abstract when compared to other validation methods, is the most relevant method for use in psychological assessment. In construct validity, the relationship between the test and the job is not direct. Rather, the test measures an employee characteristic believed to be instrumental in effective job performance. The characteristics measured by a personality test, such as self-confidence or sociability, are examples of constructs. The relevant constructs important to effective job performance would be identified through the job analysis. To be valid, the characteristic must be shown to be integral to doing the job effectively. Also, the score on the test measuring the construct would be systematically related to relevant measures of job performance. The systematic relationship is determined by a statistical procedure called correlation. (Correlations are discussed later.)

Content Validation. Another type of validation is called content validation. Here, the goal is to show that the test content is similar to the job content. The test should reflect what the person would actually do on the job. For example, the managerial in-basket test is popular because the behaviors on which the candidate is assessed are actually part of a manager's job. This test would be developed from an in-depth job analysis and an accurate job description.

Criterion Validation. The third method is called criterion validation and is conducted by showing that there is a systematic relationship between the test scores from a sample of workers and performance appraisal scores, or other measures of job performance, from these employees. The performance scores are called criterion scores. This type of validity can be demonstrated by two methods: predictive validation and concurrent validation. In predictive validation, test scores are obtained from applicants. Test scores of the hired applicants are compared to criterion scores obtained later after the new hires have been on the job a while. This method is called "predictive" because the test scores are used to predict how the employee will perform at a later date. This is the strongest method of validation because the success of the applicant is directly assessed.

However, a company might not have the time or the resources to obtain the predictive criterion scores. Concurrent validity is useful in this case. In concurrent validity, the test is given to people already on the job, and their criterion scores are also obtained at that time. The two measures are statistically correlated to determine the level of validity.

Although the methods of validation are presented separately, they are closely related. There is a fine line between construct and content validity. The difference is that content validity measures more observable components of the job, whereas construct validity is abstract. Also, criterion validity is, in essence, a specific type of construct validity, because employee characteristics are directly observable through their actions and abilities. Therefore, construct validation is often combined with subsequent criterion validation to further bolster a test's validity. The important point for the manager to remember when working with a psychologist is that the strongest possible type of validity measure should be used.

Validation Guidelines

Due to the legal importance of using valid tests, a manual or report should explain the research performed to validate the job-relevant inferences. The following standards, taken from *Standards for Educational and Psychological Testing* (1985), are specified by the number in parentheses and describe specifically what a company should be aware of:

- Evidence for the validity of all the major inferences of the test should be presented. The manual should also explain why the researcher used the methods described (1.1).
- If an inference being made by the test has not been validated, the psychologist should be made aware of this through the manual, and should have an explanation of why the evidence was not obtained. This way, the psychologist can be cautious interpreting test results that are not supported with proper evidence (1.2).
- The validation study performed by the test developer should be described with as much detail as possible, and any outside factors that could influence the results should be described (1.5).
- When the test is based on information from job experts, or if several people were used to judge the test, the qualifications of all people involved should be reported. If the judgments made were compiled to one score, the method of compilation should be described (1.7).

In addition, several other standards related to test construction are important to mention:

- Tests and testing programs should be developed on a sound scientific basis (3.1). The psychologist constructing the test should make available all the evidence used to relate the test to the KSAs and any other information that has a bearing on the use of the test.
- Domain definitions, which are the positions or people the test can be used for, and other test specifications, should be clear so that other experts can judge whether or not the test is relevant (3.3).
- When items are selected for a test, the content and type of item should be considered with respect to previous experiences and cultural backgrounds of the ethnic groups that would be applying for the positions (3.5). For

example, language in a test should have the same meaning for all groups being tested.

Test Reliability

Reliability is the other element of a test that should be known. Reliability is a measure of how dependable or consistent the test is at measuring characteristics of the candidate. A test is highly reliable if, for example, the test-taker obtains almost identical scores when taking the test at different times. A test that is not reliable could not be demonstrated to be a valid test. Therefore, if a test is demonstrated to be statistically valid, it is assumed the test is also reliable. A detailed description of reliability is beyond the scope of this chapter. The manager, however, should be familiar with a few of the relevant guidelines, because the manager may be held accountable for the use of an invalid or unreliable test. When examining the results of reliability studies for a published test, keep in mind the following standards that psychologists should follow:

- Reliability measures and possible errors in measurement should be reported for any type of score that is presented for a test. This would allow the test user to judge whether the test is reliable enough to use (2.1).

- A description of the population used to obtain the reliability should be presented, including the number of subjects, their demographics, and how the subjects were obtained (2.2).

- All the statistics relevant to a reliability measure should be reported, along with the condition in which it was obtained and the situations to which this measure can be applied (2.3). In other words, is it relevant to your work?

Correlation Coefficients

Validity and reliability are reported as a statistic called a correlation coefficient, and are represented by the letter r. Simply stated, a correlation coefficient is a number that describes the extent to which two factors are related (or co-related). A good example is the relationship between height and weight. As a general rule, the taller you are, the more you weigh. That would indicate a positive correlation (since both numbers get larger together) and a fairly strong relationship. Since there are exceptions to the height-weight rule, the correlation is not a perfect one. For example, there are short-heavy people, and tall-light people.

Another example that is more business-oriented is a correlation coefficient that relates a measure of assertiveness to the volume of sales. If the measures are perfectly related, the correlation coefficient would equal 1.00. This means every time someone scores higher on assertiveness, the person would have a higher number of sales than the person scoring lower on assertiveness. If the two measures were not related at all, the correlation coefficient would equal

0.00. A zero correlation does not help the manager, because it indicates that someone scoring high on assertiveness could do well or poorly in sales. The other extreme is a correlation of -1.00. A negative correlation means as the candidate scores higher on assertiveness, the number of sales will be lower than the person with a lower assertiveness score. This latter example is unlikely to occur, but is presented to complete the illustration.

When reporting the correlation coefficient for validity and reliability, the number will always range between -1.00 and $+1.00$. If a number is reported outside that range, there is an error. It is nearly impossible to get perfect correlations in psychological research, and any test that reports high validity coefficients (greater than .70) should be examined with great caution. Most validity coefficients will be between .10 and .50. Reliability coefficients can range between .70 and the mid-.90s.

This brief description of validity and reliability gives the manager background information to guard against the use of poorly developed tests. To remain within ethical guidelines, a psychologist must minimize the possibility that results from research would be misleading.

This section was intended primarily as an introduction to test construction for the manager working with a psychologist. It is important to be familiar with these and other standards specific to validation to know if the test that is being used for the psychological assessment is appropriate. A manager seeking more information on test construction can refer to a text on testing such as *Psychological Testing*, by Anne Anastasi (1988).

ADMINISTERING THE TEST

Pre-Administration

Once a test has been selected (or developed), and it has been demonstrated to be a valid measure of the behaviors and skills necessary for the job, the psychologist administers the test. Some tests might have specific instructions for administration. Special qualifications needed for administration should be noted in the manual (6.6). Other tests require special training on the part of the administrator. The Rorschach Ink Blot Test is an example of a test requiring specialized training. The manager should be certain the psychologist is properly trained to administer the test being used. As a safeguard, most test publishers will require evidence of proper training before allowing the test to be purchased.

Prior to the administration of the test, the psychologist should review the written documentation on the test, including the test manual and research reports, to make sure the test is being used for the reason it was intended (6.1). If, for any reason, the psychologist made *any* changes to the test format, the instructions for using the test, or the manner in which the test was scored, the psychologist would have to revalidate the test to support the changes or show proof that revalidation was not necessary (6.2 and 6.3). The psychologist should also be aware of any possible unintended uses of the test, such as using test scores for demotions instead of hiring (6.5).

The applicants should be made aware of a number of things before being administered the test. Informed consent, which represents the applicants' permission to be administered the test, is implied for employment testing. The applicants should be informed, however, of the testing procedure (16.1). The test-taker should also be aware of how the test results will be used (6.4).

Administering and Scoring the Test

Standardization. When the above standards have been met, the psychologist is ready to administer the test. The administrator should follow all the instructions in the manual for administering the test (15.1). This is important to ensure standardization of the test. Standardization means everyone takes the test under the exact same conditions, or as similar as possible. This helps to control other factors that could affect the outcome of the test, such as loud noise or poor lighting. Similarly, the test should be administered in a comfortable environment, away from distractions (15.2).

By using standardized instructions, the results of the test are easier to compare across different testing times and between different groups of people. All efforts should be made to eliminate the chance of cheating, because this would affect the validity of the test scores (15.3). If, for any reason, the test user must administer the test under different conditions, the user should verify that the changes have not made the results inappropriate for use (6.7).

A psychologist should not use any other type of interpretation of the test except for those provided in the manual (6.13). If a cut-off score is used for selecting applicants, the method and rationale for that cut-off score should be presented, at least in the manual (6.9). For more information on legal issues concerning the use of cut-off scores, see Cascio, Alexander, and Barrett (1988).

Combining Test Scores with Other Assessment Components. A final point on the use of the test scores involves how the scores are combined with other components of the selection procedure. One method examines each component of the selection procedure separately. Each component requires a "passing" rating. This method is known as a multiple-hurdles selection method, because the candidate must pass one component before proceeding to the next one. Another method examines all the components simultaneously. Each component contributes to an overall rating. This method is called the compensatory method, because a high score in one area of the assessment might make up for, or compensate for, a low score in another area. The selection policy should describe which method is used. If the compensatory method is used, the policy should explain how the components are combined to arrive at the overall rating.

Confidentiality

After the test has been administered, the critical task of protecting the rights of the test-takers arises. This includes confidentiality and proper handling of test results. It is the responsibility of the company to ensure that confidentiality is not breached and to protect the security of the tests and results (15.7). Here are the major standards related to test handling:

- When test data are retained, both the actual test and any reports and answer sheets should be preserved (15.9).
- The company using the test should have an established policy on the handling of test results, who has access to the results, how the results are stored, and how long the results are kept (15.11).
- If the results are kept in data files or on a computer system, access should be restricted to assure confidentiality (16.5).
- If the results from a test are released, all effort must be made to ensure that the scores are interpreted properly and that there is minimal chance of misinterpretation (6.8 and 15.10).
- If the results of a test must be canceled, perhaps due to misadministration, test irregularities, or possible cheating, the evidence and procedures of canceling the scores should be fully explained to the applicant whose scores are being canceled (16.7).

In a business environment, restricting who has access to test results is often difficult. Various departments will want access for research purposes or to assist in the hiring decisions. Everyone involved in research or hiring might not be familiar with ethical guidelines. The best way to avoid problems is to minimize access and educate those who see the test results. By following these guidelines and ethical principles, the confidentiality of the applicant is maintained, and the chance of mishandling information is greatly reduced.

ASSESSMENT INTERVIEW

Interview Bias

The assessment interview is the single most important part of a psychological assessment. It allows the psychologist direct contact with the applicant. This makes it possible to get information not obtained from the psychological tests and gives the psychologist an opportunity to get in-depth information on hazy areas of the applicant's profile. The assessment interview is also the most subjective part of the psychological assessment, thus making it more susceptible to rater biases and legal action.

Many managers will claim (and believe) that they are excellent interviewers, that they can obtain reliable and pertinent information from an applicant, and that their decisions are objective. Yet, research shows that some forms of interviewing are not very objective (see Arvey & Campion 1982 for a review of interview research). The objectivity of some interview techniques is compromised by interviewer biases and mistakes.

Stereotyping. There are several major types of biases that can arise in the interview process. The most common is stereotyping. Stereotyping occurs when the interviewer makes a judgment of the applicant based on the person's race, sex, age, or background. These judgments are made early in the interview process and can bias the information obtained during the rest of the interview. Another type of stereotyping occurs when the interviewer has an unrealistic image of an ideal candidate and tries to find an applicant that matches that ideal. Since the image is unrealistic, the interviewer's standards become too high.

"Halo" Bias. Another type of bias is called "halo." The halo effect is the tendency for the interviewer to rate the applicant the same on all interview dimensions based on only one dimension. For example, if an applicant has low self-confidence, the interviewer might perceive all of the applicant's attributes as being poor.

Recency/Latency Effects. Some information might be forgotten by the interviewer, depending on when during the interview the information was presented. The recency effect occurs when the interviewer recalls more information presented at the end of the interview. It is based on the idea that information that is more recent will be fresh in the mind of the interviewer. On the other hand, the latency effect occurs when information that was presented first in the interview is best remembered. This effect is similar to the idea that a first impression carries the most weight.

Similarity Bias. A bias that occurs frequently is called the similarity bias. It refers to the tendency for an interviewer to prefer applicants that have interests similar to the interviewer. For example, an interviewer might reason that an applicant is the best candidate because the applicant enjoys sailing, as does the interviewer.

Other Biases. Other factors that bias an interview include having the interviewer give too much weight to one piece of information, especially if it is negative information. Also, enough weight might not be placed on positive information. Sometimes, interviewers will make a conclusive generalization on the quality of the applicant after only a few minutes into the interview (Webster 1982). Interviewers must be properly trained to avoid making decisions or judgments before all relevant information is collected. The interview also contains more common sources of bias due to physical attractiveness or grooming of the applicant.

Reducing Bias. There are several ways to reduce the amount of bias resulting from the interview. One way to reduce bias is to conduct several interviews and use more than one interviewer. After all the interviewers have completed their interviews, the ratings obtained would be averaged. A variation to this procedure is to compare ratings across all the interviewers. If all the interviewers rated a characteristic similarly, then the average rating would be fairly accurate. If the ratings were different among the interviewers, it would be difficult to make a good judgment of the applicant based on those raters' judgments of that characteristic.

The use of multiple raters assumes that the interviews are being scored in some manner. Scoring the interviews is a good way to reduce possible discrimination, because the basis for a selection decision can be defended by the scores. If the answers to some questions are weighted more than others, they should be explicitly described in the formal selection policies prior to use in any selection process.

Interview Questions

A major area of possible legal problems with interviewing is the type of questions asked. Any question that could potentially discriminate against an applicant based on sex, race, religion, marital status, or handicap should not be asked. Here are some guidelines that must be followed to remain within legal boundaries:

- Do not ask questions that address issues of race, religion, ancestry, sex, marital status, or handicaps. Be careful not to address these areas indirectly. For example, it would be illegal to ask if an applicant is not available to work on Saturdays due to religious reasons. Similarly, it is illegal to ask questions pertaining to future plans of a woman (or man) in terms of starting a family or needing child care.

- Employers are required to make reasonable accommodations for handicapped employees or employees who observe religious holidays. Before any question referencing these can be asked, it must be a necessary condition of the job.

- Do not ask questions concerning arrest records. Employers can only ask questions about felony convictions that are job-related.

- Questions asked must be consistent across candidates. If inconsistency is demonstrated in a court case, it makes it difficult for the employer to defend.

One way to assure consistency in interviewing is to use a structured interview. A structured interview has predetermined areas of inquiry. Although limiting the topics for questioning might make it difficult for a psychologist to delve into areas of the applicant's history that need embellishing, it can reduce the risk of breaking legal guidelines. A happy medium can be found between the risks the manager is willing to take and the information the psychologist needs to obtain. Sometimes an applicant offers information that is not pertinent to the job;

information that would have been in an illegal area of inquiry. In these cases, it is best not to pursue more information in this area. Do not write the volunteered information. Although it is important to take notes during an interview so as not to forget relevant information, it would be wise to take care in what is written. For instance, if an applicant later charged the company with discrimination, and the psychologist had written that the applicant was married, it would be more difficult to prove that information was not used in the selection decision than if it had not been written.

Although some of the guidelines seem more appropriate for general interviewing as opposed to psychological assessment, the guidelines are important to know, because interviews and assessments are both subjective in nature.

LEGAL ISSUES

The manager is now aware of how to develop a selection procedure that identifies candidates with both the necessary KSAs for a job and characteristics similar to those of a successful incumbent. Ideally, the selection procedure should be accurate and result in decisions that cause the least amount of adverse impact.

Adverse Impact in Assessments

Adverse impact exists when a selection standard is applied uniformly to all classes of applicants, but the overall result is a different rate of selection for a particular class. Adverse impact can be determined using statistics that compare the hiring dates of different ethnic groups. One such statistic is called the "4/5ths Rule of Thumb." It states that adverse impact exists when the hiring rate of a protected class is less than 4/5ths, or 80 percent, of the majority class.

If adverse impact is shown to exist, the employer has several options. The employer may modify the current procedure to eliminate adverse impact. The employer may try to defend the current procedure with validation information. This might include demonstrating that the job characteristics being assessed are a business necessity. This means success of the business is dependent upon having the job characteristics in question. The employer may also choose to get rid of the current procedure and replace it with a new one. The new procedure must then be shown to be valid. In any case, any procedure that has adverse impact must be validated.

Federal Regulations

The primary goal of legislation dealing with employment is to ensure equal opportunity of employment for all people. These laws and regulations are directed primarily at human resource personnel because of their direct involvement in hiring decisions. However, any manager who interviews job candidates or assists in selection and promotion or uses the services of a psychologist should also be familiar with the laws.

Civil Rights Act of 1964. Title VII is the relevant section of the Civil Rights Act of 1964 for employment purposes. The most important element of Title VII is that which prohibits discrimination against any person based on sex, race, color, religion, or national origin. Minority groups, such as women or blacks, are considered protected classes because, historically, there has been discrimination against them. There have been several additions to the list of protected classes through other legislation. The Age Discrimination in Employment Act of 1967 helps to promote the employment of people over the age of 40 and prohibits discrimination against them. The Rehabilitation Act of 1973 prohibits discrimination against the handicapped and requires affirmative action for handicapped people. (The Rehabilitation Act was directed toward the federal government and federal contractors.) In 1974, the Vietnam Era Veteran Readjustment Act added anyone who served during the Vietnam War (though not necessarily in Vietnam) to the list of protected classes.

Another major part of Title VII was the creation of the Equal Employment Opportunity Commission (EEOC). Its function is to enforce the laws under Title VII and respond to any allegations of discrimination. In 1978, the EEOC formalized a set of guidelines to assist in defining discriminatory acts, as well as proper procedures for presenting, avoiding, and defending charges of discrimination.

Uniform Guidelines on Employee Selection Procedures

The establishment of the guidelines (1978) set a uniform Federal position on the issue of discrimination in the workplace. The main function of the *Uniform Guidelines* is to describe what evidence is considered when judgments must be made concerning charges of discrimination. The guidelines also established a statistic to measure adverse impact. The statistic, the "4/5ths Rule of Thumb," was presented earlier. Some organizations will try to maintain this percentage by hiring a number of minorities in lower-level positions to offset a low percentage of minority hires in middle- or upper-level positions. However, the EEOC has contended that hiring some minorities does not justify discrimination against other minorities.

Only a brief review of the standards is described due to the length and detail of the guidelines. There are three major sections to the guidelines:

General Guidelines, Technical Standards, and Documentation

General Guidelines. The first section defines the three major types of validity. Also, the general standards of selection procedure validation are presented, such as documentation needs and standardization practices. Several issues of validation are described, such as the use of selection procedures that have not been validated, the use of other validity studies, and the use of employment agencies in selection.

Technical Standards. The second section presents the more technical standards for validation. Each major type of validity is explained in more depth, including the criterion measures that are acceptable for each type.

Documentation. The final major section describes the necessary documentation. For example, employers must maintain and have available for each job information on the adverse impact of the selection procedures for that job. If a procedure causes adverse impact, validation evidence must be shown. Requirements are slightly different for employers with less than 100 employees. Also, adverse impact checks should be conducted annually (by the employer) on each applicant group that constitutes more than 2 percent of the local work force. Documentation is also necessary for a measure of adverse impact different than the 4/5ths Rule. This is important because other statistics can be used to indicate adverse impact.

Any manager working closely with a business psychologist should take the time to review the *Uniform Guidelines*. The guidelines should be available in the company human resources department or the legal department.

Defending Against Claims of Discrimination

As defined earlier, adverse impact is the equal application of a selection procedure resulting in unequal hiring rates for protected classes. Another type of discrimination is called disparate treatment. This form of discrimination occurs when different standards are applied to various groups of applicants. Although both can result in claims of discrimination, defense of these claims is approached differently.

Burden of Proof for Disparate Treatment Cases. Both types of discrimination suits begin by having the burden of proof rest on the plaintiff (the person claiming discrimination). The plaintiff must present arguments that the defendant (the employer) engaged in practices that violated Title VII of the Civil Rights Act. For a case of disparate treatment, the plaintiff must show the following:

1. He/she is a member of a protected class
2. He/she was qualified for a job in a company that was actively seeking applicants
3. He/she was rejected, despite being qualified
4. After being rejected, the position remained open and the employer continued to seek applicants

These requirements were set forth in the case of *McDonnell-Douglas v. Green* (1973). If the applicant can prove this, the burden of proof shifts to the defendant. The defendant must then provide an explanation for the actions taken against the plaintiff. If the company is successful in defending its position, the burden of proof would shift back to the plaintiff, who must demonstrate that the defendant actually did not follow the course of action described.

Burden of Proof for Adverse Impact Cases. A case of adverse impact also begins with the burden of proof on the plaintiff. However, the plaintiff must show statistical evidence that the selection procedure resulted in different hiring rates for protected classes with respect to the distribution of these classes in the labor market. Once this occurs, the burden of proof is shifted to the defendant.

The defendant must provide validation evidence for the selection procedure, show that the characteristics measured by the procedure are bona fide occupational qualifications (BFOQs), or that the characteristics are a business necessity. Following this, the burden of proof shifts back to the plaintiff, who must demonstrate that an alternative selection procedure is available that has less adverse impact.

Intention of Discrimination. Another important issue in discrimination litigation is intent. Even if a company had no intention of discriminating against a protected class, it is held liable for its selection practices and the resulting hiring rates. Therefore, a company claiming it had no intent to discriminate because it was following the recommendation of a psychologist consultant would not constitute a valid defense.

Court Cases

It may be seen that an adverse impact case is easier for a plaintiff to prove than a disparate impact case. For this reason, some discrimination cases have fought to have specific selection procedures tried under adverse impact. Other cases have tried to shift the burden of proof. Since the enactment of the Civil Rights Act of 1964, several landmark court cases have succeeded in shifting the burden of proof, or have set precedents in civil rights cases. Here are a few of the more important cases and their decisions:

Griggs v. Duke Power (1971). This was the first landmark case decided by the Supreme Court according to Title VII litigation. In this case, 13 black employees filed suit against Duke Power claiming that the requirements of the job were arbitrary and helped to screen out a higher proportion of blacks than whites. A high school diploma was listed as a prerequisite, yet some current employees who were hired before the requirement was set were successfully performing the job. Therefore, the requirement was judged as not related to job performance and was prohibited.

It was this case that set the precedent for burden of proof by stating, (1) the applicant carries the burden of proving adverse impact of a selection procedure, and (2) the burden of proof shifts to the employer to prove job-relatedness or validity of the procedure.

Connecticut v. Teal (1982). The issue of contention in this case revolved around the use of a multiple-hurdles selection procedure. The Connecticut Department of Income Maintenance used an exam as the first step of their procedure. The passing rate of the minority group (blacks) did not meet the 4/5ths Rule. Connecticut defended its procedure by stating that the remaining parts of the selection procedure ensured a final pass rate that met the 4/5ths Rule. The court ruled, however, that the defendant could not discriminate against an individual even if the minority group was not discriminated against. According to Title VII, discrimination is focused upon the individual, not the group. Therefore, Connecticut had to ensure that each step of its selection process was nondiscriminatory.

Watson v. Ft. Worth Bank & Trust (1988). This case addressed whether a claim of discrimination should be tried under disparate treatment or adverse impact. Clara Watson, a black, was consistently turned down for job postings while employed at Ft. Worth Bank & Trust. The case was originally heard as a disparate treatment case. Most selections for the positions for which Watson applied were made based upon the judgments of supervisors. While Watson carried her burden of proof, the Bank & Trust successfully defended its practices and Watson was not able to refute this. Had this case been heard as an adverse impact case, the Bank & Trust would have had to supply validation data to support its selection decisions.

Watson then appealed the case, claiming it should have been tried as an adverse impact case. The Fifth Court of Appeals stated that the case had been heard correctly, referencing citations stating subjective criteria (e.g., interviews) in selection would be heard as disparate treatment cases while objective criteria (e.g., tests) would be heard as adverse impact cases. The Supreme Court opposed this view, and stressed the need to study this issue. In its ruling, the Supreme Court stated that the label of "subjective" or "objective" cannot be used to distinguish the type of case. A procedure using multiple parts might contain only one subjective part, but this would make the overall process subjective, thus making it easier for an employer to defend against discrimination because it would be categorized as a disparate treatment case.

Wards Cove Packing Company, Inc. v. Atonio (1989). This case had a major effect on the burden of proof issue. The Supreme Court ruled that the defendant's burden of proof should be less demanding in cases of adverse impact. Also, the burden of proof for the plaintiff should be greater for showing that discrimination occurred. This case, in essence, shifted the ruling that had been set in *Griggs v. Duke Power.*

The burden of proof currently rests as it was set in the *Wards Cove v. Atonio* case. A bill proposed by Congress in early 1990, called the Civil Rights Act of 1990, attempted to revert the burden of proof back to the defendant, as was originally stated in Griggs v. Duke Power. This, in addition to new legislation with the bill, would increase pressure on employers to show validation and business necessity of every selection test and procedure. Defense of discrimination cases would be more difficult than it has been in the past. It is predicted that businesses would resort to "quota-filling" to avoid claims of discrimination.

This would, essentially, negate the purpose of selection procedures: to identify the most qualified applicants. Although President Bush successfully vetoed the bill in late 1990, it is presumed the bill will appear again in the future with slight revisions. All employers should be made aware of exactly what the ramifications of this bill would be in terms of current selection practices.

SUMMARY

This chapter provided information to a manager involved in psychological assessments. Ethical guidelines help set standards for selecting a properly trained psychologist to conduct assessments. The review of the validity and reliability of tests is intended to make the manager aware of important issues in testing for legal and professional purposes. The review is not intended to be a complete description of test statistics. Several references were provided throughout the chapter for managers seeking more information on that and other topics. Issues of administration and confidentiality are important because of the direct liability of the company, and are helpful should the manager decide to assist the psychologist with testing.

The assessment interview, a crucial part of the complete assessment procedure, was treated separately because of a number of biases unique to this subjective method. Stereotyping, "halo," and other rater biases were addressed to make interviewers aware of problems in interviewing. Also, legal issues in interviewing address a number of questions that are inappropriate to ask an applicant.

Finally, the legislation specifically pertaining to selection was included as a reference for the manager, should any questions of legality arise. The legal department of a company is an excellent source of further information.

The goal of this chapter was to make the manager aware of the many pitfalls and snares of psychological assessment and selection. The chances of having to defend a claim of discrimination can be greatly reduced by being familiar with this material.

REFERENCES

American Psychological Association, American Educational Research Association, & National Council on Measurement in Education (Joint Committee) (1985). *Standards for educational and psychological testing*. Washington, D.C.: American Psychological Association.

American Psychological Association, Division of Industrial and Organizational Psychology (1987). *Principles for the validation and use of personnel selection procedures* (3rd ed.). Washington, D.C.: American Psychological Association.

Anastasi, A. (1988). *Psychological testing* (6th ed.). New York: Macmillan Publishing Company.

Arvey, R. D., & Campion, J. E. (1982). The employment interview: A summary and review of recent research. *Personnel Psychology* 35: 281–322.

Cascio, W. F., Alexander, R. A., & Barrett, G. V. (1988). Setting cut-off scores: Legal,

psychometric, and professional issues and guidelines. *Personnel Psychology* 41:
1–25.

Connecticut v. Teal, U.S. Reports, 1982, *457*, 440.

Griggs v. Duke Power Co., U.S. Reports, 1971, *401*, 424.

McDonnell-Douglas v. Green, U.S. Reports, 1973, *411*, 792.

Society for Industrial and Organizational Psychology, Inc. (1985). *Casebook on ethics
and standards for the practice of psychology in organizations*. College Park, Md.:
Society for Industrial and Organizational Psychology, Inc.

Uniform guidelines on employee selection procedures (1978). *Federal Register* 43,
38290–38315.

Wards Cove Packing Co. v. Atonio, U.S. Reports, 1989, *490*.

Watson v. Ft. Worth Bank & Trust, U.S. Reports, 1988, *487*.

Webster, E.D. (1982). *The employment interview: A social judgment process*. Ontario,
Canada: S.I.P.

Tomorrow's Job Market and Psychological Assessment

Curtiss P. Hansen

WORKFORCE 2000

In 1987 the Hudson Institute completed its study of future business conditions and the characteristics of the future labor force. The result of this research, *Workforce 2000* (1987), details conditions quite unlike those of today. Many of the conclusions from this study have been widely publicized and quoted during the past few years. However, many businesses are just now beginning to grapple with the implications of these conclusions. This chapter reviews some of the Hudson Institute's research findings, especially as they are relevant to psychological assessment.

WHERE WILL PEOPLE BE EMPLOYED?

One of the main findings of the Hudson Institute is that the U.S. economy is undergoing a shift from being primarily manufacturing-based to being primarily service-based. This fact is widely known, though often misinterpreted. There is a widespread perception that "service industry" equates to minimum wage jobs in fast-food restaurants. While restaurants are part of the new service economy, there are larger service industries.

What are the main service industries? In order of the number of people employed at the present time, they are: retail; education; health care; general government; finance, insurance, and real estate; bars and restaurants; wholesale trade; transportation and public utilities; and business services. In the mid–1980s, these service industries employed 66 million people. Hudson projects that most of the new jobs in the future will be generated by these businesses.

The Institute also predicts that many new jobs will be created by smaller companies. In the future, the growth of large bureaucracies will slow and give way to firms with 20 to 100 employees becoming the primary generators of new jobs.

WHO WILL BE AVAILABLE TO EMPLOY?

Perhaps the most striking and well-known of the Hudson Institute's findings are its projections regarding the composition of the applicant pool in the future. Applicants and the employees hired will be much more diverse than at any time in our history. This conclusion is not really a prediction that might or might not come true, but is a fact dictated by present and future demographics.

The demographics show that fewer people will be entering the labor force. Of those who do enter, the majority will not be white males, but will be largely female, Hispanic, and black. Immigrants are another large, future employee group often ignored as the focus turns toward female and minority employment issues. The United States will be forced to open its borders and ports more widely to accommodate the increasing manpower needs of the burgeoning service economy in the future. Finally, another source of employees in the future could be retired people. However, because many individuals in this group will not have to work, it is unclear whether they will rejoin the work force as Hudson predicts.

WHAT SKILLS AND CHARACTERISTICS WILL BE REQUIRED?

As the United States leaves the twentieth century and the industrial age to enter a century of technology and service, there will certainly be a need for different skills than were needed in the past. Whereas once an uneducated man could earn a good living in a raw material processing or manufacturing plant, the future will hold fewer jobs for this type of worker. Even today, it is becoming increasingly evident that jobs are demanding more of employees. Some companies are discovering this fact by observing that many employees are having difficulty adapting to and succeeding in the constantly changing work environment.

The United States has been shifting to a service economy for many years. These service jobs have recently become more complex as business begins fully utilizing technology. Service jobs created in the future will require even higher skill levels just for entry. "The fastest growing jobs will be in professional, technical, and sales fields requiring the highest education and skill levels" (Hudson Institute 1987, xxi). The new jobs will demand greater math, language, and reasoning skills.

THE BUREAUCRATIC ORGANIZATION

What other skills are indicated by this economic shift? To fully appreciate the dramatic change in the job requirements of potential and current employees, let us look at what was required to succeed in the not too distant past (which, for many companies, is still the present). In a manufacturing environment with a low degree of competition and technological change, hierarchical (bureaucratic) management worked best, with labor functions broken down to the smallest units in an assembly-line fashion. When the business environment is stable and profits are high year after year, large bureaucracies appear to be an efficient and functional way to manage an organization.

What is it like to work in a bureaucracy? Most organizations of this type are built along the lines of a military division. The emphasis is on training each person to carry out a small number of work behaviors. Each employee has a clearly and narrowly defined role. Even the managers' jobs are limited to a few activities. The company believes in and promotes following orders as the highest form of corporate citizenship. The manager on the rung above you always knows more and best in any situation affecting you. An employee's goal should be to follow rules and blend in with the other employees. Training focuses on learning the rules. Company etiquette is concerned with having all employees dress alike and behave as if they were cut from the same cloth. Insubordination occurs when an employee questions the wisdom of an order or procedure. Plaques can be found on the walls with inspirational messages such as, "Don't think, just do it!"

What personal characteristics and skills are required to succeed in this kind of organization? The first that may come to mind is obedience. Other traits are a need to conform, a preference to be given directions rather than make one's own decisions, a high boredom threshold, below-average to average intelligence, a need for continuity and sameness, a need for order, and a lack of personal individuality.

The skills required would vary according to company and level in the company. Managers would require most of the hard skills needed in future companies, such as math ability, verbal comprehension skill, and competencies in accounting, financial planning, manufacturing processes, scheduling, and distributing. However, the difference is in the skills required at the rank-and-file levels of the company. In a nutshell, very few skills are needed. In fact, the fewer skills possessed by an employee, the better the employee will probably fit in. The employee needs to learn the limited number of functions for which he or she is responsible and no more.

THE SUCCESSFUL ORGANIZATION OF THE FUTURE

Today and in the future, a successful company must be flexible and constantly adapting to the changing business environment. Yesterday's formula for success will probably not be relevant tomorrow, or even today. The bureaucratic structures must be taken apart and replaced with a more functional design. This design would include a "flattened" and decentralized management structure. To increase the company's speed of response in dealing with customers and opportunities, there must be fewer layers of management. Each remaining manager, therefore, must assume a greater amount and wider scope of decision-making authority.

Nonmanagement employees will be used as never before. The distinction between management and professional/technical employees will become blurred, as the latter employees take on more decision-making responsibilities in their daily activities. Management must delegate decision-making authority to these employees if managers are to cope with their own expanded domains. Nonmanagement employees will need to function as consultants to management. That is, because they are on the front line in the daily operation of the business, they will have the freshest and most insightful view on what needs to be done. This fact will be true regardless of the type of business the company is in.

In contrast to the bureaucratic organization, what personal characteristics and skills will be required of employees for a company to be successful in the future? To meet the challenges of increased international competition in the areas of new product development, quality, customer service, and production efficiency, clearly a different type of employee will be needed. This employee will be motivated to learn new things and take on responsibility. The employee will find personal satisfaction in making unique contributions to the success of the company. The employee will have highly developed interpersonal skills, with the ability to relate to many different types of people. This person will be able to influence others in a desired direction without having formal authority. This employee will be able to work effectively without close supervision, and with only general guidelines as to what needs to be accomplished. The person will be creative and above average in intelligence. Finally, the employee will be comfortable with technology and its constant improvements, and will view technology as a way to improve job performance.

The Hudson Institute focused on skills and abilities in *Workforce 2000*, rather than on the above personal characteristics. Their conclusions were that there would be a need for even greater skills in the areas of mathematics, reading comprehension, written communication, oral communication, and logical reasoning. In addition, many jobs of the future will require a specialist's knowledge and competency in not just one discipline, but in several. This means that employers will be seeking people with even higher levels of education and formal training than they are today.

HOW IS PSYCHOLOGICAL ASSESSMENT RELEVANT TO WORKFORCE 2000?

Will there be people available in the future with the above skills and characteristics? The Hudson Institute unequivocally concludes that these desired individuals will not be available in sufficient quantities to meet the needs of U.S. business. There are two reasons why they feel this conclusion is true. One, there are not and will not be enough people entering the work force to replace those workers who are and will be retiring. Two, if current trends continue, many of the new workers will not have the basic skills required by the companies with jobs to be filled.

It is well-known that the United States is at the bottom of the list of industrialized nations when its young people are compared, based on educational achievement in various areas. For 25 years, high school and college curriculums have been "dummied down" to better appeal to students. Concurrent with these changes has been the slow deterioration in markers of educational attainment, such as Scholastic Aptitude Test (SAT) scores. The nation's daily newspapers are replete with stories about high school and even college graduates who cannot read or perform basic arithmetic functions.

Focus on Retaining Qualified Employees

How can a company cope with the two problems of a reduced applicant pool and a lack of basic skills in those who do apply for jobs? One solution to these problems is to focus on the retention of good employees. To implement this strategy, a company must begin the process at the selection stage. Greater care should be taken in screening applicants, given the novel mix of skill levels and background diversity found in today's and tomorrow's applicant pools. The psychological assessment is useful here. As described in previous chapters, a thorough assessment can not only determine current skill levels, but also an applicant's potential to learn new skills and develop greater competency.

After a promising new hire is brought on board, the real work begins. No longer can companies afford to provide temporary residence for "revolving door" employees. The luxury of choosing from an unlimited supply of "baby boomer" talent has ended. The new corporate maxim will be to retain your talent. Achieving this goal will require money and effort, though not as much of either as would be required if the goal is not addressed.

Talented employees will be in short supply and will be aggressively recruited by headhunters. To keep these desired professionals, a company must focus on meeting their needs for satisfaction, growth, and development. Paying higher salaries or bigger bonuses is the traditional approach to keeping a person from leaving the company. This tactic will no longer be sufficient, because there will always be a company willing to pay your employee more money. Instead, the focus should be on the less-tangible aspects of job satisfaction and company commitment. These intrinsic motivators include liking one's daily work, enjoying the company of co-workers, getting along smoothly with one's boss, having a clear career path laid out, finding that career path to be challenging and exciting, having opportunities for meaningful developmental experiences, identifying with the company and feeling proud to be on the "team," and respecting the company's products or services.

Does the typical manager understand what and how his or her subordinates feel about the above issues? Probably not. Even more unlikely is the possibility of a hiring manager or company recruiter delving deeply into these issues with potential employees. It is in meeting this critical need that psychological assessment becomes a useful tool. As part of the assessment process, the psychologist routinely discusses the above issues with both candidates and current employees. In fact, the content of the assessment session can be tailored to explore whatever issues have been determined to be of critical importance to the company in retaining its best employees.

The psychological assessment process is uniquely structured to identify those less-tangible characteristics critical in predicting an employee's tenure with a company, as well as overall performance. Research has found that individuals with the highest levels of intelligence and hard skills often do not make the highest performing professionals in their fields. The intangible personal traits combine with IQ and knowledge to dictate how far the person will go. These critical traits include many of the characteristics discussed in the previous chapters, such as motivation, drive, energy, independence, self-confidence, need for achievement, integrity, personal commitment, self-discipline, endurance, work ethic, and a host of others. In addition, the projected streamlining of management levels within a corporation will require employees to be more responsible for their work than in previous times. Also, fewer managers means that employees will have to know how to function comfortably and effectively in a team environment.

These traits are very difficult for busy managers to effectively assess, because they might conduct selection or performance review interviews only a few times each year. In fact, it is hard for trained psychologists to accurately measure these characteristics in employees. However, the psychologist, working closely with a manager, is in the best position to assess all aspects of a job candidate or employee. The manager is in a position to understand what level of these personal characteristics is required for success on the job. The psychologist is in the best position to assess these traits in job candidates.

The Corporate Psychologist

The demographic changes now occurring in the United States make it increasingly clear that conducting business as usual will not be an adequate response to the challenges ahead. If companies are to select employees with the most skills, as well as with the greatest likelihood of remaining with the company, then a formal psychological assessment program must be instituted. There are three ways to accomplish this objective. First, the company can contract with one of the established psychological consulting firms specializing in assessment services to business. This choice is the best one for small and medium-size companies who can't afford to hire a psychologist full-time. The company pays for services only when they are needed, and is not saddled with a permanent expense.

The second option is best suited to large companies and would require the establishment of a corporate psychological services department. This department would be the corporate home for an on-staff psychologist responsible for conducting selection assessments with key position candidates and developmental assessments with selected employees. In addition, the department could also employ psychologists working in the areas of employee counseling (e.g., crisis intervention or career counseling), ''soft skills'' training (e.g., interpersonal skills or communication), and the traditional areas of industrial-organizational psychology (e.g., selection test programs, employee attitude surveys, or performance appraisal system development).

The final option is a hybrid of the first two. The company would establish a one- or two-psychologist corporate psychological services unit. However, this unit would not be comprehensive in its scope, but would provide basic selection assessments, and counseling and testing for middle- and lower-level employees. The company would contract with an outside psychological consulting firm to provide assessments at the higher levels in the company, though. The external psychologist could also be involved in succession planning at the executive level. The relationship between the internal and external psychologists would be one of cooperation. The internal psychologist would be the coordinator of all psychological services. This psychologist might even work closely with the external consultant in arriving at assessment conclusions about each individual.

The corporate psychologist's role does not end with one-shot selection or developmental assessments, however. The value of an in-house psychologist is in providing a number of integrated services to a given employee over the years. That, in itself, will demonstrate the level of the company's commitment to its employees, and should result in increased employee satisfaction and loyalty. While it is worthwhile to give an employee a list of developmental recommendations following the psychological assessment, it is even more effective to hold regular follow-up sessions with that employee to facilitate awareness of and progress on the developmental targets.

CONCLUSION

This chapter has reviewed the changes occurring in the demographics and personal characteristics of the work force. These changes have great implications for future business viability. The psychological assessment was proposed as a tool to use in offsetting some of the negative effects of these changes.

The Hudson Institute concluded, ''With fewer new young workers entering the work force, employers will be hungry for qualified people and more willing to offer jobs and training to those they have traditionally ignored'' (Hudson Institute 1987, xxvi). The implication of this statement is that there will be a greater need to carefully assess these candidates to identify those with the highest motivation, intelligence and potential to adapt and be successful in the future. As the work force ages, companies will be forced to hire more older workers and middle-aged people between jobs. It will be critical that companies can identify the older and middle-aged workers who are most flexible and able to adapt to changes.

REFERENCE

Hudson Institute. (1987). *Workforce 2000*. Indianapolis: Hudson Institute.

Conclusion

Kelley A. Conrad

In this book we have examined the many facets of the use of psychological assessments in business settings. The application of psychological knowledge and expertise started in the mid-1940s and has become widely used. As implemented by many business psychologists, the assessment model is derived from the pioneering version established by the Chicago-headquartered firm of Rohrer, Hibler and Replogle. The popularity of this method comes from the fact that it meets several practical business needs. These include developing an understanding of work-related capacities, predicting the potential work performance of new hires, and guiding development of current employees.

In Chapter 2, Dr. Curtiss Hansen interviewed three of the founders of the science of business psychology. In his interview with Drs. W. J. Humber, Edward Glaser, and J. Richard Porter, we had the opportunity to learn first-hand some of the key elements these psychologists considered and evaluated in the design and improvement of the psychological assessment process. In their definitions of psychological assessment they described:

- The opportunity that assessment provides for individuals to describe their interests, values, abilities, personality, and motivations
- The opportunity for individuals to be given job assignments that will maximize their strengths and will support advancement to their highest potential
- The opportunity for individuals to be successful in job situations that fulfill their potential

- The opportunity for people to make significant contributions and achieve happiness in their work

- The opportunity for a company to identify and develop people with the abilities to do the job that needs to be done, to find people who want to stay with the company and those with potential to be future managers and executives

In the last chapter of the introduction, Dr. Hansen reviewed the research that supports the validity of psychological assessments. Surprisingly, this popular technique has not generated much published research. Of the studies that have been published, all except one generated results supportive of the psychological assessment as a predictor of future job performance. Most of the published studies demonstrated a positive relationship between ratings based on the assessment reports and later ratings based on job performance.

COMPONENTS OF A PSYCHOLOGICAL ASSESSMENT

Part two of the book examined each portion of the typical psychological assessment in detail. Dr. Richard Miller identified and described the three tasks that are completed in the interview itself. The typical interview involves the interviewer gaining information about the candidate, giving information to the candidate, and generating and maintaining good will.

Dr. Miller continued by describing in detail five approaches to interviewing. These were stress interviews, historical interviews, behavioral interviews, unstructured interviews, and structured interviews. He concluded by describing the steps through which an interviewer hunts for key information and the traits that are related to successful job performance.

This was followed by Dr. Stephen Guinn's description of many of the tests and measures that business psychologists use to support their interview observations. Finally, Dr. Hansen discussed the contents of a typical assessment report and presented an example report prepared on a ''perfect'' candidate.

APPLICATIONS OF PSYCHOLOGICAL ASSESSMENT

The third part described in some detail a number of the specific applications where psychological assessment is the primary tool. Applications described in detail included the assessment of first-level supervisors, middle managers, top executives, professional salespeople, technical personnel, and advertising and marketing professionals. Special situations discussed included in-house assessments, assessment for international businesses, developmental assessments, career development assessments, and the assessment of groups in a management audit.

This wide diversity of applications demonstrates the versatility of the assessment process. When properly prepared, the business psychologist is able to adapt and tailor the approach so that it can be applied to many different positions and to several different business needs. Some of the power of psychological assessment comes from the ability to generalize information obtained in very specific individual assessments. The aggregated information can prove meaningful in examining the organization's strategic positioning, national and international trends in the work force, and the importance and effectiveness of its management activities.

PROVIDERS OF PSYCHOLOGICAL ASSESSMENTS

Part four of the book provided snapshots of three of the major firms conducting psychological assessments for businesses. While the three firms—Rohrer, Hibler & Replogle; Humber, Mundie & McClary; and PSP Human Resource Development—have many similarities, there are some differences as well. RHR and HM&M have maintained the philosophy of starting with the top management of an organization wherever possible. PSP feels comfortable starting at almost any level in the organization. RHR is expanding internationally, and has opened offices abroad.

USERS OF PSYCHOLOGICAL ASSESSMENTS

Part five provided the insiders' perspective. Managers from four firms that are current users of psychological assessment described the various ways they use the tool.

Time Insurance uses assessments to help identify people with the potential to be future leaders for the company. Lesley Keegan, vice-president of human resources for Time, finds that assessments provide insights that are hard to obtain elsewhere. Time uses assessments primarily for broader organizational development, for determining placement fit for internal and external candidates, and for specific developmental planning with employees. Time believes that assessments yield more and better information about people than do other organizational processes, help the company deal with people in a more comprehensive and effective fashion, and provide information critical to the identification and development of the leadership and management skills Time needs to be successful in the future.

Aqua Chem uses assessments primarily in the selection of new employees and in the promotion or development of existing employees. Charles Zwerg's experience with assessment as the vice-president of human resources for Aqua Chem, has convinced him that a crucial factor in the success of assessment is an absolutely straightforward, bottom-line relationship between management and their psychologist. The most effective psychologist must be an extension of management. The psychologist must understand the unique characteristics of the business, as well as those of the top management team. Mr. Zwerg believes that "this relationship is so important that any management team considering using psychological assessments should not make the decision lightly."

THE FUTURE OF PSYCHOLOGICAL ASSESSMENT

The last part of the book addressed the future. It began with a summary of the legal guidelines now in effect and how these impact the uses of psychological assessments. One conclusion from this review was the observation that the field could benefit from more and improved validation studies. Publishing these would help advance the field by establishing clearer, more substantial evidence for this popular, practical technique. Such evidence is needed even more today because of the rapidly changing demographics of the workplace. The typical worker of the present and future is very different from the typical worker of the past. To maintain and improve the validity of psychological assessment predictions of people's work performance will require the best clinical and statistical efforts of business psychologists.

The future of psychological assessment is bright. It is made so by the versatility, power, and practicality of assessment as a management tool. The demands placed on the business psychologist doing assessments and on companies using them are guaranteed to increase with the new challenges presented by today's work force. Happily, psychological assessment has proven its robust nature in the fifty years of its popularity in business and organizations. It is unlikely to be abandoned. Instead, the future promises improvement and refinement. We can expect the tool to become better, more accurate, and more consistent than it has been. Employees, management, organizations, and business psychologists will all benefit from these developments.

Index

About the Contributors

JOHN D. ARNOLD is vice-president of HRStrategies, Incorporated. Prior to joining HRStrategies, he was the Detroit practice leader of Arthur Young & Company's Human Resources Consulting Practice. He also served as professor of Organizational Behavior in the Management Department of the University of Cincinnati. Dr. Arnold's professional experience includes consulting work in both the public and private sectors.

RICHARD J. BRUNKAN is president of Human Resources Development Corporation, a subsidiary of Humber, Mundie & McClary. During the past 25 years, he has conducted psychological assessments, as well as research at Marquette University, some of which was published in the *Journal of Counseling Psychology* and other journals.

KELLEY A. CONRAD is an industrial-organizational psychologist and partner at Humber, Mundie & McClary, a firm of business psychologists headquartered in Milwaukee, Wisconsin. Dr. Conrad is a vice president of Human Resources Development Corporation, a firm specializing in management and individual development. He has completed research in several areas of applied psychology with results being presented at professional conventions and published in professional books and journals.

STEPHEN L. GUINN is a principal and managing director of PSP Human Resource Development, a Pittsburgh-based consulting firm, which provides organizational consulting services to a variety of industries throughout the United

States. Dr. Guinn is an adjunct professor at the University of Pittsburgh where he teaches organizational psychology. His research activities include studies of managerial effectiveness, outplacement, and dual career employment. He has published articles on a wide variety of topics.

CURTISS P. HANSEN is an industrial-organizational psychologist with Lincoln National Corporation, a large, multiline insurance holding company, where he directs the Human Resources Research and Planning function. Prior to employment at Lincoln National, Dr. Hansen was a consulting psychologist with Humber, Mundie & McClary, and he also spent a number of years working as a psychotherapist and mental health diagnostician. He has published research in books and professional journals such as the *Journal of Applied Psychology*. His primary area of research and application interest is the relationship of personality and individual difference variables to organizational outcomes.

PIERRE JACQUES is a doctoral candidate in industrial/organizational psychology at the University of Connecticut. He completed a one-year internship at Lincoln National Corporation, a large insurance company in Indiana. Mr. Jacques has presented papers on test bias at the Eastern Psychological Association's and the Industrial/Organizational Psychology Conference conventions.

LESLEY S. KEEGAN is senior vice president of corporate services and planning at Time Insurance Company, a Milwaukee-based medical and life insurance company owned by the Netherlands-based N.V. Amev. Ms. Keegan directs the corporate services and strategic planning function. She has spent much of her career in various areas of human resource management.

BARBARA KRUSE is manager of the Personnel Research Department of the Life Office Management Association, where she has spearheaded several large insurance industry consortium projects dealing with selection methodologies.

ROBERT J. LUEGER is an associate professor of psychology and director of the Center for Psychological Services at Marquette University, where he chairs the graduate training program in clinical psychology and coordinates the activities of faculty supervisors. Prior to this position, Dr. Lueger was the manager of Career Development at First Wisconsin, training, and placing management trainees. Dr. Lueger has published over a dozen studies in professional journals, including the *Journal of Consulting and Clinical Psychology*, has written several book chapters and presented many conference papers.

SUSAN A. LUEGER is the manager of compensation and benefits at Wisconsin Electric Power Company, where she is responsible for all direct and indirect compensation. This includes benefits and salary administration for employees.

Prior to this position, Dr. Lueger was responsible for succession planning, and she coordinated the performance appraisal process at Wisconsin Electric.

RICHARD McDONALD is the co-founder, president, and chief executive officer of McDonald Davis & Associates, Inc., where he is involved in both management and strategic planning. A frequent lecturer and guest speaker, Mr. McDonald is co-author of three best-selling books on interpersonal relations. He has been the co-host of a weekly talk show on Milwaukee's ABC affiliate, and has been featured on the national morning talk shows. In addition, he was co-host of a nationally syndicated television program on humanistic issues, and co-authored a nationally syndicated newspaper column. He is a former commissioner of the United Nations Education and Science Commission (Unesco).

RICHARD E. MILLER is a principal and managing director of PSP Human Resource Development, an independent consulting firm based in Pittsburgh, Pennsylvania, where he works with corporate clients in all business areas from coast to coast. Dr. Miller has been a college instructor in industrial psychology and has made numerous presentations to civic and professional groups on employee motivation, stress management, and psychological testing. He has authored articles on outplacement counseling, motivation, and employee opinion surveys.

JOHN B. MINER is Donald S. Carmichael Professor of Human Resources at the State University of New York at Buffalo, and heads the Organization and Human Resources Department within the School of Management. His responsibilities include serving as faculty director of the Center for Entrepreneurial Leadership. Dr. Miner has published over 40 books and 100 papers in journals and books, and has authored a number of instruments for psychological assessment.

DEBORAH L. PARKER is an industrial-organizational psychologist with Humber, Mundie & McClary, a management consulting firm in Milwaukee, Wisconsin. Before joining HM&M, Dr. Parker was a member of the Management Development Department at Frito-Lay, Inc. She has presented research papers at the Pennsylvania Academy of Sciences and the Southeastern Psychological Association conferences.

M. GORDON PEDERSON is the managing partner of Humber, Mundie & McClary, a management consulting firm in Milwaukee, Wisconsin, where he began as a licensed psychologist in 1967. Previously, he was on the faculty at Marquette University and worked in the University Counseling Center. Dr. Pederson's current work activities involve consulting with top management on a variety of human resources problems. He has published several articles in professional journals and books.

PATRICK R. POWASER is currently completing a Ph.D. in industrial-organizational psychology at Iowa State University. He has worked with Humber, Mundie & McClary in the validation and evaluation of assessment tools, and in the development of assessment-related computer software for in-house use. He has presented his research on pay satisfaction at the International Psychology Congress in Sydney, Australia.

WILLIAM P. SULLIVAN is the director of research for PSP Human Resource Development. He contributed to the development of the *Uniform Guidelines on Employee Selection Procedures* and has made presentations on selection issues to the EEO Coordinating Council in Washington, D.C. He served as Assistant Director of Research at the U.S. Military Academy at West Point prior to joining PSP in 1969. He has published articles on a variety of topics including the practical application of psychological tests and measures in assessments.

RICHARD J. VICARS is senior vice-president and director of Corporate Human Resources for Lincoln National Corporation, a large insurance holding company. He joined LNC in 1963 and through a number of promotions reached his present position in 1983 and was elected senior vice-president in 1987.

CHARLES A. ZWERG is vice-president of human resources for Aqua Chem, Inc., a leading international manufacturer of water purification, desalination, energy recovery, incineration, and packaged boiler products. He has much experience in line and staff management, and has been a corporate officer since 1974. Prior to joining Aqua Chem in 1987, he was vice-president of Human Resources for Giddings & Lewis, Inc.